Russian Research Center Studies, 96

Worker Resistance under Stalin

Class and Revolution on the Shop Floor

Jeffrey J. Rossman

Harvard University Press

Cambridge, Massachusetts, and London, England | 2005

Library of Congress Cataloging-in-Publication Data

Rossman, Jeffrey J., 1965–
    Worker resistance under Stalin : class and revolution on the shop floor /
Jeffrey J. Rossman.
        p.   cm.—(Russian Research Center studies; 96)
    Includes bibliographical references and index.
    ISBN 0-674-01926-1 (alk. paper)
        1. Strikes and lockouts—Soviet Union—History.   2. Industrial
relations—Soviet Union—History.   3. Working class—Soviet Union—
History.   4. Soviet Union—Politics and government—1917–1936.
I. Title.   II. Series.

HD5395.R67 2005
322'.2'094709042—dc22   2005046084

To the memory of
Reginald E. Zelnick
mentor, friend, colleague

Contents

Abbreviations

Cheka   Soviet security police, 1917–1922

CUC   Central Union of Cooperatives

FFYP   First Five-Year Plan, 1928–1932

FOL   functional organization of labor

FY   fiscal year (began on October 1 until 1931, when it was changed to coincide with the calendar year)

IIR   Ivanovo Industrial Region, 1929–1936

IVR   Ivanovo-Voznesensk Region, 1918–1929

NEP   New Economic Policy, 1921–1927

OGPU   Soviet security police, 1922–1934

RSFSR   Russian Soviet Federal Socialist Republic

USSR   Union of Soviet Socialist Republics

Worker Resistance
under Stalin

Introduction

On April 11, 1932, Nikolai Shvernik, the secretary of the Soviet Union's Central Council of Trade Unions, informed Iosif Stalin, the general secretary of the Communist Party, that workers in a number of major industrial regions were in a state of rebellion against recent severe food shortages and the sharp cut in rations implemented on the first of the month on all but the nation's most privileged shop floors. In the Ivanovo Industrial Region (IIR), the Lower Volga Region, the Urals, Western Siberia, Ukraine, and Belorussia, workers were refusing to operate machinery, denouncing food-supply officials, laying siege to food-storage facilities, publicly demonstrating against the new "hunger rations," and fleeing for towns rumored to have even meager supplies of bread. There was no need for Shvernik to offer details about the most serious episode of unrest—a weeklong wave of sometimes violent strikes by twenty thousand textile workers in six IIR mill towns—because reports from the scene would soon be filed by the official whom Stalin dispatched to orchestrate its suppression: the party's second-in-command, Lazar Kaganovich. Endeavoring to underscore the severity of the crisis, Shvernik concluded with a warning. "In all the above-cited cases," he informed the leader whose policies were its root cause, "counterrevolutionary and Trotskyite elements attempted to exploit the temporary difficulties in worker supply."[1]

The labor unrest of April 1932 laid bare the absurdity of the party's claim that it was building a socialist workers' state, and Stalin insisted that not even oblique reference be made to it in the press. But the rumors racing through the halls of the Ninth Congress of Trade Unions, which coincidentally convened the same month in Moscow, could not be ignored. After Ian Rudzutak, chairman of the Central Party Control Commission, conceded in his address to the congress that Soviet workers were "steeped in foul moods," Kaganovich hastened to attribute the crisis to the "petit-bourgeois" mentality of new workers and the persistence of "bourgeois influences" among their veteran counterparts. Even more ideologically palatable analyses were offered by Shvernik, who heaped blame on incompetent local officials, and by the congress's auditing commission, which reported that "class-alien elements" recently had infiltrated the labor force so as to "conduct their subversive work."[2] Although it gave the delegates talking points to use once they returned to their respective enterprises, such folderol is unlikely to have persuaded many of them. The problem was not so much that the explanations raining down from the podium contradicted one another, but that the delegates knew from their own experience what the speakers knew from the top-secret reports piled on their desks: namely, that the unprecedented collapse of living standards had sown bitterness among *all* strata of the labor force.

It was a circumstance that sowed concern in the ranks of the party, many of whose members recoiled from the violence and suffering visited upon the population by Stalin's revolution "from above."[3] Nowhere did this concern find bolder articulation than in "Stalin and the Crisis of the Proletarian Dictatorship," the two-hundred-page treatise by Moscow party official Martem'ian Riutin, who offered a searing indictment of the current leadership:

> Adventurous tempos of industrialization, involving a colossal decline in the wages of blue-collar and white-collar workers, unbearable explicit and implicit taxes, [market] inflation, the raising of prices [by state cooperatives], and the devaluation of [the currency]; adventurous collectivization attended by unbelievable violence, terror, and dekulakization . . . and finally, the expropriation of the countryside by means of . . . forced [grain] requisitioning have led the entire country to the most profound crisis, to the monstrous impoverishment of the masses, and to hunger in both the countryside and the city . . .
>
> Peasant insurrections in which [even] Communists and Komsomols [members of the Communist Youth League] participate have been spreading in an uninterrupted wave in recent years across the entire Soviet Union. Despite savage terror, arrests, dismissals, and provocations, strikes by workers are breaking out now here, now there . . .
>
> Even the most daring and ingenious provocateur could devise nothing better for the destruction of the proletarian dictatorship, for the discrediting of Leninism, than the leadership of Stalin and his clique.[4]

Evidence from the industry that suffered the most severe labor unrest in April 1932 confirmed the validity of Riutin's observation. Russian textile workers had long since concluded that the party had betrayed the ideals of socialism, Soviet power, and the October Revolution. That conclusion, in turn, was based on their own traumatic experience of revolution "from above."

Stalin's Radical Program

As the largest and most profitable branch of the socialized economy—and one whose focus on producing goods for consumption assigned it the status of a neglected stepdaughter in the Bolshevik value system—the Soviet textile industry had but one fundamental assignment during the First Five-Year Plan (FFYP, 1928–1932): to produce a massive surplus for the development of heavy industry.[5] The tribute demanded of cloth—3.5 billion rubles, or more than one-fourth of the capital investment targeted for industry by the plan—represented almost the entire value of the industry's gross annual output, and almost double the value of its fixed capital stock. According to the Supreme Economic Council (Vesenkha), such a sum could be accumulated—if, indeed, it could be accumulated at all—only by increasing the size of the labor force by 13 percent, slashing the costs of production by 31 percent, boosting annual output of cloth by 86 percent, and doubling the productivity of labor.[6]

Although it was devised in haphazard fashion over a period of months, the strategy for achieving these goals was relatively straightforward. Savings would be accumulated, first, by sourcing raw materials domestically and, second, by increasing the rate of exploitation and minimizing the cost of the factors of production. In practice, this meant halting purchases of raw cotton on the international market and relying on the new collective farms of Central Asia to make up the difference; making existing supplies of raw cotton go further by reducing the density of thread and recapturing waste; increasing the productivity of workers and machinery; deferring capital investment for as long as possible; and restricting growth in wages as well as in the size of the labor force. Increases in worker productivity, in turn, would be accomplished by elevating workloads, compressing work schedules, and reorganizing production along Taylorist lines.[7] As for boosting the output of cloth, that would depend not only on gains in productivity, but also on the opening of several new mills and, more important, on rapid conversion of existing mills from two-shift to three-shift (round-the-clock) production.[8]

Like the plan that gave birth to it, the strategy of forced capital accumulation as applied to the textile industry suffered fatal flaws. First, it was too ambitious. The Soviet Union was economically backward compared with the world's major industrial nations—indeed, it was to overcome such backwardness that the revolution "from above" was launched in the first place—and not even the United States or Germany could have successfully carried out in five years such a far-reaching transformation of their own, much wealthier and more advanced, textile industries. Second, the strategy lacked internal coherence: for technical reasons that industry experts understood even if party leaders did not, some goals could be achieved only at the expense of others. For example, factor productivity inevitably would suffer as a result of: the substitution of low-quality domestic for high-quality imported raw cotton; the reduction in the density of thread; the deferral of capital investment; the introduction of round-the-clock production; and, at least in the near term, the implementation of unfamiliar, if theoretically superior, Taylorist methods of production. Finally, the strategy relied on a flawed assumption—specifically, that each measure would yield the anticipated outcome—that resulted in there being no margin for error or failure in an undertaking that was bound to entail plenty of both. To be sure, there was no challenging the party's assumption that collectivization would have a salutary effect on worker productivity and production costs by making bread cheap and abundant. But just as collectivization produced the opposite from intended effect, aggravating rather than eradicating food shortages and price inflation, so too did some measures specific to the textile industry, such as the reduction in the density of thread and the Taylorist reorganization of labor. As for elements of the strategy that were effective—for example, round-the-clock production—these often fell short of expectations.

It was the strategy's flaws rather than failure to implement its various components that prevented the textile industry, like every major branch of the Soviet economy, from fulfilling the targets laid out for it by the Supreme Economic Council. Implementation, in fact, was rapid and aggressive. A crash program of conversion of mills to three-shift production with elevation of workloads was launched in January 1928. That same year, two new mills came on line, domestic production of raw cotton rose 14 percent, and imports of the same declined by 11 percent. Beginning in April 1929, a new round of labor intensification got under way in the form of the shock work and socialist competition campaigns. Before the verdict on those campaigns was in, however, several tens of thousands of operatives were dispatched to the Labor Exchange in a desperate attempt to reduce production costs.[9] Also in 1929, three new mills came on line, domestic production of raw cotton climbed by 5 percent, and imports of the same fell by 21 percent. The major campaign of 1930–1931 was the reorganization of labor along Taylorist lines, although this period also witnessed the opening of four new mills, a 28 percent rise in domestic raw-cotton production, a 53 percent decline in raw-cotton imports, and—in a reversal of the earlier wave of layoffs and a rare piece of good news for unemployed operatives—a 7 percent increase in the size of the labor force.[10]

So exhausted were the factors of production by 1932 that not only could no new campaigns be launched in the textile industry, but some recently implemented ones—such as the reorganization of production along Taylorist lines—had to be repealed. Meanwhile, imports of raw cotton declined by a further 55 percent even as domestic output of the same, ominously, was flat. When the FFYP drew to a close on December 31, 1932, a balance sheet revealed how far short the textile industry—even more than other major sectors of the economy—fell of the targets set for it in the heady days of "bacchanalian planning."[11] Instead of rising, the output of cloth and the productivity of equipment declined. Even the few achievements fell short of expectations: employment in the industry climbed by almost 11 percent; labor productivity—at least in cotton mills—increased by two-thirds instead of doubling; and domestic raw-cotton production rose not by 166 percent but by just more than half. Worse, dividends that were supposed to accrue to textile workers failed to materialize: rather than increasing by two-thirds, real wages declined by half; and what capital investment did take place—such as the opening and equipping of new mills—often was wasted as a result of poor planning.[12]

Although the tribute rendered by cloth inevitably fell short of the sum demanded by the Supreme Economic Council, the burdens imposed on textile workers scarcely could have been greater. At the level of the shop floor, the party's radical policy of forced capital accumulation resulted in: the relentless elevation of workloads; the cannibalization of wage funds, hence the rapid growth in wage arrears; severe shortages of raw materials, hence the unexpected furlough of mills; and the rapid deterioration of equipment, hence the working conditions. Meanwhile, the party's simultaneous wars on the peasantry and the market yielded not an abundance of inexpensive foodstuffs, as promised by Stalin, but chronic shortages of bread and rampant inflation, as predicted by the Right Opposition.[13] To be sure, few if any of the Soviet Union's 2.7 million factory workers were spared the burdens of revolution "from above." But by virtue of their unsought role as the deputy financiers of industrialization, the 716,400 of them employed in the textile industry were condemned to bear the heaviest burden of all.[14]

The Workers' Opposition

How did Russian textile workers respond to this unprecedented situation? In short, with fierce resistance. A term of no small controversy, "resistance" in this book signifies individual and collective efforts by workers to alter, undermine, or abolish policies or practices implemented by local, regional, and/or central authorities, and to compel the same to fulfill what were popularly perceived to be their obligations to the industrial labor force. Common forms of resistance by textile workers during the FFYP—that most crucial period of "socialist construction"—included mass demonstrations, bread riots, strikes, slowdowns, industrial sabotage, subversive speeches at factory assemblies, acts of violence against local authorities, written protests to party leaders, anonymous leafleting, and the composition and circulation of subversive works of the imagination (chiefly, songs and poems). Triggering such resistance were specific components of the strategy of resource extraction outlined above (for example, the elevation of workloads and the reorganization of labor) as well as the inevitable if unintended consequences of that strategy (for example, wage arrears, food shortages, and plummeting real wages) and of the broader revolution "from above" from which it sprang.

Although all segments of the labor force engaged in acts of resistance, at the forefront of collective action were the basic crafts upon whom the burdens of forced capital accumulation fell most heavily: spinners and weavers. Typically, their leaders—that is, the individuals who spearheaded acts of resistance as well as those whom protesters chose to articulate their demands and negotiate with the authorities—were veteran male and female workers in their thirties or forties who commanded respect among their colleagues and whose respective biographies included some component, such as service as a soldier in the Red Army or as an elected deputy to the city soviet, that signified fundamental loyalty to Soviet power.[15] A handful of these leaders were former anarchists, Mensheviks, or Socialist-Revolutionaries; a somewhat larger number were current or former members of the Communist Party; but most, significantly, had no current or past political affiliation whatsoever. Prominent in their ranks were female ring-frame spinners, male and female weavers, and a disproportionately large number of male mule-frame spinners, weaving overlookers, and machinists.[16]

Although collective action often resulted in concessions from above, such as the immediate distribution of bread or back wages or the modification or repeal of labor-intensification measures, these came at a high price: over time, retaliatory dismissals and arrests deprived workers of their most effective leaders. But just as resistance from below failed—at least initially—to halt the process of working-class immiserization, so repression from above failed to avert collective action on a mass scale. The climax of the textile workers' struggle to defend their well-being—indeed, their survival—arrived in April 1932, when twenty thousand went on strike in the IIR.[17] Although the rebellion ended in bloodshed and repression, it also prompted Moscow to respond to the multifaceted crisis on Soviet shop floors.

Underpinning resistance to Stalin's revolution "from above" was the moral economy of the Russian textile worker. Moral economy is a concept developed by E. P. Thompson that refers, in Padraic Kenney's concise formulation, "to a set of values—generally embracing ideas of egalitarianism, social justice, and basic collective rights—embedded in the culture of a community (a moral community) that enable collective, usually spontaneous action against those whom the community holds responsible for disrupting its ability to maintain a standard of living."[18] The moral economy of the Russian textile worker manifested itself in myriad acts of resistance during the FFYP. For example, it drove: 2,000 Sereda spinners to go on strike when their take-home pay fell even as workloads rose; 1,300 delegates at a special session of the Ivanovo City Soviet to threaten collective action when bread shortages became life-threatening; 800 Vichuga weavers to reject socialist competition (a form of labor intensification) as unbearable, hence "exploitative"; 600 Navoloki operatives to storm out of an assembly upon being asked to sacrifice half a month's wages for the state; and general strikes to erupt in six mill towns in response to the implementation of "hunger" rations. Collectively, such acts signaled rejection of a development program that violated the values of the working-class communities it was supposed to benefit.

Embedded within the moral economy of the Russian textile worker was an implicit contractual understanding of the relationship between the working class and the party. The terms of what in this book will be called the October Revolution's social contract were defined concisely in 1928 by a rank-and-file operative: "We give to you, and you give to us."[19] In other words, the willingness of the labor force to sacrifice in the name of Soviet power and in the manner prescribed by the party was predicated—at least in the absence of war—on a condition: that a floor be set beneath which living standards would never fall and a ceiling erected above which workloads would never rise. When the party stopped honoring the terms of the Revolution's social contract in 1928, textile workers responded in kind.

Although it threw myriad obstacles in the party's path, the moral economy of the Russian textile worker was infused with a certain understanding of Soviet values. This was a paradox but no mere coincidence. From the perspective of the shop floor, "Soviet power" was understood to mean not a dictatorship by the party collectively or Stalin personally, but rather the abolition of the workers' suffering: their hunger, humiliation, penury, and exploitation. Given the insistence on social justice that lay at the core of their moral economy, Russian textile workers found within the October Revolution—indeed, within *their* revolution—all the justification they needed to oppose policies that resulted in their immiserization.[20]

That move is what made worker resistance subversive. The message could not have been misinterpreted because it was so often uttered in precisely these terms: the party has betrayed the Revolution, turned its back on the working class, and made a mockery of Soviet power. Those advancing such claims were, from the regime's perspective, "anti-Soviet," hence subject to prosecution under the notorious Articles 58 and 59 of the Criminal Code.[21] But there was nothing anti-Soviet, objectively speaking, about those who spearheaded resistance: men and women who viewed and presented themselves as the true "defenders of Soviet power," who based their claims on "the slogans and oaths of October 1917," and who posed questions that cast in sharp relief the enormous gulf between the radiant promises of official ideology and the grim realities of everyday life.[22] How could the self-proclaimed workers' state, which the workers brought to power and for which they sacrificed so much, fail in the absence of war to provide them with bread? How could a program that sapped the workers' vitality and shattered their standard of living possibly be compatible with the ideals of socialism? Such questions underscored what was at stake in this struggle: not just a loaf of bread, an eighty-ruble wage packet, or an extra pair of looms, but ownership of the October Revolution and the right to author—and cast final judgment on—its outcome.

If worker resistance was grounded in a specific moral economy and a specific conceptualization of the Revolution, appeals for collective action were articulated in the language of class. The effectiveness of such appeals underscores one of the most important socio-discursive phenomena of the FFYP: the reemergence of class "as a signifying system through which [workers] perceived and acted upon the social world."[23] The point is not that class suddenly superseded other categories of identity, such as gender, generation, ethnicity, region, and craft; in fact, these and other systems of signification continued to coexist, interact, and interpenetrate in complex ways. Rather, it is that class, after a decade of dormancy, reacquired valence on shop floors by giving meaning to—and, crucially, facilitating resistance against—the immiserization that was the inevitable legacy, if by no means the promise, of revolution "from above."

Just as textile workers insisted on their own interpretation of the October Revolution, so too they forged a language of class that was distinct from, if nonetheless profoundly influenced by, the party's.[24] Theirs was a hybrid language that appropriated symbolic content from official ideology—that is, Marxism-Leninism—as well as from an unofficial discourse of "us-versus-them" populism that "had deep roots in Russian culture."[25] Grounded in a fundamental dichotomy between (suffering) workers and (exploitative) elites, the language of class demonstrated its potency in many ways: in the reinvigoration of an oppositional culture within the physical spaces that the party found it difficult, if not impossible, to penetrate (above all, the factory washroom and smoking lounge); in the crystallization of perceptions of the new elite as the beneficiaries of the workers' labor and as the "other" against whom the workers' interests were defined; in the forging of alliances between segments of the labor force (for example, male overlookers and female weavers) whose relations had been chronically antagonistic; and, above all, in the constant resort to collective action to defend what were perceived to be common interests.[26]

While neither stationary nor impenetrable, the boundaries of class were well defined at the point of production. As a rule, anyone from a lower-class industrial or even agricultural background who had been employed in a factory for a substantial period of time, and who had never been deprived of his or her civil rights by the Soviet regime, could reasonably claim the social identity "worker." Significantly, the "working class" also included the dependents—especially the children—of such individuals. By contrast, three narrow strata of the industry's labor force tended to be excluded, or viewed as "other": peasants who were not members of the local community, but who had recently migrated from distant regions to secure a position in industry; seasonal workers; and *lishentsy* (individuals who had been stripped of their civil rights, typically because of their class origins).[27] The boundaries of class are important to keep in mind because resistance at the point of production was shaped by popular understandings of who was—and was not—a "worker."[28]

Since dependents were included in popular definitions of "the working class," the language of class was infused with familial references. Time and again, male and female workers condemned revolution "from above" and threatened to withdraw their labor because "the children are starving." (Not just any children, but the *workers'* children.) If the language of class derived its legitimacy from the October Revolution, its moral force was augmented by the relentless invocation of the working-class family.[29]

Given the values of the textile worker's moral economy—not to mention the breathtaking display of class consciousness and collective action on shop floors in 1917—one might have predicted that the policy-driven assault on living standards that got under way in 1928 would precipitate unrest. Why, then, has the prevailing assumption been that Russian workers responded to Stalin's revolution "from above" with ineffective grumbling, apathy, or even enthusiasm? To answer that and related questions, we turn our attention to the historiography.

As far as Soviet workers are concerned, the history of the revolution "from above" has been written from several perspectives. During the heyday of the totalitarian model (the 1950s and 1960s), the focus was on the state—specifically, its various attempts to exert control over the labor force—and the prevailing assumption was that workers were too atomized to engage in collective action even when they harbored grievances against the regime. Although more nuanced in their interpretation of state-society relations than critics allowed, scholars working within the totalitarian paradigm had little to say about the experience of industrialization at the point of production.[30]

Workers became the object of serious attention once social historians took the field by storm in the 1970s. One of the leaders of that assault was Moshe Lewin, who did not reject the totalitarian model so much as nuance it. For Lewin, the key point about the FFYP is that it was profoundly disruptive for society and, paradoxically, frustrating for the regime that launched it. With millions of peasants moving to cities to secure employment and labor turnover skyrocketing as workers fled one dismal job site for another, the party found itself presiding over a "a 'quicksand' society" in which "all social groups and classes were . . . partially or totally 'destructured' and unhinged." The resulting fragmentation of social identity was most advanced on the shop floor, where the labor force "was neither a class nor an assortment of individuals, but simply a mass" that, in the final analysis, was "easy to control." But if one effect of the revolution "from above" was to disorient the working class, thereby rendering it "passive and defenseless," another was to generate so much turmoil that no longer could those at the apex of power effect outcomes on the ground. The result: resort to coercion on a mass scale and transformation of the state "into a Leviathan."[31]

While Lewin implicitly accepted the totalitarian paradigm—or at least its model of a state that made a total claim on the human and material resources of an increasingly atomized society—the so-called revisionists rejected it. Unlike Lewin, these scholars tended to subject workers and their milieu to close examination. The result was that influential and sometimes controversial studies emphasized the integrative functions of state policy and the mobilizational capacity of official ideology. By moving away from the totalitarian model, the revisionists effectively highlighted the social bases of Stalin's revolution "from above," and of Stalinism itself. Still, their tendency to focus on a narrow stratum of the labor force—one that embraced and/or substantively benefited from state policy—raised questions about the broader applicability of their findings.[32]

Even as revisionists were plumbing the experiences of workers whom the party successfully mobilized for the project of "socialist construction," Donald Filtzer offered a very different interpretation of the shop floor. Writing from a Trotskyist perspective, he argued that workers actively resisted the revolution "from above" because it was accompanied by labor policies that intentionally shattered their class solidarity. While his emphasis on atomization drew inspiration, or so it would seem, from the totalitarian model, Filtzer concluded by emphasizing—as did the revisionists with whom he is sometimes categorized—the limits of state control. In his view, the regime's insistence, for ideological reasons, on eradicating unemployment had the unintended effect of granting workers leverage they used—with disastrous results for the economy—to maintain control over the labor process. Although Filtzer was unpersuasive in his argument that Stalinist labor policies were designed to undermine working-class solidarity—after all, there was little evidence of such solidarity during the era of the New Economic Policy (NEP, 1921–1927)—his claim that workers resisted the revolution "from above" was groundbreaking.[33]

A decade after Filtzer and the revisionists moved the field beyond the totalitarian model, Stephen Kotkin entered the debate with his monumental study of the steel city Magnitogorsk. Inspired by Michel Foucault's studies of discourse in modern Western society and Pierre Bourdieu's theory of practice, Kotkin endeavored to demonstrate that Stalinism was a "civilization" that emerged from the complex and unpredictable interaction of, on one hand, the "grand strategies" of the state and, on the other, the tactics of adaptation and survival elaborated by workers in the course of daily life. In Kotkin's view, the support-resistance paradigm is irrelevant to this period because ideological "unbelief" was "impossible" and Soviet identities were "unavoidable." This was the case for three reasons: first, because Soviet values were broadly popular; second, because alternative points of view were inaccessible due to the closed nature of the society and state control of the media; and third, because getting by necessitated mastery of "the little tactics of the habitat"—such as how to "speak Bolshevik"—that furthered the individual's identification with the regime and its goals.[34] Vigorously argued and brilliantly executed, Kotkin's study has been influential. Indeed, it has inspired a new cohort of scholars to place at the center of their agenda an important question: how did processes of identity construction operate in daily life to bind the individual to the Soviet regime and its values?

The most compelling of the recent Kotkin-inspired studies is Jochen Hellbeck's work on diarists such as Stepan Podlubnyi, a young man who abandoned his native Ukrainian village on the eve of collectivization. After settling in Moscow, Podlubnyi endeavored to overcome the stigma of his origins as the son of a "class enemy"—his father had been dekulakized and deported—by working in a print factory, enrolling at a medical institute, and becoming a Komsomol. Podlubnyi used his diary during the 1930s to gauge how far he had come in transforming himself into a "new Soviet man." By means of a close and theoretically informed analysis of Podlubnyi's diary, Hellbeck achieved the singular feat of laying bare the self-generated process of identity construction that Kotkin postulated but never demonstrated was taking place under Stalin. Yet while Hellbeck's reading illustrated "how the Soviet system of social identification pervaded . . . the individual's personal domain," turning even the son of a dekulakized peasant into a witting "carrier of the Stalinist system," it fell short of proving the claim that "most people lacked even the most basic precondition for the articulation of dissent: an outside frame of reference against which to evaluate the performance of the Stalinist regime."[35]

While Hellbeck has been criticized for making generalizations about a complex and rapidly changing society on the basis of a narrow and uniform source base, the fundamental shortcoming of his work is conceptual. Hellbeck asserts that the Soviet self was merely "an effect of the Revolution."[36] Besides being indefensible on psychological grounds, that assumption disembeds the individual from the complex social environment in which he or she was located and which the Soviet state, for all its totalizing intentions, never fully monopolized. One can reasonably pose the question: when did the Bolshevik attempt to create a new Soviet man become so effective as to wipe out alternative frames of reference, such as memory of life under the old regime, or alternative fulcra of identity, such as confession, community, and family? While Hellbeck does not deny the limits of totalitarian control, he problematically maintains that the October Revolution so thoroughly disrupted alternative sources of meaning that individuals were left with little choice but to define themselves in terms dictated by the state. Although that assumption is shared by other members of the "neo-totalitarian" school that emerged in the late 1990s and of which Hellbeck is a founding member, it is one whose emphasis on the capacity of the Soviet regime to monopolize the processes of identity construction would have given pause to card-carrying members of the paleo-totalitarian school such as Fainsod.[37]

Albeit with qualifications, that problematic assumption is shared by Sheila Fitzpatrick. One of the most prolific and influential historians of the Stalin era, Fitzpatrick has argued in recent work that a key category of social identity during the 1920s and 1930s became one only because the Bolsheviks made it so. Having come to power "in a country where class structure was weak and social identity in crisis," the world's first proletarian dictatorship found it "could know its allies from its enemies" only by reviving the dormant, if ideologically vital, concept of class. By insisting that the individual be identified in censuses, voting records, and passports as "factory worker," "white-collar worker," "bourgeois," "landowner," and so on, and then regulating access to scarce material and social goods on the basis of such classification, the party turned class into "a basic category of identity for Soviet citizens." In conditions of backwardness and social turmoil, however, the deployment of Marxist categories entailed their transformation: rather than defining individuals on the basis of their location within production relations, class in the Soviet context functioned like a prerevolutionary *soslovie* (estate) category, defining them on the basis of their relation to the state. The argument is persuasive as far as it goes, but Fitzpatrick errs in assuming that there can be only two forms of class identity: a Marxist one that emerges organically from (capitalist) production relations, and an "ascribed" one imposed from above by state socialist regimes.[38]

While Fitzpatrick concludes that the Bolsheviks saved class only by destroying it, most other social historians follow in Lewin's footsteps by concluding that they merely destroyed it. Unlike Fitzpatrick, these scholars neither ignore the processes of identity construction at the point of production nor disregard the capacity of class to function even in inhospitable (from the Marxist point of view) conditions as a framework for the interpretation of experience. Yet they agree with Fitzpatrick that class as a category of social identity in its traditional—that is, its non-*soslovie*—incarnation lacked potency after the October Revolution.[39]

Their argument runs as follows. After cresting during the autumn of 1917, class consciousness on Russia's shop floors soon gave way to fragmentation along lines of gender, ethnicity, generation, workshop, craft, and region. That outcome was the inevitable result of the political emasculation of the working class by the new regime and the tremendous social flux that accompanied the Civil War (1918–1921) and postwar reconstruction. If the political and socioeconomic effect of the Bolshevik seizure of power was fragmentation of the working class, however, its ideological effect was the debasement of class as a language of opposition. Being citizens of "a proletarian state," Russian workers could not complain about "their political disenfranchisement or economic exploitation." To be sure, they still had grievances. But the victory of Soviet power meant, first, that there were no superordinate exploiting classes to blame for these, and second, that appeals for collective action could not be grounded in the language of class without coming across as "irrational," or, even "psychopathic." The coming to power of the world's first Marxist-Leninist regime thus had the paradoxical effect of rendering "class consciousness unnecessary" and worker "opposition impossible."[40]

The assumption that resistance was impossible informs some, though not all, of the objections to the study of it in the Soviet context. The objections are either conceptual or methodological. Hellbeck claims that those who endeavor to study popular resistance in Stalin's USSR "project their own liberal values on historical actors, endowing them with a liberal self-understanding and a striving for autonomy from the surrounding political environment." The result is a Soviet subject "strangely detached from [his] social and political environment," whose "articulations and actions" have been stripped "of [their] specific frames of meaning." If Hellbeck sees resistance as existing primarily in the imagination of contemporary Western historians, Michael David-Fox sees it as existing primarily in the imagination of the Soviet security police (OGPU). In this view, Bolshevik political culture was a didactic one that endeavored to "transform both the self and society" by ritually unmasking real or imagined enemies and whose dubious legacy includes myriad accounts, accessible to historians only since 1991, of "fictional or exaggerated opposition."[41]

Hellbeck and I agree on this much: most workers who engaged in acts of resistance were committed to the illiberal values of the October Revolution. Where we differ, profoundly, is in the interpretation of what type of behavior was possible for such individuals under Stalin. According to Hellbeck, anyone who had internalized Soviet values—he assumes that most of the population had done so by the 1930s—faced a stark choice: they could either join "the chorus of the Party's general line" or resign themselves (pitiful doubters!) to "self-marginalization and atomization." Even if one were to concede that this was the case for the narrow milieu that produced Hellbeck's diarists, there is no question that other possibilities existed on the shop floor, where workers routinely claimed authority as supporters of Soviet power to contest the party's claim that it alone had the right to determine the meaning and outcome of the Revolution. Far from ignoring ideology or the rupture of 1917, this book places both at the center of attention. The result, however, is a "dissenting self" far different from the paralyzed and psychologically troubled one depicted by Hellbeck.[42]

Unlike Hellbeck, David-Fox understands that one must never lose sight of the particularities of social context—especially the proximity of a given collectivity to "the emerging Soviet political culture"—in interpreting the actions of the individual under Stalin. David-Fox errs, however, in insisting that historians read evidence of resistance as a mere reflection of "the culture of masking and unmasking that emerged out of Soviet communism's didactic thrust." The objection is not so much that David-Fox fails to acknowledge that studies of resistance rely on much more than OGPU sources to interpret the individual's experience of Stalinism; it is, rather, that his understanding of the functions of the security police in the Stalinist context is too limited. Both David-Fox and Peter Fritzsche advise against use of the term *resistance* because it led, in the German historio-graphical context, to "the false impression that popular views of the Nazis were anything but supportive."[43] But the implicit claim that the historio-graphical dividends of resistance studies will be no greater in the Soviet field than they were in the German one stands only so long as one ignores a crucial difference between the Stalin and Hitler regimes: whereas the for-mer implemented a socioeconomic revolution at home, the latter did noth-ing of the sort.

State-mandated socioeconomic revolution impinged directly on the ac-tivities of the security police. While the Gestapo busied itself making "all sorts of grumbling" that could, in fact, be found in any modern society sound like subversive dissent, its Soviet counterpart was confronted with the task of maintaining or reestablishing order among workers and peas-ants for whom the impact of the revolution "from above" was unimaginably disruptive. To ignore protests by collectivities whose traditions, cultures, and ways of life came under attack by a party determined to remake soci-ety in its own ideological image, simply because often we have no choice but to view such events through the "distorted lens of the security police," is to render invisible for specious methodological reasons phenomena that for decades were invisible for unfortunate political ones.[44] Since there are no undistorted lenses onto the past—above all in the field of Soviet his-tory—the historian's task must be to adjust for the imperfections of each lens rather than to shut his or her eyes to the refractions generated therein.

The critics of resistance studies are right to point out the biases of the sources, even if the issue is one of which the field has long been aware. Still, their contention that reports of resistance were merely a misleading effect of Soviet political culture suffers a glaring weakness. If applied nar-rowly to the documentation that served as the basis for show trials of spies, wreckers, and saboteurs—fabrications that obviously *were* meant to serve primarily a didactic function—it is more or less persuasive. But the same argument applied indiscriminately to all OGPU sources, including reports whose contents were never meant to be publicized, is not. Far more nu-merous than those intended, in one form or another, for public consump-tion, these sources served primarily a bureaucratic function: to convey information that the various organs of state needed to discharge their re-sponsibilities.

An example from the IIR illustrates the point. Soviet trade unions could not fulfill their function under Stalin—to make the labor force as quiescent and productive as possible for the sake of rapid economic development—

without thorough knowledge of what was taking place on the shop floor. Such knowledge often was in short supply, however, because trade unions were starved of resources and, more important, alienated from the workers whose interests they claimed to serve. A partial solution to the information deficit was provided by the OGPU, which filed a report with the regional trade-union council whenever workers engaged—or threatened to engage—in collective action. Though sometimes infused with Bolshevik ideological categories, such as "backward workers" and "kulak moods," these reports described events and the individuals participating in them in terms that never could have been used in public. For example, the withdrawal of labor was characterized as a "strike" rather than an "anti-Soviet event," and leaders of the strike were identified—if such was the case—as veteran workers who commanded "tremendous authority" on the shop floor and served as elected deputies to the city soviet. The purpose of these reports was not to launch a show trial, but to convey to the trade union the information it needed to reduce the likelihood of further disruptions to production. (If the workers complained of a shortage of food, for example, the trade union would be advised to facilitate increased deliveries of bread to the district where the unrest occurred.) Highly classified, the content of these reports could not be divulged, even obliquely, without severe penalty. At the same time, the events described therein often found direct or indirect corroboration in other types of sources, such as party memoranda, trade-union strike reports, diaries, and workers' letters to government leaders and the press.[45] In this book, these and other types of sources have been used—and, whenever possible, triangulated—to demonstrate that collective resistance grounded in the language of class was a dominant leitmotif of the shop-floor response to Stalin's revolution "from above."

The Textile Workers

The site of inquiry for this study is the IIR (Figures 1 and 2), a mono-industrial megaprovince that came into being in 1929 as a result of the merger of four of Russia's oldest textile regions (Iaroslavl, Ivanovo-Voznesensk, Kostroma, and Vladimir). Boasting a land mass four times the size of Belgium and a population of 4.7 million, the IIR was second only to the provinces of Moscow and Leningrad in terms of the level of industrial employment and the value of industrial output. Of the region's 327,980 factory workers—one-eighth of the Soviet total—209,964 were employed by

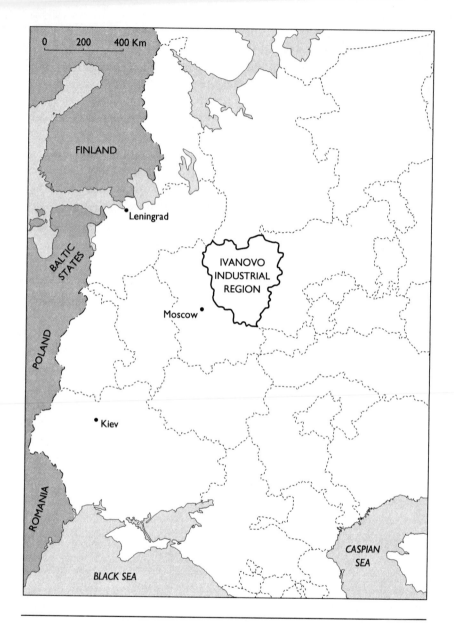

Figure 1. Map of western USSR, showing the location of the Ivanovo Industrial Region, 1929–1936.

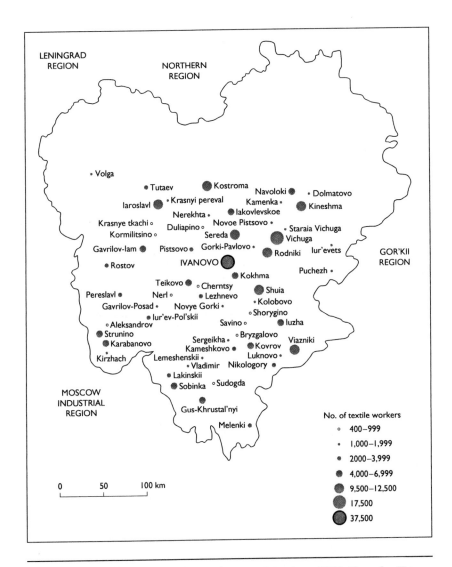

Figure 2. Mill towns of the Ivanovo Industrial Region, 1932. Data for Kovrov includes 1,424 workers from three nearby villages. Data for Viazniki includes 5,021 workers from ten nearby villages. Data for Novoe Pistsovo includes 480 workers from the nearby Chertovishchi Mill. (Source: *Raiony Ivanovskoi promyshlennoi oblasti* [Moscow-Ivanovo, 1933], explanatory notes to cartograms 5 and 6.)

105 cotton mills, and 59,791 were employed by 42 linen mills. As the source of nearly one-third of the Soviet Union's textile output by value, this "calico republic" to the northeast of Moscow was destined to fulfill a crucial if most unenviable role in the program of forced capital accumulation.[46]

Although the oldest IIR textile mills were built during the reign of Peter the Great, most were vintage nineteenth century. Unfortunately, so was much of the technology contained therein. The Lancashire power loom may have been considered obsolete in the West, but as of the 1930s it was still standard equipment in the region's weaving sheds. Most such looms, moreover, had been installed before 1910. The situation was even more dire in linen mills, 70 percent of whose equipment dated from the previous century. In other words, the industry that was supposed to produce a massive surplus for "socialist construction" was itself in dire need of capital investment and modernization. Despite promises to the contrary, neither took place on a significant scale during the FFYP.[47] The result: production problems that suppressed earnings and sowed shop-floor discontent.

The aged and often obsolete capital stock of the textile industry was housed in mills that were large or even massive in scale. This was especially the case in the IIR, where the typical cotton enterprise employed 2,430 workers. While that figure exceeded the national average by one-third, it concealed the scale of the region's seventeen "giants," each of which boasted from five thousand to twelve thousand workers apiece. Large mills gave rise to economies of scale that helped Soviet planners reduce the costs of production. But the extraordinary concentration of labor in and around such mills also made it easier for workers to view themselves as members of a distinct collectivity, or class—and for labor unrest to spread rapidly.[48]

Cotton was by far the largest branch of the Soviet textile industry; in second place was linen. This was also the case in the IIR: three out of four operatives worked in a cotton mill, and one out of four worked in a linen mill. Within the industry as a whole, weaving mills were the largest—and spinning mills, the second largest—employers. Again, the same held for the IIR, where every other operative was a weaver and every fourth was a spinner. Like the geographic concentration of operatives, their concentration by craft—especially in an industry that long boasted resilient *identities* of craft—could be destabilizing since a protest by, say, weavers in one shift, shed, or mill tended to echo in protests by their counterparts in other shifts, sheds, and mills.[49]

No major branch of Soviet industry boasted a higher proportion of women than textiles. Nationwide as well as in the IIR, slightly more than three out of five operatives were women. Since women in a given craft tended to earn about one-eighth less than their male counterparts, the gender profile of the labor force helped Soviet planners keep a lid on production costs.[50] But like the geographic and craft concentration of operatives, the high proportion of women in the industry could be destabilizing. The reason: lower-class women were more likely than their male counterparts to engage in acts of protest. This phenomenon requires explication. Socialized to carry out the bulk of her household's unpaid domestic labor alone—or at least without the assistance of male relatives—the lower-class Russian woman was acutely sensitive to measures (such as the elevation of workloads) that depleted her stamina, and to conditions (such as bread shortages) that made her obligations as mother, wife, or daughter more difficult to fulfill. Given her relatively low wages, she was no less sensitive to measures (such as increased fines for defective output) and conditions (such as low-quality raw materials) that suppressed take-home pay. When pressed against a wall, moreover, she knew how to exploit an old gender stereotype—namely, that she was a victim of her emotions, predisposed to unruly behavior, or of "dark" (male) forces controlling her from the shadows—that stripped her of agency but also rendered her less vulnerable to dismissal and arrest. The lower-class Russian woman thus had greater license and, with the advent of revolution "from above," impetus to rebel.[51]

Gender identity was reinforced on the shop floor by the segregation of the sexes by craft: most piecers, creelers, overlookers, dyers, repairmen, and machinists were men, while most drawing-frame tenders, ring-frame spinners, flyer-frame spinners, winding-frame tenders, doffers, and weavers were women.[52] Antagonism between the sexes—in particular, between male overlookers and female weavers—was not uncommon on the industry's shop floors during the NEP era. As the fundamental values and interests of the working-class community came under assault during the FFYP, however, identities of craft and gender tended to give way to—or to reinforce rather than undermine—an identity grounded in the language of class.

Textile workers were the Soviet Union's most experienced in terms of *stazh* (length of engagement in wage labor). Within the cotton industry, the most experienced operatives were to be found in the IIR: three out of five had joined the labor force when the mills were still in private hands (that is, before 1918), and more than a quarter had done so before the Revolution of 1905. Notwithstanding the virtual idling of the industry during the Civil War, therefore, "the basic, prerevolutionary industrial cadres were still at the bench" during the FFYP.[53] To the extent that these cadres were socialized to the work and time discipline of the shop floor, they were an asset for Soviet planners. To the extent that they drew upon their authority as members of the generation of workers that brought down the old regime to denounce the party for having betrayed the October Revolution, they were a liability.

Besides being highly experienced, the textile industry's labor force also was exceptionally stable. As of 1929, for example, the average IIR operative had been with his or her current employer for 7.4 years (in Soviet industry as a whole, the figure was 6 years). Contrary to Bolshevik assumptions, the most settled operatives were women and those employed in rural mills: the former, because so many men had been mobilized to serve in the military during the Civil War; the latter, because of ties to the land and the lack of alternative local employment opportunities. Labor-force stability had a salutary effect on productivity and so was viewed favorably by the party. Nonetheless, it gave rise to conservatism, which manifested itself during the FFYP in fierce defense of shop-floor traditions and routines.[54]

Further reinforcing the stability and conservatism of the labor force was that a narrow majority of operatives consisted of second-generation factory workers. Given that the IIR had been a center of textile manufacturing for more than a century and that children often traced their parents' footsteps to the mill, this is no more surprising than the fact that most of the rest hailed from the peasantry. The key variable was generation: the younger the operative, the more likely he or she was to be the offspring of a full-time factory worker. There was a benefit here for Soviet planners: since parents and children often worked alongside one another, the former as a rule assumed responsibility for the training and discipline of the latter.[55] But there was a risk as well: shop-floor traditions often were *family* traditions, which magnified attachment to them and opposition to policies that undermined them.

Having a large proportion of women in the ranks was helpful in terms of labor-force stability, but came at a price: textile workers were the least literate and among the least educated in Soviet industry. Overall, one in five IIR operatives was illiterate. The crucial variables were gender and generation: the illiteracy rate was four and a half times higher among women than men (27.9 percent versus 6.3 percent), and fourteen times higher among operatives aged forty and older than among those twenty-two and younger (44.3 percent versus 3.2 percent). Though less stark, differences in the level of education were analogous.[56] To augment the skills of the labor force and the effectiveness of official propaganda—an illiterate worker, after all, could read neither a technical manual nor a Soviet newspaper—the regime endeavored to educate the labor force during the

1920s. Advances on the "cultural front" were substantial during this period, but the outcome was not without irony: although literacy facilitated the dissemination of views that were favorable to the party, it did the same for views that were hostile.

In textiles as in other Soviet industries, the family was a fundamental working-class institution. Seven out of ten IIR operatives had families of their own; the rest were single (unmarried, no dependents). Although food shortages and earnings volatility hit "family" workers harder than "single" workers, kinship ties were important to both: almost all the former (93.1 percent) lived under the same roof as their dependents, while a majority of the latter (52.2 percent) boarded with relatives. There is no need to idealize the Russian working-class family, which exhibited chronic pathologies such as wife-beating and alcoholism, to appreciate the crucial role it played in offering succor to its members at moments of acute social crisis.[57]

While the overwhelming majority (82.4 percent) of operatives lived with kin, the textile industry had more nontraditional families than other major industries. (Often headed by a woman, nontraditional families tended to cluster in female-dominated industries such as textiles.) Data is not available for the IIR, but a 1926 study of textile-worker families in Moscow found that only 56.6 percent were headed by a husband-wife dyad, whereas 27.7 percent were headed by a single parent (typically, a widow) and 14.8 percent, by a nonparent family member (for instance, a surviving child).[58] As a rule, nontraditional families suffered more acutely during the FFYP because they had fewer potential and actual wage earners—and often no male wage earners at all—hence less of an opportunity to take compensatory action as living standards collapsed.

As in other major industries, worker housing was in short supply, especially in urban areas, and living conditions were primitive. Historically, operatives in the IIR solved their housing needs by building a small private home for themselves (typically, a wooden "pygmy" hut of six or seven square meters). For every seven of the region's operatives, three lived in their own homes, two leased a room or apartment from a private (typically, peasant) landlord, one lived in factory housing (usually, a barracks or dormitory), and one lived in either municipal or cooperative housing. Because the only way to get around in working-class communities was by foot, operatives tended to live relatively close to the mill: four out of five had a daily round-trip commute of less than six kilometers. The key variable was enterprise location: employees of rural mills were twice as likely as their urban counterparts to live in their own homes, and eight times as likely to have a round-trip commute of more than ten kilometers. (One reason rural mills tended to be less productive than urban ones was that their workers expended more time and energy on the commute.) Regardless of where they lived, however, operatives had to contend with filth, overcrowding, and other conditions that, according to a trade-union functionary, sowed "politically backward" moods on the shop floor.[59]

Ties to the land were a constant focus of attention in Soviet sociological literature of the 1920s. The issue merits attention here not because it was predictive of shop-floor unrest, as the Bolsheviks assumed, but because tensions surfaced from time to time between "peasant" workers and "proletarians." Unfortunately, the sources reveal little about how operatives defined these terms. We therefore must rely on the imperfect definition employed in the 1929 trade-union census, which equated ties to the land with formal land ownership.[60] By this definition, "peasant" workers constituted 19.3 percent of the labor force in IIR mills. (In Soviet industry as a whole, the figure was 25 percent.) The key variable was enterprise location: in urban mills, 5.7 percent of operatives owned land; in rural mills, 44.1 percent. Most linen mills were located in villages, and most cotton mills were in towns of one size or another. Consequently, more than a quarter of operatives in the former, as opposed to just one in six in the latter, were tied to the land.[61]

Regardless of where they worked, operatives who owned land invariably put it to use: nine out of ten sowed crops, three out of four maintained a kitchen garden, and two out of three possessed livestock (a cow, or less often, a horse). Such activities were time-consuming and, for one in nine operatives, amounted to a second full-time job. Poor soil and climatic conditions, however, meant that the dividends rarely were sufficient to support a family. As such—and the point is a crucial one—"peasant" workers were, as a rule, only marginally less dependent on wages than were their "proletarian" colleagues. That *stazh* was 16.2 years among the former and only 13.3 years among the latter indicates that it had long been thus.[62]

The rural influence on shop floors was greater than the data in the preceding paragraph imply, for twice as many IIR operatives (39.1 percent) lived in the village as owned land. The overwhelming majority (from 65 to 80 percent) of these "rural" operatives lived in their native village; the rest rented living quarters relatively near the mill and traveled home on days off. (Most likely to rent were operatives whose native village was situated more than ten kilometers from the mill.) Further elevating links between field and factory was that operatives who had a connection to the village endeavored to maintain it for as long as possible, since access to a kitchen garden improved one's standard of living and served as a buffer against urban food shortages.[63] Rural ties thus were stabilizing insofar as they kept the labor force in better physical condition than it otherwise would have been, but destabilizing insofar as they embedded so-called peasant moods in the factory itself.

Official levers of influence were weaker in textiles than in other major industries. Although most operatives belonged to the official trade union, nowhere was the rate of party affiliation lower. In the IIR, for example, only 13.3 percent of cotton operatives were members or candidate members of the party or Komsomol. (For Soviet industry as a whole, the figure was 20 percent.) As with literacy, the gender and generation gaps were stark: those affiliated with the party included one in five men and one in three operatives younger than twenty-three, but only one in ten women and one in twenty operatives older than fifty. The party may have assigned veteran female textile workers a crucial role in the program of forced capital accumulation, but its capacity to mobilize them was limited.[64]

Historically, the constitutive regions of the IIR were among Russia's "reddest." According to David Mandel, "the workers of the [Ivanovo-Kineshma] region showed their affinity for the Bolsheviks both before [the First World War], in elections to the State Duma, as well as in 1917, in elections to the soviets, trade union conferences, organs of local self-government and the Constituent Assembly."[65] As was the case on shop floors across Russia, support for the party peaked in the region during the autumn of 1917, when 300,000 of the operatives employed there joined a nationwide strike wave to convey their desire for a transfer of "all power to the Soviets." Support for Lenin's party was not unconditional, however, but sprang from a perception, first, that the Bolsheviks were responsive to local demands, and second, that their radical program offered a solution to the economic crisis that had shattered popular living standards.[66]

The party's failure to deliver on what operatives understood to be the promises of the October Revolution, identified by William Husband as "economic betterment, the redress of inequities, and the prosecution of social antagonisms," inevitably generated disillusionment. IIR shop floors were relatively quiescent during the Civil War, however, because the economic crises triggered by that conflict idled much of the industry even before its nationalization was complete. When recovery finally got under way, it was slow but steady: within five years of the introduction of the NEP in 1921, employment in both the cotton and linen industries surpassed prewar levels.[67]

The fragmentation of social identity during the NEP era limited but did not eliminate the potential for collective action. For example, a strike wave swept Russia's cotton mills in 1925 after the party implemented Taylorist measures in an effort to boost the output of the vital consumer good (cloth), upon which its policy of using the market to coax grain out of the peasantry was based.[68] According to Chris Ward, this event reflected nothing along the lines of "class consciousness," however, but rather a "coincidence" of "discontents."[69]

Although the NEP era provided plenty of evidence of textile workers' ability to emasculate state policy at the point of production, the Bolsheviks concluded that a combination of class-war rhetoric and targeted repression would suffice to prevent a backlash against their program of forced capital accumulation.[70] Given the labor force's fragmentation and the delusional assumptions about living standards embedded in the plan, it is not difficult to fathom why the party miscalculated. The focus of the chapters that follow are the extent, severity, and consequences of that miscalculation.

1

The Workers Mobilize

The year 1928 was one of crisis for the textile industry. Although the conversion of mills to round-the-clock production was welcomed by operatives insofar as it increased the level of employment, enthusiasm soon gave way to anger as it became clear that the measure was to be accompanied by elevated workloads and a sharp deterioration in working conditions that suppressed take-home pay. Operatives responded to the threat to their physical well-being and living standards by engaging in myriad acts of protest, the most significant of which was the Sereda strike of August 1928. No sooner had that challenge to the program of forced capital accumulation been overcome, however, when a much greater one—incapacitating food shortages caused by Moscow's abandonment of the New Economic Policy (NEP) in agriculture—descended on industry shop floors.[1] Unable to feed themselves or their dependents, operatives denounced what they understood to be a betrayal of the October Revolution and insisted on immediate fulfillment of the implicit contract governing their relations with the party. Moscow got the message and, in November 1928, restored a semblance of order on shop floors by implementing a food-rationing system in Ivanovo and other major industrial regions.

If it had been implemented alone, the reduction in the length of the working day by 12.5 percent (from eight hours to seven), which was announced in the Jubilee Manifesto of October 1927, would have been popular, especially since it was accompanied by a promise that the new schedule would have no effect on workers' daily earnings. As it turned out, however, this measure was tarnished by two others that accompanied it: the intensification of labor and the introduction of a third (night) shift. It soon became clear to operatives that the shorter workday was not intended to alleviate their burdens, but to facilitate forced capital accumulation by enabling higher rates of exploitation of both labor and machinery. In the best circumstances, these measures would have taken months to implement smoothly. Faced with a policy-generated grain crisis, however, Moscow insisted that scores of mills make the transition in a matter of weeks. Such haste created a host of problems that stoked severe discontent on the shop floor and cancelled some of the anticipated gains in output and productivity.[2]

Less controversial than the intensification of labor was the introduction of the night shift, which, to the surprise of party leaders if not industry experts, failed to boost the output of cloth as much as anticipated. Blame for the measure's failure to live up to expectations lay with the party, whose impatience resulted in thousands of workers being hired and thrown onto shop floors with only rudimentary skills and training. The result was predictable: working conditions deteriorated sharply, which in turn suppressed productivity and earnings.[3]

From the shop floor's perspective, the most negative effect of round-the-clock production was that it severely aggravated living conditions. According to trade-union reports, the housing crisis was most acute in barracks and dormitories attached to mills that had recently added a night shift. Many families were sleeping on the floor, and the commotion caused by workers coming and going at all hours made it impossible "to get a good sleep." Complained those living in such facilities: "This isn't life, but torture."[4]

Although "the severe housing crisis" was a topic of discussion in April 1928 at the national trade-union congress, the party paid no attention because the decision had already been made to devote the industry's profits to new factories. That summer, some Ivanovo operatives found themselves living with their children "under the open sky."[5]

The effect on shop-floor morale was acute: in October 1928, a speaker at a regional trade-union congress noted that living conditions were provoking "counterrevolutionary protests" and "transgressions against the Soviet regime." But when the trade-union chairman, Grigorii Mel'nichanskii, broached the matter with Central Party Committee Secretary Lazar Kaganovich, he was curtly informed that "a huge sum" had already been earmarked for resolution of the problem. ("That's nonsense," retorted Mel'nichanskii.) Keenly aware that the crisis was as much economic as humanitarian, the trade union filed an urgent appeal with the Central Party Committee. Without an increase in spending for new dwellings, asserted the union, the output and productivity goals of the FFYP would remain beyond the capacity of the labor force.[6]

Despite the deterioration of living conditions, support for a third shift was substantial in Russia's textile regions. Concerned by a perceived decline in economic opportunities for their offspring, operatives saw in the measure a solution to the problem of youth unemployment, as well as a means to boost family income. Naturally, unemployed workers also were pleased by the measure—so much so, in fact, that a crowd of them marched on Shuia's Palace of Labor on January 2, 1928, to demand that it be implemented.[7]

Ironically, the strongest support for round-the-clock production came from the one group that was banned from it. Industry and trade-union leaders understood that night work was harmful to a worker's health and productivity. As a result, they forbade managers from assigning to the third shift women who were more than six months pregnant or who had been nursing for less than five months. Where officialdom spied danger, however, these women saw opportunity. At night, there were fewer supervisors to monitor one's performance, so workloads were lighter and the opportunities to rest or nurse an infant were more frequent. The third shift also offered a solution to the lack of child care because it was easier to find a sitter at night than during the day. For these reasons, many women concurred with economic planners, who were struggling to infuse the third shift with skilled labor, that the ban should be repealed.[8]

The battle lasted for months, with women and planners on one side and the trade union and the Labor Commissariat on the other. Under pressure to hire hundreds of workers quickly, managers stifled objections when pregnant and nursing women—or, for that matter, juveniles younger than seventeen, who also were covered by the ban—applied for a job. For their part, women seeking employment on the third shift evaded questions about their reproductive or nursing status. In the end, worker-management collusion and "the protest of the women workers themselves" rendered the ban toothless.[9]

Although the government considered amending the ban, it was affirmed as originally written. Why were the protests of women and planners ignored? The answer seems to be that the ban carried symbolic significance. Although most workers initially welcomed round-the-clock production, night work evoked bitter memories. "We always fought against night shifts," declared the weaver Krasilova during a "very stormy" assembly at Vichuga's Nogin Mill, "but now they're foisting them on us." Elsewhere, trade-union officials and operatives expressed alarm after seeing women whose daytime domestic responsibilities and nighttime employment left them on the verge of collapse. These "exhausted workers are swaying like drunks," observed a Red Perekop operative. "Soviet power is worse than tsarism; it's wearing the workers out."[10] One way the party responded to such criticism was by pointing to labor-protection laws, including the partial ban on night work. That such measures were unevenly enforced was not accidental. Their function was symbolic.

The Intensification of Labor

While many operatives welcomed round-the-clock production, the attitude toward labor-intensification measures—in particular, the requirement that workers service three or four spinning frames or weaving looms instead of two—was negative. Indeed, such measures were the primary source of discontent on shop floors before the severe food shortages of autumn 1928. Resistance, which took "more or less organized forms" and was often led by "veteran worker-proletarians," was most pronounced among three groups that found the extra workloads unbearable: peasant workers who had long commutes or substantial agricultural duties; women who were intensely burdened by domestic obligations; and older workers whose bodies were in decline. Also opposed were those for whom intensification meant assignment to unfamiliar equipment and/or work teams, a decline in earnings, or layoffs. Because they interpreted it as a source of their suffering, unemployed operatives spoke out as well, albeit beyond the confines of the mill.[11]

More receptive to intensification were those whose primary concern was to maximize wage earnings: *sumochniki,* or peasant workers who rented living quarters near the factory and commuted to their native village on days off; peasant workers who needed money to improve their land; and individuals so poor they would do anything to better their standard of living. Obviously, the complex patterns of opposition, tolerance, and support cannot be understood merely in terms of the binary categories (peasant/proletarian, conscious/unconscious, party/nonparty) employed in official sources. Responses from below were shaped not just by ties to the land and the party, but by other factors as well, including age and physical condition, standard of living, family size, length of commute, current workload, and access to alternative sources of income.[12]

While certain members of the labor force stood to gain from intensification and therefore welcomed it, their enthusiasm withered. Even under ideal conditions, elevating workloads would have been difficult without temporarily disrupting production. In the context of a reorganization of work schedules (the seven-hour day) and a massive expansion of production (the third shift), it was impossible.

Determined to forge ahead with the program of forced capital accumulation, the Central Party Committee dismissed local officialdom's appeals for more time to prepare mills for round-the-clock production with elevated workloads. By no means were such appeals unreasonable: the party had been advised by experts that these measures should be implemented only after a year of preparation. That advice was too "bourgeois" for the Stalinists, however, who demanded implementation within three to eight weeks.[13]

Operatives who underwent intensification were assured that their machines would be renovated and maintained, that the supply and quality of raw cotton would be satisfactory, that their auxiliary functions would be taken over by others, and that their incomes would rise. Inevitably, they were disappointed. In a June 1928 memorandum to regional bureaus, trade-union secretary Voronova made note of "the tense state of workers in seven-hour mills" and "the unceasing demands by workers for an improvement in working conditions, remuneration, and living conditions." Only by addressing these problems, she concluded, might failure of the new production regime be avoided. Moreover, the haste with which it had been implemented "lessened to a considerable degree the political significance of the Jubilee Manifesto in the eyes of the workers" and "in the end, provoked conflicts and strikes."[14]

How bad were conditions on the shop floor? A study of seven-hour mills found that workloads per employee rose 14.3 percent in spinning sheds and 16.1 percent in weaving sheds. The effects, however, were unevenly distributed. While auxiliary workers and new hires got by relatively unscathed, veteran operatives saw their workloads climb by 50 to 100 percent.[15] This explains why spinners and weavers were at the forefront of job actions in 1928. On top of the various labor-intensification schemes implemented under the NEP, the basic crafts now were told to do more.[16] We have already seen that several segments of the labor force were inclined to make sacrifices, primarily for reasons of material self-interest. What was the fate of that support?

In short, it was sacrificed to haste. With no time to upgrade equipment, to retrain workers, or to improve the quality of inputs, managers could not elevate workloads without negative repercussions. The results were as experts anticipated: the hourly productivity of labor and machinery declined as exhaustion overcame the human and material factors of production; on-the-job accidents climbed by more than a third; the proportion of defective product rose; and wage earnings either fell or failed to rise enough to compensate for the additional burden operatives now bore.[17]

Of course, the impact of labor intensification varied substantially by mill, shed, and job category, which in turn shaped the patterns of response from below. As we explore these patterns, three summary points should be kept in mind. First, a central promise of the Jubilee Manifesto—that daily income would not suffer as a result of the 12.5 percent reduction in working hours—was not fulfilled. Instead of rising by the necessary amount of 14.3 percent, average hourly earnings increased by only 9 percent. In other words, the switch to the seven-hour day was accompanied by an average 4.6 percent *decline* in daily earnings. Second, those suffering the greatest drop in income were workers who for one reason or another did not undergo intensification. Though not surprising, given the overall decline in productivity, that outcome had an important consequence for collective action: whether or not intensification directly affected them, most workers had reason to oppose it. Finally, a substantial portion of those subjected to the measure, such as weavers who added a fourth loom to their stable of three, "received almost no compensation" for the additional output.[18]

Although the influx of new workers and the implementation of round-the-clock production contributed to the problems cited above, intensification bore the brunt of the blame. For the most part, this was justified: while workers on night shifts and new workers on any shift put in the worst performance, veteran workers on day shifts also failed to fulfill expectations. More important, mills that intensified labor without converting to the seven-hour day or adding a night shift were spared neither complications nor unrest.[19]

How did workers respond? Resentful that they bore the brunt of the burden and that their earnings had been dragged down by new hires, veteran operatives insisted that each machine's output be measured at the end of the shift instead of the end of the day. When implemented, this adjustment strengthened the correlation between individual performance and compensation—which, in turn, increased the pressure on new hires to improve their performance. As well, labor discipline declined in "almost all" seven-hour mills as workers' exhaustion from heavier workloads and the barracks' descent into chaos drove rates of unauthorized absenteeism up by as much as 43 percent.[20] Yet these responses—one divisive, the other passive—paled in comparison to the opposition that erupted when intensification was first announced.

The first wave of protest occurred in December 1927, when Communist and nonparty overlookers fell into an uproar as the new collective contract came up for ratification. Of the provisions they opposed, the most unpopular required them to service 20 percent more looms than before (that is, forty-eight looms instead of forty). In Vichuga, the overlookers of the Red Profintern Mill held "illegal meetings in apartments to work out a common protest." In Sereda, they vowed to oppose the measure "no matter what the Communists decree." In Ivanovo, they demanded the summoning of "an all-city conference of [weaving] overlookers" and threatened to go on strike. In Teikovo, delegates to a similar conference denounced the measure, lambasted the trade union for allowing it to be included in the contract, and praised Leon Trotsky for having foreseen that the seven-hour day would allow management to "pile extra work on the worker." At the Navoloki Mill, meanwhile, an assembly of four hundred worker-delegates broke into "thunderous applause" as overlookers condemned management, the trade union, and the seven-hour day—and declared that "socialism must not be built on the workers' backs."[21]

Equally strident was the rhetoric at Kineshma's Red Volga Mill, where the overlooker Burmistrov mobilized opposition to intensification on the grounds that "we're already choking . . . with work, and now it'll be worse than serfdom." The effect of such agitation became apparent at an assembly during which the Communist Sirotkin accused class enemies in the State Textile Trust of endeavoring "to agitate the workers and lead them to resistance against the Soviet regime," and the ex-Communist Kiselev accused the party of loading "the burden of . . . industrialization" on "the workers' shoulders." Similar sentiments were expressed by overlookers at the Iuzha Mill, who conveyed their opposition to management "in a sharp and categorical manner" and, aside from expressing concerns about the consequences for their health and earnings, complained that the pressure being put on the shop floor demonstrated that "we have coercion and exploitation . . . [in] the Soviet Union."[22]

Concerned that the elevation of workloads would increase the proportion of defective product, suppress wage earnings, and hasten the demise of their bodies and machines, overlookers protested with more unanimity than they had summoned in years. Faced with a serious rebellion among a crucial category of workers, the regional trade-union bureau convened a conference of overlookers and deleted the measure from the contract.[23]

In contrast to the experience of the overlookers, spinners and weavers learned of intensification only when newspapers published the relevant decree on January 7, 1928. Opposition erupted immediately. At the Red Perekop Mill, operatives at an all-factory conference denounced the party for "wringing the sweat out of the working class" and for industrializing the nation "on the backs of the workers." Vowing to "toss the Communists . . . out the window," they also passed a resolution that rejected the new workloads as "impossible." Because the response was so negative, even among party members, implementation was postponed there for several months.[24]

Fearing a similar response, the party cell at the Upper Sereda Mill advised management to proceed cautiously. This was sound advice: at all eleven assemblies convened in mid-January 1928 to discuss the measure, female spinners praised the reduction in working hours but categorically rejected intensification. When management responded by drafting nine volunteers from the Lower Mill and four unemployed women from the Labor Exchange to service four frames apiece, the spinners blocked access to the equipment, beat up the new hires, and tossed them out the gates. Later, when one of their number defected, they shut down their frames for an hour.[25]

As was the case in many mills, Sereda's spinners—including a number of party members—offered several justifications for their "stubborn resistance against the government's measure." First, not enough auxiliary workers were available to take over the time-consuming duties, such as retrieving supplies and sweeping debris, that made it difficult to operate more than two frames apiece. Second, the mill's capital stock was too dilapidated to tolerate the reduction in individual attention that resulted from intensification. Finally, the new workloads were unbearable, especially for those confronted by difficult living conditions or burdensome domestic or agricultural obligations.[26]

The second round of assemblies held in Sereda to discuss the measure was even stormier than the first, with local party officials cowed into submission by the "shouts of individual women." In an emotional speech that brought many of her colleagues to the verge of "hysteria," the ring-frame spinner Palitsina argued that "we can't go over to intensified work because it's got death in store for us. It'd be better to be taken to a field and shot with machine guns than to go over to four frames. That way, we'd perish together." Added her colleague, Rumiantseva: "We struggled for years for the Revolution, we're living under Soviet power, we're trying to get socialism, but it's not socialism that comes out of our comrades, but the oppression of the workers—serfdom." Similar complaints were voiced by male operatives. "The Soviet regime was headed for socialism," noted the nonparty mule spinner Kudriashchov, "but halted before reaching it, headed for capitalism, and began struggling for money." Since audiences responded to such remarks "with concerted applause," managers disbanded the assemblies before putting the measure to a vote.[27]

Soon the district trade-union chairman delivered a message to Sereda's spinners: he would neither support their position nor defend those who had attacked the new hires; furthermore, he would authorize implementation with or without their approval. Despite the tough rhetoric, only 17 of the Upper Mill's 612 ring-frame spinners agreed to take on elevated workloads. Among the flyer-frame spinners, opposition remained firm.[28]

Although some of the most vocal critics of intensification hailed from the mule-spinning department, all 442 of its employees submitted to the measure within several weeks. Why did they turn out to be relatively pliable? Two factors appear to have been decisive. First, most of the mule spinners were men, who as a rule were less burdened by domestic respon-

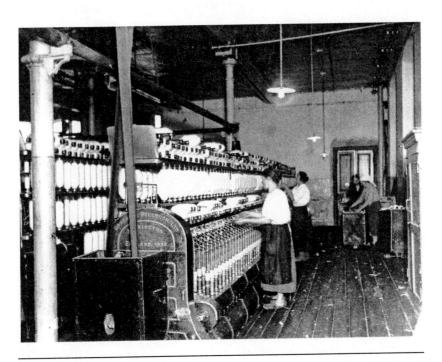

Figure 3. Flyer-frame spinners at an Ivanovo mill, 1926. Russian State Archive of Documentary Films and Photographs.

sibilities, hence less threatened by intensification than the exclusively female ring-frame and flyer-frame spinners. As well, mule spinners enjoyed more control over the labor process—theirs was an older, less automated type of production—which made it easier for them to customize intensification to the idiosyncrasies of their machines, work teams, and bodies.[29]

Notwithstanding the mule spinners' defection, operatives continued to voice support for the resisters, whose ranks now consisted primarily of female spinners and operatives with burdensome ties to the land. For example, the weaving overlooker Suslov condemned "the Soviet regime" for oppressing the workers "worse than the merchants"; the shuttle adjuster Kisiakov accused Moscow of "pushing the workers to go on strike" so that it could "up and close the mills"; and the greaser Katin predicted that "the end will come to [the Communists] . . . because not only the workers but also the peasantry is against [them]." Still others accused intensification enthusiasts—yes, there were a few—of endeavoring to win promotion into the ranks of management, or cautioned that elevated workloads "cripple[d] the workers" and exacerbated unemployment. Such agitation undoubtedly gave encouragement to the mill's (female) doffers, whose own anti-intensification protests soon yielded concessions.[30]

During the initial phase of implementation, other mills—especially those that failed to give workers a voice in the matter—also had rocky experiences. At the Shorygino Mill, female weavers and male overlookers jointly refused to submit to intensification, and bullied those who did. At the Teikovo Combine, "sharp protests against intensification" and hostility toward volunteers prevented managers from subjecting more than 2.3 percent of the looms to it. Moods also were sour on the shop floors of the Gorki-Pavlovo Mill. "It's . . . a mockery of the workers," declared the weaver Vikhrev. "They oppress us with intensified labor worse than under the old regime." In Lezhnevo, weavers insisted that the new workloads be rescinded immediately: "Down with three looms, three frames, and the forty-eight looms that they foist on the overlookers!" they shouted during an assembly. Similar protests were reported among weavers and flyer-frame spinners at the Kovrov Mill and among weavers at Kineshma's Dem'ian Bednyi Mill, where threats of a strike on account of "the bad equipment (looms) and the bad warp" prompted managers to authorize everyone to switch back to two looms apiece. Repeal of the measure likewise followed a series of protests by ring-frame spinners at Shuia Mill No. 1.[31]

That was not all. In Kokhma, a group of disenchanted former Bolsheviks descended on their mill's factory committee. "You [Communists] are beginning to oppress the workers worse than the capitalists," declared their spokesman, Salandin. "You're intensifying labor, dismissing workers, and introducing three looms and three frames against the workers' wishes." At an assembly held at Ivanovo's Sosnevo Mill, the ex-Communist and former oppositionist Vanchikov brought down the house when he called on the audience to elect trade-union delegates who could turn back the "attack taking place in all spheres against the workers." At Kineshma's Red Branch Mill, mule spinners responded with outrage when intensification was announced at a production meeting. In a moving speech, one of the fifty operatives in attendance demanded: "How many are ill now and how many will become ill under intensified labor? Will intensified labor be carried out forcibly or voluntarily? Will there be dismissal of workers under intensified labor? To what will this intensified labor lead: to the exhaustion of the people, or to socialism?" Quipped another speaker: "If workers in other countries find out that we've been treated like this, don't expect them to go down the path of revolution."[32]

Although overlookers did not participate in these protests, they offered support. For instance, when weavers at Vichuga's Shagov Amalgamated Mill responded to the intensification announcement by calling on colleagues "to fight for their achievements" and declare a strike, the overlookers denounced management's resort to "brute force" and its attempt "to enserf the entire working class." The mutual support offered by overlookers and weavers at this juncture underscores the capacity of these crafts to overcome, if fleetingly, the gender conflict that traditionally characterized their relationship.[33]

Factory managers responded to the anti-intensification protests of early 1928 with ad hoc concessions: the measure was delayed, scaled back, or made voluntary. Collective action thus bore fruit. Still, victory was elusive. This was not because managers were eager to press ahead—most were not—but rather because the party was unwilling to back down from its radical program of forced capital accumulation.[34]

An example of the new, firmer approach came in May 1928, when the Central Party Committee ordered the Iaroslavl Region Party Committee to elevate workloads in all sheds of the Red Perekop Mill. Because the new workloads were unbearable, the technical shortcomings severe, and management's behavior inflammatory, moods grew "foul" in the preparatory department and scattered work stoppages erupted among flyer-frame spinners and drawing-frame tenders. This time, however, all complaints were ignored.[35]

The Deterioration of Working Conditions

Following the unrest over implementation came the unrest over unintended consequences. In April 1928, operatives at the Red Perekop Mill and 241 flyer-frame spinners at Shuia Mill No. 2 threatened to strike when their postintensification earnings failed to rise as much as promised. No sooner had these conflicts been quelled when discontent over intensification-related technical difficulties, including sharply elevated rates of thread breakage, prompted 25 ring-frame spinners at Shuia Mill No. 1 to unilaterally switch back to three frames apiece and 411 others to idle their machines for two hours. Similar problems provoked "sharp discontent" and a strike threat from 200 ring-frame spinners at Ivanovo's Dzerzhinskii Mill.[36]

Job actions over working conditions often ended badly for the workers. Managers took a tough line because they understood that the strikers' demands typically were too narrow to trigger sympathetic protests among operatives in other departments. Two back-to-back strikes at Ivanovo's Balashov Mill illustrate the point. After weeks of grumbling over high rates of thread breakage, sixty-nine ring-frame spinners launched a two-day strike. Their demands: higher-quality raw materials and a wage supplement to cover lost earnings. The protest was quashed rapidly by managers wielding threats of dismissal, although the situation remained volatile. "You drink our blood," the organizer of the protest, veteran spinner Kotova, told the director. "We're wearing ourselves out, and if the breakage doesn't stop, then we'll give up work again."[37]

No sooner had Kotova uttered her threat when a strike erupted over the same issue among seventy-one winding-frame tenders in the weaving shed. After forcing two Komsomols who opposed the job action to stop working, the women appealed to the beam warpers for support. Rebuffed, they maintained solidarity for the rest of the day by singing, dancing, and taunting officials who repeatedly threatened to sack them. Later, a commission established to investigate the conflict conceded that the women's complaints were justified—and, in the same breath, condemned the protest, sacked ten of the strikers, and reprimanded the rest. Whether that sent a message to other operatives at what, in 1927, had been the region's most strike-prone mill, it certainly sowed hostility. "They don't have the right to dismiss workers because our demands [were] justified," the striker Gubanova told a group of her colleagues. "What sort of damned worker's regime is this when 'the bosses'—the workers—are driven out of the mill?" The same question could have been posed at the Great Kokhma Combine,

Figure 4. Winding-frame tenders at Ivanovo's Balashov Mill, 1926. Russian State Archive of Documentary Films and Photographs.

where ten ring-frame spinners found themselves headed to the Labor Exchange after spearheading a two-day strike over dilapidated equipment.[38]

Whatever the outcome—and managers did grant concessions from time to time—such protests paled in comparison to the massive strike that crippled the Upper Sereda Mill for two and a half days in August 1928. During this event, more than two thousand spinners idled their machines to protest working conditions and wages that had deteriorated sharply following the elevation of workloads and the implementation of round-the-clock production. Although discontent had been brewing for months, the strike stunned officials accustomed to protests that were relatively easy to contain. More important, the strike—the largest by Russian cotton workers in twenty months—illuminated a fundamental contradiction: the program of forced capital accumulation denied managers the resources required to fulfill promises made to secure workers' compliance with the program's demands.

The management of the Upper Sereda Mill won the mule spinners' agreement to elevate workloads only after promising to take steps—such as procuring higher-quality raw cotton that would be less susceptible to breakage, and hiring more auxiliary workers—that would prevent the measure from suppressing earnings. Initially, management fulfilled its obligations, and the mule spinners' income rose. Then, under pressure from the party to cut costs, industry officials began to supply mills with poor-quality raw cotton. Rates of thread breakage increased, and earnings decreased. In Sereda, the problem was compounded when, in May 1928, the Upper Mill implemented round-the-clock production. The spinners now had to earn a living in seven hours instead of eight, and share their equipment with poorly trained recruits from the night shift.[39]

Angered by the situation, the mule spinners demanded, and received, a monthly wage supplement of 3.5 to 7 percent. They were satisfied until management, under pressure to cut costs despite the expense of converting to round-the-clock production, suspended the supplement. The mule spinners appealed to an arbitration court, and won. Management now found itself in an impossible situation: on one hand, it was being ordered to honor an agreement about living standards that it struck with the spinners to get them to take on elevated workloads; on the other, it was being deprived by the center of funds required to fulfill that agreement. Since there was no denying Moscow its tribute, management secured permission from the State Textile Trust and the regional trade-union bureau to cancel the supplement as of August.[40]

Informed of management's plans, a group of mule spinners who had substantial authority on the shop floor—including Sorokin, a former instructor for the regional trade-union bureau who recently had been expelled from the party for political reasons—began agitating for a strike. The response of the district party committee was predictable: it formed two commissions—one consisting of operatives, the other of trust officials—to study the matter. Sorokin and his colleagues had been betrayed too often, however, to put faith in such measures. As a result, they convened "illegal meetings" to plan their next move.[41]

While these events were under way, the mill's annual summer furlough was coming to an end. Returning to work after a two-week absence, the mule spinners discovered that management had inadvertently allowed the roving (coarse thread) to dry out, which threatened to further elevate the breakage rate. After many broken promises, this indignity was too much to bear. Spearheaded by Sorokin, the ex-Communist Peunkov, and six other mule spinners, appeals for a strike coursed through the shed.[42]

Alarmed, several Communists raced to the factory committee and the party cell and demanded that the roving be replaced. Officials soon arrived on the shop floor and endeavored to convene an assembly. The mule spinners' response revealed the immediate, if unintended, effect of the internally contradictory program of forced capital accumulation: a breakdown in worker-management relations.

> You promised us a lot when we went over to intensified work, but . . . didn't fulfill the promise, carried out the seven-hour day at the worker's expense, [and] gave out bad cotton so that it was harder to work and so that the worker bit the dust sooner. So . . . we won't make any more deals with you and won't get back to work until our demands are fulfilled by central authorities. We only hope that the [trade union's] central committee will come and look into all of this and then whip . . . you by the neck.

When mule spinners from the next shift began arriving at the mill, their colleagues appealed to them for support: "Don't begin work! We've nothing to talk about with local representatives. They've deceived us." These appeals were successful: the overwhelming majority of mule spinners joined the strike, and stood by their promise to one another—"We won't let anyone work!"—by sabotaging the strikebreakers' frames.[43]

By 1:45 PM on August 16, all the Upper Sereda Mill's mule-spinning frames were idle. The strikers' demand was straightforward: immediate fulfillment of the promises, such as satisfactory working conditions and average daily earnings of four rubles, fifteen kopecks, that had been made when they initially agreed to intensification. (In recent months, the strikers' earnings fell shy of that figure by 17 percent.) Unexpectedly for the authorities, and perhaps for the mule spinners themselves, operatives from other departments also idled their machines. By late afternoon, 700 of the mill's 5,800 workers—including the mule spinners, ring-frame spinners, flyer-frame spinners, winding-frame tenders, and beam warpers—were on strike. Alarmed by this evidence of shop-floor solidarity, party officials ordered all Communists and Komsomols to get back to work. As a rule, they were obeyed, though more by the latter than the former, and only after resistance by strike enforcers was overcome.[44]

The next day, August 17, two thousand workers were on strike. The solidarity was remarkable, but there were limits to it, as there had been in other strikes triggered by a postintensification deterioration in working conditions. For example, operatives whose workloads had not been substantially elevated—card, picker, and drawing-frame tenders, repairmen, greasers, and certain types of overlookers—stayed on the job even as they

Figure 5. A beam warper at Ivanovo's Dzerzhinskii Mill, 1932. Russian State Archive of Documentary Films and Photographs.

voiced sympathy for the strikers' demand. Also absent, it seems, were the mill's weavers, whose shed was located some distance away. As for the handful of spinners who broke ranks with the strikers, their machines were a constant target of sabotage.[45]

At 11:00 AM, local and regional leaders of the trade union and the trust asked strikers from the various departments—who by now were meeting collectively—to return to work and elect representatives to participate in negotiations. The strikers balked. "We won't work until you give us a final answer," they declared, "and we call for a representative of the [trade union's] central committee to settle" the conflict.[46]

A group of mule- and ring-frame spinners now submitted a list of formal demands—which included higher wages, higher-quality raw cotton, more auxiliary workers, and better supplies of production materials—to the factory committee. Spotlighting its alienation from the workers whose interests it claimed to serve, the factory committee rejected the wage demands out of hand. Understandably, this response further inflamed shop-floor passions. When regional party officials arrived in Sereda later that day, they found it impossible to end the strike.[47]

Although all spinning crafts were represented in the strikers' ranks, the mule spinners were viewed as leaders of the conflict. Traditionally, mule spinners commanded respect because they were among the oldest, most experienced, and best compensated members of the labor force. The following illustrates the esteem in which the mule spinners were held: when the factory committee asked striking ring-frame spinners to complete an urgent order for the military, it found that they would do so only after securing the mule spinners' permission.[48]

During an expanded plenum of the factory committee on the evening of August 17, officials of the regional trade-union bureau and the district party committee condemned the strike. While conceding that there were problems to overcome, they claimed that operatives elsewhere had won concessions without resort to such tactics. Though misleading insofar as small-scale work stoppages were not uncommon at this time, that line of argument contributed to the passage of a resolution condemning the strike. (It was promptly posted throughout the mill.) As for the handful of carefully vetted speakers, one—a collective-farm peasant—called on strikers to return to work lest their actions jeopardize the worker-peasant alliance (*smychka*).[49]

The number of strikers reached 2,263 on August 18, the same day Smirnov—a representative of the trade union's central committee—arrived in Sereda. After debriefing the factory committee, Smirnov went to see the mule spinners, who bitterly recounted management's failure to honor the agreement reached prior to implementation of the new workloads. Smirnov responded by declaring that the strike was illegal and insisting that everyone get back to work. During the two hours of stormy negotiations that followed, management threatened dismissals and word arrived that the Lower Sereda Mill—which had yet to implement round-the-clock production and whose mule spinners were divided in their opinion of the strike—continued to operate at full capacity. Endeavoring to make the best of a bad situation, the Upper Mill mule spinners called off the strike after receiving assurance that their complaints would be reviewed.[50]

All departments returned to work after learning of the mule spinners' agreement with Smirnov. That evening, a special assembly was called to order. Among the four hundred delegates in attendance were the strike's most active participants, who laid blame for the conflict on "the economic and administrative officials" who failed to live up to their promises. After several officials defended their grievance-handling procedures, the assembly voted to create a commission whose task was to solicit and review petitions. Prominent strikers from the mule-spinning department were elected to this body, as were the outspoken ring-frame spinner Razgulina and a single rank-and-file party member (Kholostov, one of the strike's zealous defenders). Eleven of the commission's forty seats were reserved for officials from the factory, the trade union, and the trust, which guaranteed a strong voice for the authorities.[51]

At an assembly held a week after the strike, the commission announced its findings. As a rule, requests for minor technical improvements were fulfilled, and demands for higher wages and lower output norms were sent to arbitration or rejected. Convinced that management had hijacked the commission's proceedings, speakers from the floor protested. Under pressure from the presidium, however, a majority voted to approve the official protocol.[52]

Not surprisingly, classified reports written in the strike's aftermath failed to identify the internally contradictory program of forced capital accumulation as its cause. Instead, blame was placed—as it always would be in such cases—on local officials, who were accused of ignoring the workers' needs and failing to mobilize support for revolution "from above." Meanwhile, the trade union publicly accused the Sereda spinners of having made a "mistake" that brought irreparable "harm" upon "the state." Operatives scoffed at articles published in the trade union's mouthpiece, *Voice of the Textile Worker*, which blamed the strike on "the evil will of a small group of adversaries of the worker's state who strove by all possible means to disorient the backward workers." But they knew better than to ignore warnings that insubordination would be punished.[53] In fact, such warnings probably played a role in preventing workers from acting on the ubiquitous strike agitation that, as we shall see, swept shop floors in response to the severe food shortages of autumn 1928.

To be sure, the Sereda strike inspired a wave of lesser protests against intensification. In Rodniki, mule spinners stormed out of an assembly and threatened to strike after months of elevated workloads left them with depressed earnings and a lack of auxiliary workers. In Vichuga, weavers descended on the factory committee and disrupted assemblies, demanding bitterly that intensification measures be repealed. Similar demands poured forth in Kokhma and Ivanovo, where scattered work stoppages broke out in spinning sheds.[54]

While the Sereda strike raised alarms at the highest levels about the "very unhealthy" moods provoked by the program of forced capital accumulation, it also laid bare the limits of rank-and-file solidarity. The failure of the strikers to win the allegiance of workers from the Lower Mill—or, for that matter, of workers from certain other departments of the Upper Mill—underscored the tenuousness, at this juncture, of class identity. Comforted by what seemed to be the fragmentation of the labor force and the fact that major strikes were far from being a "mass, universal" phenomenon, the party revealed not a hint of doubt about the textile industry's ability to finance forced-draft industrialization.[55]

Publicly, the trade union clung to its position that intensification be implemented "with a firm hand," and to its claim that doing so would solve the goods famine, boost wages, and generate profits with which to develop heavy industry. Privately, though, it warned the party of "the tense situation with regard to [worker] moods . . . which manifests itself in strikes and disturbances that sometimes grip entire mills," and requested that the pressure on operatives somehow be relieved. "All the time we have intensification, intensification, intensification," trade-union chairman Mel'nichanskii complained at an emergency conference convened by Kaganovich on October 10, 1928. "When you have a tête-à-tête with economic planners, [even] they say that 'it's gotten hard to work in the enterprise.'" The root of the problem, he concluded, was the government's effort to boost labor productivity without major new investments in the industry's dilapidated capital stock.[56]

Even as Kaganovich summarily rejected such analyses, resistance passed from enterprises that had implemented intensification to those next in line to do so. At Ivanovo's Balashov Mill, for example, three hundred ring-frame spinners erupted in "sharp indignation" when the director informed them that they would have to service four frames apiece, and that noncompliance would be rewarded with a one-way ticket to the Labor Exchange. "Bloodsuckers!" shouted the women, as they surrounded their superior and threatened to beat him. "You only scoff at us! We won't work under intensification and won't go to the exchange!" Once order was restored, speakers from the floor protested that intensification was always implemented haphazardly and "at the expense of their health," and that "many workers" were already "working to the point of exhaustion." After firmly noting that "we won't give up our pair of looms," the spinners rejected the factory committee's resolution.[57]

The response was no less strident when the matter was put to a joint assembly of one thousand of the mill's spinners and weavers. After ridiculing official claims about the "triple exploitation" of the working class in the West, speakers condemned the measure. "Remember how our fathers fell victim in 1905 because they didn't want to work on four looms?" demanded the weaver Kirillova, whose red kerchief initially provoked catcalls from the audience. "How many Cossack whips did we get? We struggled for socialism then. But what do we see now? Oppression. We won't accept four looms; we won't put our brother-workers out." Confronted by an audience on the verge of riot, presidium members turned on their heels and fled.[58]

The Food-Supply Crisis

The shortage of food was the most common source of disaffection on shop floors during the FFYP. The first signs of trouble surfaced in early 1928—that is, months before the plan formally got under way—when the Trade Commissariat failed to fulfill its delivery commitments to most Russian mill towns. Although the resulting shortages were not critical, they were bad enough to sow "discontent" among "individual groups of workers." In Teikovo, calico operatives warned that "we won't allow the comrades to create famine for us again" and threatened to go on strike, while overlookers denounced the incompetence of "our rulers, the Communists," and demanded that they "stop feeding us with promises." At the Iuzha Mill, angry women attending a general assembly noted that "we've endured mockery for ten years" and warned that "we'll stop working if they don't give us bread." In Shuia and Rodniki, male operatives told colleagues that the Soviet regime was a "coercive" one "that drinks our blood" and whose fate was to "fly away . . . like Nicholas II flew away." In

Kostroma, the failure of cooperatives to fulfill obligations to shareholders provoked "great discontent." Rumors that the Communists were again using force to requisition grain from peasants, and that famine and war were just around the corner, further exacerbated tensions.[59]

District party committees and the leadership of the trade union responded to the simmering discontent by pressuring the Trade Commissariat to fulfill its delivery commitments. This seems to have had some effect, for supplies improved briefly during the spring of 1928. No sooner had the crisis in the industrial regions of European Russia subsided, however, when an even more serious one was reported elsewhere. In May, sixteen "mass protests" that were organized by women and featured demands for bread took place in various parts of the country, while "serious discontent" bordering on "strike moods" was reported among Urals and Siberian workers, who suddenly found themselves confronting bread queues of up to 1,500 consumers and skyrocketing flour prices. This time, the Trade Commissariat was unable to respond effectively, for the first wave of Stalin's assault on the peasantry had triggered a severe imbalance between supply and demand. Inevitably, shortages and discontent spread. By the summer of 1928, "a mood of panic" beset urban areas, which provoked a wave of hoarding as well as destabilizing rumors "about famine, hunger riots, insurrections in other towns, the proximity of war, [and] the introduction of a rationing system." Predictably, major centers of industry reported "strike tendencies" on shop floors, where labor discipline plummeted as the desperate struggle for food got under way.[60]

The pattern of unrest in the Ivanovo-Voznesensk Region initially was favorable to the authorities. Although moods on shop floors there were "especially tense" during the summer, protests tended to dissipate in one location before breaking out in another. In June, for example, workers at Vichuga's Nogin Mill became agitated and probably went on strike when the cooperative ran out of produce. Next month, bread shortages triggered threats of violence against authorities at the Novye Gorki Mill, while operatives attending stormy assemblies at two Ivanovo mills condemned the reappearance of "queues, like in 1917," and accused "the government" of looking after its own needs while "our brother-workers" went without "a slice of bread."[61] By August, however, isolated protests such as these gave way to what trade-union chairman Mel'nichanskii characterized as "a wave of strikes" in the major textile regions. Alarmed by the rapid deterioration of shop-floor morale, and the threat this posed to the party's ambitious program of forced capital accumulation, regional industry officials demanded that "the most urgent and radical measures" be taken to normalize supplies.[62]

On September 4, 1928, the governing body of the country's consumer cooperatives—the Central Union of Cooperatives—sounded the alarm. In an urgent memorandum to party, state, and trade-union leaders, it noted that deliveries of staples to industrial towns in European Russia were running 50 to 70 percent below plan. Since industry could accomplish nothing in such conditions, "the most serious attention" had to be paid to "the extremely grave state of food supply in working-class centers." To its credit, the Trade Commissariat drafted a proposal to improve supplies in the textile regions.[63] Inevitably, however, this proposal failed to address the underlying cause of the crisis—that is, Stalin's violent, ideologically driven assault on the market and the peasantry. The industry that was supposed to produce a massive surplus for industrialization thus plunged into crisis even as the party prepared to celebrate the formal launch, on October 1, of the FFYP.

The crisis was acute in the four textile regions—Iaroslavl, Ivanovo-Voznesensk, Kostroma, and Vladimir—that soon would merge to form the mighty Ivanovo Industrial Region. Confronted with dwindling supplies and a "very tense" mood in the mills, district party committees fired off urgent memoranda beseeching their superiors to arrange immediate deliveries of flour "to calm the agitated workers." The shortages did not affect all operatives equally—hardest hit were those with children, those whose workloads had recently been elevated, and those lacking ties to the land—and sometimes laid bare tensions within the labor force. Their main effect, however, was to prompt workers to draw together in defense of their shared interest in adequate supplies of food.[64]

The workers' solidarity in the face of this crisis is not difficult to fathom. The shortages violated the values of their moral economy. Bread, moreover, was loaded with symbolic significance. The party's failure to provide workers with the first item in the slogan that brought it to power in 1917—"bread, land, peace, all power to the soviets"—sowed doubt about the legitimacy of its rule and the wisdom of its policies.

A report on the mood of Vichuga operatives illustrates not only the severity of the crisis, but also the extent to which bread was a collective concern of the labor force. At the Red Profintern Mill, each group of disaffected workers coalesced around a different issue. For instance, 500 machinists wanted to be reimbursed for the cost of their work clothes;

300 spinners and weavers wanted to be transferred from the night shift to the day shift; and 120 spinners wanted to be supplied with higher-quality raw cotton. As for the food situation, however, the district party committee reported that it had given rise to complaints among *all* of the enterprise's eight thousand employees.[65]

Not surprisingly, much of the anger on shop floors was directed at cooperatives, which bore primary responsibility for supplying workers with bread, and at members of the local elite—including party officials, executives, and their wives—whose private shops remained reliably well-stocked. Antagonism toward authorities, who were reviled for living off the workers' labor while failing to fulfill the workers' basic needs, was reflected not only in the discourse that accompanied strike threats, but also in the observation by a Kokhma weaver that his colleagues "had stopped believing in the possibility of securing improvement in the situation with assistance from the administrative apparatus." Official attempts to blame the crisis on class enemies provoked ridicule. "The lecturer spoke about some 'enemies,' but where are they?" queried the old-time Sereda labor activist Golubev at a factory assembly. "There's no clergy, [and] Soviet power is everywhere." Operatives astutely attributed their suffering to the suppression of private trade and the peasantry, reluctantly concluding that "our regime . . . has reduced the people to starvation."[66]

Events in Teikovo illustrate the typical pattern of unrest at this juncture. After watching routine assemblies at the cotton combine get hijacked by workers incensed at having to contend with overnight bread queues—those with large families spearheaded the protests—authorities endeavored to restore order by calling an all-factory assembly. On the evening of September 9, 1928, one thousand workers packed into Teikovo's Palace of Labor. When the session opened, speakers from the floor bitterly contrasted the dismal performance of the cooperative with the privileged supply channels enjoyed by officialdom, demanded the repeal of punitive taxes that recently had been imposed on the peasantry, and called for retribution against "the saboteurs of grain procurement" in the government. District party officials were pleased that "speculators"—that is, private traders who had taken advantage of the shortages by jacking up prices—also came under attack, and that the announcement that food packets would be calibrated to family size was applauded. They urgently informed the regional party committee, however, that "the workers' mood around the matter of supply is very aggravated, [and] can be eliminated only by issuing a sufficient quantity of the required grain products."[67]

As bad as the food-supply crisis was in towns such as Teikovo, it was even worse in the surrounding countryside, which gave rise to "a lot of discontent and censuring of Soviet power among . . . groups" of peasants, who were spreading rumors of "riots [triggered] by hunger" and predicting that the party's assault on the village would provoke "a new revolution." In an indication of the close connection between field and factory, peasant moods were darkest in the same districts—including Teikovo, Vichuga, and Sereda—that reported severe labor discontent. Most alarming from the party's perspective, "unhealthy moods" in the civilian population were triggering "disturbances" among Red Army troops stationed near the mills.[68]

By October 1928, a rank-and-file Communist's warning that "hunger" would turn "60 percent" of the labor force into "malcontents" no longer seemed unduly alarmist. At an emergency conference convened that same month in Moscow by Kaganovich to discuss the crisis in Soviet mills, Mel'nichanskii bluntly identified bread shortages as the primary source of "the very unhealthy atmosphere," "the great discontent," and "the difficult situation with regard to worker moods." The signs of crisis were manifold: a plummeting rate of productivity; a skyrocketing rate of absenteeism; a surge in the number of strikes; and the appearance at trade-union headquarters of so many worker delegations bearing demands for food that "our central committee has begun to look like the [one] of 1920," when the country last found itself on the brink of famine.[69]

Confirming Mel'nichanskii's assessment were reports from the key textile regions on "the extraordinarily foul . . . mood" in the mills and the alarming economic and political implications of the shortages.[70] The opening paragraphs of an urgent memorandum to the Central Party Committee from the Ivanovo-Voznesensk Region Party Committee underscored the severity of the crisis provoked in one of the cradles of the Revolution by Stalin's revolution "from above":

> The mood of the workers of both the city of Ivanovo and the region *has sharply deteriorated recently as a result of the shortages of basic grain products* . . .
>
> The discontent among the workers is being provoked . . . by reduced flour and bread distribution, and queues. The [queues], moreover, are growing as a result of all kinds of rumors . . . being conveyed by anti-Soviet elements . . . which exacerbate . . . the panic of the population. [Worker] assemblies . . . have largely been reduced to discus-

sion of the question of foodstuffs, and . . . the problem of bread supply is serving—and especially in recent days—as the principal topic of
conversation not only among workers, but among the general population.

*Worker assemblies devoted to matters of bread supply proceed stormily
and often [include] sharp attacks against the Soviet regime and the
Communist Party, accompanied by appeals for the declaration of a
strike.*[71]

Given the legendary role played by the Ivanovo workers in the struggle
against autocracy and capitalism—they had established Russia's first workers' soviet during the Revolution of 1905 and led the general strike that
crippled the region's mills on the eve of the Bolshevik seizure of power—
it is no wonder that the regional party committee was alarmed by the dire
shortages, the wild rumors, the threats of collective action, and the chal-
lenges faced by local authorities as they struggled to contain the mounting
discontent.[72]

Reports from district party committees confirmed that the crisis was
severe. In Teikovo, the "very tense" mood on shop floors—now manifest
in public denunciations of the party's management of the economy—
prompted officials to convene the second all-factory assembly in as many
months. On October 21, 1928, one thousand operatives convened "in a
very stormy mood" and proceeded to overwhelm with "shouts" and
"heckling" both the official speaker and the rank-and-file Communists
who had nothing but "words" to offer. As at the previous assembly, speakers from the floor denounced the party's policies, such as the heavy taxation of the peasantry and the suppression of private trade, as well
as officialdom's disregard for the workers' needs. They also called for the
sacking of local officials, the recall of deputies to the city soviet, and the dispatch of an all-worker delegation to Moscow for direct talks with the
government.[73]

The raucous all-factory assembly held in Lezhnevo followed a similar
script, with speakers from the floor calling for a suspension of the war on
the market, demanding a new local government, and expressing astonishment that "the Communists" would fail to feed the workers after all that
the workers had done for the party. "If you want to govern, then give us
bread," demanded the worker Pestov. "Otherwise, go to hell [and] give us
the old 'exploited' life!" Should the crisis not be alleviated promptly, the
community was prepared to engage in collective action. "The workers

have been abandoned, the whole population has been abandoned," concluded Pestov's colleague, Mukhina. "If we're not given bread, then we'll march on the Soviets."[74]

One point bears emphasizing about most assemblies that took place at this time: a widespread complaint was that the party was violating the implicit contract that governed its relationship with the shop floor. After all the sacrifices that the workers made to bring down the old regime and to defend and strengthen Soviet power, how could the party now confront them with the prospect of starvation? Did it regard the workers as mere "beasts of burden"?[75] Had not the October Revolution been about securing dignity and respect, no less than bread? The sense of injustice—indeed, of betrayal—experienced on shop floors was no less profound than the pangs of hunger that provoked it.

Although the food-supply crisis of autumn 1928 affected some segments of the labor force more than others, it tended to propel operatives to band together in defense of their collective interest in adequate food supplies. As in Teikovo and Lezhnevo, assemblies held in scores of mills saw workers speaking in one voice—and threatening to idle production—if the party did not fulfill its minimal obligations. Yet the fact that no strikes broke out at this time suggests that something was holding workers back. Fear of the consequences, which included dismissal and arrest, played a role, as did explicit warnings from the trade union that strikes were illegal. Events in Sereda indicate that cleavages within the labor force also served as an impediment to collective action.

Confronted in October 1928 with severe bread shortages, operatives in Sereda responded, as did their counterparts elsewhere, with rage. When assemblies convened to discuss the crisis, participants hijacked them, threatened their superiors with violence, and demanded that agricultural taxes be reduced and that restrictions on private trade be repealed. The party stood condemned for "deceiving the workers" and for "having begun to oppress [them] worse than under capitalism." Strike threats were issued, as were prophecies of a "fourth revolution."[76]

The crisis affected all strata of the shop floor, and disaffection was widespread. But while authorities were the target of most criticism, some also was directed at other workers. In Sereda, two lines of demarcation came to the fore: one separating "proletarian" from "peasant" workers, and another separating "permanent" from "seasonal" employees. Although some scholars have questioned the sociological significance of binary identity categories such as these, they clearly bore meaning for operatives.

For example, the worker Semenov argued at an assembly convened at the Lower Sereda Mill that the cooperative should remove "peasant" workers from supply rolls and increase distributions to "proletarian" workers with large families. Once Semenov's proposal began to garner support, four speakers cautioned against steps that might "provoke hostility among the workers," and defended the right of "peasant" workers to receive supplies from the cooperative. Considering that half of Sereda's operatives were classified as having ties to the land, it is not surprising that Semenov's proposal was defeated. Still, the assembly did vote to remove seasonal workers—migrants from other towns who boasted almost no allies on the shop floor—from supply rolls.[77]

The Sereda assembly demonstrated that there were limits to shop-floor solidarity even in the face of severe food shortages. Although proposals to remove "peasant" workers from the rolls were not reported elsewhere, envy of those perceived to be protected from the shortages—or worse, to be benefiting from them—was not uncommon. In most cases, the target was local officialdom, which had a unifying effect on the labor force. Occasionally, however, it was *other workers:* seasonal migrants, those with strong ties to the land, or those considered to be favored by virtue of their residence in the regional or national capitals. By the same token, "peasant" workers sometimes expressed envy of their "proletarian" colleagues. "If they gave us the same rights as the proletarian, then we'd go hand in hand with him," explained a peasant employed at the Iuzha Mill. "But they dismiss us first and don't hire our children." Although they varied in severity from one mill to another, such cleavages help to explain why major strikes failed to erupt at this time even though shop-floor discontent was high and agitation for collective action was widespread.[78]

As for the envy directed toward Ivanovo workers, it was misplaced. The peak of the crisis in the region's capital came during the second week of October, when bread became so scarce that mills and schools all but closed as thousands of workers and their children queued for bread for hours at a time. Although no strikes were reported, "rumors of a rationing system" gave rise to "panic" on shop floors, with discontent acquiring "a mass character in some places" and giving rise to scathing critiques of Moscow's policies.[79]

A typical emergency assembly was the one held on October 10, 1928, at the Red Talka Mill, where the worker Ivanov took the podium before 236 colleagues. "They look upon the working class as they do upon animals," he declared. " 'Go and work,' they say, 'but don't ask for bread.' "

Ridiculing official claims that the country was "getting stronger," Ivanov instructed local authorities to "tell the government and the party" that "there's nothing to feed the children," and that the crisis was their own fault. "We're now carrying out a battle for the destruction of the private market, but without it we're sitting in hunger," he observed. "If [state organs] are unable to supply us, then let the private trader live!"[80]

When the applause subsided, party member Kolesov pinpointed trade policy as "the root of the evil." In his view, the government had "gone bankrupt" trying to exchange grain for "the machines" with which to expand industry and agriculture. "But where are the tractors?" he demanded. "The peasants don't have any." Far from having strengthened the economy, "export-import" had instead propelled it to the brink of "a rationing system."[81]

Equally infuriating to the Red Talka workers was that the party treated them like idiots by having "the press" feed them "lies" instead of reporting "the matter like it is." Besides laying bare the hollowness of the party's claim that it was only "backward" workers who opposed the revolution "from above"—presumably, such workers were illiterate and therefore not consuming official propaganda—these comments underscored the paradox that educating operatives made them more difficult—not easier—to control. As Kolesov himself put it: "You can't deceive me. In 1918, I was stupid; you could pull the wool over my eyes. But now I read the newspapers, I've become literate, and I listen to the radio every day. I get foreign stations—and they're laughing at us, comrades," because "we're bankrupt." By angrily silencing two officials who endeavored to rebuke him for these remarks, the audience communicated that it, too, would tolerate no more lies or false promises from above.[82]

After a week of endless queues and stormy factory assemblies, the Ivanovo City Soviet finally endeavored to defuse the crisis by inviting central and regional officials to address an extraordinary conference of 1,300 worker-delegates. The keynote address was given by the head of the regional party committee, Nikolai Kolotilov, who acknowledged that "panic" had descended upon shop floors and that workers, as a result, had begun to question the wisdom of the party's policies. After vigorously defending these same policies, Kolotilov condemned those who claimed—as many workers now did—that the current shortages signified a return to the desperate conditions of the Civil War.[83]

After an official from the Trade Commissariat spoke, the workers offered their own, very different, interpretations of the crisis. To applause and shouts of "Correct!" delegate Kotov of the Zinov'ev Mill invoked the October Revolution's social contract when he insisted that "the higher organs" that "demand output from us" had an obligation to "furnish us with the most basic necessities." Applause also punctuated a series of speeches that blamed the crisis on Moscow's abandonment of the NEP. "Our rulers are committing flagrant errors," noted delegate Kapralov. "[Lenin] was a sharp fellow. He understood . . . that you have to turn the land over to those who know how to work it . . . In 1923, there was more bread. In 1924, it was, 'Take as much as you want,' and the same in 1925–[19]26. [But] in 1927 . . . they squeezed the kulak [prosperous peasant] and taxed everyone." After noting that peasants had responded by refusing to sow their land, Kapralov laid out the implications for the party of its failure to supply the shop floor with bread: "Let even the devil himself govern us, but we'll be pleased with that ruler who has a correct policy, when there's enough of everything."[84]

The political implications were further spelled out in a speech by the weaver Malysheva of the Great Ivanovo Combine. "The leaders of the Soviet regime don't care about us at all," she declared. "They say, 'we're building everything,' but they've forgotten to think about us. They've intensified work on three to four looms . . . but they haven't filled our bellies . . . So what did we fight for?" Rebuked by the presidium for "telling lies" even as delegates applauded her speech, Malysheva demanded that those who "seized power" in 1917 once again put the interests of workers first, and pointedly warned that "if they aren't going to give us bread, then . . . we'll idle the mills."[85]

Seeking to elucidate the source of the gulf separating workers from the regime, a spinner from the same enterprise, delegate Sidorova, took the stage. "The lecturer from Moscow indicated that the worker gets a decent salary," she bitterly recalled. "No, that's not correct. *You* do, but we don't. (Stormy applause.) You've forgotten about us, about how we live. You've lost contact with us, escaped from the stuffy walls [of the mill], and forgotten how to stand at the looms and work. (Applause.)" Thus alienated, party leaders had "run" the Soviet ship of state "aground," and despite fleeting "improvement in 1925–[19]26," workers again lived as "badly" as they had under capitalism. "It's a disgrace . . . for Soviet power," concluded Sidorova. "Shame on you, comrades! (Voices: 'Correct!') We fought for something, you know, and there was a revolution for a reason. But in the tenth year, we're sitting without bread. (Loud applause.)"[86]

After Sidorova took her seat, delegate Kliuev turned the audience's attention back to the party's policies. "When will we have enough grain?" he inquired. "Probably never, because they're sending so much [of it] abroad." According to Kliuev, it made no difference that Moscow was funneling profits from foreign trade back into industry as long as there was "real hunger" on the shop floor. Referring to mills recently completed or still under construction in Ivanovo, he asked: "How much did the Dzerzhinskii [spinning shed] cost? The Red Talka [spinning shed] also will cost us dearly, and the Mixed Yarn Combine, too." If new enterprises offered little solace to those who might one day work in them, enthusiasm for forced-draft industrialization must be counted among the casualties of the food-supply crisis of autumn 1928.[87]

To make certain that delegates understood that Stalin's revolution "from above" was to blame for their suffering, a party member from the New Ivanovo Mill, Vagin, reminded them that no less than Politburo member Nikolai Bukharin had warned that the FFYP's "ideal" targets for capital investment would result in a "goods famine." Echoing another of the Right Opposition's concerns, Vagin pointed out that punitive taxation of the village was destroying producers and provoking "a colossal [political] divergence . . . between the peasants and the workers." Vagin blamed the current leadership of the party for these "incorrect" policies, and appealed for a change of course.[88]

Although Kolotilov bit his tongue as one speaker after another lambasted the party, Vagin's suggestion that "abuse" at the highest levels was to blame for the crisis prompted him to intervene. "It would be great if this were America, but we don't have the resources for that," he insisted. "Do [the speakers] want to undermine Soviet power? Although we have a shortage of bread, still we mustn't fall into panic."[89]

The bad news for Kolotilov was that even workers with impeccable revolutionary credentials understood "panic" to be the only rational response to the crisis. "I've been a first-rate fighter since 1905," delegate Kotova of the Balashov Mill declared. "I experienced hunger in 1918, but not like this." Now, she noted bitterly, even her own children were starving.[90]

While speakers at the conference repeatedly expressed sympathy for the peasantry, jealously of seasonal workers surfaced in at least one speech. According to delegate Maralova, peasants were abandoning the land, coming to Ivanovo to work in the factories, and sending all the bread they could get their hands on back to the village. This parasitical relationship was leaving "bench workers . . . without a slice of bread." The only solution, she argued, was for the authorities to earmark separate supplies for each group.[91] Though the effort to blame bread shortages on seasonal workers had been successful in Sereda, it fell flat in Ivanovo, where popular anger focused almost exclusively on the party and its policies. This seems to reflect the higher degree of political awareness among workers in the regional capital, or at least among the delegates they chose to defend their interests.

Another speech that fell flat was delivered by Solov'ev, a pattern maker from the Zinov'ev Mill. Identified at the highest levels of the trade union as a routine instigator of shop-floor unrest, Solov'ev drew attention to the party's disrespect for one of the Revolution's most precious achievements: the workers' civil rights. "Lenin promised us freedom of speech, freedom of the press, freedom of assembly, but now what?" he demanded. "Now we have freedom of the queue. Comrade Stalin promises us the right to criticize our superiors [*samokritika*]. But . . . who among you workers voices criticism? And *where* do you voice it? Not in the press. You speak only on street corners and in queues—and so you speak nowhere at all." Curiously, Solov'ev's remarks were greeted neither by catcalls nor an ovation; there was only an unspecified "loud noise" in the hall as he descended from the podium.[92]

A speech that seems to have resonated, by contrast, with delegates was delivered by Zolkin of the Great Ivanovo Combine, who suggested that saboteurs at the regional or national level may have triggered the food shortages "in order to idle our factories . . . and drive the matter to strikes." Such comments terrified presidium members, who potentially had a lot to lose from a hunt for "class enemies" within the ranks of officialdom. The chairman of the regional trade-union bureau, Bol'shevikov, thus commandeered the podium and changed the subject by offering two proposals for the delegates' consideration. The first, that workers who owned livestock be ordered to stop feeding bread to their animals, elicited objections from those it affected and support from those it did not. The second, that food packets be calibrated to family size rather than to the number of shares owned in the cooperative, was greeted—as it always was during this crisis—enthusiastically.[93] Since the traditional peasant commune distributed resources according to the same principle, which placed the right to subsistence above ownership rights, it can be said that rural values were still prevalent in Russia's largest mill town.

Taking advantage of Bol'shevikov's success in getting at least one of his proposals approved, Kolotilov drew the emergency conference to a close with another unyielding defense of the party's policies, including the suppression of the kulak and the private trader, the financing of technology imports with grain exports, and the intensification of labor. In an implicit rebuke of Solov'ev, moreover, he argued that the conference itself demonstrated that workers' civil rights had not been curtailed. "You can curse the government, you can charge it with the most diverse demands, both well-founded and unfounded," he insisted. "You know very well that nobody threatens anyone for that ... The OGPU [security police] fights only against counterrevolution, not against the working class's criticism, however incorrect it may be ... Freedom of speech [for the workers] exists here to a greater extent than anywhere else."[94] Given the remarkably blunt speeches delivered that day from the podium, Kolotilov certainly had a point.

Or did he? Just two weeks later, a congress of the regional trade-union bureau, meeting in the very same hall, issued a resolution that condemned "the moods of panic taking place among the mass of workers" and "the attempts by some groups of workers to subject the foundation of socialist construction—the policy of industrialization . . . to doubt and reconsideration." The message was unmistakable: policy critiques such as those voiced during the Ivanovo City Soviet conference were now unwelcome. Nor would the trade union tolderate further strike appeals, since the withdrawal of labor was "absolutely impermissible in the conditions of our socialist construction."[95] Nothing better illustrated the gulf separating Soviet trade unions from the workers they purported to represent than the contrast between this resolution, which was drafted by a party-controlled presidium, and the speeches delivered earlier the same month by the duly elected representatives of Ivanovo's shop floors.

Although the congress's leadership proved only too willing to echo the party line, rank-and-file delegates did not refrain from confirming that moods and conditions in mills across the region were grim. Several, however, also offered the party a fig leaf. "When I left for the congress," reported delegate Milovanova, "the women workers said to me, 'If they give us bread, give us decent work, etc., we'll work.'"[96] The implication was clear: if supplied with satisfactory working conditions and sufficient quantities of bread, workers would endeavor to produce a surplus. In other words, the party could secure compliance, if not necessarily enthusiasm, by honoring the terms of its implicit contract with the shop floor.

The Central Party Committee got the message and endeavored, in November 1928, to rescue its faltering industrialization drive by implementing a rationing system in major urban areas. By providing workers with 13.6 to 15.9 kilograms of flour per family member per month, the rationing system "provided fully for the laboring population of the towns" and "brought about a considerable calming in the moods of the workers and the other strata of the population," according to the Ivanovo-Voznesensk Region Party Committee. Before the year drew to a close, "the panic . . . subsided," "queues grew shorter," and "much less censure of the party and the Soviet regime was heard."[97] If the outcome was a victory for the workers, whose right of subsistence had been affirmed, it likewise was a victory for the party, which undermined lower-class solidarity by augmenting the discrepancies of privilege between field and factory.

Although the new policy did not distinguish between workers who had ties to the land and those who did not, local officials sometimes did, which provoked tensions on the shop floor. For instance, "peasant" workers in Shuia voiced "sharp discontent" when their "proletarian" colleagues received extra flour from the cooperative, while the ire of their counterparts at Red Perekop was sparked by the announcement that their dependents would be dropped from supply rolls. As arbitrary and unfair as it was universal, the classification of workers according to the extent of their involvement in agriculture had important consequences: by creating gradations of privilege on the shop floor, it shaped the state's emergent hierarchy of supply; by providing operatives with a further incentive to be viewed as "proletarian," it altered the politics of social identity; and by endowing some members of the labor force with special privileges, it undermined working-class solidarity.[98]

Whatever its long-term impact, the rationing system achieved the immediate objective: no food-related unrest was reported on shop floors in the weeks following implementation. But while the crisis of autumn 1928 was overcome, shortages of basic necessities were now—thanks to the unintended effects of the revolution "from above"—a permanent feature of lower-class life. In Ivanovo, cooperatives had no greens to sell, eggs were rarely available, and queues for salt and butter formed before dawn. More worrisome, implementation of the rationing system for dependents was delayed, the Trade Commissariat failed to make shipments on time, and workers found it difficult to procure even the cloth that they manufactured. The situation was worse in the countryside. As party member Skotkin of Ivanovo's Zinov'ev Mill observed: "The peasants are cursing the Communists for the deficit of produce and goods."[99]

Stalin's revolution "from above" did not get off to an auspicious start. In the textile industry, implementation of the program of forced capital accumulation provoked some of the worst unrest in years.[100] Initially, operatives balked at intensification because they perceived the new workloads to be exploitative. Then, as it became clear that the choice was either intensification or the Labor Exchange, they chose the former on the condition that managers took steps to prevent it from resulting in higher rates of thread breakage, hence reduced earnings. It soon became clear, however, that the program of forced capital accumulation put these same managers in a bind: they could secure workers' compliance with certain of the program's components (intensification) only by making promises (higher-quality raw cotton) that other of the program's components (reduction in the costs of production) made it impossible for them to fulfill. The party denied the existence of this contradiction, but its impact at the level of the shop floor—a breakdown in worker-management relations—was undeniable. Likewise the horrible truth of forced-draft industrialization: despite claims to the contrary, it would be financed at the expense of the workers' living standard.

Not all operatives underwent intensification, so earnings suffered in some segments of the labor force more than others. For this reason, the class rhetoric that was audible in shop-floor protests, such as the Sereda strike, often collided with craft identities. The situation changed, however, in the autumn of 1928, when other components of Stalin's revolution "from above"—specifically, the assaults on private trade and the peasantry—exposed working-class communities to life-threatening food shortages. Although tensions were reported between "peasant" workers and "proletarians," and between locals and recent migrants, the effect of the crisis was to prompt operatives to speak with one voice against what they correctly understood to be a policy-driven assault on their well-being. How could the party that the workers brought to power embark on a course that threatened mass immiserization? What was the value of a socialism that financed industrialization with exports of grain that the workers needed for their children? By posing such questions, operatives voiced their concern that the party and the trade union were theirs no more, their fear that the Revolution was being betrayed before their eyes, and their conviction that the only socialism worth its name was one built in a manner consistent with their interests.

Bread shortages violated not only the values of the workers' moral economy, but also the implicit contract governing their relations with the party. Confronted with a breakdown in discipline in the industry that had been assigned a pivotal role in the program of forced capital accumulation, the party endeavored to piece the contract back together by introducing a rationing system in major urban areas. There was no shortage of skepticism, but once it seemed that Moscow was again prepared to fulfill its obligations, operatives responded in kind. As the new year approached, a tense calm descended on shop floors. Would it last? Given the orgy of "bacchanalian planning" under way in the corridors of power, it would have been a miracle if it did.[101]

2

The Klepikov Affair

A report prepared on March 2, 1929, for the central committee of the All-Union Trade Union of Textile Workers raised alarms about the sharp rise in disaffection among operatives. The evidence of crisis, which caught factory committees and party cells off guard, was overwhelming: the size and intensity of strikes was up in 1928 compared to previous years; agitation against the regime and its policies had become common on shop floors; workers at assemblies often refused to turn the podium over to Communists; and fewer than one in six workers bothered to attend production meetings. Low morale was a problem among all sectors of the labor force, and especially among women, veteran workers, and those with ties to the land.[1]

The immediate causes of the crisis—severe food shortages, sharply elevated workloads, declining real wages, the deterioration in the quality of raw materials, and the recent influx of tens of thousands of new recruits into the mills—were diverse, but each of them sprang from the policy of forced capital accumulation. There were long-term contributing factors as well, such as the relative weakness of the party and the trade union on the shop floor, and the relative decline since the October Revolution in the status of certain crafts (specifically, mule spinner, fabric printer, overlooker, and machinist).[2]

What most worried the report's authors, however, was the emergence in a number of mills of outspoken opponents of Moscow's policies. The profile of these disaffected workers spelled trouble for the party. Literate, skilled, and relatively well-paid, they boasted long and distinguished factory careers and strong ties to Soviet power. Their influence on the shop floor was immense.[3]

Of the five activists mentioned in the report, two—Solov'ev of Ivanovo and Peunkov of Sereda—made an appearance in chapter 1. Another, Liulin of Iaroslavl, is the subject of chapter 3. As for the fourth, Parfent'ev of Pavlovskii-Posad, Moscow Region, all we know is what this lone report tells us. Employed as a driver at the Lenskaia Worsted Wool Mill, he once had been a party member and instructor in the district trade-union bureau. Affiliated with Trotskyites in Moscow, he was well-read, energetic, and effective at mobilizing, via speechmaking and leafleting, opposition to Moscow's policies. As a result, pined the authors, "he enjoys great popularity among the workers."[4]

This chapter tells the story of the fifth rebel mentioned in the report: the forty-nine-year-old weaving overlooker Klepikov of Rodniki, who emerged in the 1920s as one of the most prominent shop-floor critics of the Bolshevik dictatorship. Klepikov was deeply committed to the practical and utopian ideals of the October Revolution. The former he understood to include the establishment of civil rights and the expansion of educational opportunities for workers; the latter, the immediate emancipation of workers from poverty, humiliation, oppression, and exploitation. Klepikov's critique was blunt and powerful: the Bolsheviks had betrayed the ideals of the Revolution and the workers in whose name they ruled. Though tragic, his story is important for two reasons: first, because Klepikov eloquently articulated the sense of betrayal that consumed shop floors during the FFYP; and second, because the silencing of his voice was a pivotal moment in the party's struggle to enforce its exclusive right to define the meaning—and determine the outcome—of the Revolution.

Kapiton Vasil'evich Klepikov was born to a peasant family in 1880 in a village near Rodniki, an old mill town situated to the northeast of Ivanovo. His formal education did not extend beyond elementary school, and he spent his twenties and thirties, as did many lower-class men of his generation, moving between positions on the shop floor and in the army. When not serving in one of the major military conflicts of the era—the Russo-Japanese War, the Great War, or the Civil War—he was employed as a weaver at the giant Rodniki Mill.[5]

Klepikov was involved in the underground labor movement from an early age, and accumulated authority on the shop floor by serving as an organizer of strikes in 1907 and 1914. "For as long as he's lived in Rodniki," a group of his supporters wrote in 1920, "Klepikov has been . . . a good comrade and . . . vanguard worker [who] everywhere defended the workers' interests before the old factory administration." Although he never affiliated with a party, Klepikov voted before the war—as did most of the region's workers—for Bolshevik Duma candidates. In terms of values, though, he was an anarcho-libertarian—or, as he put it while under interrogation in 1920, "an extreme leftist"—who opposed the party dictatorship, which he perceived to be a betrayal of the Revolution's promise of emancipation for the lower classes.[6]

When the era of war and revolution drew to a close, Klepikov enjoyed success in both his personal and professional life. At the height of the NEP, he built a home near the Rodniki Mill for his family, which included a wife, who also worked as a weaver, and five children born between 1912 and 1929. Equally impressive, he fulfilled the lifelong ambition of most male weavers—such opportunities being rarely available to women—when he was promoted, in 1928, to the rank of overlooker, which put him in charge of his own work team. It was to be his best job on the shop floor—and his last as a free man.[7]

Klepikov's favorite leisure activity was to write politically informed poetry. A weaver who wrote subversive poetry in a provincial mill town was, by all accounts, an extraordinary figure. Yet Klepikov also was a personality type that became familiar in working-class life after the turn of the century: the worker-author. An ordinary member of the working class who evinced an extraordinary passion for written self-expression, the worker-author, by definition, was a marginal figure: though more than just a worker, he was not quite an *intelligent* (member of the intelligentsia). The characteristic that gave the worker-author his liminal social identity—his reliance on the pen as an instrument of self-expression—also made him, according to Mark D. Steinberg, "an important conduit of ideas, vocabularies, and images across the boundary between the educated and the masses." Typically, the worker-author felt that it was his responsibility to enlighten the lower classes and give voice to their concerns. Though he sometimes felt alienated from peers, the passion with which he chronicled the suffering of the people and the perfidy of the privileged gave him moral stature in the community and an important role in the formation of working-class consciousness.[8]

Klepikov's stature was substantial, and the cotton workers of Rodniki routinely elected him to office. At one time or another, he was a member of the mill's factory committee, the chairman of its wages and disputes tribunal, a member of the board of the regional trade-union bureau, and a delegate to district congresses. He thus enjoyed the institutional authority to voice his constituents' concerns and to mobilize resistance against policies that were perceived to be inimical to their interests.[9]

Voice of the Shop Floor

Klepikov was a prominent spokesman for the workers during most of the conflicts that took place at the Rodniki Mill in the 1920s. His earliest act of defiance occurred before the Bolsheviks solidified their hold on power. In 1920, as shop floors endured severe food shortages stemming from the Civil War and the coercive policies of war communism, he gave a speech to colleagues who had just voted to send a protest delegation to Lenin. "The current regime is not a people's regime," he declared, but is "worse than the monarchist [regime]. [It] is composed of some sort of small band of people who call themselves Communists . . . and . . . procure . . . essential goods for themselves, but don't care at all for the people." Although his comments were well received, they got him into trouble: he was arrested by the Cheka (security police) and sentenced by a revolutionary tribunal to six months of forced labor.[10]

With the introduction of the NEP in 1921, the workers' living standard began to improve. Though satisfied that at least now there was enough to eat, Klepikov remained critical of the party for failing to fulfill the bold promises it made during the Revolution. Practices viewed as exploitative were of particular concern to him. For example, he "endeavor[ed] by all means" in his capacity as chairman of the wages and disputes tribunal "to block" the introduction of individual piece rates in 1924. After losing that battle—piece rates were implemented in all the region's mills by end of the same year—he decided to run for a seat on the factory committee. His platform: only Klepikov could stand up to management. As he put it in his June 1924 campaign speech: "In the old days the workers . . . didn't witness such exploitation as now. The factory committee operates in lockstep with administrators [and] doesn't defend the workers' interests." He won in a landslide.[11]

After joining the factory committee, Klepikov renewed the attack on the party, which he accused of "back[ing] down from its slogans . . . of the October Revolution." "Lenin and Trotsky were wrong," he declared at a July 1924 conference. First, they "destroyed private capital and led the country to total collapse. And now, having recognized their mistake, they've begun to create anew the very same capital, only under a different name." As a result, "things were bad for the worker, but now they're . . . worse: wages are falling, taxes are rising, [and] exploitation is absolute." A key revolutionary aspiration—freedom from suffering and want—had been abandoned, insisted Klepikov.[12]

The next year Klepikov drove home the theme of betrayal at a local trade-union congress. "The Soviet regime has tormented the peasant in the countryside with taxes [and] created an entire network of parasites in the factory," he declared. "Instead of feeding the workers, the party exports all the food and leaves us hungry." So successful was the speech, which included a denunciation of the trade union for failing to "defend the workers' interests," that it enabled Klepikov to wrest control of the congress from Communist delegates and secure passage of resolutions put forth by the opposition.[13]

Klepikov's speech—and the victory it secured for him at the congress—got him into trouble with the security police. In March 1925, he was arrested by the OGPU and detained for several weeks. Under interrogation, he traced his alienation from the party to its retreat from the revolutionary ideals of 1917:

> I heard the fundamental slogans of the workers and of . . . Lenin: "Down with the Kornilov affair and the Kerenskii [regime]! Down with war and capital punishment!" To this day I haven't betrayed these . . . convictions. And now I boldly say: Down with war, down with capital punishment, [which] are a disgrace to the workers' regime . . . There have been great mistakes on the part of the Communist Party, but to this day they still haven't been . . . corrected.[14]

This second encounter with the security police did not intimidate Klepikov, and in late 1926 he repeated his criticisms of the party in a rousing speech to 530 constituents:

> We're in the tenth year of Soviet power. They told us before that under the old regime nothing was done in outlying worker districts [such as ours]. And now, under the Soviet regime, almost nothing is done. We're wallowing in filth . . . They say that nothing can be done, but in the past everything was cheaper and better . . . Now all the achievements of the October Revolution have come to naught.

For good measure, he added the following to the list of betrayals: elections were "fraudulent," and a new elite of "party bosses" lived in luxury while the workers went "unpaid."[15]

Anger at such betrayals underpinned Klepikov's opposition to his son's application to the Komsomol. As he explained to an official from that organization:

The Communist Party has deviated to the right and all its members have turned into old dignitaries and despots. All the promises of Great October have been forgotten and the path of force of the Stolypins, Trepovs, Arakcheevs, etc., is being followed—and the Komsomol is an assistant to the party in these matters. And if my son is going to be a Komsomol, then I'll consider him an enemy of the people.[16]

Klepikov's willingness to disown his own son revealed the depth of his attachment to the Revolution's emancipatory promise—and his hostility toward the party that betrayed this promise soon after it seized power.

Klepikov turned his attention back to the shop floor when, in 1927, a fresh round of labor intensification got under way. "The workers are tormented and loaded up like animals," he declared at a factory assembly. "This, comrade workers, is exploitation one and the same as in capitalist countries." When, on another occasion, he lambasted the trade union for failing to do anything to block such measures, officials endeavored to rebuke him. Klepikov would have none of it. According to the security police, he "ripped his shirt open from the collar . . . [and] shouted, 'Here's my chest! Shoot, I'm not afraid! I have spoken—and will speak—the truth! This is the workers' opinion! Let them persecute me! I've been to the Cheka and the OGPU . . . and will go again!'" A willingness to sacrifice oneself for noble ideals was a standard trait of the worker-author.[17] For Klepikov, martyrdom would come soon enough.

Given his commitment to what he understood to be the practical and utopian ideals of the October Revolution, Klepikov found much to criticize during the NEP era, including the suppression of shop-floor democracy, the elevation of workloads, and living standards that fell short of expectations.[18] Some scholars have argued that such disaffection generated enthusiasm for the "great turn" of 1928. As chapter 1 illustrated, however, this was not the case. Since it decimated living standards and led to even more acute exploitation on the shop floor, Stalin's revolution "from above" was not experienced as a fulfillment of the October Revolution, but rather as a betrayal of what the workers understood to be the promises of Soviet power. The Klepikov affair further illustrates the point.

The origins of the Klepikov affair lay in a fact-finding tour of nearby mills that Klepikov took with a group of weaving overlookers in July 1928. (He had been promoted to overlooker earlier that year.) At an assembly convened at the Rodniki Mill on August 7, Klepikov reported the group's finding to sixty-eight colleagues: earnings and working conditions were worse in Rodniki than elsewhere. "We work like oxen, [but] earn little," he declared. Therefore, "we must organize all the overlookers and seek a wage increase by means of a work stoppage." If Klepikov had ended his speech with these words, he never would have attracted Moscow's attention. Strike threats were common on the industry's shop floors—especially among overlookers—and there was nothing exceptional in what he said. It was what came next that got him into trouble. "The factory committee doesn't defend the workers' interests, [but] fulfills the duties of the old . . . gendarmerie," he asserted. This was so because the trade union had "sold out" the workers and now facilitated their "cruel exploitation." As for the party, it had "deceived the working class." In fact, "for eleven years everything has been built on . . . a lie." And because "Stalin . . . has deported the best defenders of the working class to 'frying pans' in Solovki," management now enjoyed free rein "to wring the last juices out of the worker."[19]

Klepikov concluded his denunciation of "the despotic system and government in our country" by reciting three poems that he recently had composed. Two of these were short works that celebrated liberty ("Freedom eradicates evil," "defends the truth," and "creates a better life") and the virtues of a free press ("The press protects freedom," "leads to a new culture," "shatters thrones," and "corrects mistakes").[20] The third was a lengthy denunciation of the Bolsheviks, who, in Klepikov's view, had betrayed the October Revolution by stripping workers of their civil rights, ignoring their demands for dignity, economic security, and cultural enrichment, and placing them under the thumb of a new class of parasitical exploiters:

Polemic

In Russia, truth is trampled in the dirt
And falsehood prevails.

. . .

Flatterers are applauded
And those who speak the truth are scorned.

Scoundrels get cushy jobs,
And the honest ones are sent off

Now to Solovki, now to Turkestan,
To cool down from the heat.

. . .

The free press is barred
Behind seven locks.
The official press is inclined
To flatter the Bolsheviks.

There's no freedom of speech,
Or assembly, and no free trade unions.

. . .

We've no more tolerance now
To keep from cursing the Bolsheviks—
Those "venerable" Communists.
These scoundrels are like none other,

And are comparable to the fascists.
There's no wheat flour
And not enough rye.
Instead of rice,
They give us vodka.

They booze us up to drunkenness,
Afraid of giving us an education.

. . .

The labor contract
Is a fictional piece of paper,
Unfulfilled by employers,
Who say it has nothing to do with them.

Every year Soviet Communists
Go annually in piles
To health resorts in the Crimea, the Caucasus, and
the Urals.

. . .

Some workers are sent as well,
But only as a ploy.
We're told, that "Everyone's equal—
It's just that few workers apply."

. . .

Institutions sprout like mushrooms
In warm weather.
The worker sees no good in them,
Only misfortune.

No one attends assemblies anymore,
Saying they've had enough.
The Bolsheviks chatter for a long time,
But it's all beside the point.
There's no sense of reality at all
In what the Communists set out to achieve.

. . .

The Soviet Foreign Trade Office trades at random,
Without logic or proper accounting;
It thoughtlessly exports everything,
Without regard for the consequences.

According to Klepikov, this poem reflected "what the workers are saying." The claim was credible: witnesses testified that "Polemic" won "loud approving applause" from the overlookers and was cited widely in the community in the days and weeks that followed.[21]

The Anti-Klepikov Campaign

Retaliation came quickly. A week after the assembly, Klepikov was branded a "counterrevolutionary" by the factory committee, five of whose members insisted that he be expelled from both that body and the trade union. Permitted the opportunity to defend himself, Klepikov reiterated his views but denied having called for a strike. Rather, he insisted, "I . . . only said that we must be more organized and firmly defend our interests." After a supporter spoke in Klepikov's defense, a compromise ensued: as punishment for casting "discredit" on "the regime and the party," he was expelled from the factory committee but allowed to retain his membership in the union.[22]

The matter did not end there. Before the month was out, the trade union's central committee reprimanded the factory committee for being lenient with an individual who levelled "a series of slanderous attacks against the Soviet regime, the trade-union movement, and the Communist Party." Klepikov had crossed a line:

> [The central committee] considers this . . . punishment insufficient, for while our trade union unites within its ranks [all] wage laborers "regardless of their political persuasions" . . . someone who considers the union to be "the old . . . gendarmerie," who calls on union members to violate union discipline and the labor contract "by means of a work stoppage," [and] who intentionally disrupts socialist construction by slandering the party and the Soviet regime cannot be considered a member.[23]

Although the leadership wanted Klepikov expelled from the union, it hesitated to act without the consent of the workers who had elected him as their representative. Local functionaries were ordered to secure such consent.

On September 1, the factory committee put the matter of Klepikov's "continued presence . . . in the ranks of the union" before an assembly of Rodniki workers. Again, Klepikov spoke in his own defense. "For what did we fight, . . . perish, and tolerate privation," he demanded, if not for the right to criticize policies that were inimical to the workers' interests? "We must work like the Communists," he concluded. "All for one and one for all!" After rousing speeches by two of what the trade union characterized as his "comrades-in-arms," Ivan Mikhalev and Aleksei Kornilov, the assembly voted decisively to keep Klepikov in the union.[24]

Alarmed by the outcome, the central committee endeavored to undermine support for Klepikov by launching a campaign that branded him an "unsolicited 'defender'" and "enemy" of the working class. "Such an overlooker has no place in the factory," intoned the trade union's mouthpiece, *Voice of the Textile Worker*. "Klepikovs—out of the union." Although the language of the anti-Klepikov campaign was harsh, it failed to have much effect on the shop floor. As a result, the Klepikov affair was deleted at the last minute from the agenda of the Rodniki Mill's October 14 assembly, which—according to the district party committee—"created the opinion among certain groups of workers that the presidium was afraid to submit this matter to discussion."[25]

The anti-Klepikov campaign was taken up two weeks later at a forum that was more sympathetic to the party line: a congress of the regional trade-union bureau. Spearheading this phase was Buianov, a member of the trade union's central committee, who rejected the view that Klepikov was "a victim of the Soviet regime" and insisted that he was, in fact, a counterrevolutionary who had taken a position of authority entrusted to him by Soviet power—factory committee member—and turned it into "a platform from which forces and strata hostile to the working class . . . [and] the proletarian dictatorship speak." Buianov insisted that there would be no tolerance of those who placed themselves "outside the ranks of the working class" by voicing "unprecedented slander of the party and the Soviet regime and the working class as a whole," and demanded that "all comrades who carry out counterrevolutionary work alongside the Mensheviks . . . be mercilessly suppressed." Delegates promptly approved a resolution calling for Klepikov's expulsion from the union.[26]

Seeking to capitalize on Buianov's victory at the congress, the factory committee convened a special assembly, on November 1, to reconsider Klepikov's fate. According to a trade-union memorandum, it was an extraordinary occasion. "The hall was jammed" with 966 workers, and "even those who had not been to an assembly for ten years came."[27]

Factory committee chairman Kuznetsov opened with a review of Klepikov's "anti-Soviet" speech of August 7, and asked the workers to expel him from the union. He then yielded the podium to the accused, who invoked his decades of work at the mill and his service to the Revolution. "I myself strove . . . for the overthrow of the tsarist-capitalist regime," Klepikov declared, "and served honorably in the ranks of the Red Army." Although he acknowledged having uttered the words attributed to him, he insisted on his right to free speech and declared that his only mistake was to have believed in the sincerity of the party's *samokritika* campaign. "It seems very strange . . . that they want to expel me for this," he confessed. "We [have] the right, after all, to criticize everyone." He concluded by warning the workers of what would happen if they followed the factory committee's recommendation: "To expel me from the trade union means to deprive me of all rights. . . . At that point I can expect the most severe consequences, that is, they'll be able to consider me a counterrevolutionary and . . . use against me Article 58 . . . which permits the application of the highest measure of punishment, that is, execution."[28]

Others who spoke that day gave voice to the range of opinions in the hall. Trade-union, party, and mill officials denied that Klepikov would be fired or arrested, and argued that expulsion from the union was commensurate with the crime. Several workers echoed these sentiments, but most came down in favor of the accused. "They want to wipe Klepikov off the face of the earth, but we won't allow this," vowed the weaver Mikhalev. "If we surrender Klepikov, then gradually they'll consume all of us."[29]

According to officials who were present, the speeches in Klepikov's defense inflamed passions, and soon "the whole assembly essentially turned into a political demonstration against the Communists." As a result, "the overwhelming majority" of workers voted in favor of a resolution declaring Klepikov "not guilty and not deserving of expulsion . . . from the union." The next day, tensions spread to the shop floor, with fistfights nearly breaking out between nonparty workers and Communists, who found themselves "manifestly outflanked."[30]

Unwilling to concede defeat, the trade union's central committee ratcheted up the pressure. In a series of articles published in *Voice,* the editors reported that "ignorant people" in the nation's mills—especially "the many new workers" who were "tied to the land"—had fallen under the influence of "enemies" such as Klepikov, who "use each of the workers' discontents to undermine . . . the Soviet regime." The good news, however, was that "conscious" workers rejected these individuals, whose transgression was to have engaged in *krytika,* which aimed "to mock, to laugh at us and our endeavor" and "to undermine our work," instead of *samokritika,* which identified specific problems in an effort to strengthen Soviet power. The message was clear: "For *krytika*—out of the workers' ranks."[31]

Criticized by Moscow for having lost touch with their constituents, the party cell and factory committee sprang into action. The results were satisfactory. Letters began to appear in the press: Komsomols demanded that Klepikov be made to desist from his "counterrevolutionary work among the unconscious workers," and a veteran operative, Bakulin, who had previously stood up for the accused, now repudiated him. Meanwhile, meetings attended by small groups of workers approved anti-Klepikov resolutions and the factory committee's proposal for another special assembly. The trade union soon registered its satisfaction. "The inhabitants of Rodniki have come to understand," declared *Voice,* "that Klepikov is an enemy who pushes the working class back to capitalism [and] to the old exploiter-boss."[32]

While the campaign against him was under way, Klepikov marked the passing of the eleventh anniversary of the October Revolution by composing a bittersweet poem on a familiar theme: the Bolshevik regime's abandonment of the Revolution's emancipatory promise and betrayal of the working class.

Forgotten Slogans

. . .

We're destroying a radiant ideal.
The ideal of fraternity and equality
Has flown away from us into the sky.

. . .

We've forgotten the slogans and oaths
of October 1917,
When regiments of our comrades roamed,
Taking vengeance on the primordial enemy.

. . .

Everywhere we defeated enemies

. . .

Who savored the thought
Of crushing the working class.
But all their thoughts turned sour,
Like spoiled kvas.

. . .

But still they whisper
Among themselves,
Saying, "Little will come of it—
Their socialism will die.

"While sitting in the palaces and armchairs,
The new leaders will learn how to rule.

. . .

"They too will be bourgeois,
And carry out exploitation.
They'll prove deaf to the needs of the masses,
And the slogans of October will perish."[33]

After eight weeks of intensive preparation, the factory committee and party cell convened the last of three assemblies to consider Klepikov's fate. Details are sketchy, but clearly nothing was left to chance. The event was chaired by Bol'shevikov, the head of the regional trade-union bureau, who demanded retribution for "class enemies" and demanded greater enthusiasm from party and trade-union activists. The twenty workers who spoke from the podium dutifully criticized Klepikov's work performance and his "anti-Soviet" agitation. The accused had nothing to say—and may well have been absent. It is not known how many workers attended the assembly, but most were affiliated with the party. At any rate, all but one voted to strip Klepikov of his union membership.[34]

The outcome was a victory for the factory committee and the party cell, whose authority Klepikov had relentlessly assailed. For all intents and purposes, this thorn in their side had been removed: without a union card, Klepikov could no longer attend most worker assemblies. To be sure, Klepikov's allies, such as the weavers Mikhalev and Metelkina, carried the flame by agitating and organizing protests against one or another of Moscow's antilabor policies.[35] Still, there can be no question that the virtual silencing of Klepikov was a blow to Rodniki's working-class community.

The outcome also was a victory for Moscow, which was struggling to contain the wave of unrest that had been sweeping shop floors since the program of forced capital accumulation was launched in 1928. The Klepikov affair had didactic value. The first lesson was that even "backward" textile workers could be made to understand that the party was fulfilling, rather than betraying, the Revolution. "At first, the whole factory defended him," reported *Voice*. "And then the workers themselves threw him out of the union." Though misleading insofar as it ignored the crucial role of officialdom in orchestrating Klepikov's defeat, this narrative had the benefit of being consistent with Bolshevik theory: those who opposed the party did so only because they lacked proper "consciousness." The second lesson flowed from the first: local party and trade-union activists needed to engage in a massive campaign to "enlighten" the labor force. Failure was not an option. "Klepikovs must be exposed and driven out of the union's ranks," intoned *Voice*, "because they hinder the great . . . work of socialist construction."[36]

Arrest and Imprisonment

Klepikov's final protest as an employee of the Rodniki Mill occurred on January 17, 1930, when he denounced socialist competition (a form of labor intensification) and led a walkout of twenty colleagues from a joint conference of overlookers and engineers. Three days later, he was sacked.[37]

Even this act of retaliation did not silence Klepikov, who barely a week after losing his job stormed into the district party committee and "declared that here in the Soviet Union we have the same fascism as abroad, that he . . . disagrees with the line of the party and the Soviet regime, [and] that he fears nothing and will fight to the end for truth." He also continued to write anti-Bolshevik poems, which condemned the despotism of the industrial plan and the workers' material conditions.[38]

Five months later, the OGPU concluded that Klepikov no longer enjoyed the support of "the overwhelming majority of workers" in Rodniki. Nonetheless, the atmosphere of crisis that prevailed in the wake of collectivization as well as Klepikov's continued intransigence inspired a decree "to liquidate the Klepikov affair" once and for all. Local party officials concurred, but to avoid disturbances insisted that Communists first denounce him on the shop floor. Finally, at 1:30 AM on June 15, 1930, Klepikov was dragged out of bed and arrested. A search of his home resulted in confiscation of his manuscripts.[39]

During the first interrogation, Klepikov defended himself as he had so many times before: by denying that he was "anti-Soviet" and insisting that he always spoke the truth:

> I consider myself guilty neither of agitation nor of counterrevolution. I consider the thoughts expressed in my poetry to be correct because I wrote everything from what I saw personally in my life and in [the lives of] others. As for criticism: in worker assemblies and private conversations with Communist comrades, I criticized individual managers and indicated in general terms the Communist Party's mistakes, which for twelve years have proceeded one after another.

Klepikov then delivered an extraordinary monologue that ridiculed Stalin for his apparent lack of ideological consistency over the years:

> I'll never understand . . . what comrade Stalin writes: right deviation, left deviation, overstatements, understatements. . . . How does comrade Stalin get by? There must be a mechanical apparatus installed in his head: something like an astrolabe or a solar chronometer for the precise measurement of a ship's whereabouts in the ocean. Comrade Stalin considers himself to be neither a rightist nor a leftist, but how can that be? Before I understood things like this: under the imperialist regime the Bolsheviks [and] the workers were considered extremely

leftist, and the bourgeoisie [and] the imperialist regime were rightist. But now we have no bourgeoisie, [and] there are no [other] parties. [Nor] are there any precise . . . directions. So then how does one . . . guess [what] to say and do so as not to make a mistake, so as not to be considered a rightist, so as not to be considered a leftist, so as not to overstate or understate? It's very difficult without a tuning-fork to set the tone correctly, and it's difficult without a thermometer to tell exactly how much the fever of the typhus patient has climbed. You have to be a sage of sages to guess exactly how to speak.

Unable to divine which way the party wind was blowing on a given day, Klepikov insisted on his right—secured by the Revolution—to speak the truth as he perceived it to be:

And therefore, dear comrades, I, neither sage nor clairvoyant, cannot say what you want me to say. I say, and have said as I could, as my heart prompted, my personal convictions. I have no tuning-fork, also no astrolabe, and therefore I beg your pardon if what I said and wrote is not according to your design. The October Revolution gave me the right as a worker to express my personal convictions openly.[40]

During the next interrogation four days later, Klepikov acknowledged authorship of the confiscated manuscripts and stated that he had used the tool of literacy to express his "personal opinion" and to convey "what I saw and heard among the workers and peasants." As for his political views, he maintained that the "comrades" (Communists) were indistinguishable from "the jailers, nobles, [and] fascists" [sic] who once ruled Russia, and reiterated his devotion to "the slogans of October," which he concisely formulated thus: "freedom of speech; the inviolability of self; freedom of the press, assemblies, and [trade] unions; freedom of conscience; the plants and factories to the workers; the land to the peasants."[41]

For the first time on record, Klepikov criticized the collectivization of agriculture. His argument was straightforward and, ironically, appealed to the party's self-interest. If ambitious industrialization goals were to be fulfilled, he maintained, then the current bread shortages had to be eradicated, for the crisis precipitated by the regime's assault on the peasantry was inflicting harm on the economy. He bolstered this argument with an historical analysis and prescription that underscored his anarcho-libertarian ideology. Since the Bolsheviks had crushed their enemies during the Civil

War, there was no need for them to rely on coercion to implement policy. (Besides which, he noted wryly, "repression" had thus far failed to fill the nation's grain "elevators.") Only the renunciation of force and the implementation of civil rights for the workers and peasants could pull the Soviet Union out of its economic crisis. As for class enemies in the countryside, there was nothing to fear: "The kulak is terrible for neither the worker nor the peasant. He'll become extinct of his own accord."[42]

Given Klepikov's opposition to collectivization, his unwillingness to acknowledge any limit on his right of free speech, and his insistence that his every word had been "correct, [but] not counterrevolutionary," the verdict in the case was a foregone conclusion. On June 21, 1930, an OGPU court convicted him under Article 58 of the Criminal Code. The relatively harsh sentence that was handed down—five years in a labor camp—reflected the party's determination to sever his ties to the community.[43]

Kapiton Klepikov was an unusually charismatic and articulate member of the generation of radical workers who brought down Russia's old regime. In his formal capacity as an elected representative of the Rodniki cotton operatives and his informal role as a worker-author, he passionately articulated the view that the party had betrayed the emancipatory ideals of the Revolution. To be sure, betrayal had long been a theme in worker discourse, as Klepikov's own history of protest illustrated. But while Russian textile workers grew disillusioned with war communism and had no shortage of grievances under the NEP, it was Stalin's revolution "from above"—or rather, the immiserization and acute forms of exploitation and coercion that accompanied it—that provoked in them the most profound feelings of betrayal.

Klepikov gave voice to these feelings more eloquently than any other member of the industry's labor force, and for this reason was viewed by the party as a threat to its radical program of economic development. The community whose interests Klepikov for so long defended returned the favor when Moscow launched a campaign to destroy him. The balance of forces was such, however, that not even a series of humiliating setbacks could prevent the campaign, sooner or later, from achieving its objective.

Although the outcome was foreordained, Klepikov and veteran workers like him were among the significant obstacles facing Stalin in 1928. The point is not simply that their activism threatened the program of forced capital accumulation. More important is that they contradicted—and by virtue of their biography, with authority—the claim that the revolution "from above" was the Revolution "fulfilled." The legitimacy of Stalin's dictatorship over the party and the socioeconomic system he was endeavoring to create would be in doubt so long as these individuals spoke freely. For this reason, it became a priority of the party, the trade union, and the security police to silence them.

3

The Liulin Affair

Of the five individuals identified in March 1929 by the All-Union Trade Union of Textile Workers as leaders of shop-floor unrest, Vasilii Liulin of Iaroslavl's Red Perekop Mill provoked the most alarm in the corridors of power. No individual mill was more crucial to the success of the revolution "from above" than Red Perekop. What made that enterprise stand out in the eyes of the party leadership was not so much its size—although, with a labor force exceeding eleven thousand, it was only slightly smaller than the massive Rodniki Mill—but that it produced specialized fabric for heavy industry. Whereas unrest in a typical Soviet mill indirectly hindered industrialization by reducing the output of consumer cloth, hence the funds available for capital investment, unrest at Red Perekop directly hindered it by bringing production lines in some of the nation's most strategically important enterprises to a halt. So important was Liulin's employer that it was supervised not by a regional industry trust like most other mills, but from Moscow by the Supreme Economic Council.[1]

Liulin was a twenty-nine-year-old lathe operator in Red Perekop's machine shop when he emerged, in 1928, as an outspoken critic of the program of forced capital accumulation and its impact on worker living standards. Like Klepikov, Liulin felt that the Bolsheviks had betrayed the promise of the October Revolution. Each of these men interpreted that promise in his own way. Whereas Klepikov was a maximalist who understood October to mean both the establishment of civil rights and institutions of higher education for workers and the workers' immediate emancipation from poverty, humiliation, oppression, and exploitation, Liulin was a minimalist who understood it to mean gradually rising living standards, gradually declining workloads, and responsiveness by officialdom to the concerns articulated by the shop floor's duly elected representatives. Once the defeat of the "exploiting" classes was at hand, Klepikov turned on the party because each version of socialism it unveiled—war communism, the NEP, the revolution "from above"—fell short of fulfilling what he understood to be October's promise. By contrast, Liulin gave the party a pass after the Civil War and was satisfied with the NEP. Only when Stalin's "great turn" shattered the workers' living standard, augmented their burdens at the point of production, and eradicated the last remnants of shop-floor democracy did he join the ranks of the party's critics.

Vasilii Ivanovich Liulin was born in 1899 in Rebrikovo, a village in Vladimir Region. Farm laborers by social origin, his parents worked at the Great Iaroslavl (later, Red Perekop) Mill for thirty-four years. Like many working-class children of his generation, Liulin completed several years of schooling and was hired at a young age (twelve) by his parents' employer. After a brief stint working as a creeler in the mule-spinning shed, he secured a position as an apprentice in the machine shop. Shortly after the Bolshevik seizure of power, he became a full-fledged lathe operator.[2]

Though not as passionate and utopian in his thinking, Liulin, like Klepikov, had been interested in politics from a young age. As a teenager, he defied his father by participating in "illegal study groups," whose secret meetings left him convinced that the Social Democrats (that is, the Russian Marxists) were "true fighters for the cause of the working class." After the February Revolution, he further demonstrated his affinity for the Social Democrats by joining the new trade union that their functionaries helped organize for Russia's textile workers. This trade union was dominated for some time by members of the party's Menshevik faction, but Liulin seems never to have objected to the October 1917 seizure of power by their adversaries, the Bolsheviks. At any rate, he had good relations with local Communists and, after a brief stint as head of the Red Perekop workers' club, volunteered for the Red Army.[3]

In 1919, while serving as a cultural operative for the military. Liulin was dispatched for training to the Moscow Party School. He dropped out, however, and, after returning to Iaroslavl, avoided the company of Red Perekop Bolsheviks. What had transpired to cool his attitude toward the party? A possible explanation can be found in testimony by his lifelong acquaintance, Nikolai Kliukin. "Liulin always said that he wasn't born to be a Communist because, [although] he imbibed with his mother's milk [a desire] to live better, to be a Communist you have to renounce . . . your family, [and] a wife has to be independent of her husband, even in sexual relations. Our society was not brought up that way." This suggests that

Liulin's alienation may have grown out of an encounter with the lifestyle experimentation that was under way within certain strata of the party during the Civil War. An apparent supporter of traditional gender roles, the idealistic lathe operator from the Russian heartland may have been shocked and embarrassed by the moral iconoclasm of the capital's cosmopolitan youth.[4]

Perhaps compounding Liulin's disaffection was his treatment at the hands of the Red Army. A year or so after his trip to Moscow, he contracted typhus while serving as a rifleman, and unilaterally extended his sick leave by two weeks. After reporting for duty, he was arrested for desertion and sent to prison for three months by a military tribunal. Although he never spoke about this experience, it is unlikely to have augmented his enthusiasm for the party. At any rate, by the time Liulin ended his four years of active duty, he knew that he was not cut out to be a Communist. "It was suggested that I should join the party, but I refused, believing myself to be politically unprepared," he testified in 1929. "To be a party member, you have to be politically literate and consistent." Whatever its origins, Liulin's alienation was typical in that it set in even before the Civil War ended.[5]

After completing a four-month course of study at the Sverdlov Communist University in 1921, Liulin secured a discharge from the army, resumed his duties as a lathe operator at Red Perekop, and settled with his wife and three children in a private home in a village near Iaroslavl. Notwithstanding his alienation from the party, he was a model Soviet citizen: he worked hard, drank in moderation, read the newspaper, enrolled in night courses, and carried out assignments for the factory committee. His cooperation with the authorities ended in 1928, however, when he began to denounce Stalin's revolution "from above" as an assault on worker interests. Liulin's slogan—"Soviet power doesn't exist for us"—bluntly accused the party of having betrayed the October Revolution. As in the case of Klepikov, activism earned Liulin "authority among the workers"—and the enmity of the party that ruled in their name.[6]

The Liulin Delegation

With severe bread shortages sowing "panic" and "strike tendencies" in Soviet urban areas, Liulin mounted the podium at a June 1928 conference whose goal was to familiarize operatives with the FFYP, and delivered a scathing assault on the recent deterioration in living standards. "They make the workers work," he declared, "but restrict the amount of bread they can buy [at the cooperative]." In Liulin's opinion, the party was to blame for the crisis because of its imprudently ambitious capital investment program, its repressive stance toward the peasantry, and its aggressive exporting of grain. Besides being well received, the speech won Liulin a reputation on the shop floor as one who "stands up for the poor."[7]

When operatives returned to work after the traditional August furlough, the mood was grim. Besides bread shortages, they had to contend with inflammatory rumors that workers in Moscow were being supplied better than those in the regions. Having spent the furlough interviewing peasants and white-collar workers, Liulin concluded that other classes were turning "against Soviet power" and would be inclined to back worker protests. After winning promises of support from friends, he vowed to take action.[8]

On August 31, Liulin persuaded an assembly of workers to disregard the objections of the factory committee and dispatch a delegation under his leadership to Moscow to investigate conditions there, and to persuade authorities that the cooperative should—especially given the recent elevation of workloads—stop imposing restrictions on bread purchases. Snubbed by the workers whose interests it claimed to represent, the factory committee proceeded to make itself even more unpopular by announcing that one of its members, Antonov, would accompany the delegation—that is, spy on its activities.[9]

News of the delegation's election spread rapidly but did little to contain the discontent. Confronted with a crisis that threatened to bring production lines to a halt, officials convened an all-factory assembly the next day. Although a third of the one thousand operatives in attendance were party members, the organizers felt compelled to cede the stage to Liulin and his allies, whose ranks included the twenty-five-year-old graser and former Komsomol Aleksandr Lytochkin. After shouting down their superiors, the workers—including "an overwhelming majority" of the Communists—rejected an official resolution and began to debate a motion to approve the dispatch of the Liulin delegation to Moscow. Interjecting himself into the debate, the secretary of the district party committee, Karin, endeavored to seize the initiative:

"If the workers trust the factory committee, then they shouldn't send a delegation," [declared Karin]. *Do you trust the factory committee?* A powerful uproar, and shouts, broke out in the hall: "No, we don't trust [it]." He then asked: *Do you trust the Communist Party or not?"* After individual shouts *("We do not!")* rang out, the clamor increased steadily and took on a mass character.

Once it became apparent that the party and the trade union commanded little authority, Liulin restored order and won support for a motion to send the delegation—under his leadership and without a single Communist among its members—to the capital.[10]

Stunned by the outcome, the secretary of the regional party committee, Bykin, concluded that Liulin and his allies were now "masters of the situation." For their part, workers underscored their solidarity in the aftermath of the assembly by "categorically refus[ing]" to purchase the government's most recent industrialization bond. Alarmed by the breakdown in discipline at a flagship of light industry, the Central Party Committee dispatched a senior investigator, Grinevich, to Iaroslavl.[11]

On September 4, the five nonparty workers elected by their peers to represent them—Liulin, Mednikov, Gudkova, Golev, and Platonov—arrived in Moscow under the watchful eye of Antonov. Their encounters with officialdom read like a Gogol story set in the Soviet period. First, they had a stormy meeting with the trade-union secretary, Voronova. "Speaking on behalf of the delegation, Liulin said that they want 'to visit Moscow enterprises and have a talk with the workers about how the Iaroslavl workers are supplied,'" reported the OGPU. "'Here you can get cooking oil at any cooperative,'" Liulin told Voronova, "'but in Iaroslavl they give out only five hundred grams per family.'" Claiming that not even *she* could procure enough food for her family, Voronova summarily dismissed Liulin's complaints.[12]

Crestfallen, the delegates next paid a visit to Pozdnyshev, chairman of the worker's section of the Central Union of Cooperatives (CUC). In Liulin's account, Pozdnyshev "sang the same tune . . . but with different words." Frustrated by the lack of sympathy for their cause, Liulin appropriated terms from official rhetoric to criticize the discrepancies in supply between center and periphery: "You have everything here, Comrade Pozdnyshev. Apparently, Moscow is America, and Iaroslavl is an American colony." Offended by the comparison, Pozdnyshev shot back: "What, you want to treat Iaroslavl the same as Moscow!?" Liulin: "What, we're a bunch of monkeys or something!?" Pozdnyshev: "There's no flour!"[13]

After visiting a working-class district to confirm for themselves how much better supplies were in the capital, the delegates went back to see

Voronova. "You're sitting here without any cooking oil," Liulin mockingly commented. "If you'd like, I'll take you out to get [some]." "That's impossible!" replied Voronova, who promptly brought the meeting to an end. After another fruitless visit to the CUC, the delegates decided to try their luck with RSFSR Trade Commissar Chukhrid. Flustered by the appearance in his office of five rank-and-file workers, Chukhrid immediately told them to go to the CUC. After hearing that they had just come from there, Chukhrid consulted his files and announced that ample supplies had been set aside for Iaroslavl, and that therefore local rather than central authorities were to blame for the crisis. Liulin would have none of it: "Give us a reason to believe that in September you'll improve the situation for the workers. Give us something in writing. After all, you're a commissar." "I'll give you nothing in writing," replied Chukhrid. "Only my word."[14]

Determined to press their cause at the highest government level, the delegates visited the Central Soviet Executive Committee on September 5. Although its chairman, USSR President Mikhail Kalinin, was away from his office, chief of staff Belov agreed to see them. After complaining about their treatment at the hands of local officials and the performance of Red Perekop's cooperative, the delegates demanded emergency food shipments for Iaroslavl. Belov provided them with a letter of introduction to Anastas Mikoian, the Soviet trade commissar, and escorted them to the door. Mikoian was away from the office, however, so a meeting was arranged with his deputy, Khinchuk, who washed his hands of the situation: "I'm a commissar of foreign and domestic trade and allocate output to the republics, not to the regions. Go see comrade Chukhrid." After finding out that they had already done that, Khinchuk summoned four subordinates, who conceded that shipments to Iaroslavl were behind schedule. Liulin now recounted the limits on food purchases at the cooperative and demanded to know if "[this] can feed a family of five?" Conceding that it could not, Khinchuk promised to dispatch one of his aides to Iaroslavl.[15]

After returning to Iaroslavl, the delegates met to review the results of their trip. Besides local and regional officials, two representatives from Moscow—Romanova of the trade union and Krichevskii of the CUC—also attended. Although the delegates disagreed as to what promises of assistance, if any, had been secured in Moscow, Liulin claimed that the CUC had vowed to dip into emergency reserves, if necessary, and that a trade commissar had agreed to raise the limit on the purchase of flour at the cooperative by 20 percent, and of cooking oil and groats, by 100 percent.

When this was denied by officials, Liulin demanded compliance with the implicit contract that governed relations between workers and the regime. "The norms . . . do not suffice for a person engaged in physical labor," he declared. "The government demands work from us. We devote all our energy to production, [so] the government must give the worker the nourishment he requires." Should authorities fail to honor their obligations, the workers of Red Perekop would follow suit: "If these demands aren't satisfied, then the intensified labor regime must be canceled—or else the workers will declare a strike."[16]

On September 12, disaster struck Red Perekop when a new power system—a Soviet-made diesel engine—exploded, injuring a worker and rendering numerous production lines idle for seven weeks. Although most of the two thousand affected operatives were reassigned to positions in other parts of the mill, the impact on shop-floor morale was severe. How would operatives survive the drop in earnings that their transfer to new machines almost certainly would entail? More generally, what did it say about the regime's plan to forcibly industrialize if Soviet mechanics could not properly manufacture and install basic equipment? Stoking the rage were the cooperative, which raised the price of rye flour, and Liulin, who publicly attributed the shortage of food to Moscow's agricultural and foreign-trade policies.[17]

On September 14, the Liulin delegation held another fruitless meeting with officials. After viewing a report on local grain supplies, Liulin demanded that reserves be released to the mill. "What makes Perekop workers so special?" sneered one of his superiors. "Why shouldn't it go to workers [elsewhere]?" "Give it to everyone!" retorted Liulin. To which another official conceded that, in fact, "there [was] no flour" in Iaroslavl.[18]

Liulin was floored by this remark. "Why are we sitting here without bread?" he demanded. "I'm Russian, I live in Russia, I have a cow, and I know that our country is agrarian." And "if a Russian were to say that there's no bread in Russia, no one would believe it." After dismissing Liulin's comment, Krichevskii of the CUC reprimanded the delegates for endeavoring to launch their own investigation and for daring, once again, to compare themselves to workers in the capital.[19]

Having resolved nothing in such meetings, each side presented its case the next day to an extraordinary conference of the mill's workers. Of the 1,300 delegates in attendance, 500 (38.5 percent) were women, and 450 (34.6 percent) were party members. Although all nonparty delegates were chosen in shop-floor elections, many Communist delegates were appointed by local party authorities, who understood that only by undemocratic means could they secure a role for their supporters. Combined with official efforts to discredit Liulin, these actions further polarized the situation. There was now "a sharp demarcation between Communists and nonparty" workers, observed Central Party Committee investigator Grinevich, with none of the latter willing to back the former's proposals or resolutions. The stage was set for a battle of "class vs. class."[20]

Liulin opened the conference with an account of the delegation's frustrating trip to Moscow. Noting, with barely concealed sarcasm, that even "[our] esteemed . . . defenders" at the trade union failed to express concern for the workers' plight, he conceded that the delegation had nothing to show for its efforts. He also ridiculed, as illogical and unfair, the regime's policy of geographically differentiated worker supply:

> I had the honor of speaking with some worker-Komsomols from the Naro-Fominsk Mill. There, they get twenty pounds of flour a month and five pounds of baked bread, even if they take it five times a day, [and] ten pounds of millet for two weeks. "But at Red Perekop we get only a kilogram of groats," I said. "That's not very much," [they responded]. Even workers from [the same] mill who came to Moscow to study were surprised. Comrade Krichevskii says, "It's Moscow, it *has* to be supplied." [But] this *isn't* in Moscow . . . The Naro-Fominsk Mill is sixty versts from Moscow. Provisions are brought there by vehicle. [By contrast you] can deliver [provisions] to Iaroslavl *directly by rail*. So to which [town] is it easier to make a delivery? To Iaroslavl, of course. And yet we're sitting [here] without any bread.[21]

Next came the CUC's Krichevskii, who found himself confronted by a hostile audience. "All the difficulties with regard to bread supply do not spring from the evil will of the party, the government, and the state," he shouted over heckling, "but depend on the complex conditions in which our country finds itself at the moment." After recounting the measures taken to improve supplies, he assailed the inflammatory rhetoric provoked by the crisis:

> All talk of there being sons and stepsons or a bourgeoisie and colonies in our country must be rejected. Where are there colonies? Only where there's a bourgeoisie, only where there are capitalist states. (Sustained murmur in the hall.) I say this so that each of you understands clearly . . . that we have no sons and stepsons in our country,

that Iaroslavl is not a colony, and that Moscow workers are not exploiting the Iaroslavl workers.

Conceding that the center was supplied better than the regions, Krichevskii claimed that it had to be that way because Moscow was the capital of an international socialist movement and the place where foreigners' impressions of the Soviet Union were formed. At the same time, he argued, it was wrong to view Moscow as "a paradise."[22]

An official by the name of Degtev endeavored to speak next, but was driven from the podium for launching into an attack on the Liulin delegation. "Away with you!" voices shouted. "You're lying!" Communists in the audience retaliated by jeering the next speaker, Gradusov, a nonparty worker who cited examples from his recent trip to Leningrad to demonstrate that there were, in fact, "sons and stepsons" in Russia. Liulin sprang to Gradusov's defense:

This is a workers' conference, and everyone has the right to speak for ten minutes. Therefore, when a party member speaks, everyone listens and no one may persecute him. . . . And when a nonparty person speaks, then especially you [Communists,] who consider yourselves to be "cultured" people who understand discipline, must maintain order. (Applause.)

Next came the worker Toropov, who wasted no time identifying Moscow's policy of forced capital accumulation as the source of the shop floor's suffering:

The newspapers say that factories never built under the tsarist regime are being built, that a lot of resources are being spent. But that's not what should have been pursued. They should have thought for a while about the mass of workers. The worker, who has adopted the seven-hour day with intensification, is expending all his forces. But if he doesn't eat, he'll hardly be able to work.

Noting the "antagonism" between "the two camps" in the hall—the nonparty workers and the Communists—Toropov ascribed it to the food shortages, which, in his view, exacted the heaviest toll on "family" operatives such as himself. "How will I feed my children?" he demanded of party officials. "If you dish out the slogan, 'Air, water and sun,' without any meat, our children will hardly turn into the 'flowers' you write about." After denouncing the factory committee and the cooperative and demanding that "the center start thinking about industrial Iaroslavl," he concluded with a spirited defense of the implicit contract between workers and the regime:

If we were enemies of Soviet power, we wouldn't have adopted the intensified seven-hour day and wouldn't have started working without bread. We're doing our share, but have a demand to make of you: Don't forget us. *We give to you, and you give to us.* Now put that in your pipe and smoke it.[23]

In a ham-handed effort to seize the initiative, an official by the name of Stameikin renewed the assault on Liulin. "I'd like to say a few words about our delegation that went to Moscow, although it wasn't a delegation, but 'Liulin and company.'" This was followed by shouts of "Away with you!" Remarkably, none other than the target of his criticism restored order: "It's Stameikin's right to reproach Liulin however he likes. Insofar as he insults me, I'll respond in my closing remarks." After justifying grain exports as necessary to finance imports of machinery and raw materials for industry, Stameikin accused Liulin of exploiting the nation's economic difficulties to undermine Soviet power, and insinuated that only "backward" workers supported him: "Liulin has tremendous authority among women, but look how workers in the machine shop view [him]." Judging from the heckling that ensued, this attempt to divide the audience along lines of gender backfired. Equally unsuccessful was a speech by Kerov, a party member who provoked a hostile response when he accused Liulin of anti-Soviet agitation and accused those who supported him of harboring "a political rather than an economic mood."[24]

After Mednikov offered a spirited defense of the delegation, Liulin rejected the criticisms leveled against him and reiterated his demand for ample food supplies and a dignified living standard. The conference's presidium then introduced a resolution acknowledging the supply crisis but insisting that workers refrain from using it against the regime. Although a third of the audience consisted of party members, the resolution failed to pass until it was amended to include Liulin's suggestions. This outcome persuaded officials that the effort to marginalize Liulin had failed. "The members of the delegation (Liulin and the others) are still far from dethroned," lamented the secretary of the Iaroslavl Region Party Committee, "and thanks to the difficulties associated with supply and the breakdown of the diesel engine, they command authority among many workers in the mill."[25]

*　　*　　*

Moscow became concerned about the situation in Iaroslavl soon after Liulin rose to prominence in the late summer of 1928. Efforts to monitor events at the mill began immediately. Shortly after the Liulin delegation returned from its trip to the capital, the OGPU Information Department circulated a summary of its activities to OGPU, party, and trade-union leaders. After the conference of September 15, regional party committee secretary Bykin filed a report with the Central Party Committee on the "extraordinarily difficult" conditions at Red Perekop. Although acknowledged that the mill was mired in an economic and political crisis, Bykin guaranteed that the district party committee would set matters straight.[26]

In contrast to Bykin's report, the one by Central Party Committee investigator Grinevich was pessimistic. Grinevich bluntly concluded that "anti-Soviet elements" had taken control of the situation because the party and the trade union were alienated from the shop floor. As evidence of this alienation, he cited the recent factory-committee elections: "No interest in [them] was observed," and the handful of workers who bothered to vote reflexively opposed resolutions put forth by the Communists. In short, concluded Grinevich, the party would be unable to mobilize support for the program of forced capital accumulation until such time as local officials became responsive to workers' needs.[27]

On October 10, Central Party Committee Secretary Kaganovich signaled the leadership's concern over the "very unhealthy" moods on the industry's shop floors by convening a special conference in Moscow. In addition to alarming evidence of unrest in Leningrad, Moscow, Ivanovo, Rodniki, and Sereda, the participants—leaders from these regions and from the industry as a whole—discussed recent events at Red Perekop. "The workers don't see the fruits of the Revolution," confessed Bykin of the Iaroslavl Region Party Committee. "In the eleven years since the Revolution, there hasn't been any improvement at all." After listening to such comments—and to criticism from trade-union chairman Mel'nichanskii of the demands being made of operatives—Kaganovich defended the party's policies and blamed the trade union for the crisis. Although the conference ended on a note of acrimony, it was not without achievements of a sort: it made regional and trade-union officials aware that the Kremlin was going to ignore pleas for moderation, and conveyed to the Kremlin that the revolution "from above" would have to be implemented over the workers' objection.[28]

The Workers' Choice

The next phase of the Liulin affair began on October 21, when an all-factory conference of 812 workers—half of whom were women, and one-third of whom were party members—rejected the Communist candidate and chose Liulin to serve as Red Perekop's representative to the Eighth All-Union Congress of Trade Unions, which was to convene in Moscow in December. Liulin's election was remarkable because authorities had rigged the outcome by distributing conference passes to what were considered to be the mill's "conscious" operatives—that is, "male and female workers who always attend assemblies." That this strategy backfired underscored the hollowness of the claim that Liulin's support was confined to the shop floor's "backward" segments.[29]

On the day after the conference, the regional party committee upbraided local officials for failing to prevent another victory by Liulin. To get to the bottom of the situation, it established a commission to investigate. A behind-the-scenes effort to sack the secretary of the district party committee (Karin) failed, however, because a qualified candidate could not be found to replace him.[30]

Moscow, too, viewed Liulin's election with alarm. During the ensuing weeks, the Central Party Committee ordered the regional and district party committees to organize a campaign that would discredit Liulin and mobilize support for the FFYP. Meanwhile, a commission consisting of two Central Party Committee investigators—Rozental and Tarasova—was dispatched to Iaroslavl.[31]

Although the Red Perekop party cell responded to the pressure from above by vowing to improve its performance, some Communists complained in a closed assembly that the mill's director and "bourgeois specialists" were at least partly to blame for the crisis because they had been treating the workers poorly.[32] Such comments illustrate not only that indignities suffered at the hands of management played a role in the crisis, but also that rank-and-file party members were skeptical of the official line, which attributed most problems to an alleged deficit of "consciousness" on the shop floor.

After being approved by the regional party committee, a campaign to discredit Liulin was unleashed in mid-November 1928. It began with small conferences of carefully vetted workers, who dutifully approved resolutions that denounced Liulin as an anti-Soviet hooligan "not worthy of being a union member." The resolutions then were published alongside explanatory articles in the regional party newspaper. Like the campaign against Klepikov, however, this one inadvertently mobilized sympathy for its target. Angered by the lies being spread about their spokesman, workers attacked the press and demanded that Miller, a district party committee official who branded Liulin "a bandit," be sacked.[33]

Far from being intimidated by the campaign against him, Liulin savored the exposure. He boasted to friends: "Soon all of Russia will be reading Liulin's words!" As for the trade-union congress, he told constituents that his priority would be to condemn all policies—from grain exports to financing of the Comintern—that had a negative impact on workers' living standard.[34]

Liulin conceded that he had other plans for the congress as well—namely, to establish contact with like-minded party officials. "So I'll go to Moscow and call on comrade Mandel'shtam of the MK [Moscow Party Committee] and tell him that I know his father, the professor, [quite] well, from Kostroma. He's always agreed with me." This reference to Nikolai Mandel'shtam, a leader of the Right Opposition, indicates that Liulin was familiar with the battle under way within the party over the direction of economic policy—and eager to turn it to his constituents' advantage.[35]

Liulin looked favorably on the Right Opposition because the rightist objection to the revolution "from above"—that it would cause severe disequilibrium in the economy, shatter living standards, and sow social unrest—echoed his own. He provocatively told colleagues on the eve of the congress: "Stalin is bringing back the times of Peter the Great. Just as Peter built Petersburg on the bones of the workers, so the Communists are building socialism on the back of the working class."[36] As we have seen, denunciations of the party's "exploitation" of the workers became common once the program of forced capital accumulation began. Although it was only the exceptional worker, such as Liulin, who endeavored to make contact with rightist leaders, support for their priorities was widespread on the industry's shop floors.

After several weeks of intensive preparation, officials convened a conference, on December 1, to reconsider Liulin's election as Red Perekop's representative to the trade-union congress. In attendance were 998 delegates, half of whom were women and a quarter of whom were party members. Although Bykin claimed that this conference was "more democratic" than the previous one, Central Party Committee investigators Rozental and

Tarasova disagreed. To demonstrate that the district party committee had rigged the outcome, they noted that the vote to replace Liulin with the nonparty spinner Makhanov was, incredibly, unanimous.[37]

Far from putting Liulin's supporters in their place, the election of Makhanov inspired them to fight harder. Within days of the conference, shop floors were abuzz with denunciations of the vote and rebuttals against the anti-Liulin campaign. "[We]'ve known Liulin for a long time," declared his supporters. "He's no hooligan, but a worker—a pure proletarian."[38]

The Liulin affair intersected at this point with battles taking place in the upper ranks of the trade union. On December 7, *Voice of the Textile Worker*—the trade union's national daily—reported that "the hooligan Liulin won't go to the congress" because young workers at Red Perekop had managed to unmask and depose him. Incensed by this claim, the chairman of the trade union's regional bureau filed a petition challenging the legitimacy of Makhanov's election. When Mel'nichanskii himself approved the petition, the editors of *Voice* issued a retraction. "The legitimate delegate to the congress," they conceded, "is comrade Liulin."[39]

In a textbook case of workers' ability to turn fissures within the elite to their own advantage, Liulin's supporters brandished copies of the retraction. "The Communists have confessed that Liulin should be the one to go to the congress," they declared. "The center is for Liulin." "Large groups of workers" agreed, prompting authorities to schedule yet another conference to resolve the matter of who should represent Red Perekop at the congress.[40]

On December 15, an assembly of Communists voted to stand behind Makhanov, notwithstanding the objections of a trade-union official and several rank-and-file party members. The factory committee followed suit. Meanwhile, scores of "stormy" assemblies held on shop floors and in barracks gave voice to the workers' rage, as speakers castigated the Communists—many of whom were frightened into silence—for conspiring against their candidate: "The Communists are to blame for the rejection of his candidacy." "[They] don't like Liulin because he points out their deficiencies and lays bare all the filth." After humiliating the few party members who dared put themselves up for election—"We must not elect Communists to the all-factory conference!"—operatives demanded strict and transparent democratic procedures, and let it be known that "all the workers are for Liulin!"[41]

The passion with which workers defended Liulin was motivated not just by support for his views, but also by a collective sense of grievance over having been deprived of one of the most precious gains of the Revolution—namely, shop-floor democracy. Speakers took advantage of the moment to advance their own agendas. Echoing rumors that Liulin belonged to an underground organization, one declared that "the Bolsheviks have their party, and we nonparty workers must build our own and send Liulin to the congress because we outnumber the Bolsheviks." Another explicitly linked Liulin to the anti-Stalinist, albeit left rather than right, opposition: "Long live Liulin and the Liulinites! Give us Trotsky, and no arguments about it!" Liulin's allies swept the elections, giving workers a rare opportunity to exult: "Even though [the Communists] said that Liulin is a hooligan, a drunkard, and a demagogue, it didn't turn out their way!"[42]

Hours before the third and final conference, on December 18, to determine who would represent Red Perekop at the trade-union congress, a dispute erupted over whether Liulin himself, who somehow was defeated in the election held in the machine shop, should be permitted to attend. Not surprisingly, an assembly of nonparty delegates voted to include him, and an assembly of Communist delegates voted to exclude him.[43]

Before the dispute was resolved, the conference convened in an atmosphere of "extraordinary chaos." Under intense pressure from the floor—of the 1,001 delegates in attendance, a quarter were party members—district party committee secretary Karin reluctantly threw the doors open to Liulin, who received a thunderous ovation as he strutted to the stage, surrounded by a throng of supporters. Turning to face the delegates, Liulin commandeered the proceedings. "Don't accept the list of presidium members they propose," he declared. "You yourselves must select the presidium." Karin offered a slate of party loyalists, but Liulin cut him off: "That's enough! Don't deceive [us]." During the next eighty minutes, each side maneuvered to win seats on the presidium. Signaling the hostility felt toward those who played the most visible role in suppressing their voice, workers denounced candidates proposed by local officials, and applauded those put forth by central authorities. In the end, thirty-eight individuals were elected to the presidium: twenty-five were allies of the party, and thirteen were worker-delegates, such as Golev and Lytochkin, who supported Liulin. Also elected, by acclamation, was Liulin himself.[44]

The first formal address was made by the regional trade-union council chairman, to whom fell the unpleasant task of making the case for

Makhanov, who was already in Moscow representing Red Perekop at the congress. As soon as he made his views known, however, the delegates heckled him into silence and endeavored to drag him off the stage. During the commotion that followed, an operative lashed out at Central Party Committee investigators Rozental and Tarasova for paying little more than lip service to a key revolutionary idea: "Is it possible that you, representatives from the center, don't see and hear what the workers want?! Why don't you want to do it the way we want to do it? For once, let it be done our way! Where is your 'democracy' you talk about?"[45]

Thus addressed, Rozental and Tarasova asked the delegates to draft a list of grievances. "Let the representatives from the center know that everything here is terrible," replied a voice from the floor. "Instead of explaining things, party members only stir up the nonparty mass. The election of Makhanov . . . was a fraud. We elected Liulin, and we'll send him. I appeal to the representatives from the Central Party Committee: Look at the mood of the workers!"[46]

Speaking on behalf of the trade union's central committee, a certain Rishchev endeavored to mollify the delegates by acknowledging his organization's shortcomings. His plea for cooperation was rejected, however, prompting Rozental to motion for a recess. As authorities conferred on stage about how to gain control over the proceedings, and as frightened Communist delegates cowered in the rear of the auditorium, Liulin's supporters lobbied for their candidate: "Vote for Liulin!" they bellowed. Eventually, word leaked that local officials wanted to disperse the delegates, which further inflamed passions. "You want to break up the conference!" a worker shouted at the presidium, "[but] we won't leave here until we vote for Liulin!" Wisely, Rozental called the conference back into session.[47]

District party committee secretary Karin now drew further attention to his alienation from the shop floor by offering a resolution that denounced *Voice* for backing Liulin and confirmed Makhanov as Red Perekop's delegate to the congress. A competing resolution was offered by the opposition: it replaced Makhanov with Liulin, ordered the district party committee to apologize for having branded Liulin a "bandit," and insisted that Liulin's wife be granted access to the Labor Exchange. Not surprisingly, the opposition's resolution passed by an overwhelming margin (70 percent).[48]

Having accomplished their goal after five hours of battle, the delegates

broke into cheers and disbanded. Although the sense of elation was genuine, realists knew what would ensue from this victory. "Now wait for the
revenge of the Communists," they warned. Liulin got the message: antic-
ipating a midnight visit from the OGPU, he arranged to spend the night
at a friend's apartment.[49]

No sooner had Liulin been reelected than the various authorities issued
their analyses. While some members of the regional party committee
shrugged off the event by saying that unruly, anti-Communist worker assemblies were "not a novelty" anymore, Rozental and Tarasova insisted
that such a situation was "unacceptable, especially in 1928." Their own
analysis of the crisis, however, was riddled with contradiction. Unable to
concede the truth—namely, that the Liulin affair was a mobilization by
workers against the party's policy-driven assault on living standards—they
instead blamed the crisis on the "suppression" by local officials of shop-
floor democracy, the "backwardness" of Liulin's supporters, and the continuing presence in the mills of "hostile" strata and "hooligan elements."
Though ideologically correct, this analysis ignored facts of which Rozental and Tarasova were aware: first, that Liulin, his allies, and many of their
supporters were "conscious" by the party's standards (that is, they were
veteran workers, literate, and deeply engaged in the life of the mill); and
second, that shop-floor democracy had to be suppressed because otherwise workers would elect opponents of the revolution "from above" to
represent them. As a result, the remedies that Rozental and Tarasova proposed—respect for "the fundamental principles of worker democracy,"
responsiveness to the legitimate demands of the labor force, a compre-
hensive campaign to "enlighten" operatives—either could not be implemented, or would fail to improve the shop floor's "very bad" morale if
they were.[50]

Since the Central Party Committee blamed a subordinate entity—
namely, the regional party committee—for allowing the situation at Red
Perekop to spin out of control, each level of the hierarchy followed suit.
For example, Bykin and Mel'nichanskii readily agreed that the district
party committee bore most of the blame for the workers' "sharply negative" opinion of "party organizations."[51]

Even more so than Mel'nichanskii, Bykin had a lot at stake in preventing further victories by "Liulin's petty-bourgeois group." As a result, he
endeavored to fulfill at least some of the Central Party Committee's recommendations, such as that local party officials and the mill's most un-

popular managers and specialists be sacked. He also went beyond these recommendations by establishing a commission to gather intelligence about conditions in *all* of Iaroslavl Region's major enterprises. He justified this step in a January 1929 letter to subordinate party organizations: "Given the economic difficulties we're experiencing, the feeble deployment of *samokritika* and the alienation of party organizations from the toiling masses create objective conditions for the type of phenomena . . . that took place at Perekop." Bykin understood that the policy-driven assault on living standards had sown discontent throughout the labor force, and he could not afford having another "Liulin type" surface in his jurisdiction.[52]

Aware that his days in office were numbered, district party committee secretary Karin made a last-ditch effort to save himself. In a direct appeal to Kaganovich, he recited the litany of problems he had inherited when he took over his post. While accepting ultimate responsibility for the situation, he insisted that shop-floor support for Liulin was weaker than the evidence of recent events suggested. Unfortunately for Karin, this argument was contradicted by the findings of the Central Party Committee investigators; moreover, the party needed a scapegoat. His plea for mercy was ignored.[53]

In contrast to party officials at every level, the OGPU Information Department composed a narrative, the purpose of which was neither to scapegoat nor to save face, but rather to convey as much information as possible. Its relatively straightforward reports—which were sent directly to top officials of the OGPU, the Central Party Committee, the Council of People's Commissars, the Central Council of Trade Unions, and the textile workers' trade union—enabled the leadership to grasp the severity of the situation. This, in turn, facilitated the evaluation of remedies proposed by various parties.[54]

The outcome of the December 18 conference was a blow to party members, who immediately found themselves subject to ridicule. "Soon we'll throw the Communists out the window," gloated nonparty workers. "Now we—not they—are the leaders." Unable to endure the humiliation, some former Makhanov supporters proclaimed their allegiance to Liulin.[55]

Meanwhile, Liulin raced to Moscow and replaced Makhanov as Red Perekop's delegate to the Eighth Congress of Trade Unions. The trip deepened his alienation from both the party and the trade union. After returning to Iaroslavl, he berated the congress as a "routine talking-shop" that was of "no benefit at all" to his constituents because the podium was never surrendered to "nonparty workers" such as himself. So disillusioning was the experience that Liulin abandoned his plan to contact leaders of the Right Opposition. "It was politically unprofitable for me to speak with members of the government," he told colleagues. "All these leaders are nothing but scum, and there's no point expecting help or protection from them." A visit to the headquarters of Taylorism in the Soviet Union—Aleksei Gastev's Central Institute of Labor—did nothing to improve his spirits. "This is an institution [that develops] scientific methods for wringing the last juices out of workers," he reported. "There, they study the system of [Frederick W.] Taylor, the American capitalist. We won't employ the institute's method on the shop floor because it reduces the worker to . . . a skeleton."[56]

Although he expected to be arrested by the OGPU in either Moscow or Iaroslavl, Liulin remained unconcerned about his fate. The following statement highlights the degree to which he had assimilated the prerevolutionary ideal of the self-sacrificing labor activist: "I'm not afraid that they can arrest and exile me because I work for the commonweal of the working class, and not for my family." Looking forward, he hoped to institutionalize his network of underground political contacts: "The time to create an organization and speak out has yet to come, but the time will arrive and I'll scream: 'Comrades, organize yourselves and crush these vermin (the Communists)!'" Though an unwavering supporter of the October Revolution, Liulin harbored fantasies—as did many operatives at this time—of Soviet power without the party dictatorship.[57]

In the near term, Liulin's goal was to enforce the implicit contract between workers and the regime by including its terms in the 1929 labor contract. His strategy for accomplishing this goal was straightforward: he would "rabidly" oppose ratification of the collective contract until it was amended to include higher wages and "an unlimited quantity of fats" and "baked bread," and his allies would agitate aggressively among the rank and file. "[Our] demands are fundamental," he insisted, "and we must prepare the workers to stand up for [them] at the conference." Given that the regional party committee warned Moscow that there would be unrest at Red Perekop when the collective contract came up for ratification, shop-floor support for Liulin seems to have been as strong after the congress as it was before. If the party was to have its way, that would soon change.[58]

The Anti-Liulin Campaign

Shortly after the congress, Mel'nichanskii ordered *Voice* to launch a public assault—similar to the one under way against Klepikov—against Red Perekop's popular shop-floor spokesman. Although nonparty operatives tended to be skeptical of the press, the move signaled an escalation of the anti-Liulin campaign. *Voice* was read widely in Soviet mills, and therefore was an appropriate vehicle for turning the events in Iaroslavl into a case study of worker "backwardness." Still, by making Liulin the focus of attention, Mel'nichanskii inadvertently risked increasing his popularity: if past experience was a guide, operatives would rise to their leader's defense. More worrisome, the campaign would broadcast some version of Liulin's views to every mill in Russia.[59]

The first salvo came in a December 30 article, "The Lessons from Red Perekop on the Struggle with the Class Enemy," which characterized Liulin as a more subtle version of Klepikov:

On more than one occasion we have exposed the speeches of Klepikov—and those like him—in our newspaper. The residents of Rodniki now understand that Klepikov is an enemy who pushes the working class back to capitalism, to the old exploiter-boss. But Klepikov is not alone.

An enemy of the working class who is like Klepikov, but more clever and more cunning, is Red Perekop's Liulin. Liulin approaches the workers differently. He doesn't come out openly against Soviet power. He pretends to be the workers' friend.

The article noted that the Liulin clique had come into existence in September 1928, when it traveled to Moscow to petition for food. The problem was that since then it had been acting against workers' fundamental interests by engaging in strike agitation and condemning "our socialist construction." Both Liulin and Klepikov were agents of "our class enemy, the Nepman and the kulak," but only Liulin had managed to disguise himself as a supporter of Soviet power: "Liulin is no less dangerous than Klepikov. And dangerous, above all, because the workers have not seen through him yet."[60]

How had this threat to shop-floor tranquility arisen? Echoing the line of the Central Party Committee, *Voice* argued that blame lay with enterprise-level trade-union and party organizations, whose "inactivity and alienation from the masses" had enabled "the rightist danger" to flourish. "The lesson of Red Perekop is a lesson for many, many factories," opined the editors, and action had to be taken immediately to persuade operatives to support Moscow's policies.[61]

The effect of the campaign could be seen in events the machine shop. On January 8, 1929, Liulin gave a speech to two hundred male colleagues in which he endeavored to defend the community's living standard by demanding that workers be granted the right to renegotiate the labor contract should real wages decline. Although this demand would have won widespread support in the spinning and weaving sheds, no one protested when the factory committee cut Liulin off before he finished speaking. Nor was Liulin able to win passage of a resolution that sought a one-year guarantee of price stability. These defeats were followed by another one several days later, when the machine shop failed for the second time in as many months to elect Liulin as its delegate to an all-factory conference.[62]

Though embarrassing, the outcome did not dampen his self-confidence. "You didn't elect [me], and I don't give a damn about you," he retorted. "The other workers will carry me in their arms to the conference!" He had grounds for optimism: outside the machine shop, most of his allies prevailed in the election.[63]

As it turned out, the conference, which convened on January 13, demonstrated that the party now enjoyed the upper hand. There was no demand that the doors be thrown open to Liulin, and no protest when the presidium rebuffed a challenge to its composition from his allies. More significant, the collective contract—against which Liulin had been campaigning—was approved without substantial changes. Apparently, the most recent phase of the anti-Liulin campaign had turned the tide. It was "a big day at Red Perekop," crowed *Voice*. "The Liulinites have suffered a defeat."[64]

Or had they? True, the conference had not devolved into chaos, even after Liulin's allies abandoned the hall to protest what they considered to be the presidium's antidemocratic procedures. If passage of the collective contract represented a defeat for the Liulinites, however, it was one that the party secured only by first offering delegates a chance to vote on a resolution that called for a higher living standard. Since this resolution passed overwhelmingly, the real lesson of the conference was that authorities could gain leverage over Liulin only by co-opting the values of the moral economy that lay at the heart of his critique of Stalin's revolution "from above."[65]

At any rate, the trade union conceded that the tide had yet to turn.

Within a week of the conference, the editors of *Voice* lamented that the Red Perekop labor force still did not understand, let alone support, Moscow's policies. Their prescription: more agitprop to eradicate, once and for all, the virus of "unconsciousness" borne by Liulin.[66]

What form should this agitprop take? *Voice* offered a template when it published a front-page caricature of "the Liulin forces"—a drunk and vomiting worker, a devout peasant woman, and a priest—engaged in mock procession. The slogan of this pathetic crew: "Drink up, brothers!" A caption interpreted the image for the reader:

DRUNKEN ASSISTANCE
At the Red Perekop Mill (Iaroslavl), the drunkard-spinner Golev, a fervent Liulin supporter, introduced a motion not to conduct a battle against hard drinking.
He argued that hard drinking is essential for the workers.[67]

The message—that only "backward" workers supported Liulin—was no less clear for having been often repeated.

On January 20, a conference of eight hundred worker-delegates—more than one-fifth of whom were Communists—convened at to consider the results of the Eighth Congress of Trade Unions. Although Liulin again failed to win a majority of votes in the machine shop, authorities had to invite him because he had represented Red Perekop at the congress.[68]

When Liulin mounted the podium, he was warmly applauded by the delegates—especially, according to the OGPU, by the women among them. Demonstrating that he had not been cowed by the press campaign, he contradicted almost every claim made in the keynote address—which he must have enjoyed doing, since it was delivered by none other than his nemesis from Moscow, trade-union secretary Voronova—and stated bluntly that Moscow's economic policies had made the workers' lives unbearable.[69]

After defending his record as the workers' representative, Liulin ceded the podium to allies. "Everyone has taken up arms against Liulin," declared Matveev, "but the masses won't treat those who are against [him] kindly." Golev denounced the caricature of "the Liulin forces" that appeared the day before in *Voice*. These comments were well received, but a resolution by Lytochkin that called on authorities to desist from further attacks on "the Liulinites" was rejected, and an official resolution that hailed the results of the congress was approved.[70]

No sooner had the conference ended when its legitimacy was challenged in a letter by the weaver Kozlova. Cosigned by eighty-seven other Red Perekop worker-delegates and published in *Voice*, the letter accused officials of packing the hall with employees from other enterprises and, for good measure, condemned the practice of branding as a "Liulinite" anyone who tried to voice shop-floor concerns. "We . . . aren't 'Liulinites,'" insisted Kozlova. "We were elected by the worker-masses." Her point was that delegates who supported Liulin's platform did so on behalf of their constituents. As for Liulin, Kozlova vouched for the purity of his class origins: "Reading the newspapers, one might conclude that he has his own party. But that's not true. Liulin hails from a proletarian family, like all the workers whom they insult and call 'Liulinites.'"[71]

Kozlova's letter did not go unanswered. In two accompanying commentaries, the editors of *Voice* summarized their position. First, the conference at the mill had been fair: most delegates were nonparty, and all decisions had been made democratically. Second, given the country's current economic conditions, all measures implemented in the industry were justified. Finally, support for Liulin's attacks on the party and its policies was confined to workers who bore a grudge against Soviet society because of a past criminal conviction or job reprimand, and to "sectarians of all colors, evangelists, priests, [and] former members of the bourgeoisie and the nobility."[72]

That was not all. *Voice* soon published excerpts—under headlines such as "Who are the friends and enemies of the workers?"—from some of the many letters it claimed to have received from across the country. Signed by groups of two to three dozen party loyalists, the missives endeavored to persuade Liulin's followers to transfer their allegiance to the party and to support "socialist construction." Recent events in Rodniki were cited as an example to be heeded:

> Your backwardness also is evident in that you're standing up for Liulin. We've read that there was a similarly harmful type at the Rodniki Mill—Klepikov. He also confused the workers. At first, the whole factory defended him. But then the workers themselves expelled him from the union.
>
> There are still many of these Liulins and Klepikovs in the mills. All of them just pretend to be the workers' defenders. We must scorch them out of our environment with hot iron.[73]

Although such appeals had little impact on the shop floor, they increased the pressure on local officials to produce a breakthrough in the battle against Liulin.

The breakthrough came on January 30, when *Voice* published a recantation by one of Liulin's prominent allies. "'I must confess: I was wrong!'" screamed the headline. "Aleksandr Lytochkin is against Liulin and his supporters." Confirming that the protests had been the work of "anti-Soviet elements," the former Komsomol repudiated his mentor and promised to support the party's policies. Having converted overnight from defender of the workers to supporter of the general line, Lytochkin endeavored to inoculate himself against humiliation by parroting official slogans and expressing gratitude to the women who had "saved" him:

> I express tender thanks to *Voice*, my wife Katia, [and] the secretary of [my department's] party cell (Akhmatova) for having clarified [things] for me and thus gotten me back on the correct path.
> I CALL ON BOTH THE OTHER MALE WORKERS AND THE FEMALE WORKERS OF RED PEREKOP TO FOLLOW MY EXAMPLE.
> Long live the Communist Party!
> Long live Great October!

In other letters from Red Perekop, an operative called on Liulin to restore the mill's honor by following Lytochkin's example, and a group of thirty-two ring-frame spinners vowed to "correct their mistake"—and demonstrate their fealty to Soviet power—by reversing their previous rejection of elevated workloads.[74]

The campaign produced mixed results. In yet another example of the unintended consequences of official propaganda, rumors that Liulin soon would "be arrested as a counterrevolutionary . . . created the impression among workers and individual party members that Liulin is *not* the enemy." Lytochkin's capitulation also backfired, leaving him ostracized on the shop floor, where, he reported, "they promise to smash my snout because of this letter."[75]

Even if it was true, as the district party committee claimed, that Liulin's supporters were compelled to lower their profile as a result of the campaign, by no means had they dropped out of sight. An assembly of one thousand workers held in February to publicize the results of a recent Central Party Committee plenum illustrates the point. After the keynote speaker, Nazarov of the Central Party Control Commission, denounced Liulin in the strongest possible terms, several of Liulin's supporters mounted the podium. According to the OGPU, a typical comment was the one offered by the worker Antropov:

> I myself am a former party member . . . but I can't bear the bureaucratism that has developed at present. A consequence of it is that the Communist Party is losing authority among the working class. A lot's been said here about criticism, but criticism must be put forth very carefully—for criticism can land you in Solovki. The entire toiling mass is behind Liulin. Liulin shouldn't be punished, he should be pardoned. Liulin has authority, and only he shook up our local organizations.

Other speakers vouched for Liulin's Soviet identity. "[He's] a bench worker and his father worked right here at the factory," insisted the thread lugger Gol'dberg. "[H]e's no counterrevolutionary."[76]

Having anticipated such protests, officialdom arranged for its loyalists to rebut them. The most dramatic speech was delivered by the turncoat Lytochkin, who offered evidence to back up the claim that his former mentor was a "counterrevolutionary":

> Indeed, I raised Cain alongside Liulin, but I learned [the truth] about him not so long ago . . . A worker once said to me: "Join the party with us." I said to him, in response, that "I'll never join the party," but he answered me back: "Not the Communist Party, but the party against [it], to fight with the Bolsheviks."

Confirming their dominance of the proceedings, authorities won passage of a resolution that vaguely approved Moscow's policies and stated that unrest directed against the program of forced capital accumulation had been orchestrated by "elements who are hostile to the Soviet regime and the party."[77] What prompted the victory—the resolution's repudiation of labor activists such as Liulin, its criticism of local organizations for ignoring the workers' needs, or its demand that the regime improve living standards—is unclear. The editors of *Voice* thus seem to have been victims of wishful thinking when they claimed that "the workers of Red Perekop have acknowledged their mistake" and turned, "together with the Bolsheviks, against Liulin."[78]

Because the crisis had not been overcome, another round of reports had to be filed. In his memorandum to other members of the Central Party

Control Commission, Nazarov elucidated an issue that had been broached time and again, though not yet systematically investigated: the mill's notorious bourgeois specialists.

> Under the tsarist regime, there was a small but strong Bolshevik group at the [Red Perekop] Mill. At the same time, there was a very substantial organization of the Union of Russian People [a right-wing political party]. Almost the entire [mill] administration . . . joined the ranks of the latter. . . .
>
> A significant part of the administration stayed behind and is in the mill to this day, and it seems to me that this circumstance, in particular, explains to a great extent why the mill has come to the state in which it now finds itself.

By underscoring the workers' resentment of the bourgeois specialists, Nazarov gave voice to a line of interpretation that was gaining currency in the corridors of power: by launching a campaign against this stratum, the party might be able to improve its image on the shop floor, if not mobilize support for revolution "from above."[79]

The new district party committee secretary, Koltun, focused on a different stratum in the mill. "It's no surprise that individual Communists and the cells as a whole don't enjoy authority among the workers," he noted in his report to Moscow. "The latter don't view the party organization as their leader." In Koltun's Leninist view, the source of the problem was not policy but rather the rude, immoral, and "unconscious" behavior of party members, and only by means of a purge could "the alienation of the party organization from the nonparty toiling masses" be liquidated.[80]

Although the regional party committee supported Koltun's recommendation, the Central Party Control Commission authorized nothing more than a verification of party documents. While the sources shed no light on Moscow's thinking, they confirm that pressure from below for a purge, which the Sixteenth Party Conference finally approved in April 1929, had been building for months. It is not difficult to understand why. Forced to implement a program of forced capital accumulation whose internal contradictions made their organizations the target of working-class hostility, regional and district party bosses could only hope that the cause of their problems was the human content of the party rather than the content of the party's policies.[81]

Although a brief article in the March 3, 1929, issue of *Voice* claimed that calm had finally descended on Iaroslavl's shop floors, a report submitted

only the day before to the trade unions central committee was far from san-
guine about the situation there or, for that matter, in any of Russia's mill
towns. After noting the "tense state of [workers'] moods" and describing
several recent episodes of unrest, the report concluded that the working-
class political landscape had undergone an alarming transformation:

> What is extremely important is that these fermentations set the stage
> for the mounting and crystallization of anti-Soviet groups that come
> forward with increasingly candid critiques of the entire policy of the
> party and the Soviet government. Existing almost openly in many en-
> terprises, such groups (the Liulin group at Red Perekop, Klepikov at
> the [Rodniki] Mill, Peunkov at the Upper Sereda Mill, Parfent'ev at
> [Pavlovskii-Posad's] Lenskaia Mill) serve as the organizing center for
> all sorts of disturbances, openly and systematically incite and head
> these disturbances, give shape to the demands of individual groups of
> workers, [and] conduct daily demolition work.[82]

Having monitored shop-floor morale for years, the party and the trade
union understood that the proliferation of Klepikovs, Liulins, Peunkovs,
and Parfent'evs posed a practical and symbolic threat to the program of
forced capital accumulation. The only questions still to be answered were:
When, and by what means, would this threat be eliminated? In the case of
Liulin, the answers would come soon enough.

Liulin's Last Stand

The final chapter of the Liulin affair began in the aftermath of the Sixteenth Party Conference, which formally approved the maximum variant
of the FFYP and, not coincidentally, launched a vicious campaign against
the Right Opposition. The victory of the Stalinists did not immediately
put an end to rightist sentiment at Red Perekop. "Having seized a large
number of Perekop's party members in the beginning," observed the district party committee, "the Liulin affair, as an expression of the petty-
bourgeois vacillations of the workers, was still quite strong and manifested
itself sharply even in the period of the party conference (May–June)."[83]

Having maintained a low profile for several months, Liulin decided that
he could no longer refrain from speaking out against the "great turn," the
radicalism of which was now apparent. An appropriate forum presented itself on June 10, when the party cell convened an open assembly to an-
nounce the plan's goals. After the keynote speaker extolled the virtues of

Stalin's revolution "from above," Liulin took the podium. "Judging from the lecture," he acidly remarked, "all of us . . . supposedly are moving up in the world, but in fact we see just the opposite." Notwithstanding the experience of Soviet bureaucrats, who "get a big salary at the expense of the working class, but do nothing themselves," and the claims of official propaganda, life was grim. "The workers' situation has become more difficult. There's deception all around, and nowhere to complain. Earnings are falling and prices for every good and food item are rising faster than [anticipated] in the . . . plan." Since the most urgent problem was the shortage of food, moreover, there could be no talk of boosting industrial output until the party abandoned its war on the peasantry: "The state and collective farms that the Bolsheviks are building in the countryside give us nothing. We must develop individual, private holdings."[84]

Having defended the NEP in agriculture, Liulin turned his attention to the policy of forced capital accumulation. "He sharply criticized the party's policy (the Five-Year Plan)," recalled his ally Bobrov, and "said that the entire policy of the party is built on the blood and sweat of the working class, the exploitation of which is becoming more and more acute." *Voice* offered a similar account:

> In Liulin's words, the Five-Year Plan is bondage [*kabala*] for the workers. The reduction of manufacturing costs and the increase in productivity indicated in the plan allegedly deteriorate the circumstances of male and female workers.
>
> "It would be more profitable for us to be under someone's heel, to become a colony or a semicolony of England or France," declared Liulin at the workers' conference.[85]

How did the audience respond to Liulin's critique? Although *Voice* reported that Liulin was repudiated by those present, the district party committee conceded that "his speech, which was directed against the Five-Year Plan, met with sympathy on the part of a significant portion of the delegates." Indeed, delegates were so agitated by his remarks that they refused to let officials address them for some time. Order was finally restored, and an official resolution on the FFYP was put to a vote. Its fate, however, is uncertain: two sources indicate that it passed; another, that it was rejected.[86]

That night, Bobrov warned Liulin that his "very harsh speech" could land him in jail. Lacing his comments with provocative references to his contacts in the underground, Liulin answered with equal parts pride and equanimity:

I kicked up a hell of a storm. I won't avoid prison, but there's nothing that can be done about that. The organization mobilized me; I came forward at its request. I've done a good job sowing at the mill. Now may it take hold. And much good these sprouts will do the Communists . . .

The organization will not abandon my family. My children and wife won't go hungry. My comrades will give [them] money.

The "organization" to which Liulin referred probably consisted of nothing more than an informal network of like-minded acquaintances. Liulin was a pillar of the working-class community, and he knew that its members would support him in his hour of need just as he had supported them in theirs.[87]

Alarmed by the destabilizing effects of Liulin's speech, one of the most audacious of his life, the district party committee filed the last of a series of applications for his arrest. This time, it was approved. On June 10, 1929, the regional party committee issued a decree authorizing the dismissal and arrest of Liulin for engaging in "counterrevolutionary agitation . . . among the mill's workers against the fundamental measures of the party and the Soviet regime." The next day, the district OGPU bureau arrested the target at his home under Article 58 of the Criminal Code. Shortly thereafter, Liulin was convicted and sentenced to three years of exile in the Northern Region.[88]

Concerned that the arrest of the shop floor's popular spokesman could ignite protests, the district party committee launched a campaign to persuade workers "of the counterrevolutionary essence of the Liulin affair" and inform them of the consequences "of speeches on his behalf." Doing its part, *Voice* published a didactic article for the "male and female workers of Red Perekop" who may have been tempted to "believe Liulin." For the benefit of these "semiliterates," the trade union explained that the FFYP promised prosperity rather than, as Liulin argued, impoverishment. There would be short-term sacrifices, but these were preferable to the alternative:

Yes, Liulin, life is still difficult and it will be even more difficult to build new factories and plants, but the workers and peasants of the USSR will never exchange freedom for a "golden cage."

Liulin, for a long time you have wanted this, for a long time you have confused the workers—so go and work in any one of England's colonies yourself.

There's no place in the workers' ranks for counterrevolutionaries, like you, who impede and harm socialist construction.[89]

The threats, if not the propaganda, were effective. Although "individual groups of workers" complained that "Liulin is a victim of *samokritika*," efforts by his "accomplices" to organize demonstrations failed. Most of the credit for neutralizing opposition belonged to the OGPU, whose agents scored a coup when they confiscated all "the anti-Soviet leaflets" that "were scattered on the grounds of the mill" before workers had a chance to read them. Drafted, apparently, by Liulin's allies, the leaflets invoked the ideals of the October Revolution to justify their call for a violent uprising against regional elites and their demand that the center reverse its assault on the conditions of work and daily life:

Comrade workers, have you not forgotten what you fought for, what you spilled blood for? For freedom, for the improvement of the worker's way of life . . . for emancipation from the yoke of capital, and for freedom of speech. Now everything is regressing to the past, to serfdom: they've stopped giving the worker what he needs to live . . . [t]hey've started intensifying labor beyond what's [humanly] possible . . . and they're beginning to arrest the advanced and just workers who speak out at assemblies and tell the truth.

Comrade workers . . . you must prepare yourselves for the day and hour of action . . . [W]e'll idle the mill, take out the [regional trade-union bureau], disperse the [regional party committee], and . . . smash the Soviet capitalists, big-bellies, mugs, and deceivers, the oppressors of the laboring masses. We're going to demand that the center increase wage earnings, put an end to work on night shifts and labor intensification, [and] provide a good and proper food supply . . . Down with the yoke, Soviet capitalism! Long live a genuinely free life and existence!

The leaflets revealed the degree to which the revolution "from above"—identified in the text, ironically, as "Soviet capitalism"—radicalized working-class critics of the regime.[90] Having crystallized months before during a food-supply crisis, the Liulin faction now found itself issuing appeals for a violent uprising. Although the means proposed may have exceeded those approved by its leader, the ends—more food, less work, higher pay, and civil rights for workers—remained the same.

Although the regional party committee claimed that workers welcomed Liulin's arrest, OGPU sources told a different story. On July 10, the security police discovered that Liulin's wife had given a petition to a sympa-thetic female relative, Loginova, who worked at the mill. The petition confirmed the validity of Liulin's complaints about the deterioration of liv-ing standards, vouched for his working-class credentials, asserted that his only mistake was to have engaged in *samokitrika*, and requested that his fate be decided by the mill's workers. In the forty-eight hours that it cir-culated before being confiscated, it drew 166 signatures. That many were willing to publicly support Liulin at this juncture, despite the obvious dan-ger of doing so, illustrates the resilience of the working-class community, whose members continued to offer succor to one another in times of cri-sis, and the depth of the shop floor's commitment to its leader. The days when Liulin's followers could defeat officialdom, however, were over: within several weeks, the factory committee convened an assembly of 857 workers, a majority of whom approved a resolution that denounced the petitioners and approved Liulin's prosecution as an "anti-Soviet element" who erroneously opposed the party and its economic program.[91]

A significant episode of resistance against fundamental aspects of revolu-tion "from above," the Liulin affair sent Moscow a message: its policies would be opposed by large numbers of workers acting in the name of So-viet power. What was to be done? Certainly, popular support had to be mobilized if the program of forced capital accumulation was to be fulfilled. To that end, the party endeavored to legitimize the program by linking it to Lenin and the heroism of the Civil War, and to stigmatize dissent as the work of "class enemies."[92] The party's resurrection of the language of class war in 1928 was a response to the shop floor's opposition to revolution "from above" and the sacrifices it would impose.

Another conclusion that Moscow drew was that the organs of political repression had to be mobilized against workers—and their leaders—at the first indication of resistance. The delay in responding to Liulin enabled him to acquire enough popularity to defend himself for some time against official countermeasures. The internal contradictions of the program of forced capital accumulation, moreover, left those condemned to imple-ment it—local elites—too reviled to function effectively as neutralizers of dissent. To prevent more Liulin types from springing into existence and posing a threat to revolution "from above," the OGPU had to be given resources to monitor shop floors closely, and authority to make arrests swiftly—indeed, preemptively.

Speed was of the essence because unrest, and the demands that accompanied it, had a tendency to escalate. At Red Perekop, a protest over food shortages gave way to a protest against the suppression of shop-floor democracy, which in turn gave way to demands that the implicit contract governing relations between workers and the regime be given binding, and explicit, legal form. Escalation was a constant threat during the FFYP because shop-floor discontent was deep and its causes, multiple. If public order was to be maintained and the program of forced capital accumulation implemented, a lid had to be kept on it at all costs.

The Liulin affair underscored the importance of reliable sources of information. The discrepancies among the reports filed by various levels of the party hierarchy showed that regional officials would do everything to underestimate the severity of problems in their jurisdiction and overestimate their ability to cope. Yet accurate accounts of conditions in the regions were vital to the success of the planned economy that the Stalinists were endeavoring to build. Clearly, the best way to procure such accounts was to maintain independent and direct reporting channels. Leaving aside the significant role played in these events by Central Party Committee investigators—who were, of course, merely ad hoc agents—the only organization that fulfilled Moscow's thirst for information was the OGPU.

A monopoly over politically sensitive information, once procured, was vital to the longevity of Stalin's dictatorship. In September 1928, a dozen officials received OGPU circulars on the Liulin affair. By the end of the same year, the figure dropped to nine. By August 1929, it fell to seven. Besides signaling the eagerness of the Stalinists to keep damaging information out of the hands of real and imagined adversaries, the distribution list showed which individuals and organizations were viewed as trustworthy. Recipients included Stalin, either directly or via his chief of staff, Ivan Tovstukha; OGPU leaders Genrikh Iagoda, Viacheslav Menzhinskii, and Meer Trilisser; and Politburo members Lazar Kaganovich and Viacheslav Molotov. Mikhail Tomskii, chairman of the Central Council of Trade Unions, and Grigorii Mel'nichanskii, chairman of the textile workers' trade union, were dropped from the list by the end of 1928; soon thereafter, so was Mel'nichanskii's colleague, trade-union secretary Voronova. That leaders of the official labor movement were denied information about unrest in a flagship of industry is evidence of the ruling clique's wariness of them. By the summer of 1929, only Stalin's trusted lieutenants enjoyed access to reports whose politically explosive message was that the priorities of the Right Opposition were also those of the shop floor.

The Liulin affair captured the Kremlin's attention because the program of rapid industrialization could not be accomplished if the crucial Red Perekop Mill was in turmoil. No less alarming than the unrest was that its leader was a veteran worker who opposed the revolution "from above" in the name of Soviet power. In other words, the stakes were symbolic as well as economic. Though Liulin was less radical than Klepikov, he likewise perceived Stalin's program to be a betrayal of the October Revolution. This perspective enjoyed currency on shop floors and won authority for those who articulated it. Workers bearing such authority posed a threat to Stalin's plan to cement his dictatorship over the party with an unprecedented program of economic development. For this reason, they were destroyed.

4

Battle at the Point of Production

Willfully ignoring the lessons of 1928, Stalin pressed forward in 1929 and 1930 with his revolution "from above." For operatives, the consequences were catastrophic. Confronted with deteriorating food supplies, serial labor-intensification campaigns, shrinking wage packets, and incapacitating shortages of raw cotton, they endeavored to defend their living standard and well-being as best they could: by rejecting party policies at the point of production, hijacking or storming out of assemblies, laying siege to the offices of the factory administration, and launching job actions.

Moods were volatile, the crisis severe. Nonetheless, the number of strikes in the industry declined. How to explain this paradox? Certainly, the OGPU was more active on shop floors, hence more effective at containing conflicts before they escalated.[1] But the decisive factor was the trauma visited on the shop floor by the mass layoffs of 1929. While there is no evidence that central planners had any goal in mind other than to slash the costs of production—as per the dictates of the program of forced capital accumulation—the immediate effect of the layoffs was to sow anxiety in the ranks. Not since the Civil War had the level of employment in the industry declined in absolute terms or operatives so feared for their livelihood. In these circumstances, the ultimate weapon in the workers' arsenal was only rarely unsheathed. Until the painful memory of the layoffs faded—which, by 1930, it did—weapons other than the strike were used to defend the interests of the working-class community.[2]

"Sharp discontent" swept through Ivanovo Industrial Region (IIR) mills when it was announced that, as a result of shortfalls in grain procurement, ration levels would be cut by 12 to 25 percent for workers, and by 41 to 50 percent for dependents, as of March 1929. The negative reaction to the announcement—compounded in Ivanovo by a decision of the city's cooperatives to remove workers who had ties to the land from supply rolls—underscored the risks inherent in the state rationing system.[3] By enabling workers to calculate month-to-month fluctuations in the food supply, it gave them a simple, if crude, instrument with which to measure the party's success in fulfilling an important obligation. Just as a worker's sense of well-being waxed and waned with the size of her ration, so too did her willingness to comply with demands from above.

The shop floor responded to the reduction in ration levels with rhetoric and behavior with which we are familiar. Assemblies convened in mills across the IIR to discuss the crisis proceeded "most stormily," and witnessed sharp attacks on the organs of authority: cooperatives were denounced for incompetence, callousness and corruption; management, for "exploiting [the workers] more and more"; the trade union, for ignoring "the workers' needs and requests"; and the party, for having no idea how to "lead the Republic."[4]

Compounding the workers' anger was a conviction that the reduction in ration levels signified a violation of the implicit contract governing their relations with the regime. "Why don't they give out enough bread," a Sereda operative demanded of a trade-union official, when "the worker and the peasant support this or that summons of the state?" Given the sacrifices they were being forced to endure for industrialization, operatives expected Moscow to establish a floor beneath which living standards would never fall. Yet instead of fulfilling its obligations, the party was "blabbering about socialism" even as it drove the economy "to famine and collapse." Accompanied often by the claim that life had been better under the old regime—and less often by the assertion that Trotsky or some other fallen party leader was "the true defender" of the workers' interests—such rhetoric reflected passions so inflamed by the implementation of "semi-starvation rations" that assemblies convened in at least three Ivanovo mills dissolved into chaos.[5]

Some scholars have sought to minimize the significance of such unrest. The objection is that workers confined themselves to economic demands and failed to imagine an alternative to Soviet power. While technically correct, the objection suffers from one preposition too many. The crucial point about resistance at the level of the shop floor is not that workers failed to imagine an alternative *to* Soviet power; it is, rather, that they imagined an *alternative* Soviet power—in particular, one that placed workers' interests, as defined by the workers themselves, ahead of the party's. This vision was subversive because it contradicted a core tenet of

Bolshevism—namely, that the workers' interests were coincident with the party's—that led, in 1918, to the subordination of local soviets to the will of the center and, a decade later, to the implementation of the program of forced capital accumulation. Having already visited upon them so much grief, this tenet was one that the workers were only too willing to consign to history's dustbin.

Because the cut in ration levels was experienced as a dual violation—of, on one hand, the implicit contract governing workers' relationship with the party and, on the other, the values of their moral economy—it unleashed a flood of anti-Bolshevik agitation. According to a report to Moscow from the IIR Party Committee, "the import of [such] agitation boiled down . . . to the following: 'The . . . Communists can't pilot the ship of state. They're driving the country to ruin with their policy. The Revolution has come to naught. It's time to overthrow the Bolshevik regime.'" Although the same report attributed "the multitude" of such attacks to "the most backward working-class strata," and to "anti-Soviet elements" who were now "endeavoring, by all possible means, to disrupt our [socialist] construction," it conceded that the behavior of the "conscious" stratum of the labor force likewise left much to be desired:

> Many party members still don't understand the true causes of our difficulties, and therefore can't carry out explanatory work among nonparty persons. And there are many . . . party members who, speaking in debates, advance the line of the backward strata of the working class . . . and go against the party's decisions . . . while others, not wishing to get involved in an argument with nonparty persons or to explain to them the . . . correctness of the party's policy, simply *hide* their party identity.[6]

So devastating was the impact on the shop floor of the revolution "from above" that often it was no longer safe to disclose one's affiliation with the party that had launched it.

Reports from mills across the region confirmed that among those questioning the "correctness" of Moscow's policies and agitating for collective action to "secure improvement in [the workers'] way of life" were myriad current and former rank-and-file Communists. One of these was Malin, a machinist at the Great Ivanovo Combine and deputy to the Ivanovo City Soviet, who was expelled from the party for decrying the simultaneous cutback in ration levels and elevation of workloads, and for predicting that "soon they're going to send Soviet Cossacks against the workers."

Another was the overlooker Smirnov, who explained in a private conversation with colleagues why he intended to "throw out" his party card as soon as "the [next] war" began: "The Bolsheviks have come to a dead end. We should have confessed a long time ago that they don't know how to govern the country. I, too, am a party member, but I admit that everything's coming to ruin, that they want to starve the workers."[7]

If the implementation of rationing made it possible for workers to quantify the party's success or failure in fulfilling an important obligation, it also made it possible for them to quantify the privileges showered on certain members of the population. While envy often was directed at local elites, occasionally it focused on workers living in the Soviet capital cities. As a Sereda operative demanded of Grigorii Mel'nichanskii during the trade-union leader's March 1929 visit to his mill:

> What's the difference between the workers of Moscow and Petrograd and those in the regions? Workers there get a bigger salary and as much foodstuffs as they want, while we get a ration . . . that doesn't suffice . . . We live in one Union and there ought to be one set of conditions, but it turns out to be the other way around. The government divides up the workers, making some into aristocrats who are supplied at the others' expense.

By no means were such charges unfounded. During a plenum of the trade union's central committee the same month, an official from the Central Union of Cooperatives confirmed that geographically differentiated supply was a matter of policy:

> The norm for all regions is the same: 600 grams for blue-collar and white-collar factory workers, and 300 grams for the rest of the population, with the exception of Moscow and Leningrad, in view of their status as capitals. In these cities, it's necessary . . . that the population feels greater security in terms of bread, for the question of bread supply can be a political question. And if we're going to spread a tense atmosphere from the capital to all corners of the Union because of 200 grams of bread per person, then it's better to use up the extra 200 grams instead of having a hot-bed that'll spread panic.

The policy was only a partial success: it kept a lid on discontent in the center, while fueling resentment in the regions.[8]

Confronted during the spring of 1929 with "a rather complicated and tense environment" that featured mounting violations of labor discipline as operatives spent hours each day searching for food, local authorities responded with a typical combination of repression and reform: "anti-Soviet elements" were swiftly purged from shop floors even as state stores and private traders were granted the right to sell up to one kilogram of bread per consumer at market prices. As "bagmen"—mostly peasants and railroad workers—began hauling flour and bread into town, *Voice of the Textile Worker* published a front-page article promising that "there won't be any hitches or hold-ups" in ration distributions. Although these claims provoked skepticism, the measures taken were effective: ration packets, though reduced in size, were distributed in a timely manner; market prices declined from their late-winter peak; and in second-tier mill towns where the threat of strikes had been most severe, "the mood of the workers . . . improved significantly."[9]

Aware of the volatile moods in industry and the constraints that food shortages placed on his program of forced capital accumulation, Stalin was thrilled by news of the successful grain procurements of autumn 1929. Aside from adding to the government's emergency reserves, he vowed to use the surplus to appease Soviet workers. "We will raise the rations in industrial towns such as Ivanovo, Kharkov, etc.," he promised Politburo member Viacheslav Molotov in December 1929.[10] Clearly, the party leadership had gotten the message of the March 1929 unrest. But was this a promise Stalin could fulfill?

Unfortunately, it was not. Just as the political stabilization produced in late 1928 by the introduction of a rationing system lasted only several months, so too did the optimism generated by the harvest of autumn 1929. Food shortages became a chronic feature of working-class life because the regime's policies made them so. The multipronged assault on the peasantry—in particular, forced collectivization and dekulakization—led to a severe decline in agricultural output even as demand for food surged as a result of the expansion of heavy industry. The resulting discrepancy between supply and demand was exacerbated by the regime's determination to finance purchases of foreign technology with grain exports. Even when domestic supplies were adequate, as they seem to have been in late 1929, there was no guarantee that the grain would make it to the mills because the distribution system was underfinanced, inefficient, and corrupt. Meanwhile, the war on the market stripped private traders of the ability to fulfill unmet demand for food at prices that were within the reach of workers who were paid poorly—if they were paid at all.

Enthusiasm over the harvest of autumn 1929 thus gave way the following summer to concern about dire shortages. In the IIR, the shortages of mid-1930 triggered panic, hoarding, and unrest. In Ivanovo, for example, workers voiced "sharp discontent" when they discovered that there were no potatoes for sale in the city. The mood of the population became so "tense," and queues for basic necessities so long—2,400 consumers stood outside one store on July 19—that the mounted police were dispatched to maintain order.[11]

While the use of light force to clear the streets further inflamed popular sentiment, at least shop floors in the regional capital remained free of the disturbances reported in second-tier mill towns. At Shuia Mill No. 1, an assembly dissolved into chaos after an emotional speech by the bobbin winder Baklanovskaia prompted "a substantial majority" of the three hundred workers in attendance to denounce their superiors for "smothering us with work" when "there's no bread." In Melenki, workers facing "colossal" bread queues denounced "the party, Soviet power, and the Five-Year Plan," and dispatched protest delegations to the district party committee. Sharp discontent also was reported on the shop floors of Teikovo and Nerl, where female operatives lambasted local supply officials, complained about escalating market prices, and noted bitterly that "they squeeze us with work, but give us nothing to eat."[12]

Most troubling to the OGPU, however, was the unrest in Kostroma, where *"discontent overcame up to 3,000 workers of the Lenin and October Spark Mills,"* provoking a wave of "anti-Soviet moods" and strike threats. At overflowing assemblies to discuss the crisis, operatives denounced their "rulers" for betraying the "promises" of 1917, for "forgetting" about the "workers," and for "ruining the peasants." The handful of regime loyalists who dared speak up for the party were mercilessly silenced: "You Communists can die if you need the Five-Year Plan, but there's no need to starve *us*!"[13]

The shortages of summer 1930 sowed deep panic in rural mills. In Kolobovo, rumors that employees of such enterprises would be denied rations prompted three hundred angry workers to march on the cooperative. Informed that the rumor was false but that no food would be distributed for at least ten days, the protesters threatened escalation: "The worker is working like an ox, but you're starving him!" they shouted. "Tomorrow we'll idle the mill and both shifts will come for bread!" At the insistence of the OGPU, a district party official raced to the mill and somehow defused the crisis.[14]

At the Puchezh Mill, workers became unruly as word spread that supplies were running low at the cooperative. In provocative speeches at an emergency assembly convened by the trade union, employees of the machine shop noted bitterly that "the only difference" between 1905 and 1930 was that "the tsar treated us to bullets" when we "ask[ed] for bread," whereas "the Communists treat us to words." Demands for collective action ensued: "There's no reason to wait any more; we have to demand bread! We have to abandon work; then they'll give it to us!" Soon fifteen female workers descended on the factory committee, vowing to lay siege to the cooperative if rations were not distributed. As in Kolobovo, order was restored only when the district party committee intervened, this time with a decree instructing the cooperative to fulfill the shop floor's demand forthwith.[15]

Not that all district party committees were effective at quelling unrest. At an emergency assembly attended by hundreds of employees of the Navoloki Mill, a series of strident speeches rang out from the floor. "It's getting more and more difficult to endure the Five-Year Plan," noted the weaver Vinogradova. "We fulfill the . . . plan, but they give us nothing." Warning that "we'll have unrest here all the time" if the shortages continued, Vinogradova urged colleagues "to grab them by the throat and demand food!" Incensed by such threats, the secretary of the district committee endeavored to rebuke the protesters. The assembly was in no mood to listen and "a majority" of the workers stood up and demonstratively marched out of the hall.[16]

The summer 1930 crisis gave way to a pattern of unrest that persisted until the strike wave of April 1932. Each month the regional bureau of the Supply Commissariat made difficult decisions about how to divide ever-decreasing quantities of food among the districts in its jurisdiction. Inevitably, some cooperatives ended up with too little flour to fulfill monthly obligations. If rations were distributed in full and according to schedule, workers stayed on the job while continuing to demand that chronic shortages be overcome. If told, however, that crucial nonration staples were unavailable—or worse, that rations had been reduced, or that distributions had been delayed or suspended—protests ensued.

A pattern of simmering discontent punctuated by protest can be discerned in party and OGPU reports of autumn 1930. Most cooperatives seem to have fulfilled basic ration commitments at this time, although scattered flour shortages were reported and nonration staples were scarce. In Ivanovo, which as the regional capital continued to enjoy a privileged position in the supply hierarchy, factory assemblies were consumed by endless discussion of shortages, and "anxiety" spread that the opening of new stores—the so-called closed workers' cooperatives—would not improve the situation, but rather make it worse. In Shuia, the district party committee reported that "the mood of workers in the mills is bad."[17]

At one of the Red Profintern mills, meanwhile, operatives issued strike threats and stood up in assemblies to denounce the FFYP and accuse "the Soviet regime" of "drink[ing] the blood of workers and peasants more than any other government." In Kineshma, workers idled production lines and brought demands for food directly to management and the factory committee. Similar protests were reported at Iaroslavl's Red Perekop Mill, where the announcement that no rations would be distributed in November sowed "tense" moods and prompted the posting of leaflets that condemned the FFYP and called for "death . . . to the Bolshevik breed." In Kovrov, fifty women workers marched on the local cooperative, where anger gave way to astonishment when one of its administrators candidly admitted that "there's no flour."[18]

Rural mills, which were supplied least reliably, if at all, remained particularly vulnerable to unrest. In Nerekhta, for example, Communist workers refused to take on elevated workloads until supplies improved, while a daylong strike that idled the Iur'ev-Pol'skii Mill was attributed to, among other things, "the food difficulties."[19]

The Intensification of Labor

Once the food-supply crisis of autumn 1928 passed, trade-union leaders endeavored to persuade planners to delay intensification measures until conditions were in place for these to be implemented effectively. Given the dilapidated state of the industry's capital stock and severe shortages of raw cotton, the fear was that further efforts to elevate workloads would inflame passions "among backward groups of workers" without achieving the desired effect of higher output and productivity. The warnings were ignored, however, and the themes and patterns of protest established in 1928 recurred.[20]

Operatives' most pressing worry was that the new workloads were unbearable. "Under the seven-hour day, you make the worker produce seventeen hours' [worth of goods]," a Sereda operative, upset over the implementation of four-loom production, wrote in a 1929 note to Mel'nichanskii. "Is [that] not 'sweating' the workers?" At Ivanovo's Balashov Mill, the weaving overlooker Zakharov won election to the factory committee in 1930 by arguing that job actions were justified insofar as "we now work like nobody has ever worked anywhere else before." Such concerns also fueled discontent in other mills, where increasingly ambitious "counterplans" and skyrocketing output norms were derided by Communists and non-Communists alike as "unrealistic" and oppressive.[21]

A related concern was that elevated workloads would have a deleterious effect on workers' well-being. "With these quadruple looms," an operative from the Navoloki Mill complained in 1929, "they're going to remove the workers from the mill in an ambulance." At the Great Ivanovo Combine, Communist city soviet deputy Malin gave substance to this fear in a speech delivered to the party cell: "Thanks to intensification being carried out, there is a constantly growing number of invalids." Similar complaints were echoed by the ring-frame spinners of the nearby Dzerzhinskii Mill, who responded "very negatively" to management's labor-intensification announcement, and by veteran female workers at Kineshma's Dem'ian Bednyi and Red Branch Mills.[22]

Health concerns became even more acute once it became clear that food shortages were not fleeting, but chronic. In Teikovo and Vichuga, as we have seen, the reduction in ration levels in March 1929 triggered protests against recently elevated workloads. In Gavrilov-Posad, the rumors of famine that swept shop floors at this juncture led operatives to protest that "we don't want to go over to intensified work, to four looms." Later the same year, the coincidence of labor intensification and food shortages fueled anti-Communist rhetoric, strike agitation, and panic among employees of the finishing shed of the Great Ivanovo Combine and weavers of the nearby Zinov'ev Mill, as well as opposition to the new labor contract among operatives at the Small Kokhma Mill and the Teikovo Combine. When the elevation of workloads provoked "sharp discontent" at the Gavrilov-Iam Mill in the spring of 1930, the bleacher Mokritsin agitated for a strike. "They're fleecing our brother like a dead dog," he noted, while "we're eating straw, which is killing people and which even the newspapers don't conceal."[23]

Another concern was that intensification exacerbated unemployment, especially among the offspring of field and factory. "As for loading up the worker, no good comes of it," declared a female employee of Iaroslavl's Red Perekop Mill in 1929. "They forcibly make us work six looms, and unemployment is growing. It's better to work on two looms: there wouldn't be defective product, and they'd take all the younger generation off the street." In Shuia, the coincidence of elevated workloads and staff cutbacks sowed bitterness and despondency.[24]

Figure 6. Engraving department of the Great Ivanovo Combine, 1930. Russian State Archive of Documentary Films and Photographs.

Although the impact of intensification on earnings triggered strike agitation among weavers at the Great Shuia Mill and a slowdown by flyer-frame spinners at the Sergeikha's Karl Liebknecht Mill, the rhetoric accompanying such protests was, at first, mild. On two looms "we received seventy rubles," noted the weaver Zaitseva of Vichuga's Red Profintern Mill in a typical complaint, "and now on four looms, our earnings are sixty to sixty-five rubles." The tone changed, however, in 1930. At the Gavrilov-Iam Mill, for example, an unexpected decline in take-home pay in the aftermath of intensification generated "great aggravation in the mood of the workers" and provoked strike agitation in both January and May. "It's time to start a row!" declared the bleacher Pershin in an informal speech to thirty colleagues. "Enough working for kopecks! They're driving the workers into bondage, squeezing the last drop of [strength] out of us!"[25]

The mood at Vichuga's Nogin Mill also was bitter. "They squeeze the worker for every last kopeck and issue reprimands, but they don't see how tormented and worn out we are," declared the ring-frame spinner Konchikova. "We'll go bust with such work!" Determined to take action to defend their standard of living, Konchikova and her colleagues marched to the director's office. "You've deceived the workers through and through!" they shouted. "You drink our last drop of blood, you make us go over to intensified labor, but you don't increase [our] wages!" At Ivanovo's Zinov'ev Mill, meanwhile, female weavers under the leadership of the Komsomols Lebedeva and Zavaeva issued ultimatums—which management later rejected—after discovering that they earned less on six looms than on four. An analogous situation among ring-frame spinners at Kostroma's Lenin Mill resulted in a brief work stoppage, the outcome of which was not reported.[26]

At the few mills where the promise of better pay was realized, anger was triggered by the realization that workloads had risen more than earnings. "Why do they carry out intensification and discount the worker's labor?" an employee of the Iakovlevskoe Mill inquired of Mel'nichanskii in 1929. "If I worked on one loom and received forty rubles, then on two I received seventy-six rubles. I lose my strength and they discount my labor. Here, we call that exploitation." Although similar complaints surfaced at Ivanovo's Dzerzhinskii Mill, the trade union maintained that this was the only way to reduce the costs of production and, ultimately, to tame consumer price inflation.[27]

As in 1928, workers often refused to consent to intensification until managers issued specific guarantees about working conditions. Also as before, managers found it impossible to honor such guarantees because the program of forced capital accumulation deprived them of the resources to do so. The inevitable result: "sharp discontent," strike threats, and job actions of one sort or another.[28]

Workers continued to draw on a rich repertoire of tactics to resist intensification. Work stoppages were not uncommon. One of the largest took place in March 1929 at Ivanovo's conflict-prone Balashov Mill, where six hundred weavers walked off the job after being told that the mill would soon implement the seven-hour day with intensification. Despite its impressive size, however, the protest failed: with the support of the party cell, management elevated workloads and sacked the strike's four female organizers.[29]

Since intensification often was introduced in piecemeal fashion, and since its effects varied from one shed to the next, most work stoppages were modest in terms of the numbers involved. This did not mean, however, that they were ineffective. At the Small Kokhma Mill, thirty weavers walked off the job on May 15, 1929, because their new workloads were unbearable; after forty-five minutes of negotiations, managers permitted them to operate one loom apiece instead of two. At Ivanovo's Dzerzhin-skii Mill, months of ineffective protest culminated in a brief strike on September 17, 1929, by female ring-frame spinners, whose requests for deintensification likewise were fulfilled. The same outcome was reported on November 1, 1930, after a strike by twenty weavers at the nearby Zinov'ev Mill. At Vichuga's Red Profintern Mill, meanwhile, a ninety-minute strike by 137 ring-frame spinners resulted in measures being "taken to eliminate [post-intensification] thread breakage."[30]

Operatives sometimes circumvented the need for a strike by refusing to allow managers to elevate workloads. At one Ivanovo mill, weavers rejected intensification until something was done about "the overlookers' bad attitude toward the preparation of the looms and toward the female workers." At the Navoloki Mill, spinners rejected a June 1929 request that they operate eight frames apiece instead of four. At Gus-Khrustal'nyi's Red Profintern Mill, women informed management that "all of us workers have decided not to accept the industrial-financial plan and not to agree to intensified work." In Kamenka, operatives justified a similar announcement in March 1930 by noting that labor intensification "won't increase our salary, but will smother us with work." At Vichuga's Nogin Mill, weavers stormed out of assemblies before proposals for intensification could be put to a vote. Such incidents make it easier to understand why Kineshma's leaders fell victim to "inertia and fear" in the early stages of their campaign to boost workloads.[31]

Keenly aware of the risks of speaking out, many operatives chose to convey their opinion of intensification—and of those who ordered its implementation—under the cover of anonymity. At the Great Shuia Mill, workers slipped a note to a visiting party official: "Comrades, the administration looks down on the working class and oppresses it mercilessly. They suck the blood out of the working class, and all that remains is a pelt, the residue of a human being . . . [M]anagement squeezes us . . . worse than the old bourgeois factory owners."[32]

While the authors of this note seem to have held out hope that officials from the center would come to their assistance, the party itself often stood accused of betraying the Revolution by ratcheting up workloads so aggressively. A leaflet posted near the Pistsovo Mill in October 1929 stated:

Comrade Textile Workers, twelve years ago they preached land and freedom, free labor, brotherhood, and equality to us. But is that how it is? Of course not. We now see unbearable labor, we now see hard labor in production, we now see GENERAL MALNUTRITION—and what's more, the closure of the private market. What does this lead to? . . . [T]o forcing the worker to starve and . . . produce that unbearable norm that the Communist masters demand. Are we going to tolerate this for long? . . . Our opinion is such: Down with Soviet power!

Five months later, a similar leaflet was found in the barracks of the Lakinskii Mill: "Comrade workers, down with extreme labor and the exhaustion of the working class! Long live the new revolution for the liberation of the workers and the peasants!" At the Small Kokhma Mill, meanwhile, operatives vented their frustration by setting their favorite melody to subversive lyrics:

In our country, the comrades are in power, / Every misfortune has befallen us. / There's no bread—and don't ask for any, / But perform unbearable labor. / When we were given three looms, / Our trousers fell down. / And when they give us a fourth, / It'll rip 'em right off.[33]

A more active form of anti-intensification resistance was to harass—or sabotage the equipment of—workers who supported it. At the Iuzha Mill, the weaver Vinogradova resigned from the party after enduring abuse at the hands of nonparty colleagues. At the Navoloki Mill, operatives undermined the performance of the weaver Gruzdeva and schemed to have her fired. At Vichuga's Red Profintern Mill, the spinner Aleksandrova fell victim to withering ridicule from party and nonparty workers alike. At Ivanovo's Balashov Mill, "backward workers" endeavoring to idle production after the elevation of workloads beat the "conscious workers"—mostly Communists and Komsomols—who refused to abandon their looms. At the Kamenka Mill, "anti-Soviet elements" issued "threats against individual Communists" who volunteered to take on "three machines" apiece. At the Gavrilov-Iam Mill, threats were directed against winding-frame tenders who elevated workloads by 25 percent. In Teikovo, Vichuga, and Iaroslavl, unidentified "class enemies"—veteran operatives, no doubt—sabotaged the looms of those taking part in the Competition for Best Weaver and Overlooker.[34]

In an indication of their ambivalence toward intensification and, more important, fear of the mass of nonparty workers, factory committees and party cells often failed to come to the defense of their besieged loyalists. By contrast, workers backed colleagues who resorted even to extreme measures to defend their well-being. At Kostroma's Lenin Mill, for example, seventy-eight female weavers "under the leadership of Nazalina, a member of the plenum of the IIR Soviet Executive Committee," signed a petition demanding the immediate reinstatement of their colleague Druzhkova, who had been sacked for responding to an order to take on a second loom by beating the shed's foreman to a pulp and hurling abuse—and a bobbin—at the chief engineer.[35]

Although workers also exploited formal channels of protest, the reward for doing so, ironically, could be a fate worse than Druzhkova's. When weavers from the Lakinskii and Sobinka mills filed a complaint with the IIR Labor Bureau in October 1929, this was acknowledged by the OGPU to be a sign of "the extraordinary tension in the workers' moods and their total distrust of local organizations." Instead of investigating the charges of unbearable workloads and unsafe working conditions, however, the labor inspector turned the document over to the security police so that "appropriate measures" could be taken against the eight men and two women who signed it.[36]

Notwithstanding policies that required managers to secure the approval of the shop floor prior to the elevation of workloads, operatives often were denied a say in the matter. Conceded the Communist Zharov of Kineshma's Red Volga Mill: "We approach the matter of intensified labor by overcoming not only the workers' unwillingness, *but their direct resistance. Indeed, in this respect, we go too far.*" A similar sentiment echoed in remarks delivered by the worker Dymov at an Upper Sereda Mill party assembly: "Sometimes we're reproached for not defending the party line staunchly enough, but the workers say that they're oppressed under the Soviet government and forced to work on four machines, and we can't respond to that." Because the involuntary elevation of workloads had a deleterious effect on shop-floor morale, this was a serious matter of concern for the leadership of the trade union.[37]

Managers who implemented intensification forcibly did so because they had no other choice. As we have seen, operatives often refused to consent to this aspect of the program of forced capital accumulation—or withheld consent until such time as managers fulfilled demands that the program would make it impossible for them to fulfill. The resort to coercion was dictated by workers' opposition to a policy that threatened to undermine their well-being, as was the deployment of retaliatory measures against the individuals who spearheaded this opposition.

What form did retaliation take? At the Navoloki Mill, recalcitrant workers were targeted for demotion; at Ivanovo's Balashov Mill, they were dismissed. As far as heavy-handed tactics are concerned, perhaps the most notable anti-intensification protest was the so-called Kochetkova affair. Besieged by complaints from their constituents about the conditions of work and daily life, the Murom Mill factory committee twice rejected labor-intensification proposals. After a series of stormy production meetings, management retaliated by firing a dozen or so of the protesters, most of whom were female, and by orchestrating their expulsion from the trade union. The victims, under the leadership of the weaver Kochetkova, responded with a petition to the trade union's central committee. Although the editors of *Voice* initially supported the petitioners, trade-union officials sent to Murom to investigate came down on the side of management. The punishments meted out to "the antiproletarian group headed by Kochetkova" were allowed to stand, and *Voice* fell into line by announcing that such individuals were, by virtue of their opposition to state policy, "class enemies" whose presence on the shop floor would no longer be tolerated.[38]

Socialist Competition and Shock Work

Not content to elevate the rate of exploitation of labor merely in the traditional manner—such would have been too "bourgeois" an approach—the party called on Soviet workers, in April 1929, to engage in socialist competition, whereby shifts, sheds, and enterprises competed with one another to boost output and productivity, slash production costs, and strengthen labor discipline. As a result of this appeal—or rather, directive—scores of mills in the IIR soon launched competitions.[39]

Socialist competition often required a substantial portion of an enterprise's operatives to organize themselves into shock-work brigades—which, in turn, were expected to demonstrate their enthusiasm by taking on elevated workloads. As in the case of traditional intensification campaigns, this one encountered strong resistance, especially among groups burdened by heavy workloads on the shop floor (for example, skilled veteran operatives) or at home (for example, women and workers with active ties to the land). Given the pressure placed on them in the months since implementation of the program of forced capital accumulation, operatives found—even if the party refused to concede—that they had reached the limits of endurance. As a participant in the uproar against socialist competition at the Great Shuia Mill explained: "A large portion of the discontent is a consequence of the workers' exhaustion."[40]

At the forefront of resistance were the overlookers, described by one IIR party official as "the most fundamental obstacle to socialist competition," and by another as "kulak-counterrevolutionary personnel who, in the majority of cases, spoil implementation of [the measure]." Evidence for these claims was not difficult to muster. In Shuia, for example, overlookers concerned about the potential effects on their health, wages, and working conditions responded to Moscow's directive by rejecting official resolutions and storming out of assemblies.[41]

Official claims notwithstanding, "conscious" strata of the labor force were deeply involved in such protests. Two organizers of the Shuia unrest—the ring-frame spinner Kozlova and the overlooker Polivanov—were popularly elected city soviet deputies—whose slogans—"The Soviet regime squeezes the workers!" "There's exploitation in the Soviet factory!"—

Figure 7. An overlooker, right, and weaving operatives at a Shuia mill, 1929. Russian State Archive of Documentary Films and Photographs.

earned them the praise of constituents and the enmity of officials. As a rule, rank-and-file Communists tended to take a neutral stance toward the campaign, or to side with their nonparty colleagues against it.[42]

So fierce was shop-floor opposition to socialist competition that trade-union functionaries often refused to endorse it. "Not only do [our] activists struggle feebly against . . . backward moods among the workers," concluded a report drafted in late 1929 for the trade union's central committee, "but, to a considerable degree, [they] are *themselves* infected with [these] moods."[43]

Several examples illustrate the dynamics of this "manifestation of the right deviation" in the trade union's own ranks. In Murom, the factory committee "categorically opposed[d]" competition until such time as management took steps to improve working conditions. At the Iuzha Mill, the chairman of the production commission vowed to fight the measure until certain manufacturing processes had been mechanized and certain bourgeois specialists, dismissed. Endorsing this position was Poliakova, a weaver and member of the regional party committee plenum, who protested that "they're putting pressure on the workers." At the Navoloki Mill, meanwhile, a senior trade-union functionary converted to the opposition after witnessing the competition's impact at the point of production. "We've worked the workers to death with [this] campaign," he conceded, "[and] it's time to put an end to [it]."[44]

Occasionally, factory committees formally approved socialist competition but made no effort to implement it out of fear of provoking "the strong peasant and self-seeking moods" on the shop floor. As a result, many operatives surveyed in late 1929 still had not heard of the campaign, and many of the competition agreements entered into by mills "were left unfulfilled." Concluded a pessimistic report by the IIR Party Committee: "For the most part, [the campaign] exists [only] on paper."[45]

As for the mills where socialist competition and shock work were implemented, the ambivalence or outright opposition of factory committees emboldened workers and sowed dismay among party loyalists. On September 26, 1929, *Voice* published an article that graphically described the dynamics of the battle provoked at the point of production by the campaign—and left no doubt in the reader's mind as to which side enjoyed the upper hand:

The kulaks are conducting unyielding agitation in the mills. They're trying to confuse the backward workers. Hiding behind their backs, they fling mud at worker-competitors, and don't stop at threats or at spoiling machines and goods, and sometimes simply beat up individual shock workers. This subversive work is especially strong where union organizations have done a bad job explaining the significance of competition to the workers. The [letters we've received] . . . indicate that the best and most advanced female workers don't always find protection in factory organizations.

Considering that enthusiasts of the campaign found themselves subject to "persecution" and "abuse," it is no wonder that their ranks were thin.[46]

As the coverage in *Voice* implied, socialist competition exacerbated tensions not only between workers and managers, but also between different groups of workers. As a rule, the lines of division were generational. At the Great Shuia Mill, for instance, the handful of spinners who came out in favor of competition sprang from the ranks of the young, while older workers opposed it. The same was true in Ivanovo, where groups of young operatives sought to demonstrate their enthusiasm by organizing themselves into shock-work brigades. Angered by the threat to their authority, wages, and working conditions, veteran workers ridiculed "the greenhorns" and sabotaged their equipment. At the Iakovlevskoe Mill, meanwhile, two female Komsomols who organized a shock-work brigade were given blunt warning in an anonymous note:

> You're . . . kicking up a hell of a row on account of competition. You're undermining our work . . . and because of you they're pressing us like in the old days. We ask you not to do this and to renounce the brigade . . . And if you don't, then we'll try . . . to hinder you and . . . smash your brigade . . . You were [also] the first to kick up a row about intensified labor. Many are being tormented because of you. If you don't give it up, then it'll be bad for you and you're mug'll be smashed or we'll kill you altogether.

Such warnings did not go unheeded. At the Tutaev Mill, "young female workers" refused to endorse the campaign out of fear that their senior colleagues "would 'torment' [them] and force [them] out of work"—a scenario that materialized in not a few mills.[47]

Although most operatives who embraced the campaign were young, there were exceptions, such as the Iuzha weaving overlooker whose unusual devotion to shock work earned him "the hostility" of colleagues—

one of whom assaulted him with a knife. By the same token, the ranks of the opposition included youth, such as the nine Komsomols from Iaroslavl's Red Perekop Mill who denounced shock work as exploitative, and Gorelev, a twenty-one-year-old ex-Komsomol from the Lakinskii Mill, who declared in a leaflet that it "shortens our life a hundredfold and enslaves us." Since Gorelev called on workers to skip the Revolution Day parade and join "our demonstration . . . at the mill at 5:00 PM," he was arrested by the OGPU.[48]

The campaign for socialist competition also exacerbated tensions among different strata of the traditional work team. In Shuia, for example, the spinners and weavers ignited a furor among the overlookers by justifying their opposition with the argument that the latter failed to fulfill their duties in a timely manner. Aware of such tensions, officials endeavored to exploit them by publishing articles in the press about overlookers who had been transformed by shock work from abusive "drunkards" into "good people."[49]

If the evidence from Vichuga is indicative, this propaganda failed to persuade the mass of workers, whose response was characterized by solidarity. At the Shagov Amalgamated Mill, two overlookers and three weavers "carried out a 'rabid' campaign for the disruption of socialist competition" in response to management's May 1929 decision to hold a competition with other enterprises. The protesters' slogan: "The working class is gripped in a vise and is being exploited mercilessly." According to a Central Party Committee report to Stalin, "party members did not respond in any way to this agitation. As a result, 800 weavers rejected socialist competition." In a letter to the trade-union newspaper *Labor*, the worker Gozhev offered an eyewitness account of the conflict:

> [The Shagov weavers] justified themselves by the fact that it is already impossible to raise output further, since the working day has been intensified to the limit as it is, while the norms have been raised. They already call current working conditions "sweating," and socialist [competition] smells directly of capitalist exploitation. As an older worker, I fully share these arguments, and that is why I myself do not participate in [competition] and do not try to outdo the others in labor productivity.

Although the IIR Party Committee endeavored to excuse the eruption of "backward moods" in Vichuga by claiming that "a majority of the workers [there] are tied to the peasantry," this was a self-serving falsehood. The truth—that only one in nine Shagov operatives reported ties to the land—had to be concealed because of the humiliating implication: the fiercest rejection of socialist competition occurred in one of the region's most "proletarianized" mills.[50]

The Shagov protest was only the most dramatic of the many that occurred at this time. At the Iakovlevskoe Combine, operatives responded to the campaign by declaring that "work under Soviet power has become more difficult than . . . under serfdom." In Shuia, protesters complained that "the worker's labor is being reduced to forced [labor]," and asserted that such measures never would have been implemented under Lenin or the tsar. At one of the Red Profintern mills, the Communist Afonin shared with nonparty colleagues his astonishment that the party would endeavor "to make [us] work" in such a manner in "the fourteenth year" of the Revolution—let alone while "we're starving." After visiting Karabanovo, an official notified the IIR Party Committee of a "most perverse" sentiment on shop floors there: "Socialist competition is seen as a wringing of the juices out of the workers." At the Red Perekop Mill, the measure was condemned as "the tenth collar on the workers' neck" and rejected out of hand by an assembly. Anonymous leaflets found later in the weaving shed derided it as "the idea of idiots, self-seekers . . . and parasites who drape themselves in oratory while taking the worker's life." Weavers at the Navoloki, Nerl, Novye Gorki, Tutaev, and Zinov'ev mills withheld approval of the campaign until working conditions and food supplies improved, while their counterparts in Krasnye tkachi complained bitterly about the expected impact on their earnings, energy, and rest breaks. "They want to thoroughly crush us with work," declared an astonished female operative in March 1930. "Not only does the administration lean on us—now they want us to urge ourselves on!"[51]

As for the ultimate effects of the campaign, the evidence is contradictory. On one hand, it seems to have enabled some enterprises to boost output, if only temporarily. On the other hand, it left most operatives embittered and contributed to the further deterioration of working conditions. The toll on operatives' well-being was heavy. As Gozhev put it in his letter to *Labor:*

> Whom do we see among the shock workers? Komsomol members, youth at peak strength and full of ardor with whom, understandably, you can move mountains. Behind them drag the hotheaded lads among the adults, who in their enthusiasm also produce record out-

put. But how long can this ardor hold out? You can work that way a month, two months, let's say six months, and then you run out of steam. Yet we, the rank-and-file workers, have to stay at the bench year in, year out.

I base myself on facts. A month ago I went to visit my wife at the sanatorium . . . and had a look there at these same shock workers. There was a woman shock worker there, Niura from the Shchelkovo Mill. For two months she "attacked"—and wound up in the sanatorium with nervous over-exhaustion. There was a weaver, a little old fellow from the Lantsutskii Mill. He was lured into a competition for the best weaver, switched from three looms to four, and worked that way for two months. His hands began to shake, his nerves were shattered.

At least the operatives whom Gozhev met were receiving treatment for the medical problems caused by Moscow's latest intensification campaign. Others were less fortunate. "I'm losing the use of my hands and feet, so how will I ever be fit to operate twenty looms?" the thirty-year-old Kokhma weaver Lobanova wrote in a note to loved ones. "They'll sack me—if not today, then tomorrow. I won't be able to earn a piece of bread, and these days it's impossible to secure an invalid's pension." Attributing her predicament, ironically, to the "damned 'freedom'" that workers now enjoyed, Lobanova concluded that it was "better to die"—and took her own life. Hers was just one in a string of suicides that the OGPU attributed to "the extreme stress imposed on the nervous system by elevated workloads."[52]

Layoffs and Unemployment

Although unemployment was lower in the IIR than in other textile regions, it rose sharply in 1929 as a result of, first, strong demand by peasants and youth for factory positions and, second, a series of cost-cutting measures that sacrificed thousands of operatives to the Labor Exchange.[53] Upset by the party's favoring of heavy over light industry as well as its failure to fulfill the Revolution's implicit promise of full employment, many protested bitterly.

A major concern was the lack of jobs for young people entering the labor market for the first time. "Two are working, but five are unemployed," a Vichuga operative complained during a production meeting. "There are a lot of girls and boys, but they aren't being hired." Workers feared that their children would be denied a livelihood and fall victim to the rough-and-tumble culture of the streets. In the words of a Iuzha operative concerned about the high rate of unemployment: "There's nothing but immorality, hooliganism, and debauchery, and Soviet power is responsible for this. It's turned all the good kids into bad ones." The solution, according to female weavers at the New Ivanovo Mill, was obvious: recent labor-intensification measures had to be repealed in order to "empty the Labor Exchange and give jobs to the kids." The lack of opportunities not only sowed anger toward the authorities, who were addressed as "blood-suckers" and "exploiters" in *anonimki* (anonymous notes passed to the podium during an assembly), but also prompted operatives to defend their traditional right—exercised at retirement—to bequeath their jobs to their offspring.[54]

Inevitably, the competition for jobs sowed tension within the labor force. In Sereda, blame was placed on workers with ties to the land. "The children of us pure proletarians aren't hired by the mill," an operative told Mel'nichanskii in March 1929. "The solution is to dismiss all the peasants and hire our children." At Kineshma's Dem'ian Bednyi Mill, the scapegoats were migrants from other regions. "You don't hire our children, but . . . only those from Samara," complained an *anonimka*. "We don't care if the devil himself is in power, so long as the workers live well." Among peasants, meanwhile, there was a conviction that mills discriminated against them and in favor of those from working-class backgrounds.[55] Whatever the validity of such views, they undermined shop-floor solidarity.

Discontent was deep among those who had long been out of work. During the February 1929 election campaign for the Ivanovo City Soviet, three unemployed workers

> used all possible means of an anti-Soviet nature (leaflets, posters, appeals, agitation . . .) to achieve their goals: the elevation of their deputies to the soviet, the rejection of the candidates nominated by the party organization, and the imposition on the soviet of their counterrevolutionary mandate, which refutes the correctness of the policy of the party and the Soviet government in fundamental matters of socialist construction.

Leaflets circulated during the campaign called on "unemployed comrades" to "elect genuine nonparty persons" to the soviet, and to "demand equal rights to labor" and "the liquidation of party members' privileges." The demand for full employment was popular, and two of the three insurgents prevailed at the polls. Their victory, however, was short-lived: the party nullified the vote and arranged for its own candidates to replace them.[56]

Notwithstanding popular concerns about unemployment, the Supreme Economic Council ordered mills to lay off tens of thousands of operatives in 1929 to reduce the costs of production and conserve rapidly diminishing supplies of raw cotton. Concerned about the potential for unrest, trade-union leaders argued against the cutbacks. Their advice was ignored and mass dismissals took place in April–May and October.[57]

Coming as it did on the heels of a series of unpopular measures, such as the elevation of workloads and the March 1929 reduction in ration levels, the first round of layoffs provoked sharp discontent. According to the IIR Party Committee, "anti-Soviet elements," including overlookers and workers with ties to the land, employed "all available means . . . [including] leaflets, poison-pen letters, demagogic shouts, and speeches in assemblies, etc., to ruin at any cost the party's measures in the area of cost reduction."[58]

The protests were widespread. In Sereda, operatives demanded that the visiting trade-union chairman explain how the party could boast about the expansion of the textile industry in the USSR and condemn layoffs in the West while dispatching thousands to the Labor Exchange. At the Pistsovo Mill, the operative Kharitonov argued in a speech to an assembly that life was worse under Soviet power because "there's no truth or stability—you're waiting each day for them to throw you onto the street." In Shuia, workers at three mills responded to the announcement of layoffs by accusing the regime of abandoning "socialism" in favor of "capitalism" and demanding "the removal of the Communists from power." Discontent also coursed through the ranks of the "conscious," with party members publicly denouncing the cutbacks and insisting that strikes were the only way to "secure improvement in [our] daily life." While no job actions materialized at this time, collective action of another sort was taken at the Iuzha Mill, where workers under the leadership of a factory committee member rejected a resolution that would have resulted in some of them making a one-way trip to the Labor Exchange.[59]

The layoffs that took place during the autumn of 1929 likewise provoked a wave of protest. In Shuia, the mood on shop floors was characterized by the OGPU as "abominable"; in Ivanovo, as "strained." "Every day," noted a report on the situation in the regional capital, "all sorts of cries can be heard: 'They squeeze the workers! Only the Communists live well! It's gotten worse than before!'" The layoffs prompted the weaver Belova to agitate for a strike at the gates of her mill. "Life has gotten unbearably difficult," she argued. "It's time for us to make short shrift of the Communists."[60]

Although Belova's colleagues were too traumatized to launch a formal protest, the "mass discontent" sowed by the measure in Kokhma inspired a degree of collective action. After 150 petitions for reinstatement had been filed with the authorities, forty weavers elected a delegation under the leadership of a nonparty colleague, Goloberdova, to take the matter up with the regional trade-union bureau—and, if necessary, with Soviet President Mikhail Kalinin. While the delegation drafted a complaint, the most embittered stratum of the labor force applied pressure by issuing strike appeals, threatening managers with violence, and scrawling subversive graffiti on party buildings: "Carry out underground work!" "Down with the Soviet consuls!"[61]

Notwithstanding the events in Kokhma, shop floors did not typically respond to the layoffs collectively because they were too paralyzed by fear to do so. Although he was given myriad *anonimki* during his March 1929 tour of the mills, Mel'nichanskii noted that operatives became "dispirited" once the layoffs were announced. Confirmation of this assessment came from one of Mel'nichanskii's subordinates, Korovin, who was dispatched to investigate the troubled state of worker-management relations at the Pereslavl Mill. "We're afraid to act," workers there confided, "because you'll wind up outside the gates [if you do]." The same fear was prevalent at the Telegino Mill, where a wave of rumors about forthcoming layoffs brought a series of wage-related protests in the weaving shed to a halt.[62]

Besides terrifying the shop floor, the layoffs sowed tension in the ranks. Faced with the prospect of a loss of livelihood, those possessing impeccable revolutionary or class credentials argued that they were more deserving than the kulaks, *lishentsy*, migrants, and loafers who, according to trade-union guidelines, should be the first to go. Workers with ties to the land likewise protested when they felt unfairly targeted for dismissal. A Sereda *anonimka* summarized the situation: "You comrades have poisoned relations between proletarians and peasants with these layoffs. There's nothing but backstabbing among the people. It's every man for himself."[63]

Did some segments of the labor force suffer disproportionately? The sources do not provide a clear answer. On one hand, some mills strictly adhered to trade-union guidelines. On the other, managers often culled the ranks without bothering to take into account either the social origins or material circumstances of victims. The entire process, moreover, was riddled with corruption. As an operative from the Smolensk Region's Iartsevo Mill wrote in an unpublished letter to *Pravda:* "Dismissal and recruitment are carried out improperly. Kinship, friendship, and even bribery play a role."[64]

While the scale was modest, a final round of layoffs occurred during the spring of 1930. Apparently having learned from mistakes of the previous year, managers targeted two groups in particular: workers with cultivated plots of land, and those whose income exceeded thirty rubles per month per family member. In Shuia, the layoff of 1,400 operatives had a devastating effect on morale, but proceeded without a hitch. Elsewhere, things did not go so well. At one unidentified mill, a female ring-frame spinner committed suicide after receiving notice of dismissal. In Nerl, a male worker who found himself in the same situation broke into his superior's office and assaulted him with a knife. In Sereda, layoffs provoked vehement attacks on the party by groups of up to a dozen workers. At Iaroslavl's Red Perekop Mill, the targeting for dismissal of workers who failed to fulfill output quotas triggered "powerful discontent."[65]

Wages and Inflation

Many types of wage conflict could be found in the mills, but the problem underlying all of them was the inferior position accorded textile workers—the majority of whom were women—in the Soviet compensation hierarchy. By 1931, the average cotton operative earned 28.7 percent less than the average Soviet industrial worker. Only the linen and matchmaking industries offered worse compensation rates. Given that the percentage of skilled and highly skilled workers, as defined by length of training, was higher in the cotton industry than in other industries that rewarded labor more generously, it is clear that the wage gap was a matter of tradition. Textile workers long had been poorly paid in Russia, and their position on the wage scale deteriorated further once the decision was made to forcibly develop heavy industry at the expense of its light counterpart.[66]

Several examples illustrate the problem. In Leningrad, where textile mills offered the best wages in the industry, skilled female spinners and weavers earned 30 to 40 percent less than unskilled and semiskilled female workers in a number of the city's other (nontextile) factories. In Iaroslavl, wage rates for workers occupying identical positions on the compensation ladder were 35 percent lower at the Red Perekop Mill than at a nearby rubber plant. Nationwide, machinists and repairmen earned from 10 to 90 percent less in textiles than in other branches of industry.[67]

The wage gap had deleterious effects. Mills reported a chronic shortage of skilled labor, as individuals with transferable skills migrated to other industries. Also morale suffered as operatives came to regard their inferior position as unfair. "Discontent will break out . . . as long as . . . textile workers are kept on low wages," trade-union chairman Mel'nichanskii warned Central Party Committee Secretary Lazar Kaganovich in October 1928. "The textile workers know from the newspapers that [their] industry is [both] profitable . . . [and] the wealthiest, that resources are being extracted from [their] industry to support deficit branches of industry. And meanwhile, wages in these deficit branches are higher than in the very industry that supports [them]."[68]

Although Kaganovich rejected the demand that the party change its approach and advanced the dubious argument that workers in heavy industry were paid more only because their jobs were more demanding, the announcement, one month later, that textile workers in a number of regions would receive a one-time wage supplement suggests that Mel'nichanskii's protest was not in vain. Still, the underlying problem did not go away. As a result, wages remained a significant source of discontent on shop floors, hence of concern in the corridors of power.[69]

In addition to occupying a low position on the compensation hierarchy, textile workers—like most Soviet workers—endured a sharp decline in real wages during the FFYP. Publicly, trade-union leaders claimed during this period that real wages were rising; privately, they acknowledged that the opposite was the case.[70] The trade union's position was irrelevant, however, because textile workers knew firsthand that their wages procured fewer basic necessities each month.

Part of what made the food-supply crisis of autumn 1928 severe was that private traders inevitably raised prices when cooperatives proved unable to satisfy the shop floor's basic needs. Since workers—especially those with large families—relied heavily on the market to supplement their monthly food packet, it is understandable that concerns were voiced at this juncture about inflation. Although the trade union remained formally committed to preventing a deterioration in living standards, it also embraced—because it had to—the party's position that all resources be funneled into heavy industry. It thus failed, in late 1928, to push for wage hikes in the collective contract. Perhaps fearing the shop floor's response to news that nominal earnings would rise by an insignificant amount in the new year, three out of eight IIR mills neglected to convene the mandatory contract-ratification assemblies. This was a smart move because mills that held such assemblies found that "counterrevolutionary chatterboxes" seized the floor in an effort to persuade operatives that "the new contract makes your situation worse."[71]

Although the trade union claimed that these appeals fell on deaf ears, the evidence suggests otherwise. At the Great Ivanovo Combine, opposition to the contract was spearheaded by the Communist city soviet deputy Malin and the roving-frame spinner Sidorova. Conveying the bitterness of workers whose expectations of a better life under Soviet power had been dashed, Sidorova recalled, during a February 1929 assembly, that under the old regime:

> The capitalists squeezed us and the Cossacks lashed us, and we thought, "Now it's going to be better." But it turns out just the same. Comrades, when will life be good? They've given us [a raise of] just two kopecks, yet everything at the market has gotten two or even three times more expensive. Let them give these two kopecks to the indigent, but we don't need them. (Applause.)

Although the protests came to naught, operatives at a number of mills again spoke out when, twelve months later, the 1930 contract came up for ratification.[72]

In the meantime, the flame was kept alive by those who sympathized with one or another of the anti-Stalin oppositions. At the Iuzha Spinning Mill, Trotskyites distributed leaflets containing an appeal for defense of the workers' living standard:

> We cannot remain silent while they exploit us, while they fail to give us a slice of bread, while our earnings fall on a daily basis . . . We must not allow this, but must collectively . . . say: "Give us bread, free trade, a reduction in prices, and an increase in pay!" This is what Trotsky fought for—and for this, he was shamelessly driven out of the . . . party.

Although expressions of support for fallen party leaders were, as a rule, uncommon, the OGPU noted with alarm that "many workers cited these leaflets and . . . [concluded] that Trotsky really was correct in his battle with the party."[73]

Besides failing to keep pace with inflation, earnings often fell short of workers' expectations because of, first, the myriad production problems caused by the program of forced capital accumulation and, second, the program's insistence that production costs be reduced. Sometimes wage packets shrunk by accident; other times, by design. Whatever the cause, operatives conveyed their anger in familiar ways: they quit their jobs, condemned their superiors, launched job actions, and dispatched protest delegations to Moscow.[74]

A typical conflict occurred at the Tutaev Mill on August 15, 1930. Upset that wage rates for the production of sackcloth had been reduced even though "life has gotten many times more expensive," 160 female weavers idled their looms. "We won't work at this price," they declared. "The rates have to be raised." Among the leaders of the protest was the veteran weaver Ushakova, who demonstratively surrendered her candidate membership in the party. "The Communists deceive the workers," she explained. "I led the workers to strike in the old days, and I'm going to continue doing so." When management capitulated, Ushakova and the others went back to work.[75]

Another successful protest occurred on February 9, 1930, in the preparatory department of the Sergeikha's Karl Liebknecht Mill. After receiving their wage packets, operatives idled their machines and demanded to know why their earnings had fallen by one-fifth. "Why have they deceived us? They said there would be an increase this month, but that proved a fraud!" The flyer-frame spinner Murkina barked at a foreman: "Bring [mill director] Petrushin to us! It makes no difference to us if we end up in Solovki—we're going to smash his snout straight away!" Order was restored only when Petrushin and the factory committee chairman arrived and announced that an accounting error had been made, and that it would be corrected.[76]

Less successful were the more moderate tactics pursued by the four hundred winding-frame tenders of Iaroslavl's Red Perekop Mill, who voiced "powerful discontent" after being told to do more, for less. "We entered into a collective contract for the whole year, and the administration isn't supposed to violate it, but here everything's done the other way around," they complained. "Not even two months have gone by, and suddenly there's a rate reduction and a norm increase." At a "stormy" assembly convened on March 21, 1930, to discuss the matter, 165 operatives

under the leadership of Afanas'eva, Belova, and Kozyreva ridiculed management and the factory committee and elected a commission to pursue restoration of the status quo ante. Tensions mounted anew when the commission
failed to secure what was demanded. "Few workers attend assemblies . . .
and now we won't go at all," declared a protester, Kalashnikova. "We elected
a commission and thought that it would help us, but the administration
does things its way, while nothing is ever done our way." In the absence of
concessions from above, warned the OGPU, a strike was inevitable.[77]

Besides lowering compensation rates, management endeavored to fulfill
the mandate for reduced production costs by imposing fees and fines. After touring IIR mills in March 1929, Mel'nichanskii addressed this practice in a report to colleagues on the trade union's central committee:

> [Workers] complained strongly about endless deductions from
> wages . . . which, as a rule, are carried out in a compulsory manner.
> The directive on the regulation of deductions . . . and the implemen-
> tation of them on a completely voluntary basis has been forgotten by
> everyone . . . At the slightest hint of trouble, a deduction is imple-
> mented . . . [As a result,] many receive but kopecks in their pay pack-
> ets—or, at best, 30 to 40 percent of their earnings. This provokes
> bitterness: you work and work, but don't see a pay packet.[78]

Despite shop-floor protests, the assault on take-home pay continued. Late
in 1929, workers were shocked to discover that the new collective contract
reduced the rate of compensation for defective output and introduced
fees for housing and utilities. At the Great Ivanovo Combine, operatives
protested that "we're going back to the old, tsarist ways. Just as there were
fines then, so they want to introduce them again." At Vichuga's Nogin Mill,
factory committee and party members joined nonparty workers in pointing
out that the mill's founder, Konovalov, had provided free or subsidized
housing to employees. "Is it really impossible to do this under Soviet
power?" they demanded. At Ivanovo's Zinov'ev Mill, opposition was spearheaded by the veteran weaver Solodkova, who accused management of violating "the workers' remaining rights" and "squeezing the last juices out of
the workers." After concluding that the contract amounted to "a reduction
in the worker's real wages," two assemblies voted it down.[79]

Resistance to the reduction in the rate of compensation for defective
output persisted even after it was implemented, in 1930, over the shop
floor's objection. At several Ivanovo mills, weavers and overlookers condemned the measure as unfair, given the poor condition of the looms, or

simply refused to acknowledge output as defective. At Vichuga's Nogin Mill, a collective protest got under way as soon as the effect on take-home pay became apparent. "Why did we fight for such 'freedom'?" the weaver Gruzdev demanded. "So they could smother us?" Under the leadership of his colleague, Prostiakova, a deputy to the city soviet and former party member who enjoyed "great authority" on the shop floor, a group of female weavers commandeered a meeting of the wages and disputes tribunal. "There are all kinds of deadwood in the factory committees," Prostiakova declared in a speech from the stage, "but no defenders of the interests of the working class!" After insisting that the trade union reverse this "reduction in wages," and silencing officials who endeavored to rebuke them, the women stormed out of the hall.[80]

Discontent over deductions from wages also played a role in work stoppages. When paltry wage packets were distributed at the Telegino Mill on April 6, 1930, six hundred weavers idled their looms in protest. The source of the problem was not the reduction in the rate of compensation for defective output, but rather the monthly advance that workers were supposed to turn over to the cooperative to fund purchases of consumer goods. Although they were to benefit from this deduction, the weavers insisted that it be repealed because they did not trust management to spend the funds as promised.[81]

Shop-floor discontent also focused on the routine collections held to raise funds for local, national, and international causes. "Time and again it's been said that it's inadmissible to carry out . . . collections in the mill," a textile worker complained in an unpublished letter to *Pravda*, "but to this day they haven't been eliminated." Even high-priority campaigns, such as those mounted by the party to raise funds for capital investment, came under attack. At one of the Red Profintern mills, opposition to an industrialization bond was led by the lugger Krasnoshchekov, who told a sympathetic audience of 150 operatives that the party "banished [trade-union leader Mikhail] Tomskii . . . because he said that we must fulfill the workers' needs before implementing the Five-Year Plan." Now, concluded the speaker, "there's nobody to defend us . . . [and] they're fleecing us of all we have left." At Iaroslavl's Red Perekop Mill, protest came in the form of anonymous postcards delivered to the machine shop:

The attack on wages is intensifying all the time. The latest deception by the dictators, who speak brazenly in the name of the workers, brings us to the point at which we must reply: HANDS OFF OUR WAGES, or we're going to do harm however . . . we can. Down with the Bolshevik yoke! Down with the latest bond![82]

Besides being fed up with the endless fundraising campaigns, workers were bitter that the state had carried out an expropriation at their expense by restricting the redemption of previously issued bonds. "When they sold the [first] bond, they said it could be sold whenever the need arose," complained a Teikovo operative, "but now they've shown themselves to be deceivers of the working class, and now nobody will believe them anymore and won't subscribe to the [next] bond." Such comments were heard widely on shop floors, and explain why mills found it so difficult by 1930 to sell bonds to Communist and nonparty workers alike.[83]

Faced with mounting opposition to bond campaigns, officials discovered that they could quench the center's thirst for funds only by pressuring operatives. "Here they force us to subscribe to the fourth state bond," complained the Sereda worker Ogurtsov, "but in the newspapers they say that it's a 'voluntary' matter." In the jaundiced view of one of Ogurtsov's colleagues, the campaign would follow an all-too-familiar course: "It'll be the same as with the collective farms. They'll use force to make us subscribe, and if we refuse and demand an end to it, then the Central Party Committee will write that this [was] an abuse by local authorities."[84]

Compounding the frustration at being pressured to tithe up to a month's wages was concern that "the money isn't used properly." Observed the fifty-year-old lathe operator Aleksandrov of Shuia Mill No. 2:

We've been awaiting a better life for thirteen years, but instead we get a noose wound with our own hands. We ourselves subscribed to the loan, and we ourselves will walk around hungry. The workers didn't have this in mind while making the Revolution. They didn't know that thousands of salaries would be paid with their money, and that their last kopecks would be torn away from them.

Operatives were hesitant to make further sacrifices for a regime whose competence was in doubt. "They haven't been able to get the economy going . . . for twelve years," explained one of Aleksandrov's colleagues, "and now they want to take it out on the worker." Embittered by the party's determination to press ahead with its program even as living standards plummeted, the forty-two-year-old Sereda worker Vozilov offered cheeky advice for the hapless hawkers of state bonds: "It'd be better if they said that they've failed with their policy . . . We'd give more."[85]

The Furlough and Closure of Mills

On October 10, 1928, the All-Union Textile Syndicate, which until its abolition in 1929 provisioned the peasant market with cloth and carried out certain planning functions, informed Central Party Committee Secretary Kaganovich that the Soviet mills might not be able to fulfill the program of forced capital accumulation. The problem: "Today we have an absolute lack of raw materials." Although the syndicate failed to identify the cause, Kaganovich knew that the government was using its foreign currency reserves to finance imports of machinery for heavy industry instead of raw cotton for the mills. In other words, the textile industry had been ordered to produce a massive surplus for industrialization and then denied the resources necessary to accomplish this task.[86]

Shop-floor rumors about the severity of the crisis were confirmed in late 1929 when industry officials found it necessary to lay off 42,000 operatives and freeze implementation of the night shift to conserve dwindling supplies of raw materials. The peak of the crisis came the following summer when most Russian mills found it necessary to shut down for up to seventy-five days and then, upon resuming production, to lay off more workers and indefinitely suspend the night shift.[87]

Operatives in the regional capital were outraged by this latest assault on living standards. At the Great Ivanovo Combine, the veteran protesters Malin and Sidorova "carried out agitation for organized resistance" in response to "persistent rumors" that compensation rates for furloughed operatives would be inadequate. "We must demand that we be paid 100 percent of our wages," they argued. "We're being deceived."[88] At the Sosnevo Mill, female spinners bitterly blamed the shortages on campaigns to boost productivity, such as shock work and socialist competition, which "used up the whole . . . stock of raw cotton faster than if we'd worked in the usual manner." At the Zinov'ev Mill, an employee of the machine shop asserted that "all the workers are dissatisfied with the regime" because "life is incomparably worse for the worker in the USSR than abroad." His evidence for the second half of this statement: "Hundreds are being let go from the mill—and soon it'll be thousands." Similar complaints were heard at the nearby Dzerzhinskii Mill, where the card tenders Gorbachev, Belousov, and Gruzdev appealed to their colleagues to send a protest delegation to Moscow.[89]

Assemblies held in Sereda likewise gave operatives a chance to vent their anger at those responsible for leading the industry off a cliff. At the Lower Mill, the sixty-year-old mule spinner Perchikov, a former trade-union rep-

Figure 8. A card tender at Ivanovo's Dzerzhinskii Mill, 1932. Russian State Archive of Documentary Films and Photographs.

resentative who, according to the OGPU, had opposed "all [the regime's] measures" since 1927, pointed the finger at central authorities: "In thirteen years our comrades have had a lot of mistakes and shortcomings. There's abuse, too. Under Nicholas [II], we had everything. But now? What suffices? There isn't even enough malt. Were the Communists really unable to take into account that there isn't enough raw cotton? Where were their heads? In no way do our rulers . . . behave toward the worker as they should." Besides drowning Perchikov's speech in applause, "the majority of those present" signaled their agreement by "demonstratively abandon[ing] the assembly" when an official began to offer the party's self-serving interpretation of the crisis.[90]

The assembly in the weaving shed initially followed a similar trajectory. "The worker has toiled at the peak of his capacity, and now suddenly he's being thrown overboard," declared the forty-five-year-old overlooker Suslov. "Did the party and the government really not take into account this situation when they undertook to fulfill the financial-industrial plan, and now suddenly there's such a crisis?" After the applause died down and a Communist who endeavored to defend the party's performance was driven from the podium, however, two speakers drew attention to the crisis's exacerbation of a long-standing cleavage within the labor force. First, the forty-five-year-old warp lugger Stepanov accused Moscow of orchestrating the furloughs and layoffs so as to purge the mills of peasants. "Where was the Soviet regime before?" he demanded. "Why didn't it take care of the cotton? Did the party really not know? It did know before, and simply wants to toss the peasants overboard as an unworthy element, and leave the proletarian, who lives better than the peasant, alone." Next came the thirty-five-year-old weaver Starostin, who argued that it was short-sighted to load a disproportionate share of the sacrifice on workers with ties to the land: "If the peasants are going to be sacked, then the proletariat also won't have anything to do, because the peasant won't make bread for him." The concerns underlying these speeches were legitimate. More important for our purposes, they illustrated the corrosive impact of the crisis on shop-floor solidarity.[91]

This impact was confined to mills—such as those in Sereda—where the labor force was relatively evenly divided between "proletarian" and "peasant" workers. Elsewhere, it was relations between workers and those destroying the economy in their name that fractured. The case of Vichuga's Nogin Mill, where the lack of raw cotton compelled management to extend a one-month furlough by three weeks, is illustrative. At a "very stormy" general assembly, operatives vented their rage. "What are you bastards doing to the workers? You get large salaries and don't look after the workers while living off their sweat and drinking their blood!" Although officials caved to demands that wage and ration packets be distributed immediately, another protest erupted when workers returned from the furlough to discover that there was enough raw cotton for only one of the mill's two shifts. "They're ready to bury the workers in a pit!" cried Zakharova, a candidate member of the party. Distraught by the shortages, a crowd of workers marched on the administration building. "You swine!" cried the operative Vinogradova. "For three months we were out of work—virtually without pay—and you've done nothing!" When a foreman, Goroshkov, threatened to summon the police, the worker Volkova responded with a threat of her own: "You've plundered the whole mill but [say] 'it's the workers' fault.' Such things never happened under [the mill owner] Konovalov, but you damn fools have quite tormented the workers. Fine, a stone can endure a lot, but our patience will be exhausted next time you damn leaders put the screws on us." Although the secretary of the party cell eventually managed to disperse the crowd, the OGPU warned the IIR Council of Trade Unions that "the entire mill of 6,000 workers" continued to be "gripped by discontent."[92]

Solidarity also characterized the response in rural mills, which were the reverse image of Vichuga's insofar as almost all their workers had ties to the land. The protests in Navoloki were typical. At a "very stormy" assembly attended by six hundred employees, speakers from the floor denounced their superiors, complained about the suffering caused by the FFYP, and refused to let any of the Communists in attendance—including the secretary of the district party committee—speak. When officials made the mistake of calling on everyone to sacrifice half a month's wages for the latest industrialization bond, moreover, "a majority of the workers" abandoned the hall to convey that further assaults on their living standard would not be tolerated.[93]

No less hostile was the response to rumors of the impending—and, by contrast, permanent—closure of the Rostov Mill. The first sign of discontent came in the form of wall graffiti: "The Communists have squandered the mill on drink." "The Communists are swine and only look after themselves." Then came the semiprivate conversations. "They gorged themselves and fell asleep at the wheel," the thirty-five-year-old dye works employee Ulitin announced in the washroom. "That's how the comrades build socialism." Warehouse employee Mialyshev told colleagues that Moscow had been deceiving the workers all along: "All the plans are written as a diversion, while in fact mills are closed and the workers are let go."[94]

Concerned by such comments, a group of workers descended on the factory committee. "Instead of giving proper explanations," however, its chairman "said, with tears in her eyes, that the mill was being closed for no reason, which created a mood of panic among the workers." Facing a collapse of discipline, the director convened an assembly to explain why the mill had to be mothballed. Far from accepting their fate, the mill's three hundred "extremely agitated" employees elected a delegation of veteran nonparty workers to file a protest with Moscow, and ordered the director "to take measures to protect the mill and to not allow machinery or equipment to be carted off until the matter . . . is resolved."[95]

A "tense atmosphere" likewise arose on the shop floors of Ivanovo's Sosnevo Mill after word spread in November 1930 that it, too, would shut as a result of the government's unwillingness to fund a sorely needed renovation. "The newspapers say that foreign capitalists are throwing workers onto the streets," noted the weaver, city soviet deputy, and former party member Vedernikova. "But isn't it just the same here in the USSR?" Although management promised that all employees would be given jobs elsewhere, operatives feared that "soon *all* the mills are going to come to a stop." Trapped by the internal contradictions of the program of forced capital accumulation, local party and trade-union officials were speechless as the accusations that they had "tormented" and "deceived the workers" rained down on them.[96]

A similar scenario unfolded at the nearby Korolev Mill, where 125 weavers attending an assembly fell into "panic" after hearing that their enterprise's days were numbered. "The Communists are still deceiving the workers!" cried speakers from the floor. "We workers always have to pay . . . for wrecking committed by higher organs!" As at the Sosnevo Mill, the promise that jobs awaited them elsewhere provided little comfort to the women, who feared being thrown "onto the street as 'temporary' workers" as soon as the next policy-driven crisis came to pass.[97]

Given the loss of seniority, hence vulnerability to long-term unemployment, that beset operatives whose mills were mothballed, the expectation was that these operatives would be awarded severance pay. When authorities failed to deliver, the response was unforgiving. At the Iakovlevskoe Mill, for example, the administration's attempts to economize by eliminating severance for anyone who was pregnant or had a job lined up elsewhere provoked demands for a general assembly. When five hundred workers gathered the next day to discuss the situation, they evicted their superiors from the hall and turned the podium over to "anti-Soviet elements," who proceeded to lambaste "the Communists" for "deceiving," "starving," and "robbing the workers." After unanimously passing a resolution that demanded severance for all employees, operatives delivered their complaints to the director during a tense meeting on the shop floor. While generous in their criticism of his administration, they did not neglect to lay ultimate blame where it belonged. "Light industry is coming to a halt because the Soviet regime doesn't pay enough attention to it," declared a male weaver. "They see that there's [economic] collapse, but don't do anything about it." A comment by another employee demonstrated that the crisis undermined the effectiveness of official propaganda: "The Communists are lying when they [boast] about the Five-Year Plan. Soon the people will see through their deceit."[98]

This concern was shared by party officials, one of whom fired off a letter to *Pravda* while serving as a delegate to the Sixteenth Party Congress:

> [Those giving speeches] are following the script . . . [saying] "the general line is correct," but when they go for a smoke . . . *these same speakers swear at the Central* [Party] *Committee and the present situation.*
>
> The masses are discontent. *We're . . . implementing the Five-Year Plan in heavy industry, but have abandoned light industry.* We're screaming about the rise in real wages, but everything is going up in price . . . [Meanwhile,] production is falling and factories are shutting down [in Ivanovo].
>
> In the event of an attack from abroad, the people will prove a weak pillar because they see that we're bad masters.

While dismay over the economy's collapse was pervasive, the threat to their livelihood that this posed frightened some workers into silence. As the weaver Larionova of the Krasnye tkachi Mill explained: "We all keep quiet so they won't do anything to us."[99]

Having correctly anticipated that Stalin's revolution "from above"—in particular, the program of forced capital accumulation that lay at its core—would shatter their living standard, operatives condemned it in 1929–1930 with a ferocity equaled only by the horror of the suffering it visited upon them.[100] Because of the terror and disorganization sown by serial layoffs and heightened OGPU activity, however, they proved less willing than before to defend their interests by collectively withdrawing their labor. It was the same in other centers of industry as well: as a Western diplomat observed in October 1930, people on the streets of Leningrad "loudly and openly abuse the regime, but confine themselves to abuse."[101]

To be sure, it was only the incidence of formal strikes that plummeted; other, less risky, forms of collective action—the sabotage or hijacking of a factory assembly, the march to the headquarters of the factory administration, the work stoppage that amounted to a strike in all but name—continued to be deployed. As in 1928, these protests were motivated by a conjuncture of policy-driven crises—relentless deterioration of food supplies and real wages, inexorably rising workloads, critical shortages of raw cotton—that threatened the fundamental interests of the working-class community. Also unchanged was the identity of those spearheading the unrest: male and female veterans of the labor force who refused to accept that it was their fate and profound misfortune to witness the betrayal of the October Revolution by the party whose rise to power they once saluted as a herald of their own imminent emancipation.

5

To the Brink of Rebellion

Incredibly, the last twenty-four months of the FFYP were even more traumatic than the twenty-seven that preceded them.[1] The countryside had been devastated by collectivization—and the market, by the war on private trade—so there was not enough food. Light industry had been denied crucial resources, so there were few consumer goods to buy. And in all sectors of the economy, wage arrears mounted even as the purchasing power of the ruble plummeted.

For textile workers, the lack of food, goods, and money was only part of the problem. As per the demands of the program of forced capital accumulation, two other threats to their interests now appeared on the horizon. The first was the influx into the mills, during the second half of 1931, of 45,000 new recruits, whose poor training inadvertently undermined the output, hence earnings, of their senior colleagues. The second was the gradual introduction, beginning in 1929, of the functional organization of labor, which deskilled spinners and weavers, and—like other Taylorist schemes that preceded it in Soviet industry—left turmoil, hostility, and thinner pay packets in its wake.

Less concerned, as a result of the expansion in employment, about the potential risk to their livelihood, operatives gradually reacquired their habit of launching strikes. Having surged from 732 in 1929 to 2,930 in 1930, the number of IIR operatives involved in job actions skyrocketed to 16,000 in 1931.[2] More important, broad swaths of the labor force now couched their grievances in strident denunciations of those held responsible for the betrayal of the October Revolution.

Food supplies continued to deteriorate, notwithstanding the leadership's claim that shortages had been overcome "thanks to the party's victory in the construction of state and collective farms."[3] The crisis was caused by the internal contradictions of Stalin's revolution "from above." On one hand, the expansion of heavy industry elevated urban demand for food; on the other, forced collectivization, surging grain exports, and lack of investment in the food-storage and distribution network precipitated a collapse in supply.

Hunger and malnutrition stalked the IIR and other centers of industry, resulting in a chronic threat to stability in the form of working-class unrest. The first protests of 1931 erupted in early spring, in Rodniki, where groups of up to one hundred unemployed operatives marched on food-supply agencies, trade-union offices, and the city soviet to condemn ration packets that were 56 percent smaller than anticipated. Following on the heels of these disturbances were others in response to delays in the distribution of bread. In Shuia, appeals for collective action prompted groups of female workers to descend on the headquarters of the town's cooperatives, where they demanded flour for their families. In Vichuga, one hundred female weavers at the Nogin Mill took their demands for food to the factory committee. At the Pistsovo Mill, angry workers hijacked an assembly devoted to the crisis and refused to let Communists address them. In Sudogda, anonymous leaflets declared that "we [linen] workers are on strike" for "bread" and "freedom."[4]

Strike agitation also was reported among weaving overlookers in Sereda and Gus-Khrustal'nyi, and among women workers at Vichuga's Red Profintern Mill, where the outrage provoked by the party's failure to fulfill its obligations was conveyed in an *anonimka*. "Give us the full ration!" it declared.

> Why do you starve the workers, why do you deceive [them]? You promised the worker seventeen kilograms and groats and . . . meat—but where are they? Half [of us] have been left without meat and bread. The worker spends his last earnings buying [bread] on the sly from the market . . . Shame on you! The worker has expended all his strength, but you torment him . . . Who's to blame for this? You rulers. You are beasts, idiots, you drink the worker's blood.

The rhetoric was no less caustic in Sereda's bread queues and at Kineshma's Red Volga Mill, where female operatives declared that "this is not a government, but a den of plunderers"; that "the regime has deceived us for thirteen years" and "is digging its own grave"; or simply that "the Bolsheviks must be driven from power." Cooler heads argued for the dispatch of protest delegations to Moscow.[5]

Because rations eventually were distributed in full, no major strikes erupted during the crisis of spring 1931. Discontent erupted anew, however, with each perceived assault on living standards. That summer, for example, cooperatives in several mill towns revealed that they lacked the resources to supply everyone with a full complement of rations. In Kineshma, angry female operatives responded by hijacking assemblies. In Iaroslavl, Sereda, and Vichuga, these announcements—and the endless queues to which they gave rise—sowed "tense" moods in the mills.[6]

Autumn witnessed another wave of discontent. In Ivanovo and Kokhma, shortages of staples triggered "strike moods." At the Teikovo Combine, they gave rise to graffiti "of an anti-Soviet character," including some that targeted the root cause of the suffering: "The Communists are leading the workers to famine! Down with the Five-Year Plan!" In Kostroma, the announcement, on the eve of Revolution Day, that an entire month's rations would be cancelled "embittered" the workers.[7]

The OGPU's overriding goal during this period was to prevent strikes on the region's construction sites and peat bogs from spreading to industry. It endeavored to accomplish this by rushing supplies to mills where protests seemed most likely to gain momentum, and by neutralizing the male overlookers, female weavers, and party members who spearheaded them. Although these tactics were effective, the grim circumstances of the workers' lives—and officialdom's increasingly frequent resort to coercion—led true believers to be "overcome by a depressed mood." As the Puchezh operative Petrov warned in a November 1931 letter to Stalin: "I am dedicated to the cause of socialism and the party," but "people's indignation is growing stronger by the day."[8]

Efforts to retard the deterioration of shop-floor morale by opening cafeterias achieved mixed results. As of October 1931, 41 percent of IIR industrial workers lacked access to a factory dining facility. With regard to the remaining 59 percent, they had little to look forward to: the fare was grim; the portions, meager; plates and utensils, scarce; and the standard of hygiene, abominable. While cafeterias may have kept a lid on discontent in some mills, they failed to halt the decline in productivity, which suffered whenever the cooperative put items out for sale. Though increasingly uncommon, such an event prompted operatives to idle their machines and take a position in the queue.[9]

Sometimes managers endeavored to minimize the impact on productivity by earmarking special rations for shock workers. This practice violated the egalitarian principles of the working-class community, however, and backfired. The result was "mass discontent"—and threats of slowdowns and strikes—among ineligible workers, who feared being left with "nothing" while their more fortunate colleagues ate "to their heart's content." Although shock workers at one of the Red Profintern mills responded by asking the trade union to defend their privileges, elsewhere they endeavored to defuse the anger by steering clear of the tables set aside for them in the cafeteria.[10]

Tensions among different strata of the labor force eventually dissipated because the practice, if not the concept, of "special" rations was rendered moot by the sharp decline, during the winter of 1931–1932, in deliveries from the center. Aware that plan fulfillment was suffering in all but the highest-priority sectors of the economy as rising levels of truancy and illness took their toll, and that "anti-Soviet and Trotskyite elements [were] using this situation . . . against the party and the state," the secretary of the Central Council of Trade Unions, Nikolai Shvernik, asked the Central Party Committee to order the appropriate agencies to improve their procurement efforts. Also at this time, the textile workers' trade union demanded that regional party committees halt the diversion to other industries of shipments earmarked for mills, and petitioned the Supply Commissariat to upgrade the classification of 160,000 operatives and distribute rations to operatives' children. Since none of these measures addressed the systemic causes of the crisis, they were without effect. Meanwhile, officials found it all but impossible to develop local sources of supply, and to overcome the inefficiency and corruption of cooperatives.[11]

The situation became critical. In Vichuga, shortages of flour prompted cooperatives to cancel rations for seven hundred working-class families in February and March 1932. Though not without precedent, this illegal act prompted many to skip work and make their way to Ivanovo in search of food. Operatives also acted collectively. A strike over shortages was reported at one mill in January 1932. The next month, the deteriorating quality and rising price of cafeteria meals ignited a sharp protest by three hundred operatives at Ivanovo's Krupskaia Mill. In Iuzha, more than a dozen assemblies of female spinners were disrupted by demands for food. The same demands surfaced during a brief strike by mule spinners and a protest by two hundred other workers at Gus-Khrustal'nyi's Red Profintern Mill. At the Teikovo Combine, an attempt to organize a strike and send a protest delegation to Stalin captured OGPU attention when Communists involved themselves in denunciations of the party.[12]

Although a wide range of workers engaged in acts of protest, discontent remained especially acute among working mothers, to whom the burden of caring for children fell, and among those whose children were denied a spot on the supply rolls—perhaps illegally—because their parents had ties to the land. Meanwhile, "anti-Soviet agitation" coursed through the region's consumer queues as empty shops, state-decreed price increases, and rumors of a forthcoming reduction in ration levels stoked concern about the prospect of famine.[13]

When workers discovered, in April 1932, that the rumors were true, they responded with a weeklong strike wave that crippled mills in Teikovo, Vichuga, Lezhnevo, Novye Gorki, Puchezh, and Nerl. Understanding this dramatic response requires examination of worker purchasing and consumption patterns.

According to surveys taken in 1932, Russian textile workers acquired three-quarters of their food supplies from state distributors (mainly, factory cooperatives) and the remainder, from private traders. Flour and baked bread, symbolically and physiologically the most important component of the worker's diet, were supplied almost exclusively (95 percent) by the state. A working-class household also looked to the state for most of its sugar (99 percent), tea (97 percent), sweets (94 percent), fish (96 percent), vegetables (74 percent), meat (67 percent), cooking oil (66 percent), fruit (61 percent), and butter (58 percent), while private traders met the bulk of demand for lard (78 percent), milk (74 percent), eggs (66 percent), and potatoes (62 percent). The surveys show that reliance on private traders—though vital given the poor performance of the state—was costly: the one-quarter of supplies acquired on the market consumed more than half the worker's food budget.[14]

We can begin to discern the difficult position in which workers found themselves. Squeezed between monopolistic state agencies that acted as unreliable suppliers of flour and bread and private traders who extracted high prices for milk and potatoes, they lived in constant fear of losing income, rations, and purchasing power. Data collected from IIR workers on the portion of their budget going to the state versus the market shows that sensitivity to shortages was seasonal. Private traders claimed the largest portion of the worker's budget (51 percent) in August, when crops were harvested and brought to market, and the smallest portion (38 percent) in March, when peasants had yet to sow their land.[15] Workers thus felt most vulnerable in late winter and early spring because that is when they were most dependent on the state for basic necessities and least able to turn to the market to cover shortfalls. That rations were cut repeatedly at this time of year—in March 1929, March 1931, and April 1932—should be interpreted not as an indication that there was no concern in the corridors of power as to how workers would respond, but as proof that the disastrous if unintended effects of Stalin's revolution "from above" made it impossible for the cuts to be made when they would have a less severe impact on living standards.

Wage Arrears

During the third quarter of 1930, Soviet industry plunged into a payments crisis from which it did not emerge for many months. The cause of the crisis was obvious: despite claims to the contrary, the Stalin regime was financing industrialization at the expense of living standards, leaving enterprises with "an absolute lack of currency" with which to pay wages. By the end of 1931, the situation became so acute that the chairman of the IIR Council of Trade Unions, Semagin, dispatched an urgent memorandum to Nikolai Shvernik, the secretary of the Central Council of Trade Unions. "The untimely payment of wages leads to the abnormal operation of enterprises," warned Semagin, "creating political complications in the workers' moods, with all the consequences arising therefrom." Noting that plan fulfillment was running at only 75 percent and that wage arrears in the IIR stood at 16,586,000 rubles, Semagin delivered an alarming message: the failure to pay wages on time was undermining production and morale.[16]

Wage arrears first rose to the top of the shop floor's agenda in late summer 1930, when the OGPU informed Semagin that "workers in factories where the payment of wages has been delayed are extremely tense." Evidence to support this claim was not difficult to muster. At an assembly of Ivanovo's Zinov'ev Mill, weaving overlookers bitterly complained that arrears had rendered the workers "ill-clad and hungry." At Iaroslavl's Red Perekop Mill, anonymous leaflets protested that "they don't give us money for a month's work: they're violating the collective contract, and turning [us] into pawns." In Gavrilov-Iam, operatives threatened to go on strike.[17]

The claims of official propaganda were among the first victims of industry's sudden inability to meet the payroll. Comments made at the Red Perekop mill illustrate the point. "Everyone says that we're growing, but in fact even money's disappeared," declared the worker Molodkin. "Yeah, sure we're getting closer to socialism!" One of his colleagues, Vologodskaia, responded: "If only this regime were struck dead. They talk about 'achievements,' but we see only shortages."[18]

The crisis also shredded the credibility of party members. In Kineshma, Communists mobilized by the district party committee to raise morale were nearly lynched when they showed their faces in working-class neighborhoods. "Go away!" shouted groups of workers. "We should take you by the scruff of the neck and throw you out of the barracks for swindling the workers!" Moods did not improve the following week when mills issued pay packets that consisted of worthless coupons instead of currency. "Look what they've led the country to!" the greaser Vinogradov shouted to colleagues at the Dem'ian Bednyi Mill. "They tricked us before, and thirteen years later, they're still trying to trick us!" Concluded the worker Gur'ianova: "All the Communists should be hanged."[19]

Workers often responded by collectively withdrawing their labor. At Kineshma's Red Volga Mill, the 120 employees of the machine shop—one-sixth of whom were Communists—refused to return to work after lunch because they had not been paid on time. During a stormy meeting with the director, the secretary of the party cell, and the chairman of the factory committee, the men demanded to know "where the money's got to?" Dissatisfied by this response, the worker Kuznetsov offered his own: "*They're* doing just fine, riding around in automobiles." Besides laying bare the hostility sown on the shop floor toward those fated to implement Stalin's policies, this comment prompted the strikers to end the meeting and go home.[20]

Wage arrears also brought production lines to a halt at Viazniki's Paris Commune Mill. Frustrated that their foreman would not summon the director, 150 female ring-frame spinners convened an unauthorized assembly. "With them, there's no use asking for something—you have to demand it," explained leaders of the strike. "Our children are hungry, and we're not going to work . . . for free." Only after extracting a promise from management that wage packets would be distributed within twenty-four hours did the women return to work.[21]

News of the strike's outcome triggered further protests. Two days later, a group of ring-frame spinners from another shift marched to the factory committee and declared that "the worker's face is gaunt, but they don't give us our money." After failing to win support from the trade union, the women settled on a course of action: "You want to starve us to death, so we're . . . declaring a strike." Upon returning to the shop floor, they screamed at the top of their lungs: "They won't pay us our money—stop the machines!" Seventy-five of their colleagues heeded the call; the rest fell victim to harassment. As with the job action that inspired it, this one ended with a promise from management that wage arrears would be liquidated forthwith.[22]

Rather than formally declare a strike as the Viazniki workers did, operatives often idled their machines spontaneously and delivered a demand for back wages to superiors. At Iaroslavl's Red Perekop Mill, 120 party and non-party weavers descended on the administration building on September 20, 1930. "We should organize a hunger riot because they don't give us what we've earned," they shouted. Seeking to defuse the crisis, the enterprise's director emerged to explain why payment had been delayed. When it became clear that he had nothing to offer but excuses, the protesters lunged at him with their fists.[23]

Management was not the only group whose image suffered as a result of wage arrears. In Sereda, two hundred angry employees of the Lower Mill gathered outside the administration building on September 25, 1930. "We don't need factory committees," declared the spinning over-looker Smirnov. "The collective contract has come to nothing. They don't pay our wages on time. We ourselves are our only defenders." Similar protests, against both management and the trade union, were reported at Kineshma's Red Volga and Dem'ian Bednyi mills.[24]

With wage arrears in some districts doubling by late 1930, another wave of protest was inevitable. On November 1, a month of relative calm on shop floors was broken by "anti-Soviet authorities" such as the worker Bychkovskii, who organized a daylong strike at the Iur'ev-Pol'skii Mill to protest, among other things, "the hold-up in wages." At Ivanovo's Dzerzhinskii Mill, meanwhile, groups of up to forty weavers launched brief strikes and promised rough justice for the director.[25]

Passions were no less heated at the Red Perekop Mill, where crowds of up to two hundred workers repeatedly "la[id] siege" to the administration building and threatened to bring production lines to a halt.[26] "Strike moods" likewise infected shop floors in Ivanovo, where workers who had recently vowed "to grab a rifle . . . and shoot all the Communists" won a promise that their demand for back wages would be fulfilled.[27]

The pattern of a month or so of silence, followed by a wave of unrest, persisted. The peak of the next cycle came in the spring of 1931, when "strike manifestations" were reported at the Kovrov Mill and demands for the liquidation of wage arrears accompanied brief strikes by Gus-Khrustal'nyi mule spinners, 100 female weavers of Vichuga's Nogin Mill, and 350 weavers of Vichuga's Red Profintern Mill. The most serious protest at this juncture occurred at the Gorki-Pavlovo Mill, where workers, distressed by a delay in ration distributions and by a rumor that the mill would be shut down due to raw-cotton shortages, succumbed to "mass discontent" after discovering that wage packets would not be distributed. Led by "anti-Soviet elements" who urged them to visit rough justice on trade-union functionaries, gruops of up to five hundred workers launched brief work stoppages over a three-day period. When this tactic failed, all 950 of the mill's workers walked off the job. Desperate to end the standoff, management capitulated.[28]

A protest in July 1931 at one of the Sereda mills followed a similar course. The first sign of trouble was when spinning overlookers voiced "discontent" over management's failure to pay wages on time. OGPU agents just managed to "localize" this protest and detain its "anti-Soviet ringleaders," when the overlookers' female subordinates took up the cause. With the support of at least one rank-and-file Communist, a delegation of twenty-two spinners delivered an ultimatum to the party cell: either distribute wage packets or "the entire mill" goes on strike. The delegation then returned to the shop floor and agitated for support. The response was overwhelming, and four hundred workers soon gathered at the gates of the mill. With the memory of the August 1928 strike still in his mind, the director dialed Moscow and secured permission to distribute wage packets immediately.[29]

Aside from the Sereda protest and "mass discontent" accompanied by appeals for a strike among workers at Ivanovo's Balashov Mill, wage arrears were not a factor in shop-floor unrest during the summer and fall of 1931. The situation changed in November, when "unhealthy moods . . . caused by delays in the payment of wages" swept shop floors and triggered a five-month series of protests. The first sign that the issue was back on the agenda came when residents of several towns complained that "we're marking the anniversary of [the] October [Revolution] . . . but they're not giving the workers any money." Convinced after listening to official speeches that their superiors had no intention of addressing the problem, operatives took matters into their own hands. At Vichuga's Nogin Mill, groups of up to two hundred workers, led by the Communist flyer-frame spinner Vlasova and others, descended on the director's office until a promise that wage arrears would be liquidated was issued. Similar protests took place in Shuia and Teikovo, where the veteran ring-frame spinner Chigunkina lambasted authorities for treating themselves to "an executive's ration" while "the worker is dying" from the shortage of food and money. "Sharp discontent" also erupted in Sereda, where two hundred overlookers and machinists took the lead in condemning the lack of currency. Of the many strike threats issued at this juncture, at least two culminated in successful job actions: the first was a strike by thirty women at the Gavrilov-Iam Mill; the second, a strike by 290 workers at the Kolobovo Mill.[30]

Despite such victories, the crisis continued. Finding it difficult to keep their families clothed and fed, workers kept up the pressure. During the first nine weeks of 1932, "mass discontent" accompanied by strike threats erupted in the mills of Gavrilov-Iam and Viazniki, and large groups of workers in Gus'-Khrustal'nyi, Karabanovo, Kineshma, and Vichuga idled their machines and took their demands for payment to administrators. Although the organizers of protests typically were expelled from the trade union and arrested by the OGPU, it was not the impact of repression so much as delays in the distribution of rations that, in March 1932, moved the issue onto the back burner.[31]

Although the number of job actions rose sharply in 1931—this was due, in part, to the failure of mills to pay wages on time—operatives tended to use their most potent weapon, the strike, as a last resort. The archival sources provide many examples of workers filing individual and collective petitions for the redress of grievances with management, the factory committee, the wages and disputes tribunal, and the courts. Not only were strikes during this period more common among the region's metal, construction, and peat-bog workers, but strikes by textile workers tended, by comparison, to be shorter in duration and smaller in size. Considering the risks involved, including dismissal and arrest, it is understandable that operatives first endeavored to exhaust legal means of protest.[32]

Compensation

Wages were a constant flashpoint on the industry's shop floors because the program of forced capital accumulation required managers, by hook or by crook, to further devalue the labor of some of Soviet industry's most poorly paid workers. Stark evidence of the tensions sown by this situation surfaced in February 1931, when an announcement that piece rates would be reduced triggered "mass discontent" among 1,400 weavers of Vichuga's Nogin Mill. At emergency assemblies convened to discuss the situation, Communists and Komsomols retreated to the sidelines as workers rejected the new rates, drove official speakers from the podium, and applauded a series of sharp speeches that included calls for a strike. "You only know how to squeeze the workers," declared the weaver Panova. "We fought [for Soviet power] because of hardship, but have fallen into serfdom. And you do with the workers as you please. We've given the Soviet regime everything we could, but it cares little for the workers." Comments by the weaver Tarasova likewise laid bare the shop floor's rage: "You've smothered [us] with work, cut rations, and now you're lowering piece rates . . . But this won't go on for long, and the time will come when we'll hang you from the gallows." Behind such comments lay bitterness over the gulf between official promises of a "radiant future" and the grim realities of everyday life. As the former party member Smirnova explained: "You promised the worker mountains of gold . . . but now each of you strives to smother the worker, who lives worse than a dog."[33]

Tensions remained high until management capitulated the following day. The significance of the outcome was not lost on Smirnova, a veteran weaver who immediately began to agitate for more collective action. "If a lone worker sticks his neck out, tomorrow he's out of a job," she explained to a group of women in the washroom. "Instead, we need to gather in groups of five, prepare the soil, and have everyone march out of the factory. After all, they can't arrest everyone."[34] Given that the general strike that swept Vichuga's shop floors in April 1932 began in Smirnova's shed, this lesson was not soon forgotten.

Because managers rarely cut the piece rates of more than a fraction of their employees at one time, the typical protest in defense of earnings was small in scale and duration. In March 1931, the veteran weaver Petrova, who had recently been stripped of her candidate membership in the party for spearheading unrest, led a thirty-minute strike at Kostroma's October Spark Mill when a dozen of her colleagues discovered that their rates had been reduced. Three months later, an unspecified number of weavers at the Nogin Mill idled their looms to protest the introduction of new sorts that suppressed take-home pay by 30 percent. "When Lenin was alive, he took care of us," one of the women complained during an assembly, "but Stalin has reduced us to extreme poverty." Protests were reported the same summer at the Krasin Mill, where it was overlookers rather than weavers who took the lead in defending rates, and at Ivanovo's Zinov'ev Mill, where four female weavers cooperated with a male brigade leader and a male cloth printer to foment "strike moods" against intensification measures that suppressed take-home pay.[35]

The next wave of protests in defense of earnings began in November 1931, when a group of Komsomols, led by two female apprentices,

Figure 9. A Shuia weaver, 1932. Russian State Archive of Documentary Films and Photographs.

marched to the director's office at Kineshma's Red Volga Mill and announced that they would not return to work until a cut in piece rates was rescinded. If the director expected that his decision to fulfill the Komsomols' demand would restore order, he was mistaken. Instead, it gave rise to calls among nonparty operatives for job actions of their own. The next month, management at the Teikovo Combine was forced to convene an emergency assembly of the weaving shed when a coalition of twenty weavers and overlookers called for a strike on the grounds that the wage rates of those who failed to meet output quotas had been cut. Further evidence of workers' unwillingness to tolerate the discounting of their labor came early in 1932 in the form of a two-hour strike by fifty Sobinka mule spinners, led by party member Shabashov, and a two-day strike by the same number of warp drawers at Kineshma's Red Volga Mill.[36]

To buttress Stalin's claim that his program amounted to a fulfillment of the October Revolution, the party adopted, in 1928, an aggressive policy of wage leveling, which reduced pay differentials among workers by channeling the bulk of raises to those at the bottom of the skill hierarchy, and by rewarding the unskilled disproportionately when their qualifications improved. The impact of this policy was dramatic: in 1913, highly skilled operatives earned four to eight times as much as their unskilled colleagues; by 1930, they earned no more than twice as much. There was an unintended effect as well: wage leveling undermined the enthusiasm of the skilled, hence their commitment to the industry.[37]

Dismayed by the loss of skilled workers, Stalin condemned wage leveling in his "Six Conditions" speech of June 23, 1931. The textile industry responded by endeavoring to restore traditional pay differentials. It accomplished this by channeling the largest raises to those at the top of the skill hierarchy. In 1932, nominal wages for the unskilled climbed by 6.25 percent; among the skilled, by contrast, they rose 21.2 percent.[38]

If the restoration of pay differentials rewarded the most skilled operatives, the introduction of progressive piece rates, on January 1, 1932, rewarded the most productive. The principle behind this reform was simple: by paying more for each additional unit of output, mills increased the incentive for workers to fulfill or exceed the norm. In a further attempt to overcome the legacy of wage leveling, the most progressive piece rates were reserved for those at the top of the skill hierarchy.[39]

Although the abandonment of wage leveling and the introduction of progressive piece rates had a salutary effect on earnings, the shop floor's enthusiasm was dampened by two factors. First, automatic withholding remained a chronic source of discontent. Given that one-quarter—and in extreme cases, three-fifths—of gross pay was withheld to cover fees and fines, it is not difficult to fathom why. Second, the methods used to calculate earnings were opaque, hence subject to abuse by managers faced with shortfalls in the wage fund. As a trade-union commission conceded in 1932, mills committed "systematic" and "deliberate accounting errors that provoke fully justified discontent among the workers." Thanks to pay-book notations that often were indecipherable, these errors were difficult, if not impossible, to correct.[40]

Conflicts over records kept by supervisors became more acute after the implementation of a new system of compensation for defective output and equipment idleness. Through the end of January 1931, operatives received the regular piece rate even when they produced defective goods, and payment equal to the average tariff rate even when production lines were down. These policies became prohibitively expensive as shortages of cotton, fuel, and spare parts—which were themselves a consequence of the internally contradictory program of forced capital accumulation—idled machinery, and as the declining quality of equipment, materials, and workmanship boosted the output of seconds. The cost-saving measures implemented in February and March 1932, however, were drastic: pay for those assigned to idled equipment was cut by 50 percent, and pay for those who produced defective output through no fault of their own was cut by one-third. These reforms were unpopular, but what sowed the most anger was another one that eliminated compensation for output that was defective as a result of employee error.[41]

Resistance began immediately. In February 1932, 30 percent of the workers attending an assembly of Vichuga's Nogin Mill voted against the new compensation policies, while their counterparts at the nearby Shagov Amalgamated Mill abandoned their looms and took their complaints to the director. At the New Ivanovo Mill, a meeting of the party cell was disrupted when the weaver Khudiakov stood up and declared that "the Communists have turned into capitalists and are going for the big money even as the workers drown in their own sweat." Protests also were reported among Vichuga spinners, Sereda weaving overlookers, and operatives in Iaroslavl, Kostroma, Rodniki, and Teikovo. Even foremen, rank-and-file party members, and enterprise-level trade-union and party functionaries were dismayed. As members of the Great Ivanovo Combine factory committee demanded in a meeting with their chairman: "How are we to justify the new system to the workers if we ourselves don't support it?"[42]

The shop floor's discontent was justified. The new compensation policies were implemented simultaneously with a new system for supplying mills with spare parts and materials, and this system created bottlenecks that, together with chronic shortages of fuel and skilled labor, increased rates of equipment idleness and the proportion of defective product. While the initial impact was mild—earnings were only 2 to 3 percent lower in February and March 1932 than they would have been under the old system—some mills and professions suffered disproportionately. Moreover, the size of wage packets became highly susceptible to unpredictable fluctuation. Conflicts over who was to blame for seconds proliferated, with managers and workers attributing shortcomings to one another.[43]

Overlookers were among the most vocal opponents of these policies. As his counterparts in Teikovo walked off the job in protest, the overlooker Ivanov of the Lower Sereda Mill spoke to colleagues about the crisis of morale in his craft: "It has become impossible to work. Wages are low, and now there's a deduction for idle machinery and defective goods . . . It's better to leave the factory, and all the overlookers probably will." Ivanov's prediction was not far from the truth: during the first quarter of 1932, earnings among overlookers were 17.9 percent below projected levels, as a result of which many quit their jobs. Managers discovered that nobody wanted to fill these positions—once among the most desirable on the shop floor. The crisis peaked during the summer, prompting Ivan Nosov, the secretary of the IIR Party Committee, to ask Pavel Postyshev, an Ivanovo native now serving as secretary of the Central Party Committee, to repeal the measure that penalized workers for machines idled through no fault of their own.[44]

A study of a mill in Vichuga laid bare the effects of the new compensation system. Initially, the news was good: the earnings of most operatives climbed in January 1932 as the impact of progressive piece rates spread through the labor force. When the penalties for idle production lines and seconds came into effect in February and March, however, take-home pay declined. By May, a day of work in most crafts was worth substantially less than it had been three months before: declines ranged from 12 percent for loom starters to 37 percent for two-loom weavers.[45]

Unfortunately for workers, the decline in nominal earnings came just after Moscow ordered factory cooperatives to raise prices on a range of staples. A provocative speech delivered by the worker Vorob'ev to fellow party members at the Sobinka Mill illustrated the cost of Moscow's decision to squeeze the labor force in this manner:

The raising of prices will make the workers' situation worse. We all speak . . . about achievements, but where are they? "We'll increase the production of soap by a thousand tons!" Yet there's no soap. "Demand has increased!" So before did none of us use soap or something? In 1926 we had everything, but now we have nothing. Where did it all go? All of us accuse the class enemy. "The class enemy! The class enemy!" we shout. But where is he, and what does he have to do with it?[46]

No sooner had cooperatives raised their prices than private traders started jacking up theirs. Surveys carried out in the IIR give a sense of the impact on the typical worker's budget. Between March and May of 1932, respondents reported increases in the per-unit price of eleven items: potatoes (up 7.7 percent), milk (up 8.6 percent), sugar (up 17.4 percent), fish (up 19.8 percent), vegetables (up 35 percent), eggs (up 42.9 percent), fruit (up 90.5 percent), meat (up 105.5 percent), shoes (up 19.6 percent), clothing (up 39.4 percent), and firewood (up 83.3 percent). By contrast, declining prices were reported for just four items: rye bread (down 7.1 percent), wheat (down 54.4 percent), tea (down 58.2 percent), and soap (down 17.5 percent). As noted in a speech delivered to an assembly of Vichuga Communists by former city soviet chairman Evtushenko, workers trapped between falling wages and rising prices were unlikely to be persuaded by claims that the party's policies had improved their lives:

> We've fulfilled the Five-Year Plan and drafted a second one. We all say, "We're growing!" but the result is that we're penalizing workers for defective output and equipment idleness. We're building [new factories], boosting labor productivity, demanding faster tempos from the workers—but we don't give anything to the worker. [Instead,] we raise the price of goods. What will the worker say to us? That anyone proclaiming growth in real wages has only a fat head of cabbage on his shoulders.[47]

The Functional Organization of Labor

Average workloads in the Soviet cotton industry were about 50 percent greater in 1930 than they had been on the eve of World War I. Much of that increase occurred during the second half of the 1920s, when the effort to raise funds for industrialization swung into gear. The results were dramatic: in just four years, from 1926 to 1930, the elevation of workloads and the compression of time schedules boosted productivity among spinners by 30.5 percent, among weavers by 42 percent, and among employees of finishing mills by 76.5 percent.[48]

Unfortunately, these achievements did not satisfy industry officials, who believed that only a thorough reorganization of production would enable the industry to achieve the productivity gains demanded by the FFYP. Seeking guidance, they turned in 1929 to the Central Institute of Labor, whose director, the Bolshevik Taylorist Aleksei Gastev, proposed implementation of the so-called functional organization of labor (FOL). By increasing the number of job categories on the shop floor and reducing the number of tasks assigned to each worker, the FOL encouraged a high degree of specialization. The benefit of this specialization was that it reduced demand for skilled labor and eliminated the unproductive pauses that occurred when workers transitioned from one task to another. Although the FOL required the presence of more bodies on the shop floor—the tasks of the spinner and weaver were now to be fulfilled by several operatives—a FOL brigade serviced more machines, and produced more goods at less cost, than the traditional work team.[49]

That was the theory, anyway. In reality, the FOL failed to live up to expectations. To be fair, it performed well when introduced on an experimental basis at the newly constructed spinning shed of the Lakinskii Mill. But the experiment was carried out under ideal conditions that could not be replicated elsewhere. To be effective, the FOL required an unbroken supply of raw materials, first-rate technical conditions, and a highly motivated labor force. These factors were lacking, however, and the FOL—like many aspects of Stalin's revolution "from above"—had the opposite from intended effect. In other words, productivity did not rise, but rather declined, after the FOL's introduction.[50]

Implemented in spinning sheds in 1930 and in weaving sheds the next year, the FOL provoked potent resistance from below. As an account published by FOL's backers conceded, "a combat environment" arose whenever managers ordered staff to organize themselves into FOL brigades. Although the press portrayed them as "the most backward elements" on the shop floor or "the class enemy," opponents of the measure included veteran spinners, weavers, and overlookers, many of whom were stripped of their trade-union or party membership—and, in some cases, their livelihood—for defending traditional methods of production. Given that the FOL disrupted shop-floor subcultures, deskilled the labor force, boosted the output of defective product, and suppressed wage earnings by as much as 38 percent, it is clear that resistance was motivated by more than knee-jerk aversion to change.[51]

On February 13, 1931, the leadership of the textile industry voted to implement the FOL nationwide. Two weeks later, the IIR OGPU bureau reported "mass discontent among [Ivanovo] workers, bordering on strike moods." On shop floors across the city, Communists and non-Communists alike were "actively resisting the implementation of the FOL," denouncing it at assemblies, refusing to abandon traditional methods of production, and sabotaging machinery intended for FOL brigades. At the Zinov'ev Mill, fifty weavers led by Agafonova, a former city soviet deputy, marched to the director's office and "refused point-blank" to work under the new system. At the New Ivanovo Mill, forty weavers bypassed their unresponsive factory committee and filed a complaint at the regional trade-union bureau. "We ask you to defend us," the women pleaded. "They're imposing the FOL against our will."[52]

The organizers of these protests were singled out and punished, and operatives discovered that they could delay, though not derail, implementation of Gastev's scheme. Soon one-quarter of Soviet looms and almost three-quarters of Soviet ring frames were being serviced by FOL brigades. The problems, however, had not been overcome. As trade-union leaders conceded at a special conference held in August 1931 to discuss the campaign, the FOL produced "a negative result in the overwhelming majority of factories in terms of both equipment productivity and workers' moods." Meanwhile, leadership of anti-FOL protests passed from female weavers to overlookers, "the most conservative and resistant stratum" as far as this and other campaigns were concerned.[53]

Evidence of the overlookers' intransigence could be found in Ivanovo. In May 1931, the OGPU reported another wave of equipment sabotage and "strike moods" on the city's shop floors. Spearheaded by the Old Bolshevik Driagin, party member Toshchakov, and former party member and underground labor activist Kornilov, overlookers at several weaving sheds endeavored to force managers to abandon the FOL. In a series of shop-floor conversations at the Krupskaia Mill, Driagin and Toshchakov appealed to their nonparty colleagues: "Nothing will ever turn out for us if we act alone, but certainly we'll get results if we boycott our duties five days in a row . . . Look how work's going now: it's nothing but torment. Our earnings are down, and why the hell anyway are we all running around like madmen?" Operatives responded sympathetically, as they did to agitation at the nearby Balashov Mill by the nonparty weavers Kitaeva and Romanova: "We've got to walk off the job and go ask for bread and eas[ier] work. We've been deceived and given unbearable work. So much was promised, but nothing besides torment was delivered." Although support for a strike was strong, it dissipated when the activists were dismissed and taken into custody by the OGPU.[54]

Joined by the cloth inspector Kashirin and the shuttle adjuster and former party member Golubev, weaving overlookers at the Vakhromeevo Mill also endeavored to organize a protest. "The Soviet regime has tormented the workers and smothered everyone," they declared. "Soon there will be an insurrection, and everything will be swept away." Sixty workers launched a slowdown and demanded an assembly. Management stonewalled, and frustration mounted. "The FOL is an act of sabotage," declared the protesters. "We must reject it." No concessions were granted, and the instigators were arrested when another conflict erupted two weeks later.[55]

Anti-FOL protests often focused on the impact on earnings. On March 16, 1931, the overlooker Trenin and the weaver Lopatina, a party member, persuaded their brigade of FOL operatives at one of the Red Profintern mills to idle their looms and march to the director's office to demand higher piece rates. During the summer, sixty female weavers at the Upper Sereda Mill launched a similar job action.[56]

Although anti-FOL protests tended to be small in scale, the rhetoric that accompanied them was bitter. Consider, for example, the strike on October 10, 1931, by sixty women from Viazniki's Rosa Luxemburg Mill, where wage packets shrunk in the aftermath of the conversion of all the looms to the FOL. At an emergency session of the factory committee, the strikers condemned the Moscow Taylorists, declaring that "whoever came up with the FOL should be shot," and ridiculed the party. "When [the Communists] seized power, they said 'oppression is a thing of the past,'" recalled the weaver Bezdelova. "Yet now they drive us harder than before. It's impossible to work under the FOL." Just as galling as the party's betrayal of its promises was the hypocrisy of rank-and-file party members, who, despite being "the first ones to abandon the FOL," continued to "walk around with their hands in their pockets . . . screaming, 'Work! Work! Work!'" Eager to restore order, management granted a one-time wage supplement. Still, the underlying issue—that the FOL had been implemented in the absence of proper technical conditions and the consent of the workforce—was never addressed, and another conflict soon broke out.[57]

Managers conceded that the FOL was a failure. As the director of the Zinov'ev Mill recalled in March 1937:

This system led enterprises to the point of breakdown. As a result of its implementation, lack of accountability (obezlichka) took root, the basic crafts were deskilled, product quality declined, the rate of defects rose, equipment was ruined, [and] earnings fell. All of this resulted in tremendous growth in the workers' discontent.[58]

Confronted by strikes and surging desertion rates, Moscow suspended the FOL campaign in late 1931. FOL operatives flooded their superiors with petitions demanding that their brigades be disbanded. These requests were denied, however, because party leaders continued to insist that the FOL was the solution to problems that, in truth, it either exacerbated or created. With living standards under assault from many directions, brigades took matters into their own hands by abandoning the FOL unilaterally. On August 16, 1932, the final wave of anti-FOL protests culminated in a strike by the Shorygino Mill's 524 weavers, who demanded restoration of traditional methods of production. Although their protest was crushed, it prompted the secretary of the IIR Party Committee, Nosov, to petition his counterpart on the Central Party Committee, Postyshev, to abandon Gastev's brainchild. What a sigh of relief operatives and managers alike must have breathed when, several months later, the party repudiated the FOL.[59]

Overtime

Having elevated workloads in 1928–1930 and reorganized production along functional lines in 1930–1931, managers could further boost output only by increasing the amount of time that workers spent in front of their machines. The shop floor's response to efforts along these lines illustrates why such efforts were rare. On March 9, 1931, 350 weavers walked off the job at Vichuga's Red Profintern Mill after being told that the length of their shift was being increased to nine hours. Besides securing repeal of the measure, the protest led to the sacking of the man who implemented it—the secretary of the district party committee. The lack of enthusiasm for longer hours also was evident when managers at Ivanovo's Zinov'ev Mill tried to get employees to work on their day off by promising that the extra output would be used to purchase deficit goods for the cooperative. Cognizant of the likely outcome of agreements that required up-front sacrifice in exchange for promised future benefits, almost the entire labor force stayed home.[60]

Even protests that ended in failure underscored the risks of making exhausted, malnourished workers spend more time on the job. At the Lezhnevo Mill, the announcement, on July 2, 1931, that the traditional summer furlough had been cancelled triggered strike agitation that, according to the OGPU, won the support of a majority of the enterprise's 1,250 workers. Although the arrest of key individuals, such as cafeteria employee Zubynina, derailed planning for the strike, a spontaneous protest erupted three weeks later. Taking advantage of an unexpected power outage, the piecers Kulakova and Shurygina led a crowd of one hundred to the director's office, where they vowed to go on strike if the furlough was not reinstated. The next day, the protesters returned with a group that was twice as large. When management balked, the workers shouted down their superiors, including the secretary of the district party committee, and elected a commission consisting of the watchman Gusev and the weaver Pestova. Monitored by the head of the factory committee, the commission went to Ivanovo and pleaded with trade-union leaders, who came down on management's side but softened the blow by promising better food supplies and timely distribution of wage packets.[61]

New Recruits

After peaking, on January 1, 1929, at 718,800, employment in the Soviet textile industry declined as labor-intensification and cost-cutting measures, as well as policy-driven raw-material shortages, exacted their toll. Two years later, employment in the mills was down 10.3 percent, to 645,100. The loss of 73,700 jobs contrasted with what was taking place in heavy industry, and represented another unintended consequence of forced-draft industrialization. The trend reversed, however, in June 1931, when the government responded to the shortage of consumer goods and the resulting shortfall in capital accumulation by boosting cloth-output targets. Finding it difficult to squeeze more effort out of the labor force, industry officials added 45,600 jobs before the year ended. Combined with turnover rates that climbed rapidly in 1931 as operatives deserted to seek better jobs elsewhere, the expansion of the labor force by 7.1 percent altered its profile, with troubling implications for morale.[62]

In the IIR, most of the new hires were literate, young, nonparty, peasant women with no previous experience in the mills. The immediate effect of their arrival on the shop floor was negative: not only were they infected with the resentments of an embittered peasantry, but the task of training and absorbing them had a suppressive effect on the productivity, output, and earnings of *all* segments of the labor force.[63]

On the eve of the strike wave of April 1932, then, IIR shop floors were younger, less skilled, less experienced, more feminized, and more in touch with the mood of the peasantry than at any time since the launch of the FFYP. This does not mean that the factory was an alien world for the new hires, many of whom came from families that had long relied on industrial wage labor to make ends meet. Nor should it be assumed that the skilled and experienced disappeared. Although a narrow majority of textile workers now had less than one year of shop-floor experience, tens of thousands of veterans remained at the bench. Their authority, moreover, was augmented among managers who required their expertise, and among novices who demanded their guidance. But if the expansion of the labor force was good news for the unemployed and consumers alike, it was bad news for organizations, such as the OGPU, whose priority was to maintain discipline in the mills.[64]

Prisms of Perception

We should pause to consider more closely how workers interpreted the material deprivations that accompanied, and were an inevitable consequence of, the FFYP. This takes us into the arena of shop-floor mentalities, which are difficult to reconstruct. Nevertheless, the sources yield intriguing clues about the prisms of perception that shaped operatives' understanding of their world.

During the FFYP, many workers paid little attention to events beyond the local community: the struggle for survival was too consuming for there to be much time for reading, debate, or discussion of the day's major issues. It is also clear that a significant portion of the labor force continued to cherish the ideals of the October Revolution, whether defined in maximalist or minimalist terms, and believed that Stalin's revolution "from above" violated these ideals.

The most common targets of worker hostility were local authorities. Although retaliation was a risk for anyone who complained, it was theoretically acceptable to expose abuse, corruption, or incompetence in the lower rungs of officialdom. Best exemplified in the *samokritika* campaign, legitimate criticism by workers of their immediate superiors was, where it was permitted to take place, a safety valve that enabled Moscow to preserve its authority by channeling popular disaffection onto those burdened with the responsibility of policy implementation.[65] Workers also had at their disposal a number of institutions—the most important were the factory committee and the wages and disputes tribunal—whose mission, in principle, was to address their grievances.

While workers often turned to these institutions for assistance, it would be wrong to assume that all politics was local or that resistance stopped at the factory gates. In propaganda that was as ubiquitous as it was unimaginative, the party trumpeted the brilliance of its economic policies and the genius of the general secretary. It was not therefore difficult for ordinary citizens to draw a connection between official policies and popular suffering. When the visions presented in newspapers, posters, and agitational speeches contradicted the experience of daily life—which, routinely, they did—workers were inclined to include Moscow in their complaints.

Favorite targets of attack were propagandists who purveyed false descriptions of everyday life. In 1931, a male worker at one of the Red Profintern mills took the podium at a conference and assailed the lack of accurate reporting: "Strikes are occurring in plants and factories, but they don't write about them in the newspapers, and the lecturers fail to mention the workers. Thus, everything takes place in the dark." The same year, a male worker and former party member from Gusev district used the opportunity of a routine factory assembly to question the wisdom of funding agitprop while food supplies were dwindling and wage arrears were mounting: "The Soviet regime and the party occupy themselves only by putting up posters, but give nothing to the workers." Although propaganda was less pervasive in villages than towns, rural audiences also cast a skeptical eye on the official media. As a male citizen who lived near Iaroslavl put it in an unpublished letter to *Pravda:*

> There's no produce, no goods, no boots, no cotton cloth, no stockings . . . There's a shortage of food and clothing, especially for children. As a result of these shortages, market prices are rising fast and don't at all suit the budget of the factory or office worker. And it turns out that the earnings of the factory and office worker are decreasing rather than increasing, since earnings rose 5 to 10 percent while produce prices have climbed by 200 to 300 percent. Everyone believes that 1920 is approaching once again.
>
> Outpatient clinics are full of sick people, but treatment proceeds poorly due to the lack of necessary drugs, and that's why the proper upbringing of children isn't possible. Thus, posters are one thing, but life is another. The discontent is growing. This year [1930] is like the end of 1916 and the beginning of 1917.[66]

By 1932, cynicism and bitterness blunted the party's message. "There was a time when we rejoiced in [the party's] posters and ourselves hung them up, when we attended assemblies," a group of female shock workers from the Gus-Khrustal'nyi's Red Profintern Mill declared in a letter to Lenin's widow, Nadezhda Krupskaia. "[But] now we oppose going to [assemblies,] and their posters are repugnant to us." As propagandists lamented that "nobody believes the party now," rank-and-file Communists insisted that they, too, be included in that statement. "I disagree with the policy of the Central Party Committee," declared the Communist operative Novikov of the Teikovo Combine. "The party drubs into you that a white wall is black, [but] I see that it's white and nobody will convince me otherwise."[67]

In addition to ignoring and contesting official slogans, workers appropriated them to underscore the party's incompetence, hypocrisy, and mendacity. How could the party reduce ration levels when all the talk was about "growth," and when Stalin himself had proclaimed, in June 1931, that it was a priority to improve living standards? How were the Bolsheviks, with their special supply networks, any less hypocritical than their ideological foes, "the Social Democrats of Germany"? Why did propagandists focus so much attention on the suffering of workers in the West when "the crisis in our country . . . is worse?" The outrage was especially fierce among former party members, such as the greaser Belov of Bel'kovo's Freedom Mill. "Why is there such a scandalous situation with regard to worker supply?" he demanded. "Because the Communist Party can't govern the state. The capitalists want to foment war, but our Communists scream, 'We're building socialism!' when in fact *nothing's* been built and there are shortages all around."[68]

The official media's lack of credibility left many struggling to locate alternative sources of information. In December 1930, a thirty-six-year-old female textile worker, Krasavina, concealed the following appeal in a shipment of cloth headed from her Iur'ev-Pol'skii mill to an oilskin plant in Leningrad:

> I want to share our woes with you . . . It has become utterly unbearable to live. There's nothing—no footwear, no clothes. There's nothing to buy. We receive a paltry wage, and they give us a very meager ration: sixteen kilograms of rye flour and nothing else—no butter, no meat, no fish, positively nothing . . . And look, dear comrades, how much we've weakened from malnutrition. We're suffering even as we walk to work. I want to know: can it be true that everywhere there is as much hunger? We've already stopped believing the newspapers . . . You may respond collectively, but I ask you to write only the truth.[69]

Anonymous leaflets circulating in IIR towns and villages were blunt in their calls for resistance at the local, regional, and national levels. Although the OGPU attributed a dozen leaflets seized at a Kovrov factory to an engineer, the real culprit could have been any of the enterprise's disaffected employees: "Workers, you must go out onto the streets and carry out an insurrection . . . Foreign capital will help us . . . drive this regime away . . . We ate and there was a lot of fish in the cooperative during the first year of the Five-Year Plan . . . By the third year, there's a piece of bread . . . and by the fifth, they'll carry the factory worker out on stretchers. *This* is the Soviet regime."[70]

Popular hostility against the new class of exploiters was captured in a leaflet confiscated at a Rybinsk factory in September 1931:

COMRADES—FIGHT AGAINST COMMUNISM! . . .

We all suffer from the violence and luxuries of the Communists. We all see clearly all the low-down tricks that the Communists commit before our very eyes. This entire fraud is clear to every unenlightened worker.

We see what the Soviet regime has brought us to. The oppression of the workers grows more and more with each passing day. A very serious hunger hangs over us. The enslavement of all the working people has intensified to the ultimate degree. At present, we still see a special class that drinks the blood of the working people . . . These parasites comprise a third of our country . . . but earn two and a half times more . . . [than we do].

I call upon the honorable workers to declare a merciless struggle against the idlers and parasites.[71]

There was sympathy for such appeals on the shop floor, where some anticipated the outbreak of a war in which the workers would "get even" with the Bolsheviks. Others, like the Vichuga operative Radnoshkina, consoled themselves with nostalgia: "There's deceit all around: they say that under the Soviet regime it's easier, but it's much worse than under Nicholas [II]. Before we had everything, but now—nothing." For those who could not bring themselves to speak favorably of the old regime, an alternative to Stalinism could be found—or so it was believed—in the visions of dead or exiled party leaders. "Lenin taught us how to fight," declared the spinner Kozlov at an assembly of one of the Red Profintern mills. "[And] now we workers . . . must fight and secure our well-being." A leaflet confiscated at Kineshma's Dem'ian Bednyi Mill echoed Kozlov's call to arms: "Our rulers of the Soviet Union are far more feeble than the bourgeoisie . . . Down with the Soviet rulers! Long live Trotskyism!

Long live Leninism and the Leninist way! But what the Communists say is *not* the Leninist way." A group of barely literate peasants pinned their hopes for salvation on another group of socialists whose hour on the stage of Russian history had passed. "Down with the Five-Year Plan!" they wrote in a leaflet that called on workers to join them in a strike against Moscow's hunger-inducing policies. "Long live the Socialist-Revolutionaries!"[72]

The party's betrayal of the values that infused socialism drove some to look back to one of the first articulations of that ideology for an explanation of—and promise of release from—their suffering. No sooner had the devastating impact of the revolution "from above" become apparent when the trade union reported a surge in "sectarianism and religious belief" in the mills. Most alarming, warned a Kineshma official, was that "[t]his influence [was] beginning to seize the younger generation." Why were textile workers, in urban and rural mills alike, donning crosses, joining sects, attending services, marching in icon processions, and collecting funds to build chapels even as the party endeavored to crush organized religion? After a disillusioning tour of regional mills, an atheism lecturer offered the following explanation: "The sectarians are strong because they speculate in the Christian slogan about equality, fraternity, justice, and so on, which don't exist now, in their view, because people are removed from the Evangelical Testaments."[73] In other words, the party's abandonment of the October Revolution's ideals was driving workers back to the church.

As for the proselytizers of Christianity, their pitch was that the collapse of living standards was "divine punishment for a godless regime." An operative who embraced the message formulated it thus: "Before, the people had God and bread. But now, there's no God, and no bread." The implication— that the road to "justice" and "a better life" began with piety instead of the party—was a subversive one whose appeal Moscow was at a loss to overcome.[74]

By the first quarter of 1932, workers had reached the end of their rope. Notwithstanding myriad signals of discontent over the relentlessly deteriorating conditions of work and daily life, Moscow pressed ahead with its breathtakingly ambitious and unbalanced economic program. As food became scarce, as wage arrears mounted, and as chaos descended on shop floors, strike activity increased and moods grew more bitter than at any time since the difficult months before the introduction of the NEP. Ironically, even the industry's one piece of good news—the expansion of the employment level during the second half of 1931—had, at least in the short term, a negative impact on shop-floor morale.

Rank-and-file Communists understood what was at stake. As an incredulous Zharkov of Ivanovo's Zinov'ev Mill put it in a conversation with nonparty colleagues: "What foolish [economic] tempos they've adopted. These could bring the entire Revolution to ruin."[75] In Moscow, however, the signals were ignored. How far could the workers be pushed? What were the boundaries of their tolerance for suffering? Having failed to pose—let alone answer—such questions, the party issued one inflammatory decree after another. Finally, in April 1932, the workers drew their line in the sand.

6

The Teikovo Strike

Facing weak procurements and rapidly diminishing stocks of grain, Moscow responded in March 1932—as it had twice before in recent years—by cutting daily bread rations. For workers on the special and first supply rolls, most of whom were employed in heavy industry, rations fell 12.5 percent, to seven hundred grams. For those on the second and third supply rolls, most of whom worked in light industry, they fell 31 to 47 percent, to four hundred and three hundred grams, respectively. As for dependents, their meager rations were cut in half—or, in some instances, eliminated.[1]

It was only fitting that the party implemented the new policy on April Fool's Day *(Den durakov)*. What better way to mock Soviet workers than to put them on "hunger rations" in the final year of a development program that by now was supposed to have put them within a stone's throw of the socialist paradise? With real wages having declined by half since the launch of Stalin's revolution "from above" in 1928, with shortages as bad as almost any of them could remember, and with their children beginning to bloat from hunger, the workers who made the October Revolution responded in a manner dictated by their wounded dignity and life-threatening circumstances. In centers of industry across the Soviet Union, they erupted in rebellion. Their message to the party: "We'll repay you for this mockery of the working class!"[2]

The IIR Party Committee received Moscow's decree on the new ration levels in mid-March. It was promptly forwarded to district party committees. Fearful of how shop floors would respond, local officials made almost no effort to inform operatives in advance. As the date for the distribution of April rations approached—typically, the tenth of the month—explosive rumors began to spread, generating what the IIR party boss characterized as "very unhealthy moods that threaten the normal course of operation of [our] enterprises."[3]

Management at the Iur'ev-Pol'skii Mill immediately held meetings with workers and posted extra Communists on the shop floor; here, at least, the panic was contained. Elsewhere, the authorities failed to act or, in some cases, tacitly endorsed the shop floor's angry response. At the Navoloki Mill, for example, managers and Communists watched in "silent agreement" during an assembly as weavers appealed for collective action: "We must carry out the struggle in an organized manner and take it to the end!" The weavers elected a delegation of five nonparty workers, and dispatched it to Moscow with a demand that rations be restored to their previous level.[4]

At the Novye Gorki Mill, meanwhile, 970 weavers piled into an assembly and listened to 42 of their colleagues condemn the policy. "How can our rulers not be ashamed of distributing such a small [ration]?" demanded Voinova. "Did Lenin really teach them to supply the workers so that they perished like fleas? Can we really survive on such a ration and fulfill the [quota] they give us?" Next Sergeeva took the podium: "How come we had everything before, but not now? All of us are waiting, [thinking] soon life will get better, but it [only] gets worse!" After Galin demanded to know why bread was in short supply even as the party boasted about the success of its agricultural policies, Vlasova threatened to visit rough justice upon those who "feed us nothing but fables": "We'll . . . teach them how to starve the workers!" Finally, Panova, who apparently had ties to the land, warned that operatives would abandon the mill until rations were restored, and offered an observation that was no less bitter for being almost universally held: "Life has become worse than under the tsar."[5]

The morale of cotton workers in Teikovo, one of the IIR's oldest mill towns (population 21,300) and the site of a large cotton combine, had been deteriorating for months. Among the factors creating a volatile situation were shortages of food, fuel, and cotton; declining output and earnings; unpopular labor-intensification measures; grim living conditions; and the recent influx of new recruits. Compounding the crisis, hundreds of peasant households recently had abandoned the district's collective farms. A local notable, Teikovo newspaper editor Nikolai Kochnev, recorded his concerns in a diary:

31.03.32: "We've built the foundations of socialism" (from a decree of the Central Party Committee). The notion is very relative, because it's not easy to understand where the foundation ends, and where it begins.

[Early] April 1932: The situation in the country is very tense. There isn't enough bread . . . For the class enemy, it's solid ground for struggle, for gossip . . . The *meshchanstvo* [lower middle class] of all ranks is urgently raising a whining grumble. The style of all work has . . . begun to resemble the era of war communism. Some sabotage is reported . . . Labor obligations have embittered the peasant.[6]

Friday, April 8

The "class enemy" began its work on this day in the machine shop of the Teikovo Combine's finishing shed, when word spread among workers that rations had been reduced. The machinists—all of whom, by tradition, were male—expressed dissatisfaction and supported the proposal of a fitter to summon an administrator. Their messenger returned with inflammatory news: the director of the factory, Novikov, refused the request for talks. Discontent over the new policy soon gave way to complaints about the way management treated workers. Informed that operations in the machine shop had ground to a halt, Novikov appeared—alongside the combine's party secretary, Bazakin—to restore order, but found that operatives from the finishing shed already had joined the protest. Queried about rations by a group of eighty workers, Novikov stonewalled: "It's a state decree, and there's nothing to explain to you." The strikers insisted, however, that he answer their questions. During the exchange that followed, Gavril Chernov, a thirty-seven-year-old joiner with eighteen years at the combine, condemned the new policy: "I knew even before that the party was carrying out an incorrect policy, and that the lowering of rations could be done by some other means—by means of a curtailment of rations in the fall. It's impossible for the worker to work with this level of rations. Indeed, it'll be starvation!" Chernov also spoke out in defense of the community's most vulnerable members: "A dependent can't live on four kilograms. You yourselves couldn't live on [that]." Though dissatisfied with management's response, strikers eventually went back to work.[7]

Saturday, April 9

The next morning, workers arrived at the finishing shed and again expressed concern about the new ration levels. At 9:30 AM, 124 of them laid down their tools in support of demands by Chernov and Vasilii Shishkin—a thirty-seven-year-old fitter with two decades at the combine—for an impromptu assembly. Members of the factory committee appeared on the scene, but their explanations fell flat. Their refusal to convene an assembly exacerbated tensions, as did the retort of a Communist foreman: "No problem, you won't kick the bucket." Their passions inflamed, the workers petitioned Novikov to convene an assembly, but displayed willingness to compromise by agreeing to meet outside regular working hours.[8]

Despite being well-informed about the crisis of shop-floor morale, Teikovo's leaders were shocked by the day's events. In his only diary entry during the strike, Kochnev admitted that he never would have believed the rumors he was hearing had the forces unleashed not confronted him in person:

> 09.04.32 . . . The rations for workers were cut back, so they started making a fuss. The Teikovo . . . Mill—it's impossible to believe—has gone on strike. Yes, yes! . . . a real Italian strike. What a horror. The fifteenth year of the Revolution, and suddenly . . . It simply can't be. But? . . .
>
> I walked around town today, agitated by the news of what was happening. My look was serious and tense. Near the cooperative . . . a worker who had drunk a fair amount stopped me and began to shout . . . "My friend, when will you let us eat, you devils!"[9]

If Kochnev found it difficult to fathom the turn of events at the combine, he must have been stunned by what followed.

Sunday, April 10

When machine-shop workers arrived at the finishing shed the next morning, they were confronted by Novikov, who rejected requests to hold an assembly, demanded an end to the strike, and threatened that anyone demanding food "can be dismissed." His remarks inadvertently added oil to the fire. By the time an unauthorized assembly came to order, calls for talks gave way to demands for rations equal to those of local metalworkers, who enjoyed a higher supply rating. The strike's most active supporters were three nonparty veteran workers with families: Shishkin, Chernov, and Vasilii Anan'ev, a thirty-year-old assistant fitter with seventeen years at the combine. By late afternoon, operatives from the finishing shed joined the discussions in the machine shop.[10]

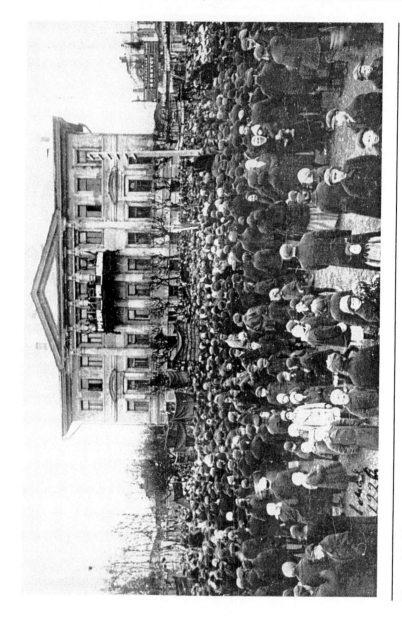

Figure 10. May Day celebration on the Teikovo town square, 1926. Museum of the Teikovo Cotton Combine and School No. 4.

As word of the strike circulated, workers in other parts of the combine began to stir. In the cafeteria, weaving overlooker Pavel Vakhrovskii openly denounced the new ration levels. Arriving for their 12:30 PM shift, spinners and weavers—mostly women—succumbed to strike agitation. Inspecting her ring frame, Praskov'ia Lavrent'eva, a spinner at the combine for thirty-six of her forty-eight years, was confronted by a friend: "None of us is going to work, and you'll be ashamed [if you do]." Shearing machines whirred around fifty-seven-year-old carding operative Pavel Asafov when a group of agitated women barged in: "Stop working!" they shouted. "Don't you want to eat, or what?"[11]

Out of feelings of solidarity or fear—or simply because their machines had been sabotaged—Lavrent'eva, Asafov, and many others joined the strike. Meanwhile, a few encounters turned hostile. "Twenty-five thousander" Aleksandr Malov, one of the Komsomols mobilized by the district party committee to keep production lines running, alleged that Shishkin called him a "strikebreaker," "self-aggrandizer," and "tormentor of collective farm peasants" as the job action got under way. Others who refused to abandon the shop floor allegedly were branded "traitors."[12]

By early afternoon, thousands were on strike. Though not coordinated, the protests occurred simultaneously in various locations, and were accompanied by an eruption of verbal activity: female workers demanded a restoration of rations in speeches at the factory courtyard, the cooperative, and the workers' club; weavers attempted in vain to persuade factory committee members to support the shop floor's demand; 250 workers from the finishing shed assembled in the machine shop, argued with the party secretary, and debated strategy; and groups of strikers marched to the town square, where they listened to speeches by female workers and by Nazar Gradusov, a thirty-six-year-old former mill hand. One of the few acts of violence by protesters occurred this day on the square, where women dragged a Communist off the rostrum after he condemned the strike. Remarkable in this diversity of action was the uniformity of the workers' demand: the restoration of rations to their previous levels, or equilibration with metalworkers.[13]

Monday, April 11

Only 130 spinners and weavers, mostly Communists and Komsomols, reported to their posts the next morning. Chernov arrived at the machine shop at 7:30 AM and sided with Shishkin and others against several mechanics who wanted to work. Soon a group of female strikers, including spinners and weavers, intervened: "You really don't want to eat?" they inquired. The debate ended, and Shishkin led everyone to the finishing shed, where discussions about the food-supply crisis were under way. Meanwhile, some five hundred workers, including many female weavers and a handful of spinners and disaffected party members, blocked entrances to the combine and broke into the various sheds, appealing for everyone to strike ("Stop work! All the workers have left the mill!"), forcibly idling equipment, and warning the card tenders to "stop work—and if you don't, they'll find your heads in the machine." Shop floors emptied quickly, and the crowd in the courtyard swelled to more than two thousand.[14]

While mobilizing the ranks, some strikers threatened party loyalists. For example, the Komsomol Malov reported that a group of women weavers attempted to defenestrate him into the river, and that he escaped only after several Communists intervened. Although such incidents were blamed on Shishkin, the workers who enforced the strike mostly acted on their own.[15]

When Chernov arrived in the courtyard, a female worker was publicly condemning the performance of the cooperative. Shishkin then called on the strikers to demand nothing besides better rations, to resist giving in to provocation (such as threats by the factory committee to deprive them of rations altogether), and to beware the OGPU, which tried to "probe" him the night before "under the pretext of having keys made." He was followed by Vakhrovskii, who told of his own encounter with the OGPU and justified his support for the strike with reference to his responsibilities as a head of household: "It's impossible for a family to survive on four kilograms of bread. I have a large family. We'll have nothing to live on." Their speeches were applauded by the crowd, but the response to party and trade-union representatives who opposed the protest was impatient ("Bread . . . give us bread, and then we'll work!" "Away with you!") and disdainful ("Down with the fat-mouthed jabberer!" "Wipe your nose, sniveler!" "Down with the whore!"). Clearly, the opponents of collective action lacked authority among the rank and file.[16]

Led by Shishkin and Chernov, the strikers—their ranks now expanded by workers from the second shift—marched to the center of town. Hundreds joined the procession as it wound past the spinning shed and through the streets of Teikovo. On the way, strikers stopped at the cooperative and demanded an audience with its director. He was away—or hiding—so they went to the city soviet instead. Although four members of the soviet's presidium, including its chairman, supported the strike, the official who appeared on the balcony insisted that everyone go back to work. Rejecting the request, strikers began calling for the blood of retailers, officials, and OGPU officers. Cooler heads prevailed, and the crowd headed to the site proposed for negotiations: the town theater.[17]

When it reached the town square, the crowd was more than four thousand strong. Though satisfied that the workers were displaying a high degree of solidarity, Shishkin felt uncomfortable that many who had no connection to the combine—in his words, "invalids, housewives . . . kulaks, and *lishentsy*"—had joined the demonstration, either out of curiosity or sympathy. He kept his concerns to himself, however, no doubt aware that the extra bodies increased the force of the workers' protest.[18]

Many bystanders—including artisans, pensioners, and peasants—agreed that "it's really difficult for a worker to live on such a ration," and responded enthusiastically to the strikers' speeches. For example, Andrian Lipin, the forty-one-year-old head of production at a cobblers' artel and a long-time critic of the regime, returned to his workshop and announced that "the workers are striking and they're right to do so. By these means they'll get their way." After asserting that operatives wanted "workers in neighboring factories . . . to strike," and declaring that "we mustn't suffer anymore," Lipin urged his colleagues to lay down their tools. He also issued a thinly veiled threat to his boss: "Soon we'll come to you asking for bread!" The head of a large family, Lipin spent many hours on the square. He joined the fray once, when he came out against the city soviet's request for the election of a strike committee. Such a move, he feared, would only make the shop floor's leaders more vulnerable to arrest.[19]

Intrigued by what he had seen thus far, the fifty-five-year-old pensioner Vasilii Khudiakov arrived at the square at 11:00 AM. The meeting had been under way for some time: Shishkin, Chernov, and others denounced the cutbacks ("It's impossible to live on such a ration!"), while a weaver and strike activist named Mokeeva attacked administrators' privileges ("We must get them to keep the old rations and make cuts in executives' [rations]—for they eat, while we starve!"). Intermittently and unsuccessfully, town officials attempted to restore order. Khudiakov then "approached the tribune." "A worker . . . asked me to give a speech," he testified. "I agreed, but first . . . found out what demands the workers made, and was told . . . that they requested that March rations be kept, and nothing else. With this directive, I gave a speech—not as one of the . . . mill's workers, but as a worker-pensioner who supported the workers' demands."[20]

Khudiakov recounted his speech for investigators:

"We've gone from Lenin's famine to Stalin's famine," I said. "There's no improvement in 1932 compared to 1919. I consider this policy of the Soviet regime utopian because at one end of the country we're digging trenches, but internally we're losing the confidence of the workers" . . .

I explained to the workers the causes of the 1919 famine and the approach of the different famine of 1932, which was caused by the unchecked exporting . . . of grain, poor inventorying, and the absence of a system of controls.

Witnesses testified that Khudiakov uttered a series of remarks that were witheringly critical of the new elite or that attributed popular suffering to the regime's policies:

We must reduce the rations of the Red Army and the OGPU, for they grow plump while the workers starve . . . The Communists and the OGPU live well, earn a lot, and get good rations.

The new bourgeoisie—the Communists—sit in the homes of the former mill-owners . . . They live well, they have their closed shops, but everyone else starves.

During the past thirty-six years I've never seen Teikovo workers go without bread, but now it's happened. Lenin certainly wouldn't have allowed this . . . But now we have not a "communist" party, but some kind of "utopia."

This regime is a "utopia." The working class is perishing.

Year fourteen [sic] of the Revolution—and we're still starving.

The policy of Lenin [sic] and the Soviet regime is incorrect.

We must declare a boycott of the Soviet regime.

We must overthrow the Soviet regime . . . Help for the strikers will come from abroad . . . Not only Soviet but also foreign miners will support our demands.

If bread isn't going to be added and we're going to stay like this, then it's better to be down with Soviet power![21]

It seems that Khudiakov's speech was infused with anti-Soviet, anti-Communist, anti-Stalinist, and perhaps even anti-Leninist rhetoric. How did the strikers respond?

Although many sympathized with Khudiakov's complaints, the stridency was alarming. Calls for the overthrow of "Soviet power"—a term that was far from being synonymous on the shop floor with the party dictatorship—punctured the boundaries of publicly acceptable speech. After the strike, Khudiakov admitted that "the workers responded animatedly" to his remarks; what he neglected to mention was that he surrendered the rostrum after some voiced objections. As for the strike's leaders, most of whom had known Khudiakov for years, they worried that his harsh language attracted "class-alien" elements, obscured the protest's goal, and handed the authorities a weapon to wield against them in propaganda and the courts. Shishkin, Chernov, Anan'ev, and others thus refused to endorse what they later characterized as these "patently counterrevolutionary" and "purely anti-Soviet" remarks.[22]

Local notables exploited this episode in their frantic efforts to break the strike. The Communist director of the Teikovo Savings Bank, for example, mounted the rostrum and argued that the uprising had become the vehicle for "class enemies" such as Khudiakov. In the language of social identity, officials found a weapon to wield against their adversaries. Despite fifteen years of work in a calico-printing artel and experience as a labor organizer during the 1905 Revolution, Khudiakov could be branded with the pejorative label "tradesman" *(torgovets)* because his father—who was still alive and receiving a worker's pension—ran a grocery store after losing his job at the combine, and because he himself had apprenticed with a tradesman and worked as a shop assistant in his youth. Moreover, some workers questioned whether a "mere" factory guard was a member of their class. Khudiakov "commanded authority" on the shop floor as recently as 1925, when he was elected chairman of a strike committee, but his provocative speech meant that authorities now could exploit the unusual aspects of his biography to label him a *byvshii chelovek* (a member of the former "exploiting" classes).[23]

Although the bank official who denounced him also was forced from the rostrum, Khudiakov had undermined his standing by making genuinely anti-Soviet remarks (for example, "Down with Soviet power!"). Vasilii Matiushkin, a forty-nine-year-old fitter with three decades on the shop floor, supported the strike but harbored reservations about Khudiakov's role in it. "I consider Khudiakov to have been the organizer and inspirer of the strike," testified Matiushkin. "His father was a tradesman, and he himself traded alongside his father. I've known his family for thirty years, and although he considers himself a worker, in fact he is a tradesman—if he did work, then it was only as a guard. At all the assemblies, wherever they occur, Khudiakov speaks out against the measures of the Soviet regime."[24]

The forty-two-year-old ex-Communist E. V. Balashev, a lugger and carpenter with two decades in the finishing shed, also supported the strike, but hastened to repudiate its radical spokesman: "We won't follow Khudiakov. He's not ours." According to Fedor Letkov, a forty-one-year-old condenser operator, "the workers supported [Balashev's] speech."[25]

Shortly after Khudiakov's appearance, Gradusov addressed the crowd: he supported the strikers' demand that "we must pressure Soviet organizations to maintain the March rations," and "called the workers to order, warning them of the consequences" of their actions. "My speech was of a purely economic character," he recalled. "I spoke on my own initiative on behalf of the combine's workers and the town's working people." Gradusov claimed that his goal was to act as an agent of moderation, and that the strikers dismissed his appeals for compromise. "[The] authorities won't make concessions," they told him. "We won't end the strike, but will strike until the first of May!"[26]

According to witnesses, Gradusov's "long speech" was more provocative than conciliatory. Their accounts, which are mutually corroborating, indicate that Gradusov called on strikers to persevere until their demand was met; ridiculed the level of executives' rations; proposed that Moscow— and foreign workers—be petitioned for assistance; demanded that Teikovo's leaders be sacked; reiterated "Khudiakov's anti-Soviet statements"; and appropriated official rhetoric in an appeal to the crowd's familial concerns ("Our children are supposed to be 'tomorrow's flowers'," said Gradusov, "but they're withering from hunger"). Apparently, Gradusov was an influential speaker who enjoyed more authority than Khudiakov. Kochnev acknowledged his abilities: "Gradusov is crazy, but the son-of-a-bitch conducts himself capably." Nonetheless, his provocative remarks and period of employment outside the combine—as a *Chekist* and, more recently, cesspit cleaner—made it difficult for some workers to see him as "ours." Concerned about the direction in which the radicals were headed, several prominent strikers criticized them. For example, Chernov distanced himself from their attacks on the privileges of select social groups: "We mustn't apply Red Army and OGPU standards to the workers, since they have more work than us."[27]

Anan'ev characterized the interaction between the crowd and its radical spokesmen as follows:

At the head of the workers on the street were Khudiakov and Gradusov, who before Shishkin's appearance wanted, by means of their anti-Soviet speeches, to send the workers on a different path altogether . . . More than anyone else, Khudiakov and Gradusov stirred up the masses. After their appearances, the masses were disposed in an unruly and anti-Soviet manner, and especially after the long and harsh speeches by Gradusov . . . Maybe their speeches could have been more successful, but the fundamental mass of workers condemned them for it. *Undoubtedly, [though,] . . . backward workers and that segment of the audience consisting of . . . non-working-class outsiders supported them.*

Anan'ev's testimony reveals much about efforts to shape interpretations of the unrest as well as the prevalent categories of social identity. After the IIR strike wave ended, a struggle over meaning began: where émigrés, diplomats, and protesters saw working-class discontent, officials spied the machinations of class enemies.[28] This contest took place within the Soviet bureaucracy itself. In a report written on April 22, 1932, by the regional party control commission, the terms "strike" and "strike movement," which carried positive valences in Marxist-Leninist rhetoric, were employed liberally. When the report arrived in Moscow, however, the Central Party Control Commission substituted neutral or pejorative terms. For example, the title of the document was altered ("Memorandum on the ~~strikes~~ *events* in . . . the [IIR]"), as was the last sentence of the introduction:

As a result of [delays in explaining the new ration policy to workers] and the existence of huge deficiencies in the performance of supply agencies and cooperatives, unhealthy moods arose among a certain segment of the workers, and these moods were used by Trotskyites and class-alien elements, who managed to put significant groups of backward workers under their influence and organize ~~a strike movement~~ *an assault against party and Soviet organizations.*[29]

Moscow's editorial changes point to the discrepancies of perspective that existed between center and periphery. Not that the procedure of political translation was alien to regional authorities; after all, the report's authors understood that it was imperative to describe working-class strike leaders as "Trotskyites and class-alien enemies," and their supporters as "backward workers." (How many problems of analysis were eliminated by such elastic categories!) If the report laid bare the process whereby observed social reality—in this case, a strike wave—was coded by officials into a language that was safe for internal or public consumption, it also highlighted the difficulty the regime had coming to terms with recent events: were these strikes by workers, or assaults by the class enemy? (Another possibility—that workers had *become* the class enemy—was conceded in some corridors of power.) At the same time, Anan'ev's use of the term "backward workers" shows that official categories also enjoyed traction in the popular psyche.

Now to translate Anan'ev's observations into an analysis of social support for the strike's leaders. Shishkin and Chernov represented the majority of demonstrators who, out of fear, exhaustion, or an appreciation of the balance of forces, wanted to focus exclusively on an economic demand (higher rations), while Khudiakov and Gradusov conveyed the views of a minority whose hostility toward the party and its revolution "from above" inclined them to approve more radical critiques. The archival sources do not allow us to determine with certainty who supported Shishkin and who supported Khudiakov, but they do suggest that a majority of strikers supported the former and that constituencies for the latter included exceptionally disaffected workers, collective-farm peasants, former supporters of anti-Bolshevik parties, disgruntled leftists, *lishentsy, byvshie liudi* (members of the former "exploiting" classes), and individuals from the various other malcontent groups that populated IIR towns and villages at this time.

Following the controversy caused by Khudiakov and Gradusov, Anan'ev condemned the performance of the cooperative and the trade union and appealed for moderation: "We must settle the supply and work situation and come to an agreement with local organs." The next speaker, the thirty-eight-year-old trade-union functionary Praskov'ia Maleeva, was less conciliatory: "Brothers, . . . have a look: our children have become lice-ridden, sugar has disappeared, there's no millet, and the children are whining from hunger. Brothers, you could say it's practically consumption." Maleeva, a Communist and former underground labor organizer, concluded that workers in such conditions "could do nothing other" than strike, at which point "the crowd applauded."[30] Shishkin endeavored to boost the crowd's resolve: "We'll strive to preserve the old March rations," but "do we go back to work or not?" A chorus of voices—or rather, according to the testimony, *women's* voices (recall that a majority of the combine's workers were female)—responded: "We won't go back to work!" Having quelled the disturbance caused by Gradusov and Khudiakov and found local authorities unresponsive, Shishkin then seized on an idea that had been circulating for some time: "We aren't in agreement with local organizations, so let's send a telegram to [Council of People's Commissars Chairman Viacheslav] Molotov in the capital."[31]

The strikers deputized a commission to draft an appeal to Molotov. No elections were held, but the most active strike participants—Shishkin, Gradusov, Khudiakov, Anan'ev, Mokeeva, and a certain Bagazhkova—were dispatched to the district party committee. Although Khudiakov suggested that the commission consider itself a formal strike committee, this was rejected by its other members as too provocative. As if in retaliation, party officials denounced Khudiakov as a "former tradesman," an "anti-Soviet person," and a "nonworker who has no relation to the workers," and refused to negotiate in his presence. Thus repudiated, Khudiakov departed for his shift as a night watchman. Nothing was resolved during the talks that followed, and officials warned the delegates that they would be held responsible for further disturbances. This frightened Gradusov, but officials rejected his request to step down. Shishkin and his colleagues then drafted an appeal to Molotov in which they requested the restoration of rations or, alternatively, the dispatch for negotiations of his representatives to Teikovo. Surprisingly, the district party committee approved the text for transmission to Moscow. Strikers were still on the square when their leaders returned. Gradusov recited the appeal and incorporated rank-and-file suggestions, while Shishkin collected sixty rubles to pay for express delivery. After voting to continue the strike until Moscow responded, the crowd dispersed: some went home for the night; others went to the combine to enforce the job action. Finally, Shishkin and Gradusov delivered the telegram to the Teikovo Post Office.[32]

Tuesday, April 12

As the new day started, scores of Communists and Komsomols and a handful of nonparty workers strove to get the combine's most vital production lines running. Their efforts met with only limited success. Since most veteran workers had joined the strike, and since Tuesday was a day off for employees anyway, equipment performed unreliably and the quality of work suffered accordingly. Strikebreakers also remained vulnerable to aggression: no sooner had the doors been locked and work begun on one floor of the finishing shed when two hundred female weavers broke in and brought operations to a halt.[33]

Although strikers often interfered with the activities of anyone who opposed them, they did not prevent essential tasks from being performed. For example, strike leader Chernov skipped several hours of speeches to fix trolleys, "since repairs are done on days off." Chernov understood that if his duties were not fulfilled on this day, then the vehicles would be unavailable when the strike ended, which would place an unfair burden on luggers and suppress the earnings of operatives whose tasks required the timely circulation of supplies. Uncompensated labor by joiners who supported the strike and the lack of opposition to them lay bare the moral universe of the strikers: theirs was not a blind rage, but a finely targeted one.[34]

Several thousand strikers and hundreds of sympathizers gathered at an early hour in the town square. Speeches by strike activists—Shishkin, Gradusov, Anan'ev, Mokeeva, Bagazhkova, Chernov (who arrived after fixing the trolleys), thirty-two-year-old auxiliary spinning operative Ivan Semenov, and a certain Iakovlev—continued until midafternoon.[35] As usual, Shishkin spoke "very well in defense of the workers." His message was one of moderation, directed at strikers who nearly came to blows with their adversaries: "It's impossible to exist on such a ration, and therefore we must demand the old March rations from the government. But don't curse and fight the Komsomols." If danger lurked in confrontations with true believers, it lay also in brushes with *byvshie liudi.* "We've assembled to request bread," he continued. "We mustn't yield to provocation because there are people in the crowd who are not ours—and we aren't against Soviet power." Shishkin's caution was matched by his determination to prevail, which itself was reflected in his threat to expand the movement if necessary: "Comrades, we'll strike until we secure an increase in rations, and if we get no response from the capital by April 13, then we'll go on the morning of April 14 to Ivanovo to resolve this issue jointly with Ivanovo workers at the Palace of Labor." Frustrated by the lack of response from Moscow—one rumor held that postal employees had been too fearful of retaliation to dispatch the telegram—the strikers authorized Shishkin to establish direct telephone contact with Molotov. Although local officials approved the plan, nothing came of it.[36]

Khudiakov, who appeared on the square at 11:00 AM, supported calls for escalation: "We've lived poorly for fifteen years in a row." "The regime won't compromise with us. We must go on a hunger march to get help from the Ivanovo workers." Some protested when Khudiakov again called for the overthrow of "Soviet power," but the reaction was more muted than before, if only because the mood now was characterized more by frustration than exhilaration. (As a witness recalled, "many women were weeping.") Gradusov also addressed the crowd. "In his speech," testified Balashev, "Gradusov agreed with Khudiakov and agitated for a hunger march and drew a series of anti-Soviet conclusions. He also demanded that Teikovo workers write a letter abroad about their situation." A bold promise concluded Gradusov's remarks: "We'll struggle with you in the front ranks until [achieving] complete victory in what we demand from the region's and the town's rulers."[37]

Although his presence provoked concern, Khudiakov continued to play a leading role in the protest. "In talks at the tribune," he recalled, "I spoke with many individuals about strike methods and advised [them] to elect a delegation for a trip to the capital." His proposal was heeded, as a result of which Shishkin, Gradusov, Mokeeva, Semenov, a worker named Prokor'ev, and Khudiakov were elected to the new body. After more inflammatory remarks, however, Khudiakov was quietly compelled to relinquish his seat.[38]

Party loyalists again called for an end to the strike, but were rebuked by angry demonstrators. Even regional leaders found it difficult to get their message across; one who started giving a speech was interrupted by Stepan Andrianov, a fifty-eight-year-old unemployed *lishenets* who had just returned from the Soviet capital in a vain attempt to get his civil rights restored. "The workers have listened to your speeches for fifteen years!" barked Andrianov. "We've had enough of that already, and even in Moscow the people are hungry!" Signaling their determination, the strikers supported calls to persevere until rations were increased or word arrived from Molotov. The only fissure in the workers' stand against officialdom surfaced when Vakhrovskii objected to calls for escalation: "It's time to back down from this bad stuff—'the hunger march,'" he declared. Meanwhile, spontaneous conversations continued to erupt across town, as residents expressed sympathy for the demonstrators and shared rumors about official efforts to quash the IIR strike wave.[39]

By 3:00 PM, an official from the IIR Party Committee, Maksimov, arrived in Teikovo with representatives of the IIR Party Control Commission and Workers' and Peasants' Inspectorate, and invited the strikers to assemble for talks in their club. The invitation was accepted, but the factory committee chairman restricted participation to current mill employees. As a result, hundreds of demonstrators, including Gradusov and Khudiakov, were excluded. As a concession to the rank and file, Komsomols also were banned from the meeting. The head of the factory committee chaired the assembly, which convened at 4:00 PM, and Anan'ev served as secretary.

After officials spoke at length about the food crisis, Chernov, Semenov, and several female workers condemned the performance of supply agencies and declared that it was impossible to survive on the new rations. Regional leaders responded by recommending that a commission of strike leaders be sent to Moscow. This was approved, at which point the workers elected Shishkin, Gradusov, Chernov, Semenov, Mokeeva, and several others to represent them. But Shishkin, who arrived late, persuaded his followers to rescind the vote. Although he had supported the idea when Khudiakov proposed it earlier, he now feared that it was part of an official effort to get the strike's leaders out of town. Besides, he asked rhetorically, what assurance did the commission have that it would be able to meet with government leaders who had failed thus far to respond to an urgent telegram? Savoring his influence, Shishkin whispered a boast to Maksimov: "The workers don't listen to you, but I can persuade the masses—and you can't." Twisting the knife, the assembly voted to reconvene at 8:00 AM and to strike until central authorities arrived. Finally, after five hours of debate, the conference adjourned.[40]

Wednesday, April 13

The next morning, Shishkin led a group of workers from the combine to the town square, where several thousand awaited his arrival. Because the collective farm bazaar was open for business and because nervousness had begun to set in, the crowd was smaller than on previous days. Shishkin opened the meeting: "We must come to an agreement . . . What do we do next?" The strikers responded with determination: "We won't go to work as long as the rations don't satisfy us." "Since you don't want to go to work," echoed Shishkin, "we'll continue the strike." After several women spoke in support of the workers' demand, Gradusov pointed out that the cut in rations would trigger a drop in output, productivity, and wages, and concluded with a thinly veiled threat of escalation: "If Soviet organs don't make concessions . . . then we must take certain measures." Chernov followed with a report that management had settled on a method of retaliation: apparently, workers who failed to go immediately to the combine's cashier would forfeit their wages, and perhaps also their jobs. Evoking remarks made earlier by Gradusov, he assured everyone that there was no reason to capitulate: "We'll have time to get [our money], but we'll strike for as long as they [refuse to] increase our rations. Soon it'll be the first of May, spring flowers will (bloom), but our 'flowers'—the children—are going to wilt from a lack of food." Chernov then excused himself from the meeting—during his absence, speeches were given by Khudiakov, Semenov, local and regional authorities, and others—to help Shishkin ascertain the fate of the telegram. The city soviet had no information, but postal workers confirmed that it had been sent. After returning to the square, they reported their finding. Anan'ev attempted to alleviate the disappointment by publicizing a small victory: the price of food at the cooperative and the cafeteria had been reduced—in the case of milk, by 67 percent.[41]

The other good news was that the public continued to support the strike. "We considered the workers' demands correct," recalled the fifty-three-year-old pensioner Ignatii Matrosov, "and deemed it impossible to survive on such a ration." Citizens listened sympathetically to appeals made at the town forge by Shishkin's wife: "My husband is suffering for the people, so you must make sure they don't put him in jail." Meanwhile, anger in the town square escalated to the point where strike activists won support for a proposal to inspect shop floors so that weavers rumored to be operating looms against their will could be "liberated." Efforts by a group of 150 strikers to penetrate the combine failed, however, because management had sealed the premises.[42]

Such provocations contributed to the radicalization of the strike. Although a "hunger march" had been discussed for days, it won popular support only after Shishkin—and, to a lesser extent, Gradusov and Khudiakov—seized on it in an effort to overcome the disappointments of April 12 and 13. "Since the authorities won't come to us a for a meeting," he declared, "we have to go on a hunger march to the Ivanovo workers to ask . . . for bread." During the debate that followed, many spoke in favor of the proposal, several against it. Finally, Shishkin motioned for a vote, at which point "an absolute majority" indicated their approval.[43]

Although the procedures were democratic, Chernov recalled experiencing some discomfort over the way the decision was reached:

Some workers in the crowd said that we don't have to go on a hunger march, but Shishkin put this question to a vote and a majority decided to go. Not only workers but also the entire audience . . . perhaps up to and including *lishentsy*—voted. I believe that the hunger march took place not through any fault of the workers, but on the initiative of Shishkin and Gradusov, who . . . stirred up the crowd of workers. And if one of them had said to the workers that we don't need to go on a hunger march, then I'm certain that the march wouldn't have taken place.

Though provocative, Chernov's testimony should not be granted too much significance. Because he was absent while most of these events transpired, he underestimated the sense of desperation that had overcome the rank and file by the sixth day of unrest. Shishkin and Gradusov were persuasive speakers, but they insisted that the decision was their followers' to make. And while the participation of *lishentsy* may have "tainted" the vote, their influence was limited because workers tended to regard them with suspicion.[44]

Having voted to march on Ivanovo, the crowd was told by Gradusov— "out of pity for the workers," he recalled—to pack "bread and mugs for the road." Seeking to include those who had families, to augment the moral force of the protest, and to make it more difficult for authorities to resort to violence, Shishkin asked everyone "to bring their children." By late afternoon, the strikers adjourned. Some went to the market, others dropped by the combine to agitate, but most went home to prepare for the thirty-kilometer trek to the regional capital. Meanwhile, rumors about the plan reached the OGPU, which made the first arrests, in typical fashion, overnight. The targets were the most radical strike leader, Khudiakov, the pensioner Matrosov, the *lishenets* Andrianov, and three cobblers— Lipin, forty-two-year-old Mikhail Gornostaev, and fifty-five-year-old Petr Kozyrin—who voiced support for the workers.[45]

The vote in favor of a "hunger march" signaled an escalation of the conflict. By taking their protest on the road, the workers threatened to arouse the disaffected peasantry; and by selecting Ivanovo as their destination, they threatened to ignite a general strike there as well. If it is true, as an IIR Party Control Commission report suggests, that officials believed that Shishkin intended to unite his followers with strikers in other mill towns, then the decision to march was interpreted in the corridors of power as a sign that the radicals in the movement had prevailed.[46] Before the vote, officials displayed little inclination to fulfill the protesters' demand; afterward, the opportunities for compromise diminished even as the potential for violence increased.

The march was less of a threat than imagined, however, because proponents reacted coolly to proposals that would have inspired a broader (urban or rural) revolt. Shishkin recalled his personal reluctance to expand the strike's basis of support:

As a result of the strike, the mills came to a standstill. And if the march per se had been organized rather than spontaneous, then the exacerbation [of the social climate] would have been greater, [but it wasn't] because participants in the march held various opinions. When the workers proposed that I serve as leader of the march, I refused. And if I'd wanted to assume a position at the head of the march, then in my personal opinion we would have had to join— and could have joined—striking peat-bog workers. And as a result, Ivanovo could have been left without electrical power. There were shouts from the crowd on this issue, about joining the peat-bog workers and even the peasants, but the crowd came to no decision at all.[47]

Shishkin's desire to limit the participation of nonworkers is reflected in his cautious attitude toward the march. He also may have been intimidated by the recent OGPU arrests. (Seeking to stay out of jail until the strike was over, he changed his clothes often to make it difficult for authorities to identify him.) At any rate, Shishkin's position prevailed: notwithstanding pleas from the rank and file for the mobilization of other social groups, the stated aims of the "hunger march" remained to meet with Ivanovo workers at the Palace of Labor and to appeal to them for support.[48]

Thursday, April 14, to Sunday, April 17

Three thousand demonstrators assembled on the square the next day. Many women brought their children, and the tears flowed freely as shouts cracked the morning air: "There's nothing to eat!" "We must go to Ivanovo!" At 8:00 AM, Shishkin called for order: "There's no reason to wait." "Whoever wants to eat, let's go to Ivanovo." A woman called for the release of Khudiakov, but Shishkin, who viewed the radical with suspicion, quashed her appeal: "The arrest of Khudiakov is the authorities' business, and the workers mustn't interfere." Sensing doubts among some, Vakhrovskii renewed his opposition to the plan: "It's not expedient to go on a hunger march. We must wait here for results." His comment launched a new debate in which Shishkin argued for perseverance: "We haven't received any responses; therefore, we have to go to Ivanovo. Otherwise, we'll get nothing." "Since we started trouble and began the strike, let's carry it through to the end." Having said his piece, Shishkin surrendered the rostrum to others, including march proponents Anan'ev and Chernov. Before a final vote was held, however, he told the strikers to heed the guidance of their own conscience.[49]

In the end, it was not debate but provocations from above that solidified support for the endeavor. Having rebuffed appeals by Shishkin and a female worker to address the crowd, the district party committee alienated itself further by publicly denouncing the strikers as "counterrevolutionary elements" and by ordering singing, banner-waving Komsomols to parade through town during the debate. Ironically, these actions made it harder for fence-straddlers to support appeals for patience. Had it not been for such tactical errors, testified Gradusov, "perhaps the toiling masses wouldn't have gone" on a hunger march that day.[50]

The strikers confirmed their resolve with a show of hands. At 11:00 AM, they assembled into rows of six, which soon became disorganized, and headed for the first designated rest spot, a stream on the west side of Teikovo. Most dissenters, like Vakhrovskii, bowed to popular opinion and joined the procession, but others required persuasion. "It's not worth being left behind," strikers told Andrei Syrov-Shishkinov, a forty-one-year-old unskilled laborer in the dye works. "You have a family and . . . [are hungry]. Therefore, it's necessary to support us." The spinner Lavrent'eva recalled an appeal from her neighbors, the Luk'ianovs: "Come along with everyone to Ivanovo!" Their enthusiasm was infectious, so she "went to ask for bread, like everyone else." The fifty-year-old card tender P. E. Romanov acquiesced after being "accused . . . of not supporting the workers."[51]

Why did so many participate in the hunger march? Some believed that a direct appeal to the Ivanovo workers, who still enjoyed higher ration levels, was the only option left after a week of failed protests at home. Others went to slake their curiosity or sense of adventure, to partake in a carnivalesque journey, to visit loved ones or buy bread in Ivanovo—or simply to enjoy a beautiful spring day.[52]

The Teikovo unrest exhibited traces of popular carnival: inversions of the social hierarchy, transgressions of the codes of publicly acceptable speech and behavior, ridicule of official culture, evocations of the symbolic role of collective food and labor, and the conquest of fear. The participants, however, were cast in a Stalinist tragedy rather than a Rabelaisian comedy. "Every act of world history was accompanied by a laughing chorus," wrote Mikhail Bakhtin. Also, we would add, by a weeping one. Among the several thousand marchers—especially the women and children— there were few cries of laughter, and many of pain.[53]

Not surprisingly, some workers refused to join the march. Of the 1,503 employees scheduled to work that morning, 628 (41.7 percent) reported to their posts. Many of these were party loyalists, but some were strikers who abandoned the movement after it veered in a radical—and potentially dangerous—direction. The Komsomol Malov was not an entirely credible witness, but he probably was telling the truth when he claimed that some workers condemned the "madness" of Shishkin's trek to Ivanovo.[54]

Although some witnesses portrayed him as an instigator of the march, Gradusov recalled the concerns he harbored once it got under way: "I walked along the road, unconfident, and I thought: this march will miscarry. And I considered it not a 'hunger' march, but a 'Susanin' [suicidal] march." Intending to participate as a mere "rank-and-file worker," Gradusov instead found himself pushed by supporters to the head of the crowd, where he assumed his usual place next to Shishkin. The strikers thus kept the reins of control firmly in their leaders' hands. Recalling how the district party committee had promised to hold him accountable for disturbances, Gradusov made a point of keeping order. He was aided by Shishkin, who periodically barked at stragglers: "Come on! Let's go! Don't fall behind!" Like Gradusov, Shishkin also endeavored to keep his head down. "When after the second vote the crowd of some two to three thousand strikers decided to organize a 'hunger march' to Ivanovo to demand that bread rations be returned to the levels of March," he recalled, "I was sympathetic [*solidaren*] with the crowd, didn't want to be viewed as a coward, and went along . . . but without actively taking part."[55] Shishkin's concern about losing face suggests that cultural assumptions about masculinity—that men should display courage and protect the weaker members of the community—played a role in determining who would undertake the arduous journey that day.

The procession of several thousand strikers crossed the town line, encountered travelers on horseback, opened its ranks to sympathizers, and made its only stop of the day in the village of Lifanovo. The delay was motivated by a need for rest, and by rumors—which turned out to be false—that officials were on their way to negotiate. During the interval, nineteen workers led by Chernov and Vakhrovskii entered a rest home and cheekily asked the maid for food. "[We] are going on a hunger march to Ivanovo," they declared. "You must give [us] dinner, [and] send the bill . . . to the district party committee." The maid, whose Old Bolshevik boss, the fifty-eight-year-old former spinner Ivan Gorbatov, had looked askance at the marchers when he rode past them earlier in the day, complied. Ninety minutes later, the march resumed.[56]

It was a solemn affair. Exhausted after months of shortages and a week of demonstrations, the marchers mulled over their sufferings, attended to children, kept an eye out for trouble, and wept. Their leaders were unusually quiet: they did not strategize among themselves, sing songs to boost morale, or agitate among the peasantry. The event was not lacking in spontaneity, however. For instance, a female marcher periodically mounted makeshift platforms and lectured to onlookers: "It's very difficult for the workers to work. They pay little. We're hungry and demand that goods be cheap and sufficient in quantity." Her appeals persuaded some peasants, including mothers and their children, to join the procession.[57]

At one point, several workers expressed displeasure toward Semen Dvorianchikov, the former proprietor of a trading enterprise and dye works: "Why are you going, *lishenets*? We're going for bread. We don't need any *lishentsy*." The old man ignored their remarks, which were fleeting, and was not challenged again. Strike activist Semenov testified that Dvorianchikov's presence proved "that *lishentsy* and *byvshie liudi* wanted to use the workers' discontent for their own purposes"—a concern shared by Shishkin as well. As former members of the "exploiting" classes, *lishentsy* endowed the protest with political overtones that made some workers uncomfortable and a favorable outcome less likely. Strikers expressed even more hostility "against the Communists who went with us," which compelled Gradusov to take defensive measures on their behalf.[58]

Inevitably, there were confrontations with authorities. At a railroad crossing near Teikovo, OGPU officers tried to block the crowd, but were overwhelmed by its size. Then came attempts to capture the strike's leaders: aided by Bagazhkova and others, Shishkin repulsed armed officers on four occasions. Notwithstanding such interference, not to mention their own fear and exhaustion, the marchers reached villages on the western edge of Ivanovo by late afternoon. They would have proceeded as planned to the Palace of Labor, but the road was blocked by hundreds of Communists and Komsomols—mostly students and workers—who had been mobilized by the IIR Party Committee to intercept them. At the head of the delegation stood Nikolai Kubiak, the chairman of the IIR Soviet Executive Committee and an Old Bolshevik member of the Central Party Committee. Backed by OGPU officers and civil police, Kubiak's cadres agitated intensively among the exhausted marchers and herded them into an empty passenger train commandeered for the occasion.[59]

Ruses to capture the strike's leaders were deployed. For example, Gradusov was speaking with one of the Ivanovo Communists when someone shouted his name; turning to see who it was, he was identified and arrested. Sensing danger, Shishkin, Chernov, Vakhrovskii, Bagazhkova, and others broke from the crowd, scuffled with officers, and escaped into the forest. Meanwhile, Semenov called on his followers to penetrate the blockade and proceed to the Palace of Labor; they shielded him from arrest, but were overwhelmed by the show of force and thus unable to heed his call. Besides Gradusov, a handful of workers who endeavored to proceed to Ivanovo were arrested.[60]

The train brought its passengers to Teikovo and released them. Several marchers who skipped the train and headed home on foot were arrested by mounted police in the village of Pelgusovo. Shishkin, Chernov, and Bagazhkova were luckier. After discussing the day's events, they fell asleep in a haystack. A sympathetic peasant woman fixed breakfast for them the next morning and listened to their remarkable story. After arriving in Teikovo at 1:00 PM, they encountered a group of female workers near the district OGPU bureau. Chernov paused to tell his story, while Shishkin publicly taunted his pursuers: "If they want to arrest me, then let them take [me]! But if they come at night to make an arrest, then let them kill me!" Shishkin and Chernov then headed for the combine's courtyard, where a crowd of some seven hundred workers demanded the election of a commission to investigate the fate of thirty individuals who had been taken into custody. By now, however, the authorities enjoyed the upper hand. Having already denounced the hunger march in assemblies throughout the combine, they insisted that the strikers capitulate. As Chernov unsheathed a knife and sliced the boots off his painfully swollen feet, Shishkin concluded that the risks of standing firm outweighed the potential benefits. "Since they won't make concessions," he declared in his last public speech, "then we have to make concessions ourselves." Reluctantly concurring, the crowd voted to capitulate. By late afternoon, half the combine's employees reported to work. The next day, "the overwhelming majority" did so. By April 17, the Teikovo strike had been "completely liquidated."[61]

The OGPU targeted three groups for arrest and interrogation: strike leaders, marchers who failed to return to Teikovo by train, and "class-alien" elements, especially current or former *lishentsy,* who in any way took part in the demonstrations. Although some women were hauled in for questioning, none appears to have been prosecuted—which is not surprising, as nonviolent female strikers rarely were subject to criminal charges during this period.[62] What price did the targets of repression pay for their "crimes"? Shishkin and Khudiakov, both of whom defended the strike to the end, were exiled to Kazakhstan. More willing to condemn it after the fact, Gradusov and Chernov were prohibited from living in the IIR and other densely populated urban areas. Punishment also was meted out to those with tainted social backgrounds, even if their role in the strike was negligible. For example, the *lishenets* Andrianov was exiled to Novosibirsk, while four cobblers who had the misfortune of being the offspring of *byvshie liudi* were sent to labor camps on the notorious White Sea Canal.[63]

After months of conflict over food shortages, intensification measures, declining wages, and the conditions of work and daily life, the Teikovo strike began spontaneously on April 8, 1932, in response to the sudden introduction of "starvation" rations. Perceiving a threat to their survival, the town's cotton workers—especially those with families to support—demanded immediate talks with their superiors.[64] When this demand was dismissed out of hand, the workers withdrew their labor and engaged in a week of public demonstrations that culminated in a "hunger march" to Ivanovo. The unrest came to an end only when the marchers were intercepted, key strike leaders were taken into custody, and a determination was made by those still at large that the risks of pressing forward were too high to bear.

Shishkin articulated majority opinion and became the strike's most influential leader. By declaring repeatedly that the strike had only one goal, he served as a beacon for workers who supported Soviet power but found it impossible to reconcile themselves to current conditions. A proponent of perseverance and moderation, he prolonged the strike by making it viable, and fought to keep it from taking the radical trajectory promoted by some.

Shishkin never retreated from his belief in the shop floor's right to resist: "I believe that the strike was necessary and consider such a strike the only correct method of mass protest for workers against the cutback in ration levels," he testified. Sarcastically employing a term for one of the regime's recently abandoned wage policies, he also condemned the emerging hierarchy of supply: "I believe there must be leveling *(uravnilovka)* in, to be exact, gastric matters, insofar as everyone works equally." In this regard, Shishkin echoed the strike's most radical leader: "It's impossible for the worker to live with existing supply [levels]," Khudiakov told investigators, "and I consider the differentiated supply of workers totally incorrect, since according to their gastric needs, all workers are the same."[65]

While Shishkin and Khudiakov shared the egalitarian values of their community's moral economy, their views of Stalin's revolution "from above" were shaped by different ethical concerns. Like Rodniki's Klepikov, Khudiakov was a libertarian socialist—or, in his own words, "a Social Democrat"—who rejected the Stalinist premise that socialism could be achieved by coercive means. "I do not agree with the policy of applying pressure," he declared, "and consider it capitalist rather than socialist." Because personal autonomy was a core value for Khudiakov—it lay at the heart of his interpretation of socialism—he rejected the party's use of coercion against workers, peasants, and Orthodox believers alike.[66] Shishkin's critique was narrower, though no less principled. A generation younger than Khudiakov and a proud veteran of the Red Army's Civil War triumph, he identified with Soviet power, whose goal he—like Iaroslavl's Liulin—believed was to improve the workers' lives. His opposition to the revolution "from above" thus focused on the calamitous impact it had on living standards.

Shishkin put his life on the line twice: first, to defend Soviet power from the Whites; and later, to insist that Soviet power fulfill its promise to the workers. Shishkin perceived no contradiction here because in each instance he fought in the name of the workers against what he understood to be an oppressive elite. But just as he erred during the Civil War by associating himself briefly with the anarchist Nestor Makhno, so he erred also in April 1932 by allowing the opponents of Soviet rule to assume prominence in a protest whose objective should have been narrowly economic. He testified:

As a former commander in the Red Army and a participant in the Civil War, I am a worker by birth and have a record of twenty-one years in the mill. And I consider it my duty to state that at the height of the strike when I, standing virtually at the head of the crowd, demanded only the improvement of the workers' economic condition (because I radically disagree with the party's policy of reducing the workers' rations), at that moment there were outsiders in the crowd, such counterrevolutionary personalities as Khudiakov. They made political demands and generally expressed dissatisfaction with the Soviet regime.

I consider my mistake to be that we carried out the strike within view of the entire region—in particular, for example, the hunger march on Ivanovo. And the whole trouble is that *lishentsy* and other anti-Soviet individuals used the strike for their agitation. I believe that we should have carried out the strike on the strength of the workers alone, so that outsiders didn't participate. Notwithstanding my deficiencies, I must say again that I am not a counterrevolutionary.

But because of my character, I don't agree with the social condition of the workers. All the same, bearing in mind the loss that the strike caused the government, I readily agree to bear punishment for my crimes. But I don't want to be considered a rebel [*buntovshchik*], because I am prepared to defend Soviet power at any moment. Therefore, I ask the OGPU not to prescribe a heavy punishment for me.[67]

Deprived of the opportunity to press their grievance in a legitimate manner, workers pursued the only possible course of action: public demonstrations against a policy that condemned them to gradual starvation. That a strike appeared on the horizon of action and was well organized underscored both the severity of popular discontent and Teikovo's history of labor militance.[68] The traditions of resistance persisted in living memory and, paradoxically, in official myth, which supplied workers with models of speech and behavior that could be wielded effectively against those who now ruled in their name.

The mood of the shop floor was so explosive by 1932 that the Teikovo strike surmounted many obstacles. Prominent among these was the lack of a formal strike committee. As in 1917, the strikers organized themselves in a radically democratic manner: everything was put to a vote. Although there was no shortage of disagreement among the workers and their most prominent spokesmen—Shishkin, Gradusov, Khudiakov, Chernov, Semenov, Anan'ev, Mokeeva, Maleeva, and Bagazhkova—official efforts to break the strike failed.[69]

Authority figures of every stripe lacked influence among the strikers. Outnumbered nine to one on the shop floor, the Communists enjoyed privileges that made them vulnerable to ridicule by a labor force that viewed them as self-aggrandizing hypocrites; wisely, all but the truest of believers maintained a low profile. Whether out of fealty to superiors, a desire to maintain privileges, or disagreement over the chosen forms of protest, 90 percent of party members stayed on the job, while just about everyone else went on strike. Discipline flagged even among the elect, however, and no less than thirty-one Communists and thirty-seven Komsomols joined the demonstrations. Not that this shielded them from popular hostility: party members who condemned the strike were physically abused, and those who sided with the workers were, at times, verbally abused.[70]

Because trade-union activists were more likely to share the shop floor's concerns, 170 out of 477 of them (35.6 percent) joined the strike, as did half the members of the factory committee. Although these individuals were viewed with somewhat less disdain than the Communists—the categories, of course, overlapped—this should not be taken as evidence that the trade union was perceived as a vehicle for the defense of working-class interests. (Nobody was surprised when the factory-committee chairman sided with management.) Most trade-union activists opposed the strike because they understood that their primary function was to keep the labor force as passive and productive as possible. As for those who supported it, they did so out of sympathy, fear of losing face, or a desire to keep class enemies at bay.[71]

The hostility felt toward management is the least difficult to fathom. Although the workers were upset by a policy formulated in Moscow, they did not go on strike in large numbers until administrators callously dismissed their concerns. On top of the physiological assault that reduced rations represented, this assault on their dignity was too much to bear.

What does the Teikovo strike tell us about the effectiveness of those in power? If the question is one of center-periphery control, then it can be said that the organs of authority fulfilled their role as "transmission belts" poorly. Orders from Moscow to prepare the population for lower rations were mostly ignored because agitprop departments had fallen into dormancy and party cells were in disarray. More over, officials at all levels were terrified of publicizing, let alone defending, the new policy on the shop floor. As a result, decrees from above were implemented furtively, rumor gave way to panic, and nothing was done to contain unrest until it was too late.[72]

While officials never lost power in Teikovo, as they did in Vichuga the same week, they were compelled to cede the public stage to the lower classes and wait for attrition and arrest to take their toll. Compared to others in positions of influence, OGPU officers were effective, if brutal, and could be counted on to produce results when everything else failed. It is no wonder that the party came to rely on them so heavily.[73]

Not that we must embrace attempts by the center to lay blame for the IIR strike wave on local authorities, who found themselves in an impossible situation: after months of implementing state-decreed assaults on society, they understood that most social groups opposed Stalin's revolution "from above." On the eve of the unrest, peasants were abandoning collective farms, workers were sabotaging intensification measures, and criticism of the party and its policies was ubiquitous in the most vibrant loci of unofficial worker culture: the factory washroom and smoking lounge. In the polarized conditions that prevailed in the regions during the twilight of the FFYP, inaction was the rational response for officials trapped between impossible decrees and embittered social groups.

Kochnev characterized the situation shortly after the IIR strike wave was suppressed: "Class stands against class."[74] A decade of Bolshevik rule followed by four years of Stalin's revolution "from above" had created a relationship of mutual hostility between workers and the party. Ironically, interpretive lenses popularized by the latter laid bare the contours of social reality, and state policy regenerated a self-conscious working class that was prepared to defend its interests by means of extralegal, collective action.

The centripetal forces that brought workers together for a week of strikes against the reduction in ration levels included the accumulated, devastating effects of the revolution "from above"; the resurgence of class identity precipitated by the collapse of living standards; and a moral economy that dictated collective action in defense of the community's vital interests. What were the centrifugal forces that sowed division even as the strike wave reached its climax? Workers occupied different positions on the spectrum of support for the regime: if some lauded Khudiakov's and Gradusov's harsh speeches, others did not. Differences of opinion about Soviet power and the Stalin dictatorship affected the viability of collective action.

Gender also influenced the strike wave in profound, if ambiguous, ways. Under the FFYP, branches of the economy in which women predominated—such as textiles—involuntarily financed the construction of male-dominated heavy industry. Moreover, Russian women, as the primary caregivers of their children, felt disproportionately burdened by food shortages, which inclined them to protest when hunger loomed. If these factors explain why the most significant unrest occurred in a region of light rather than heavy industry, so too does the fact that lower-class women were willing to take advantage of a traditional gender stereotype—that they were victims of their emotions, predisposed to unruly behavior—that made them less vulnerable to prosecution. Still, women continued to occupy a narrow space on the stage of political action—a majority of the strikers were women, but most strike leaders were men—and this diminished the movement's appeal in male-dominated industries.[75]

7

The Vichuga Uprising

The labor unrest of April 1932 marked a turning-point in the relationship between the Stalin dictatorship and Soviet society. By organizing strikes, slowdowns, emergency assemblies, and a "hunger march," the IIR textile workers expressed their willingness to engage in collective action to change the policies that had reduced them to poverty and hunger. By sending Central Party Committee Secretary Lazar Kaganovich to suppress the demonstrations, Stalin laid bare the hypocrisy of the claim that he was building a socialist workers' state. These events had profound ramifications: they transformed the government's economic program, exacerbated the crisis of public morale, and served as a pretext for the Great Terror. It took years for all the repercussions to become manifest, but word spread quickly that something unprecedented had occurred. Indeed, it had. In Vichuga, the institutions of power all but collapsed in the face of a violent, working-class rebellion. More powerfully than even the Teikovo strike, the Vichuga uprising illuminated what Stalin's revolution "from above" had sown on the shop floor: explosive hatred of those perceived to be responsible for the workers' suffering; and a willingness by the workers to engage in collective action on a mass scale to bring an end once and for all to the party's relentless assault on their living standard.

The IIR's second-largest mill town, Vichuga (population 36,000) boasted three cotton mills and a small machine-building plant; villages in the district were home to three other nineteenth-century mills.[1] By 1932, Vichuga's 17,500 cotton operatives confronted the same policy-driven threats to their well-being as did their counterparts in Teikovo and elsewhere: grim working conditions and declining take-home pay; plummeting real wages; and severe shortages of life's basic necessities. Local party officials ignored the suffering of the workers whose interests they claimed to represent. When cooperatives took the unauthorized step in February and March 1932 of canceling rations for hundreds of working-class families, the district party committee failed to intervene. It was a fateful error that made a volatile situation explosive. "[These] people don't understand that a political mood forms around a bowl of soup," observed a member of the IIR Party Committee, "that a political mood forms around an empty thermos."[2]

Although officials were alienated from the shop floor, the same could not be said for members of the local intelligentsia. On March 12, a student at Vichuga's Textile Polytechnic, Kholshchevnikov, had this to say during a meeting of his current affairs study group: "The condition of the working class isn't improving, as was stated in the decisions of the Seventeenth Party Conference, but is deteriorating. As a result of the intensifying food difficulties, the workers' real wages are falling. The workers are beginning to starve." The polytechnic's civics instructor, Aristov, seconded Kholshchevnikov's assertions, and began to include two provocative claims in his lectures: mortality was on the rise as a result of declining living standards; and blame for the situation lay with the party's economic policies.[3]

Not surprisingly, these claims created a stir at the polytechnic and in the mills, where "the starving existence of the workers" had long been a topic of conversation. Comments that the instructor Borisov made to his colleagues at Factory School No. 1 illustrate the erosion of faith among those charged with mobilizing support for the Party:

> What Aristov said is the truth, and I fully share his thoughts. I won't go to the workers to lead discussions and to convince them of something in which I myself don't believe. You won't build socialism in one country—Lenin himself wrote about that—and what is more, foreigners are convinced that the Soviet Union can be broken without a war, that they can wait quietly for a revolution in Russia itself, without intervention on their part.

Borisov concluded with a prescient analysis: "The situation in Russia is so tense now that one tremor is enough to detonate the atmosphere that has been created."[4]

When party officials convened meetings to suppress these "Trotskyite" moods, the dissenting voices were insistent. Declared the Communist Zatroev of the Shagov Amalgamated Mill: "The third decisive year of the

Five-Year Plan was critical, and, having endured it, we thought 'supplies will improve,' but it turned out precisely the other way around. Last year we received fish and meat—albeit only a little—but now we see nothing."[5]

While the Communist rank and file wrestled with concerns about what the party had sown, the mood of the nonparty labor force manifested itself in rumors that workers with ties to the land would be removed from supply rolls, in the escalation of complaints among the hundreds of Nogin operatives who had recently—and illegally—been denied rations, and, on March 25, in scattered slowdowns and work stoppages. The district party committee underscored its obliviousness by ignoring urgent OGPU reports that detailed "the signals of swelling discontent."[6]

Frustrated by the lack of response from above, a crowd of Nogin workers marched to the center of town on March 31 and demanded that back rations be distributed immediately. When the demand was rebuffed, the crowd elected a delegation to convey its complaints to Moscow. As a result of a successful OGPU operation, however, the delegation never made it out of town.[7]

Sunday, April 3, to Friday, April 8

During the first week of April, the district party committee reacted to Moscow's order to cut rations for workers and their dependents by convening closed assemblies of party and trade-union activists. Alarmed by the unrest that rumors of the cutback had aroused—manifest in a one-hour strike by the Nogin's white-collar employees—party officials made a fateful decision: the news would be announced not in all-factory assemblies, which were difficult to control, but in meetings to be convened at the level of the workshop or brigade.[8]

It was the perceived indignity of not being allowed to meet collectively that transformed discontent into rage. Informed, on April 3, of the implementation of what were already being characterized as "hunger rations," 150 Nogin operatives stormed out of the workers' club, "burst into the mill, and demanded the summoning of an all-factory conference." During the next forty-eight hours, a series of assemblies at Shagov Mill No. 1 ended in the same manner. "Why are you assembling us in small groups?" the workers demanded. "Convene general assemblies, where we, too, [will] speak!" Determined to deal collectively with the crisis, operatives gathered spontaneously on shop floors and began calling for a strike.[9]

On April 5, a crowd of weavers gathered outside the Shagov Amalgamated Mill, demanded an all-factory assembly, and echoed the appeals for a strike. Workers who happened to be passing through the factory gates joined them. Informed of the protest, the district party committee dispatched several officials to the scene; their speeches or threats must have been effective, for the crowd dispersed. Satisfied by the outcome, party leaders turned their attention to other matters. Their confidence, however, was misplaced: on shop floors and streets across town, support was surging for a collective response to this latest assault on the workers' living standard.[10]

Under the leadership of the weaver Zabelkina and the fitter Tezin—who, the previous day, April 5, had been among the first to call for a strike—almost all the workers from the weaving shed of Shagov Mill No. 1 struck from 9:30 to 11:00 AM. Their demand: an all-factory assembly to discuss the crisis. Workers from the second shift struck from 1:00 to 3:00 PM in support of the same demand. Although agitation by district party committee officials and the arrest of the organizers brought these job actions to an end, they failed to prevent the unrest from spreading to the spinning shed, where operations ground to a halt at 4:00 PM and the workers demanded an all-factory assembly.[11]

Some Communists, including a secretary of the party cell in one of the weaving sheds, joined the calls for a strike. As for those who dissented—mainly Komsomols and Communists—they were threatened with reprisals. Rumors that a general strike was being organized for April 8 raised expectations on the shop floor and concern in the corridors of power.[12]

April 7 was a day off for most workers, and the mills were empty. Pressed by the OGPU to seize the initiative, the district party committee convened a meeting of party and trade-union functionaries to settle on "tactics of struggle against the strike." A representative from the OGPU reported that strikers from the Shagov Amalgamated Mill were poised to send delegations to other factories, or to march on them collectively, in an effort to expand the protest. In the latest of a series of bad decisions, the district party committee concluded that "concrete measures" did not have to be taken because the disturbances were unlikely to spread "beyond the confines of individual enterprises." Despite their familiarity with the "sharp forms" of conflict that had just occurred, party leaders laid bare their hubris and alienation by dismissing the OGPU's warnings as "exaggerated."[13]

Events the next day, April 8, justified the stance taken by the OGPU. At

5:00 AM, when the first shift was scheduled to begin, operatives in the spinning and weaving sheds of Shagov Mill No. 1 refused to tend to their machines. Support for the strike was all but universal among nonparty workers, and it was the overlookers—all of whom, by tradition, were male—who served as the enforcers. The Communists, meanwhile, were divided: those in the spinning shed supported the strike, while their counterparts in the weaving shed opposed it.[14]

Early that afternoon, workers arriving for the second shift joined protesters at the gates of the Shagov Amalgamated Mill. At 1:00 PM, workers at Shagov No. 3 and the Krasin Mill also idled their machines. Later, so did those at Shagov No. 2 and No. 4. The demand was no longer for an all-factory assembly; it was too late for that. Instead, it was for restoration of monthly bread rations to sixteen kilograms for workers and eight kilograms for dependents.[15]

As rumors of the day's events spread, tensions rose even in mills that had yet to join the strike. Notwithstanding that several officials from the district party committee went to the Shagov and Krasin mills to organize countermeasures, the response of Vichuga's notables left much to be desired. Although he knew that trouble was brewing, the chairman of the city soviet, Filippov, proceeded with his long-planned vacation to a health resort. The district party boss, Vorkuev, suffered from chest pain after attending an assembly of angry Krasin workers—and stayed home for three days. Having received an OGPU account of the disturbances shortly after they began, the chairman of the district soviet executive committee, Aref'ev, went to visit his wife in Rybinsk. Vichuga's state prosecutor, Krutikov, disregarded warnings from the district party control commission and deserted his post.[16]

By succumbing to panic and refusing to fulfill their duties, Filippov, Vorkuev, Aref'ev, and Krutikov revealed the depth of their alienation from the shop floor and ceded the initiative to the strikers. As a result, according to Kaganovich, "the district found itself to all intents and purposes without leaders," which paralyzed the organs of authority. As for those officials who dutifully remained at their posts, they miscalculated the significance of the unrest, delayed placing the call for help to the IIR Party Committee, and quickly lost control of the situation.[17]

Ironically, the chaos in the ranks of officialdom contrasted sharply with the cohesiveness of the shop floor. Although the Vichuga general strike was the largest to occur at this time, its organizers were no less nimble than their counterparts in Teikovo. Perhaps because the authorities in

Vichuga were so disorganized, the sources tell us little about them. A member of the IIR Party Committee, however, admired their ability to mount a "counterrevolutionary organization" that commanded the allegiance of the town's workers and put the party to shame:

> It's an established fact that they convened a conference in the forest. During the strike itself, information was purveyed perfectly well, [and] they responded to our measures very flexibly. There were moments when they tapped into the [telegraph] wires, put forward their own Morse code signalers, and so on. Although all preconditions for exposing this organization had been met, the party organization slept through all of this.

In his report to Stalin, Kaganovich likewise observed that the strike's leaders enjoyed excellent "reconnaissance" and "the closest communication" with other mill towns—including, ominously, with those engulfed by disturbances of their own.[18]

Saturday, April 9

On this morning, two warp drawers from the Nogin Mill—Iurkin, a former Communist who quit the party, in 1922 on account of "political differences," and Komarov, who allegedly hailed from "prosperous peasants"—demanded that an all-factory conference be convened to deal with the crisis. All their department colleagues and a number of slasher tenders idled their machines and marched to the factory committee. "Give us bread!" they demanded. "We won't work for eleven kilograms!" Weavers at the Krasin Mill and spinners and weavers at the Shagov Amalgamated Mill, meanwhile, continued to strike.[19]

At 2:30 PM, the Shagov strikers did just as the OGPU predicted: determined to trigger a citywide strike, they marched to the Nogin Mill. On the way there, they eagerly invited passers-by to join them. Twenty-nine-year-old Grigorii Simov, a heating engineer employed at the Red Profintern Mill, spotted an acquaintance in the crowd: "How did you wind up here?" he inquired. "So you really don't want to eat?!" came the response. "We're going to get workers from the [Nogin] Mill." Attempts also were made to agitate among Red Army troops, one of whom was threatened after he endeavored to stand in the way of the strikers: "So it seems you're a Communist? Well, then, we should rough you up!" Brawls ensued when the strikers came upon a group of Communists and Komsomols who had been dispatched by the authorities to intercept them.[20]

After reaching the Nogin Mill, the strikers cast rocks through the windows, broke through a line of Komsomols stationed at the gates, and penetrated shop floors, where they demanded that everyone "stop work." Venting their anger, the intruders—led by Iurkin—smashed equipment, destroyed supplies, and beat their opponents. Outside, a crowd took control of the entrance to the mill and agitated among those scheduled to work the night shift, such as the forty-five-year-old warp drawer Pavel Korotkov. Engaging two Shagov overlookers in conversation, Korotkov learned that the strikers intended to increase their numbers or, at a minimum, to prevent anyone else from working.[21]

Most Nogin workers were sympathetic to the demands made by the Shagov strikers, and 1,500 of them—more than half of those on duty—joined the protest that day. Although most opponents of the job action maintained a low profile, a few spoke out. "Comrade workers from the Shagov Mills," shouted one Communist, "there's nothing for you to do here! We won't join you, and we cast shame on you!" As he spoke, however, a large number of workers poured out of the mill in a show of solidarity. During the next five days, most of the Nogin's production lines lay idle.[22]

When it became clear that the restoration of rations was a universal demand and that most nonparty workers supported the strike, women in the crowd demanded further expansion of the movement: "Comrades, let's go to the [Red Profintern] Mill!" Under the leadership of Iurkin, Komarov, and several of their female colleagues, the crowd of some three thousand strikers marched to the gates of that enterprise, where Iurkin issued an appeal for support:

> Comrades, we'll die from hunger in the fifteenth year of the Revolution, our children will die, and what will we do—be silent? If Stalin were put on a ration of eleven kilograms, then he would probably leave the party. Eleven kilograms don't make sixteen, and four kilograms don't make eight. They lubricate the machine with oil, but what do they lubricate us with? Will the comrades be left behind and not support us?[23]

Most workers responded by abandoning their machines. Even a small number of the Red Profintern's Communists—twenty-nine out of five hundred, to be exact—sided with the strikers. A candidate member of the party, Varentsov, led his coworkers out of the factory after assuring them that their pay would not be docked; another, Zakharov, declared that "all the Communists are self-aggrandizers" who "have forgotten the interests of the working class." Those who stayed behind—typically, either Communists or Komsomols—were beaten with shuttles, and their machines were sabotaged. Eventually, the number of demonstrators outside the mill exceeded five thousand.[24]

In his next speech to the crowd, Iurkin explained why he had joined the strike: "Comrades, I earn 200 rubles, I have a family of two, and no children. I have an adequate supply of bread, but I speak for the workers and the peasants, not for the 'briefcases' and deceivers who drive the workers to the grave." The implicit message—that workers who were not threatened by the reduction in ration levels had an obligation to fight on behalf of those who were—was a pure expression of the community's values. Iurkin understood the risks he was inviting by taking such a stand, but ex-

Figure 11. A weaver and a loom repairman at Vichuga's Red Profintern Mill, 1932. Russian State Archive of Documentary Films and Photographs.

pected the strikers to sacrifice for him just as he did for them: "I know they'll seize me, but I hope you'll support me." Inspired by Iurkin's courage, other speakers vowed that the strike would continue until rations were restored. As for the few who dared condemn the protest, they were subjected—as always—to verbal and physical abuse.[25]

By the end of the day, almost every enterprise in Vichuga was on strike. Flush with pride from their achievement—it had been fifteen years since a general strike crippled Vichuga's mills—several thousand strikers endeavored to expand the protest to the district's only outpost of heavy industry: Machine-Building Plant No. 6 ("the metal factory"), whose 425 male employees fabricated parts for textile equipment. For some reason, however, most of the metalworkers rebuffed attempts to secure their support.[26]

As for Korotkov, he stayed behind at the Nogin Mill with two hundred other strikers, including a fellow warp drawer, Golubev. The demonstrators applauded speeches by a female worker and a fitter, Kostkin, from the Red Profintern Mill, both of whom insisted that management come out and negotiate. The crowd also agitated among those arriving for the night shift, and several who endeavored to enter the mill were beaten. The strikers' calls for negotiations were rebuffed, and by 9:00 PM almost everyone—including those scheduled to work overnight—went home.[27]

After receiving word of the unrest sweeping across one of its most important mill towns, the IIR Party Committee dispatched a team of regional officials, including El'zov, Fomenko, Gribova, Kisel'nikov, Kotsen, and Sever'ianova of the committee's secretariat; Koriagin and Postnova of the party control commission; Semagin of the trade-union council; Andreev and Ivanov of the OGPU; and Novikov and Sulimov of the civil police. After nightfall, the district OGPU bureau—under whose orders is not clear—committed a fateful error when it arrested Iurkin, one of the strikers' most popular spokesmen. This inadvertently increased Iurkin's authority among the strikers and set the stage for a dramatic escalation of the conflict.[28]

Sunday, April 10

The next day, groups of strikers appeared at the gates of the mills before dawn in a coordinated effort to enforce the job action. As usual, anyone who opposed the strike was treated harshly. By 7:00 AM, every loom and spinning frame in Vichuga lay idle. The strikers then turned their attention toward the metalworkers. Although Communists were guarding the entrance to the machine-building plant, strikers somehow penetrated shop floors and cleared them of workers. To avoid "a slaughter," the metal-workers had been ordered not to resist the incursion. Most of them refrained from endorsing the strike, however, and went back to work once repairs to the boiler, which had been sabotaged, were complete.[29]

While the conflict at the machine-building plant was under way, by-standers joined the strike. "It's necessary for me to go," the former trades-man Ignat'ev explained to friends. "As an unemployed person, I'm a member of the committee, you know." Ignat'ev's reference to "the com-mittee" lent credence to Kaganovich's assertion that "the strike was led by an underground organization." As he noted in his report to Stalin: "The character of the speeches, the strikers' slogans, the rapid change of tactics, the . . . composition of the ringleaders—all this testifies to the organized character of the strike."[30]

To the extent that it existed, however, the strike committee was far less sinister than Kaganovich imagined. Essentially, it was an ad hoc and fluid group of individuals who endeavored to give shape to a spontaneous out-burst of popular discontent. More significant, therefore, was another re-mark that was made by Ignat'ev, and that foreshadowed the day's dramatic events: "If they gave us power, then we'd tear all those damned Commu-nists to pieces."[31]

By 10:00 AM, some five thousand workers fulfilled a pledge made to Iurkin the night before and gathered in the square by the city soviet to de-mand the restoration of ration levels. When it became clear that their leader had been arrested, they also demanded his release. Although a false rumor—that a representative from the Central Party Committee would give a speech—generated premature expectations of compromise, the strikers demonstrated their hostility toward local officials by refusing to let any of them speak.[32]

Seeking to regain control of the situation, authorities made a fatal error: they sent in the mounted police. Having fought so hard to gather and demonstrate collectively, the strikers refused to back down; instead, they fought back with objects scavenged from the streets. Overwhelmed, the officers soon fled. Flush with victory, the crowd marched to the Vichuga police station and, in an effort to find Iurkin, laid siege to the building.[33]

After overpowering guards at the entrance, the most active group of strikers confronted the chief of police, Mokhov, with their demand. Frus-trated by the response—that Iurkin was not there and that his where-abouts were unknown—they proceeded to beat up every officer in the building, ransack offices, rummage through arrest files, and search for an entrance to the holding chamber. "What are you looking for?" a bystander asked two young men who led the assault. "Iurkin!" they replied. "He was seen [here] only today!" Eventually, the invaders located and broke into the holding chamber, from which they liberated a group of petty criminals. Since he had already been spirited away to Ivanovo, Iurkin was never found. Their plan foiled, the strikers vented their frustration by smashing windows, tearing down doors and cabinets, and pummeling unconscious both Mokhov and his deputy.[34]

Outside, repeated attempts by the mounted police to disperse the crowd failed. Unwilling to abandon the search for Iurkin, the strikers defended themselves with rocks and sticks. After watching his men sustain "serious injuries," the police commander, Chistiakov, ordered them to pull back to the railroad tracks, and to reassemble at the fire station. They did so, although a junior officer was thrown from his horse during the retreat and beaten unconscious with his own rifle.[35]

Responding to a rumor that "a mass meeting" was under way at the district party committee, the strikers also laid siege to the headquarters of the party and the OGPU, which were situated next to each other in the center of town. The conflict now was as much about visiting vengeance upon the detested organs of authority as it was about locating Iurkin. At the district party committee, workers fulfilled the crowd's battle cry—"Beat the Chekists and the Communists!"—by pummeling the chairman of the district trade-union council, Rybakov, and the head of the IIR Party Committee's Department of Cadres, El'zov. Three other regional officials—Kotsen, Semagin, and Ivanov—fled the building in a panic just before the crowd arrived. Having been aroused from his "sickbed," the secretary of the district party committee, Vorkuev, observed the assault from afar, but made no effort to intervene on his colleagues' behalf.[36]

Still hoping to find their leader, the strikers cornered Itkin, the head of the district OGPU bureau. "Either give us Iurkin," they told him, "or we'll kill you." After talks went nowhere, the crowd ransacked OGPU headquarters and set upon Itkin and his subordinates, several of whom endeavored to burn sensitive files before fleeing. Of all the officials targeted for revenge, Itkin came closest to losing his life. Dragged into the courtyard and beaten with bricks, he fell unconscious from blows to the head. Fortunately, an unidentified worker spirited him to safety, which enabled plainclothes officers to get him into a cab, and then to a hospital.[37]

Meanwhile, a top official from the regional OGPU bureau, Golubev, "who had arrived in Vichuga the day before," appeared at the fire station and ordered the mounted police who had reassembled there to retake OGPU headquarters and liberate those trapped inside. Arriving at the scene by automobile, ten officers—now under Golubev's direct command—met fierce "resistance" in the form of "a torrent of stones," resulting in "serious injuries." After forcing their way inside and drawing their weapons, they managed to clear the building and secure the gates to the courtyard.[38]

Incensed by their treatment at the hands of these officers, the strikers "surrounded the building from all sides," bombarded those standing in the courtyard with bricks, and began to ram the gates. *"Ura!"* they shouted. With only moments to spare before again losing control of the building, Golubev ordered his men to fire their weapons into the air. Startled, the crowd pulled back. Seizing the moment, Golubev unlocked the gates and led his men outside. Although one worker lay dead in the street from a bullet wound, neither side backed down. Fearing a renewed assault on the building and dodging projectiles, Golubev permitted his men to continue firing. Either out of fear or a desire to avenge their fallen colleagues, the officers now aimed their guns directly at the crowd. Shots rang out, several more workers fell to the ground, and the crowd fled for cover.[39]

By 4:30 PM, Golubev's men had retaken all of Vichuga's administrative buildings. The strikers quickly regrouped in the square by the city soviet, at the train station, in cafeterias, and at the mills, where they drove clusters of strikebreakers from the shop floor and beat up Communists, Komsomols, and "even nonparty women" whose red scarves led some to suspect that they were party members. In an attempt to gain support from workers in other districts and to deprive the authorities of communications with Ivanovo and Moscow, they also endeavored to occupy the post office. When this failed, they dispatched delegations to nearby mill towns and ingeniously found a way to tap into local telegraph cables.[40]

After a meeting in the forest that evening, the workers again descended on the mills, where they cleared shop floors of strikebreakers, pummeled party loyalists, plundered supplies, and—in a daring move that required penetration of several lines of defense—sabotaged the boilers that powered production lines. Later, eight members of "the strike committee"—including the timekeeper and former party member Mironov of Shagov Mill No. 1—debated strategy at the home of his colleague, the flyer-frame spinner Surova. After settling on a plan of action for the next day, they dispersed, at 2:00 AM.[41]

Within a matter of days, a strike whose goal was economic had turned into what IIR officials called "political banditism" and a witness described as "a full-fledged revolt" against the guarantors of order: the party, the OGPU, and the civil police. The arrest of Iurkin, which the authorities later admitted was "a tactical mistake," infuriated the workers and gave the boldest and most discontent among them a pretext for escalation. Members of the social groups that the authorities referred to as "class-alien and hooligan elements"—*lishentsy*, the unemployed, petty criminals, and so on—contributed to the radicalization of the strike by engaging in extraordinary acts of trespass and assault. Most of the protesters were mill hands, however, and it was *their* rage that fueled the four-and-a-half-hour riot.[42]

As Kaganovich conceded in his report to Stalin, the strikers' choice of targets was "significant." They understood who wielded power in the community, hence were responsible for their suffering. At the same time—and the point is crucial—"Soviet power" was a governing ideal to which they were committed. As strike leaders explained two days later: "We aren't against the soviets. We gather[ed] on the square by the city soviet, and we sent a telegram to the Central Soviet Executive Committee. We didn't destroy the soviet, but [rather] the OGPU, the civil police, and the district party committee."[43]

This point requires elaboration. A crucial principle of the October Revolution was that workers' affairs should be managed by local soviets over which the workers had electoral control. Although Lenin subordinated the soviets to central authority after seizing power, many of the deputies who served on them were still chosen by popular vote. By targeting for destruction the institutions that imposed central mandates on the shop floor—the party, the civil police, and the OGPU—the Vichuga strikers eloquently conveyed their desire for a government that would be responsive to their needs. The uprising thus was not, strictly speaking, "anti-Soviet," as the official narrative would maintain, but rather pro-Soviet and anti-party. This was a combination that Moscow dared not admit was even possible, but it made perfect sense to the workers, whose actions were shaped as much by the party's violation of the Revolution's promise of "all power to the soviets" as by its disregard for the values of their moral economy.

A tally of the victims illustrates the extent of the violence that descended on Vichuga that day. Of the thirty to sixty rounds of ammunition fired by the officers under Golubev's command, three broke flesh. The worker Polunin, who had a wife and child, died immediately; Dolgov, a twenty-five-year-old unskilled laborer at the Nogin Mill's storage shed, succumbed to a blood infection while being treated at the hospital for a thigh wound; and a female worker suffered a slight grazing.[44] Among the forces of order, the casualties were more numerous: about thirty individuals, including half a dozen officials, sustained broken ribs, fractured skulls, and burst eardrums. As for those who had endeavored to keep production lines running, thus far seventy-two had been assaulted.[45]

If they had been unaware of it before, regional leaders came to understand how profoundly the workers detested their superiors. No sooner had they arrived in Vichuga when they found it necessary to beat a series of retreats. After learning that the strikers were headed for the center of town, they fled from district party committee headquarters to the Red Profintern Mill. Then, upon hearing that a crowd was gathering nearby, they raced to the machine-building plant, whose shop floors remained immune to the calls for resistance.[46]

To be fair, the highest-ranking official in Vichuga—Kotsen, the IIR Party Committee's second-in-command—struggled to recapture the initiative as the chaos unfolded around him. In response to the clashes, for example, he ordered the district military commissar to mobilize "a detachment of 300 Communists," and the OGPU "to rescue" his colleague, El'zov, who was stranded at district party headquarters.[47] Kotsen's decisiveness could not compensate for the fact that the organs of authority were in disarray. With almost nobody from the local establishment to assist him and almost nothing beyond "imprecise and exaggerated 'street' rumors" to guide his actions, he found it impossible to effectively deploy the resources at his disposal.[48]

Notwithstanding the turmoil, Kotsen did receive a reliable report that afternoon: the OGPU was in possession of a worker's bloody corpse. Realizing that the body could become a totem of the revolt, he ordered the security police to convey it secretly to the train station. Hoping to avert further bloodshed, he also instructed the civil police to pull back.[49]

An hour later, Kotsen himself headed to the station. On the way, he stopped at the semaphore for an emergency meeting of rank-and-file Communists. Although he forbade further applications of force against the strikers, he responded to a report that a crowd was approaching by ordering armed Communists to remain at his side. The others were told to go home and await further instructions.[50]

Moments later, Kotsen arrived at the Vichuga Station with his armed defenders, commandeered a train, and oversaw the removal of the "carefully wrapped" corpse from a delivery truck. The body was spirited into a makeshift coffin and onto the train. Loaded with corpse, armed Communists, and four high-ranking officials (Kotsen, Ivanov, Semagin, and Kisel'nikov), the train departed shortly after 5:00 PM for Gorkino, a village situated twenty kilometers west of town.[51]

From Moscow's point of view, Kotsen's actions would have been acceptable had he communicated his plan to those left behind. His failure to do so left the demoralizing impression that he "had retreated," thereby leaving "the district without leadership" at the height of the crisis. In Kotsen's defense, his intention had always been to return to Vichuga as soon as possible. He thus detached his car from the train once it reached Gorkino, ordered the conductor to convey the corpse to Ivanovo, and waited for the arrival, via Kostroma, of a "special train" of reinforcements. When that train pulled into the station a short while later, Kotsen breathed a sigh of relief, for inside its many cars were 450 fresh civil police troops and seventeen OGPU officers. Shortly after 9:00 PM, he returned with these reinforcements to Vichuga, convened an emergency session of the district party committee, and hammered out a plan to retake the town from the strikers.[52]

Monday, April 11

The next morning, a handful of workers who opposed the strike again came into conflict with strikers who were monitoring the entrances to the mills, and it was not long before production lines ground to a halt. At 9:00 AM, some two thousand strikers gathered on the square by the city soviet and demanded that the day's meeting begin and that a course of action be approved. Most of the speakers consisted of strikers who denounced the new ration levels. "We won't go to work until our demands are fulfilled!" they shouted. Several local and regional party leaders also endeavored to address the crowd.[53]

Around 1:00 PM, an official from Ivanovo announced from a balcony overlooking the square that concessions would not be forthcoming until everyone went back to work. The strikers rebuffed him—"Give a clear answer! What will you give us?" they demanded—and turned their attention to a weaver who recounted her latest experience of administrative callousness. A group of Shagov workers, she claimed, summoned the chairman of the cooperative and complained about the new ration levels. Instead of addressing their concerns, however, the official sarcastically dismissed them:

"What sort of famine is *this*," he retorted, "if we aren't eating our own children yet?" Her story provoked cries of indignation.[54]

During his speech to the crowd, Korotkov ridiculed a portly official from Ivanovo: "The comrades have brought about nothing good at all. Look at him (I pointed to the regional comrade). He's well fed, but we and our families are starving. Why shouldn't we yell at him? They get by and aren't as exhausted as the worker." A witness claimed that Korotkov threatened violence during this same official's speech—"Down with him! Drag him off the rostrum! We should tear him to pieces!"—and told the crowd to go to the machine-building plant to make another effort to win support from the metalworkers. Other inflammatory speeches by strikers ensued. The crowd responded by ignoring calls for order and refusing to let any other officials speak.[55]

Eventually, the deputy chairman of the district soviet executive committee, Smirnov, managed to win the crowd's attention with a proposal that a commission be elected "to settle the conflict." Smirnov turned the podium over to an official from Ivanovo, who explained in a conciliatory manner that the commission would be allowed to investigate local food-supply organizations. In an overt appeal to the sentiments of the predominantly female labor force, he also promised an investigation of the nurseries, the quality of which was abysmal.[56]

A long debate ensued, but the strikers found it impossible to overcome their distrust of the organs of authority. "A series of speakers," noted an OGPU report, "insisted that proposals being put forth by representatives of party and soviet organizations not be accepted, and that [the workers] not go to work until all [their] demands were fulfilled." A suggestion that the strikers send a delegation to Moscow—made by the recently "recovered" secretary of the district party committee, Vorkuev—likewise was rejected. Having fought to meet collectively, the strikers were unwilling to risk having their movement decapitated. "We'll withdraw everyone from work," they declared, and "we're going to discuss everything together."[57]

Like their counterparts in Teikovo, the Vichuga strikers were convinced by years of experience that promises from their immediate superiors could not be trusted. Their only option in the face of the current crisis, therefore, was to win a commitment of change directly from Moscow.

After waiting for a group of strikers to return from the Nogin Mill, where they drove strikebreakers from the shop floor, the crowd elected an ad hoc commission consisting of three women and two men, who subsequently withdrew to the offices of the district soviet executive committee to draft an appeal to USSR President Mikhail Kalinin. Apparently, there was some disagreement over the wording, for the male commission members stepped down and had to be replaced. Eventually, the reconstituted commission completed its task, returned to the square, and submitted the text to the crowd. It was read by Smirnov of the district soviet executive committee, whose voice carried well and who was well-regarded in the community. At 7:00 PM, the strikers voted to transmit their appeal to Moscow. As commission members rushed to the post office to complete their mission, speakers called on their fellow strikers to stand firm until their demands were met. Gradually, the crowd dispersed.[58]

The telegram that arrived in Moscow several hours later was succinct, graphic, and insistent:

> [To: President Kalinin,] Central Soviet Executive Committee. As a result of the reduction of the food ration, the mass of 15,000 workers has left their factories and ceased work for five days now. The laboring mass has clashed with the police and the organs of the OGPU, where a bloody clash—with several woundings and victims—has taken place. The workers demand that three representatives from the Central Soviet Executive Committee come immediately to the site for settlement of the present conflict. Work has been discontinued until your departure. Of the workers who have given speeches, one comrade Iurkin has been seized. The masses demand his immediate release.
>
> Signed: Bol'shakov (Shagov Mill No. 3), Obukhov, Golubev (Nogin Mill), Kostkin (Red Profintern Mill).[59]

That evening, while awaiting a response to the telegram, members of "the strike committee" convened in the home of the spinner Surova. Nearby, rural communities in which some of the strikers resided began to stir. "Tomorrow . . . the peasants from neighboring villages intend to go to Vichuga to demand bread," a peasant woman selling milk at a bazaar told customers. "We've already sent delegates to Fediaevo to teach the chairman of the village soviet a lesson. The trouble is, we don't have any weapons. We'll have to go with just pitchforks and axes."[60]

Tuesday, April 12

After a night of hasty preparations intended to jump-start production and undermine the strikers' solidarity, management opened the gates of Vichuga's mills at 5:00 AM the next day. Exhausted by a week of demonstrations, 30 to 40 percent of those scheduled to work the morning shift reported to their posts. Efforts to enforce the job action quickly cut this figure in half. During the second shift, staffing levels reached no more than 15 to 20 percent.[61]

Although "all the streets were filled to overflowing with agitated workers," the tide was turning in favor of the authorities. Kotsen ordered the troops under his command to enforce an overnight curfew. Kaganovich, who arrived at 9:30 AM, instructed these same troops to encircle the town. Meanwhile, dozens of OGPU officers set about securing state property, infiltrating the crowd, and combating "strike moods" in nearby collective farms. By blocking access to Vichuga, the authorities inadvertently delayed delivery of supplies to the mills, making it more difficult for production lines to get up and running. However, they achieved their goal of preventing supporters of the IIR strike wave from reaching its capital.[62]

Despite the effectiveness of such measures, it was too late to completely isolate the rebellious workers. As Kaganovich conceded in his report to Stalin:

> The Vichuga strikers were in contact with other districts. They wrote letters . . . and sent . . . representatives. In turn, people came to Vichuga in large groups from other mills and districts—"To study how to do this." On the day of our arrival, April 12, dozens of visitors with suitcases walked about Vichuga. All of them attended our speech at the club. There were many railroad workers in the crowd.

As if support for the strike among employees of the transportation sector was not alarming enough, some workers now were intensifying their agitation among the peasantry.[63]

Buoyed by the support of neighboring communities, Vichuga's workers chose not to be intimidated by the forces arrayed against them. In a reversal of the events of the strike's early days, a crowd of Nogin and Red Profintern workers marched to the Shagov Amalgamated Mill. Although Communists and Komsomols blocked the entrance to two of the Shagov enterprises, strikers penetrated Mill No. 3, whose shop floors emptied for the second time in five days. Other strikers responded to a rumor that Iurkin had been freed and was hiding in his apartment by heading to the nearby settlement of Gol'chikha. Before leaving town, they vowed to descend on the police station and OGPU headquarters again should their leader not be found.[64]

Eager to rally the faithful, Kaganovich spent the first part of the day meeting with workers who had reported to their posts at the Nogin Mill. Accompanying him were three notables: Isidor Liubimov, the USSR Commissar of Light Industry; Ivan Nosov, the recently appointed secretary of the IIR Party Committee; and an official from the trust that supervised Vichuga's mills.[65]

Although the workers with whom Kaganovich met had remained aloof from the strike, they sympathized with the demands made by their colleagues in the town square. Kaganovich summarized his impressions for Stalin:

> We listened attentively, and the workers who spoke out complained about outrages with regard to provisions. A portion of the women workers cried hysterically . . . The discontent was divided among a series of sore points, and mainly the shortages taking place because of bungling by local organs.

While Kaganovich took the measure of the strikebreakers, leaders of the strike gave voice to their distrust of the party's second-in-command. "There's no point listening" to Kaganovich, argued the Nogin operative Obukhov, because he was "a Jew."[66] The remark was significant not because of its anti-Semitism, but because it laid bare the disappointment that the strikers felt on discovering that it was not a top official of "our" (Soviet) government but of "their" party who had come from Moscow to address them. Kaganovich's ethnicity only confirmed his untrustworthiness, the fundamental source of which, from the shop floor's perspective, was his position of leadership in the party.

Skeptical but with nowhere else to turn for help, some one thousand workers gathered on the square by the city soviet to wait for Kaganovich to speak. At 11:00 AM, an official from the district soviet executive committee announced that Kaganovich's only public appearance would take place at the Nogin Mill. When the crowd arrived there a short while later, the police refused to open the gates. Fearing a trap, some of the women panicked, but Korotkov calmed them down: "Don't be afraid," he told them, "they won't shoot." When Kaganovich emerged an hour later from his meeting with the strikebreakers, he found before him a crowd of three thousand to four thousand impatient workers.[67]

Unable to make himself heard from where he was standing, Kaganovich led the strikers to the workers' club, from whose steps he and Liubimov spoke for ten minutes. Their remarks were by turns defensive, reprimand-ing, conciliatory, and exhortatory. First, they justified the reduction in ra-tion levels as a necessary but temporary measure dictated by circumstances beyond the party's control. Second, they rebuked the workers for endeav-oring to fulfill their goals by withdrawing their labor, committing "assault and battery," and laying siege to "Soviet institutions." Third, they prom-ised that all complaints would be addressed at the level of the enterprise and at a special citywide conference. Finally, they ordered the crowd "to disperse and go back to work."[68]

The strikers were not satisfied. Although they "listened very attentively" to what Kaganovich and Liubimov had to say, their own spokesmen en-deavored to respond. Kaganovich would have none of this, and after con-demning the attempt "to conduct a meeting . . . on the street," he and Liubimov fled into the club. What were the strikers to do? On one hand, their fundamental demand had been rejected; on the other, they had the attention of the men who made policy and a promise that their grievances would be addressed. Moreover, the mills—and Vichuga itself—were sur-rounded by well-armed troops. Weighing the options—compliance with Kaganovich's order in the hope that somehow their suffering would be al-leviated, or further resistance that could end only in tragedy—most strik-ers chose the former. Kaganovich's speech and the overwhelming display of force thus produced the intended effect: the Vichuga strikers dispersed for the last time.[69]

Having generated "a turning-point" in the crisis—65 to 85 percent of the workers scheduled to work in the mills that night reported to their posts—Kaganovich set about doing all he could to retain the initiative: he mobi-lized rank-and-file Communists, dispatched plenipotentiaries to the mills and agitators to the barracks, and arranged for workers to air their com-plaints in supervised assemblies. He also convened evening conferences at-tended by more than one thousand workers, to whom he gave assurances that food supplies would improve, and from whom he accepted petitions. He ended the day by chairing a session of the district party committee, with whom he reviewed the latest intelligence from the region.[70]

Wednesday, April 13, to Friday, April 15

Vichuga's mills were scheduled to rest on April 13, so Kaganovich spent the day rallying rank-and-file Communists and thanking the metalworkers for their opposition to the strike. The next morning, he proudly informed

Stalin that "the first shift is working normally," and that shop floors were staffed at "close to 100 percent." Subsequent shifts also went smoothly. Remarkably, the only incident reported that day was "a small hitch" at the nearby Kamenka Mill—"but it was quickly settled."[71]

At 2:00 PM on April 14, Kaganovich, Liubimov, and Nosov attended a joint conference of the city soviet and the district trade-unions council, where they addressed an audience of seven hundred functionaries and eight hundred worker-delegates.[72] The handful of workers who were permitted to speak from the podium echoed the official line as enunciated by Kaganovich in closed party assemblies: the strike was wrong, and it never would have occurred had it not been for "the abominable work" of local officials. More indicative of the shop floor's mood, however, were the *anonimki* that demanded execution of "those who shot into the crowd," raged against the "impossible" supply situation, expressed resentment that workers in the regions were supplied more poorly than those in "the center," appealed for the restoration of private trade, and warned of the bitterness in towns and villages alike.[73]

The conference's official resolution—drafted, apparently, by Kaganovich—endeavored to fulfill several goals. By promising "a radical restructuring" of local supply organizations, it tried to take the edge off the workers' discontent. By characterizing the leaders of the strike as "enemies of Soviet power," it communicated to anyone who would follow their example that the consequences of doing so would be severe. And by calling on operatives to support the party's economic program and to embrace state policies at the point of production, it showed them how they might overcome the stain that their actions left—at least from the official point of view—on their "glorious revolutionary traditions."[74]

Given that shop-floor morale could not have gotten much worse at this point—"hunger rations" were still in place and unarmed strikers had only four days before been mowed down in the streets—Kaganovich probably was not just flattering himself when he informed Stalin that delegates left the conference "in an uplifted mood." But this did not mean that the workers were now more willing to trust the party. As far as the crucial issue of the day—food supplies—was concerned, skepticism prevailed. "Will the shortcomings that were disclosed be eliminated?" delegates asked one another. "We'll see how things change," came the response.[75]

Having learned a lesson from the ham-handed arrest of Iurkin, party cells flooded shop floors with denunciations of the strike's "ringleaders," thereby setting the stage for a roundup by the security police. On the night of April 14–15, fifteen individuals were arrested. Sixteen others, including Korotkov and Nikitin, were taken into custody shortly thereafter. As usual, the OGPU targeted individuals from the most vulnerable social groups: ex-Communists who had records of "deviation"; former Socialist-Revolutionaries and anarchists; *lishentsy;* and others from the universe of "class-alien elements" who were blamed for leading Vichuga's "unenlightened" workers down the path of rebellion.[76]

During the next few weeks, the OGPU interrogated its prisoners and deposed dozens of witnesses. In June, indictments were filed under Articles 58 and 59 of the Criminal Code. Convictions were handed down by an OGPU court the following month: eight defendants deemed "fit for physical labor," including Korotkov, were sent to labor camps; twenty-four others, including Nikitin, were exiled. Most of the sentences carried a term of three years.[77]

Following months of scattered protests against the consequences of Stalin's revolution "from above," the situation in Vichuga's mills was "tense," and the prevailing mood was one of "depression." When "hunger" rations were implemented in April 1932, shop floors erupted in rebellion. The strike was small at first, but distinguished itself from earlier episodes of unrest by expanding in size. On April 6, 15 percent of Shagov Amalgamated Mill weavers idled their looms, and within several days, almost all of Vichuga's 17,500 cotton workers were on strike.[78] The protest gained momentum for three reasons: first, because the shop floor's discontent was deep;[79] second, because the leaders of the protest included effective organizers; and finally, because the reduction in ration levels posed a threat to the fundamental interests of the working-class community.

As a rule, official responses exacerbated the conflict: the refusal to convene all-factory assemblies or to negotiate with the strikers inflamed popular sentiment; the desertion of their posts by key officials meant that an effective strategy could not be implemented once the strike got under way; the arrest of the strike leader Iurkin provoked a violent reaction from the crowd; and when rank-and-file Communists were mobilized for duty by the IIR Party Committee's second-in-command, a key line of defense was withdrawn from the mills. By all accounts, the authorities' behavior was deficient. "We [made] the most flagrant errors," conceded a local official, "not only from a political standpoint, but from a tactical one as well." If nothing else, the panic that swept their ranks exposed their alienation from the class whose interests they claimed to represent. "During the strike," recalled a Communist from the Nogin Mill, "party and soviet leaders became afraid of the workers: they hid beneath tables and behind corners." The violent clash between strikers and the police generated an unprecedented collapse of authority. For a terrifying moment, noted the chairman of the IIR Soviet Executive Committee, "there was no Soviet power in Vichuga."[80]

This was a statement with which the strikers would have disagreed. After all, they had consciously spared the city soviet even as they sacked the headquarters of the party and its organs of enforcement. The distinctions they drew as they engaged in mass violence were crucial, just as the meaning of their actions was indisputable. Soviet power, for which the workers had sacrificed so much and which they understood to mean a government that was subject to their control and responsive to their needs, was not the problem. Rather, it was the solution to the problem they now faced: the party had usurped their voice and sacrificed their interests to its own.

Kaganovich, for one, got the message—and immediately endeavored to obfuscate its subversive content. Ignoring evidence gathered by the OGPU, he made certain that the city soviet conference of April 14 branded as "enemies of Soviet power" those who had spearheaded the rebellion. Like Klepikov and Liulin before them, these individuals had to be so labeled—and, ultimately, silenced—because their opposition to the party in the name of Soviet power posed a fundamental threat to the dictatorship's claim to legitimacy.[81]

The Vichuga strike was the largest to occur in the IIR in April 1932. Not only the number of demonstrators, but also the violence—carried out by individuals on both sides of the conflict—made it stand out. Although force, or at least the threat of force, was a factor in other episodes of unrest that month, only in Vichuga did it play as significant a role as speech in the interaction between workers and the state: it was used by Shagov workers who sought to bring production lines to a halt; by mounted officers who attempted to disperse peaceful demonstrators; and again by workers who sought to liberate their leader from prison. A teacher who was prevented by strikers from reporting to her post recalled their destructive rage: "My God, they spared nothing." The sabotaged looms and boilers, the piles of rocks and broken glass on the streets—and most poignantly, a worker's bloody corpse—were nothing if not the bitter harvest of Stalin's revolution "from above." The party's immediate response: a curfew and a cordon of troops, whose siege prevented outside support from reaching the strikers and the virus of rebellion from spreading to several adjacent mill towns.[82]

If the violence was purposive, it also was richly symbolic. The attack on peaceful demonstrators by mounted officers evoked bitter memories of the prerevolutionary era—and, not surprisingly, provoked an extraordinary response from below. During their attempt to find Iurkin—the charismatic warp drawer and former Communist from the Nogin Mill who served as their spokesman—the workers took vengeance on those who had so often humiliated them.

Still, it was only a minority of workers—and an undetermined number of malcontents from other strata of the population—who engaged in violence. As for the rest, they stepped back from the precipice of April 10 and focused on the singular goal of the protest: to restore rations to their previous levels. If the Teikovo workers moved in a radical direction—toward a "hunger march"—after determining that their voices were being ignored, Vichuga's retreated from the radicalism of mass violence after discovering that the center apparently had answered the call for help.

By choosing to obey Kaganovich's request that they go back to work, the strikers laid bare their understanding of the political circumstances in which they found themselves: the only hope of alleviating their misery was to persuade the center to modify its economic program. It had been gratifying to realize—if only briefly, and at the local level—the popular fantasy of Soviet power without the dictatorship of the party. Unfortunately, however, the workers could not feed this fantasy to their children. Only a strategy calibrated to the reality of the party's seemingly firm grip on power would maximize the strike wave's chances of success. Popular hostility thus was channeled against those who implemented policy, and hopes for improvement were projected onto those who authored—and had the power to change—policy. This strategy bore fruit.

Conclusion

The Central Party Committee delivered its report on the April 1932 strike wave to Stalin shortly after Kaganovich returned to Moscow. The conclusion was sobering:

> The events that took place in . . . Vichuga and Teikovo . . . from the seventh to the sixteenth of April—the strike by workers, the merciless beating of the civil police, the raid on the OGPU and the . . . district party committee, the organization of a "hunger march" to Ivanovo, the effort to exert influence on the countryside (the exodus from collective farms), the breaking of looms, the cutting of warp, the merciless beating, with shuttles, of the workers who continued to work— have graphically disclosed the alienation of the party organization from the laboring masses and the most serious shortcomings in the sociocultural and political servicing of the workers, which were exploited in public demonstrations by anti-Soviet elements.

Correctly interpreting the strike wave as evidence of alienation between workers and the regime, leaders such as Central Party Control Commission Secretary Emel'ian Iaroslavskii "attached great political significance" to it. Nonetheless, blame for the crisis was deflected from its root cause. As Iaroslavskii insisted in a post-strike address to Vichuga Communists, some of whom continued "to justify these events" even a month after their suppression: "The policy of the party and the Soviet government is absolutely correct and must not give rise to any doubts."[1]

If Moscow was not to blame for what even Iaroslavskii conceded had been "an extraordinarily grave blow for our party [and] for the proletarian dictatorship," who was? The usual suspects, of course. By willfully ignoring the needs of the workers, squandering the supposedly ample resources at their disposal, and failing to notice that "the debris of counterrevolutionary parties . . . endeavored to lay a nest for themselves and organize protests against . . . the Soviet regime," officials in the towns where the strikes occurred had demonstrated their lack of fitness to govern. So they were sacked and publicly humiliated to boot.[2]

While there was no acknowledgment of policy failure, the strike wave of April 1932 put urban living standards at the top of the party's agenda.[3] The Politburo took a number of steps immediately. First, it authorized the use of emergency grain stocks to fulfill ration commitments to workers and earmarked the summer grain harvest for "industrial centers and the army." Second, it implemented startling neo-NEP reforms—including the May 1932 reduction in requisitioning quotas and the legalization of collective farm markets—in a desperate effort to coax more produce out of the peasantry. Finally, it abandoned the "fantastic planning" that had caused so much suffering in working-class communities.[4]

Although the neo-NEP reforms of 1932 were overlaid with another round of coercive measures in the village, the shift "towards realistic planning" was a permanent one whose explicit goal, and eventual achievement, was to improve living standards.[5] In the meantime, however, there was tragedy in the form of mass famine to endure. As the party averted its gaze from the horrible harvest of its policies in the village, it relied on carrots and sticks to contain discontent in the city. By and large, such measures were effective: the Great Famine of 1932–1933 bypassed centers of industry, and the party was spared a repeat of the severe labor unrest of April 1932.[6]

Shop-floor discontent was widespread during the FFYP, and labor unrest was reported in most, if not all, sectors of the economy. That the IIR became the epicenter of worker resistance to Stalin's revolution "from above" was due to a unique combination of factors.[7] Most important was that the IIR was a locus of textile manufacturing. No industry was squeezed harder for funds or paid a higher price for Stalinist industrialization. The burden on textile workers thus was heavier even as compensation in the form of wages and rations was lower.

That no industry had a higher proportion of women on the shop floor also was important. Russian working-class women were disproportionately burdened by domestic responsibilities that made them acutely sensitive to food shortages and elevated workloads. At the same time, they enjoyed more license than men to engage in acts of protest without enduring dismissal or arrest. The gender profile of the labor force meant also that no industry had a lower rate of party affiliation or literacy. The regime's mechanisms of influence and control thus were weaker in textiles than in other, particularly male-dominated, branches of industry.

The exceptional stability of the industry's labor force was another important factor. During the FFYP, employment more than doubled in heavy industry even as it declined by 15.6 percent in Soviet cotton and linen mills.[8] IIR shop floors thus were less diluted with raw recruits from the countryside, which left veteran workers in a commanding position. Such individuals had workplace traditions and routines to defend, knowledge of how to defend these collectively, and a social identity that endowed them with authority to resist.

That the labor force was experienced was crucial. A majority of IIR operatives were veterans who had been at the bench since at least 1917. These workers initially supported the Bolsheviks because they perceived in Lenin's program a solution to the social antagonisms that offended their dignity and the economic crisis that threatened their well-being. Most also participated in the general strike that swept the region during the autumn of 1917 and facilitated the party's rise to power. The IIR thus was populated with workers who had their own experience and interpretation of the October Revolution, which they claimed as their own. From this sense of ownership sprang the conviction that it was their obligation to pass judgment on those piloting the Revolution in their name.[9]

The judgment was severe. If nothing else, workers expected the party to provide them with a better living standard, fewer burdens on and off the shop floor, and a measure of shop-floor democracy. Chronic bread shortages, mounting wage arrears, sharply elevated workloads, the Taylorist (dis)organization of production, persecution for expressing legitimate grievances—this was not what they had bargained for. Nor was there enthusiasm for new factories—even those in which they or their own children might one day work—so long as these came at such a heavy price. "The [industrial] 'giants' are for those who want to show off to the planet," an employee of Ivanovo's Mixed Yarn Combine declared at an assembly held to discuss the April 1932 strike wave. "We workers lived better before."[10]

The textile industry also was vulnerable because it employed an unusually high proportion of single-parent families, which were hit harder than their traditional counterparts by the collapse of living standards. No stratum of the shop floor was spared the suffering, however, so mothers—whether single, widowed, or married—were never alone in demanding that their children be liberated from the despotic rule of "Tsar Hunger."[11] The perception of a threat to the working-class family's fundamental interests tended to unite, if fleetingly, the sexes.

Also crucial was that the capital of the IIR was Ivanovo rather than Moscow or Leningrad. The Bolsheviks understood that labor unrest in either of the latter two cities would humiliate them in the eyes of Western diplomats and journalists, even if it fell short of having regime-changing consequences. As a result, they made certain that ration levels were higher—and the forces of order more visible—in the center than in the regions. The strategy was effective: shop-floor unrest was more common in the IIR than in either of the only two provinces—those whose capitals were Moscow and Leningrad—that surpassed the IIR in terms of the level of industrial employment.[12]

The moral economy of the Russian textile worker dictated a collective response to Stalin's revolution "from above," which from the perspective of the shop floor appeared to be nothing less than an incomprehensible conspiracy by the party to shatter the workers' living standard. But it was the language of class that gave meaning on shop floors to the experience of exploitation and immiserization, and that mobilized workers to act collectively in defense of their interests. To be sure, divisions within the labor force—among the various crafts, between "peasant" workers and "proletarians," between locals and recent migrants, between workers in second-tier mill towns and the regional capital—surfaced from time to time. As crisis gave way to crisis and the conditions of work and daily life deteriorated, however, the constraints on mobilization imposed by these divisions dissipated. By April 1932, IIR textile workers engaged in collective action as a class, excluding from their collectivity only the tiny minority among them, such as the *lishentsy*, who were perceived to be socially alien.

The solidarity did not endure. Despite everything that so alarmed the IIR Party Committee in the aftermath of the strike wave—demands that jailed strike leaders be freed; reports that party and nonparty workers approved of the strikes, and that individuals who participated in them "command[ed] great authority" on the shop floor; evidence of explosive resentment toward the elite and its privileged supply network; inflammatory rumors that one enterprise or another had secured higher rations by launching a strike, or that the OGPU filled "five rail cars" with "corpses" after opening fire in Vichuga; threats of further strikes, riots, and "hunger march[es]"; the dispatch to Moscow of protest delegations; testimony from a Viazniki official that "up to half the workers" were "opposed to the policies of . . . the party"; a warning from a Pistsovo Communist that "the workers and the peasants" were vowing to "turn [their] bayonets against the Soviet regime" should war break out—despite all this, the labor force began to (re)fragment.[13]

The causes were multiple. First, political repression deprived shop floors of their most effective leaders, and conveyed to those who would fill their shoes that a high price would be paid for doing so. Second, the experience profile of the labor force changed, as veteran workers quit, retired, or passed away, and as raw recruits took their place.[14] Third, the partial recovery of living standards after 1933—itself a consequence of Moscow's shift "towards realistic planning" in the months following the strike wave—answered the shop floor's basic demand. Finally, the security police became more effective at monitoring the population and nipping dissent in the bud.[15]

The outcome of the October Revolution was settled by 1937, at which point the party deployed political terror to complete the monopolization of its meaning. It could not have been a coincidence that one of the first regional party apparatuses to endure a mass purge was the one headquartered in Ivanovo, or that Stalin delegated supervision of the purge there to Kaganovich.[16] His assignment: to definitively absolve the revolution "from above" of responsibility for the great wave of worker resistance that swept across IIR shop floors during the FFYP, and that Kaganovich himself played a crucial role in suppressing.

On August 1, 1937, Kaganovich launched the Ivanovo purge by delivering a momentous address to a special plenum of the regional party committee. Its climax featured the presentation of startling new evidence from a recent "confession" by Nikolai Kolotilov, who had been the secretary of that organization from 1929 to early 1932. According to Kaganovich, Kolotilov admitted to having received orders in 1928 from Mikhail Tomskii, the former chairman of the Central Council of Trade Unions and leader of the Right Opposition, to turn the IIR into "a pillar of the rightists in the struggle against the Central Party Committee." Infected with "antiparty moods" himself, and eager to stymie Soviet industrialization, Kolotilov immediately set about sowing "discontent" on the region's shop floors. His pièce de résistance: the strike wave of April 1932, which the former regional party leader admitted to having organized by planting "anti-Soviet kulak elements" and creating "artificial" food shortages in the mills.[17]

Kaganovich's address made clear that Moscow's original interpretation of the strike wave had been superseded: the unrest was not the result of incompetence at the local level, but of a conspiracy by highly placed class enemies to provoke popular "discontent with the [party's] policy."[18] It had taken five years to unmask the conspirators, but at least revolutionary justice could now be served. And so it was, in the days and weeks that followed, in dark basements and secluded forests of the "calico republic."

Retribution was the explicit goal, but there was an implicit one as well: to eliminate a stratum of officials who might one day endeavor to rehabilitate themselves before the party by challenging this latest falsification of the history of Stalin's revolution "from above." But if Kolotilov and others whose task it had been to suppress worker resistance had to be annihilated because of what they knew, so also did those who had spearheaded this resistance and now refused to cooperate in the suppression of its memory. Thus was Teikovo strike leader Vasilii Shishkin, who settled with his family in Ivanovo after returning from exile in Kazakhstan, also swept up in the Great Terror. Among his "crimes": having dared relate the events of April 1932 to fellow convicts.[19]

The goal of this book has been to restore to the historical record the great wave of worker resistance that swept across the IIR during the FFYP, and whose meaning the party endeavored to distort beyond recognition. The story is important because it demonstrates that Stalin's revolution "from above" was perceived by workers to be a betrayal of the October Revolution. It also is important in that it underscores the capacity of workers living under Communism to locate within official ideology the symbolic basis for opposition to policies deemed to be inimical to their interests. Although the party made a total claim on society's human and material resources, it failed to monopolize the language of class, let alone the processes of identity construction. To the list of reasons that Communism perished before the end of the century in which it first came to power must be added this failure. And to the list of Communism's fatal flaws must be added the paradox that its legitimacy derived from an ideology that, when (re)appropriated by the workers themselves, subverted the intention and authority of the party that ruled in their name.[20]

Appendix:
How Cloth Was Manufactured

Operatives in Soviet textile mills were organized into fairly stable work teams, each of which was supervised by an overlooker (Figure 7, page 128), a veteran male operative who had worked his way up through the ranks. Just above the overlooker stood the first (lowest) level of management—the foreman, who in turn reported to the shed's director. Besides overlookers, operatives employed throughout the mill included repairmen (Figure 11, page 214), machinists, lathe operators, fitters, greasers, luggers, and cleaners.[1]

Raw fiber passes through three stages—spinning, weaving, and finishing—on its way to becoming cloth. The manufacturing process in Soviet mills began in the initial processing room of the spinning shed, where bale breakers operated a machine that broke apart bundles of raw cotton. Picker tenders then fed the cotton into a series of pickers that removed impurities and pressed what was left into a thick sheet, or lap. Card tenders (Figure 8, page 145) then fed the laps into a machine that combed the fibers and, once these were aligned, pressed them into a rope, or sliver.

When initial processing was complete, barrels of sliver were delivered to the preparatory department, where drawing-frame tenders fed the slivers into machines, or frames, that squeezed and stretched them to further align the fibers. Once drawing was complete, the slivers were fed by flyer-frame spinners (Figure 3, page 35) into a series of frames that twisted them to produce a coarse thread, or roving.

The third and final stage of the spinning process took place in the fine spinning hall, where winding-frame tenders (Figure 4, page 39) supervised the transfer of roving onto special bobbins. These bobbins then were loaded by mule spinners and ring-frame spinners onto frames that stretched and twisted the roving to produce a thread suitable for weaving. (Self-acting mule frames produced finer yarn than ring frames, but required

239

more skill and strength to operate.) Assisting the spinners were creelers, who loaded bobbins onto frames; doffers, who removed empty bobbins; and piecers, who repaired broken strands of thread. Once the thread was spun, frames operated by twister tenders gave it another twist.

Bobbins loaded with yarn were now delivered to the weaving shed. Before the yarn could be woven, cylinders, or beams, of warp—the yarn that runs lengthwise in cloth—had to be prepared for the loom. Beam preparation consisted of four steps: winding, warping, slashing, and drawing-in.

In the winding room, cone winders supervised machines that transferred thread from bobbins onto cones. Once the cones were loaded, beam warpers (Figure 5, page 42) placed them on a nonmechanical frame, or creel, in the warping room, and attached the strands of yarn from the creel to a beam mounted at the far end of a warping machine. When all the threads from the creel were in place, the warping machine was activated. By turning the beam in one direction, this machine created warp by coiling hundreds of parallel strands of yarn onto the beam.

After warping, beams were brought to the slashing room, where slasher tenders mounted them onto a machine that strengthened the threads by saturating them with chemicals.

The last preparatory step occurred in the drawing-in room, where the warp beam was attached to removable loom components, including the harness(es) and the reed. Guided by a designer's pattern, a warp drawer now threaded hundreds of yarn strands from the beam through the eyes of each component.

After drawing-in, a warp rigger mounted the assembly consisting of warp beam, harness(es), and reed onto a loom in the weaving hall. Inspections and adjustments were made by a warp tension checker and a loom starter. When everything was set, a weaver (Figures 9, 11, pages 162 and 214) loaded a shuttle containing weft (cross) thread into the loom and pulled the power lever. The shuttle now shot back and forth rapidly—and deafeningly—across the warp threads, creating cloth that coiled automatically onto an empty beam. The task of the weaver was to keep the loom operating until the warp beam was empty. Assisting the weaver in these tasks were smash piecers, who tied broken warp threads together, and battery loaders, who replaced spent shuttles. When the warp thread ran out, the beam of unfinished cloth was taken to the inspection room and examined for defects.

Unfinished cloth had to pass through the finishing shed before it was ready for the end user (typically, a consumer or clothing factory). If the cloth had to be whitened, it was taken to the bleaching room. If color was required, it was taken to the dye works. If a pattern had to be added, it was taken to the printing shop. After dyeing and/or printing, colors were made fast by machines in the steaming room. Besides bleachers, dyers, printers, steamers, and engravers (Figure 6, page 122)—the latter carved designs onto copper rollers used in the printing shop—the finishing shed also employed cloth inspectors and packers.

Archival Sources

APUFSBIaO (Archival Unit of the Iaroslavl Region Bureau of the Federal
Security Service)

APUFSBIO (Archival Unit of the Ivanovo Region Bureau of the Federal Security
Service)

GAIO (State Archive of Ivanovo Region)
- f. 119   Ivanovo-Voznesensk Region (IVR) Labor Department
- f. 1276   Ivanovo Industrial Region (IIR) Council of Trade Unions
- f. 1283   IIR Bureau of the All-Union Trade Union of Textile Workers
- f. 2888   First Ivanovo State Cotton Trust

GARF (State Archive of the Russian Federation)
- f. 374   Central Party Control Commission
- f. 393   Commissariat of Internal Affairs RSFSR
- f. 1235   Central Soviet Executive Committee RSFSR
- f. 3316   Central Soviet Executive Committee USSR
- f. 5451   Central Committee of the All-Union Central Council of Trade Unions
- f. 5457   Central Committee of the All-Union Trade Union of Textile Workers

GARF/RR2 (State Archive of the Russian Federation/Reading Room No. 2)
- f. 374   Central Statistical Directorate RSFSR
- f. 390   Commissariat of Labor RSFSR
- f. 406   Workers' and Peasants' Inspectorate RSFSR

RGAE (Russian State Archive of the Economy)
- f. 1562   Central Statistical Directorate RSFSR
- f. 8043   Commissariat of Supply USSR

RGASPI (Russian State Archive of Socio-Political History)
- f. 17   Central Party Committee
- f. 81   Lazar Kaganovich
- f. 89   Emel'ian Iaroslavskii

TsDNIIO (Center for Documentation of the Contemporary History of
Ivanovo Region)
- f. 2   IVR Party Committee
- f. 327   IIR Party Committee

Notes

Introduction

1. GARF, f. 5451, op. 42, d. 250, ll. 17–18. The date of Shvernik's report is estimated from this author's analysis of its contents. The term "hunger rations" was used by rank-and-file Communists in Kineshma. GARF, f. 374, op. 27, d. 1988, l. 63.

2. *IX vsesoiuznyi s"ezd professional'nykh soiuzov SSSR: stenograficheskii otchet* (Moscow, 1933), pp. 96–99, 194 ("steeped"), 659–660 ("petit-bourgeois," "bourgeois influences"), 708 ("class-alien . . . work").

3. The revolution "from above" was the set of radical socioeconomic policies—including forced industrialization and collectivization and the war on private trade—that the party implemented beginning in 1928.

4. Cited in B. A. Starkov, "Delo Riutina," *Oni ne molchali,* comp. A. V. Afanas'ev (Moscow, 1991), 162, 164. Dekulakization was the policy of stripping so-called prosperous peasants ("kulaks") of their property and civil rights. Many kulaks were exiled, imprisoned, or executed.

5. RGASPI, f. 17, op. 85, d. 305, l. 7; E. H. Carr and R. W. Davies, *Foundations of a Planned Economy, 1926–1929* (Harmondsworth, England, 1969), 1:914; R. W. Davies, *The Development of the Soviet Budgetary System* (Cambridge, England, 1958), 194–195. As of 1928, the textile industry was the largest in the USSR in terms of employment and gross output. *Trud v SSSR: statisticheskii spravochnik* (Moscow, 1936), 94; R. W. Davies, *The Soviet Economy in Turmoil, 1929–1930* (Cambridge, Mass., 1989), 500.

6. *Vos'moi s"ezd professional'nykh soiuzov SSSR* (Moscow, 1929), 416; Carr and Davies, *Foundations,* 1:1038; *Piatiletnii plan narodno-khoziaistvennogo stroitel'stva SSSR,* 3rd ed., vol. 2, pt. 1 (Moscow, 1930), 212–213, 251; A. M. Korneev, *Tekstil'naia promyshlennost SSSR i puti ee razvitiia* (Moscow, 1957), 144. Founded immediately after the October Revolution, the Supreme Economic Council played an important role in the management of Soviet industry until 1932, when it was divided into the commissariats (ministries) of heavy, light, and the timber industries.

7. Taylorism was a scientific approach to industrial management pioneered in the early twentieth century by Frederick W. Taylor, an American who carried out time and motion studies of factory workers to determine the most efficient way for them to execute their tasks. On the Bolshevik fascination with Taylorism, see Mark R. Beissinger, *Scientific Management, Socialist Discipline, and Soviet Power* (Cambridge, Mass., 1988), chap. 1.

8. *Piatiletnii plan,* vol. 2, pt. 1, 212–220; *Direktivy KPSS i Sovetskogo pravitel'stva po khoziaistvennym voprosam, 1917–1957gg.: sbornik dokumentov* (Moscow, 1957), 2:51–59.

9. In this book, "operatives" always signifies workers in the textile industry.

10. Statistics on the import and production of raw cotton are from Roger A. Clarke, *Soviet Economic Facts, 1917–1970* (London, 1972), 48, 116. Employment statistics are from *Trud v SSSR,* 94.

11. Naum Jasny, *Soviet Industrialization, 1928–1952* (Chicago, 1961), 73.

12. Korneev, *Tekstil'naia promyshlennost,* 144, 200; GARF, f. 5457, op. 23, d. 228, ll. 18–20; *Trud v SSSR,* 94. Target real wage figure is for textile workers. *Piatiletnii plan,* vol. 2, pt. 2, 190. Actual real wage figure is for Soviet nonrural workers. Jasny, *Soviet Industrialization,* 110. The FFYP called for 1.1 billion rubles of capital investment in the textile industry. *Piatiletnii plan,* vol. 2, pt. 1, 213. Substantially less than that seems to have been allocated. Edward Page Jr. and Natalie C. Grant, "The Textile Industry of the Soviet Union, 1913–1936" (unpublished report, U.S. Department of State, July 1937), 234. On poor planning of such investment, see GARF, f. 5457, op. 23, d. 228, ll. 21–23; and Korneev, *Tekstil'naia promyshlennost,* 154–155.

13. The Right Opposition, whose most prominent figure was the Old Bolshevik Nikolai Bukharin, opposed Stalin's revolution "from above" on the grounds that it would shatter living standards and ignite social unrest, hence imperil the party's grip on power and, by extension, the October Revolution. Stephen F. Cohen, *Bukharin and the Bolshevik Revolution: A Political Biography, 1888–1938* (Oxford, 1980); Moshe Lewin, *Political Undercurrents in Soviet Economic Debates: From Bukharin to the Modern Reformers* (Princeton, N.J., 1974).

14. Labor-force statistics are as of 1928. *Trud v SSSR,* 93.

15. Soviets were local councils established and elected by Russian workers, soldiers, and peasants in 1917. Although the Bolsheviks subordinated these councils to central control after seizing power, deputies who served on them had to stand for election from time to time. As a result, they tended to be regarded—even in the 1930s—as more responsive than the party to the needs of the population.

16. Mensheviks were non-Bolshevik Marxists; Socialist-Revolutionaries were non-Marxist (agrarian) socialists. For a description of textile industry crafts, see the Appendix.

17. The IIR Party Control Commission stated that "up to 15,000 workers" participated in the strike wave, but its report was written within days of that event and missed important parts of the story. This author's estimate of 20,000 strikers was derived as follows. First, numerous sources confirm that almost all

nonparty operatives in Puchezh, Teikovo, and Vichuga went on strike. Since these towns employed a total of about 24,000 workers as of April 1932, and since only about one in eight textile workers was affiliated with the party, a conservative estimate for these towns yields no fewer than 17,000 strikers. Second, the control commission estimated that there were 2,500 strikers in Lezhnevo district. Finally, Nerl's weaving sheds employed about 700 workers, most of whom joined the strike there. Altogether, then, about 20,000 operatives were involved in the IIR strike wave. GARF, f. 374, op. 27, d. 1988, ll. 93–85; RGASPI, f. 81, op. 3, d. 213, ll. 3–15, 64–67, 69–71, 77–78; TsDNIIO, f. 327, op. 4, d. 508, l. 3.

18. E. P. Thompson, "The Moral Economy of the English Crowd in the Eighteenth Century," *Past and Present*, no. 50 (1971): 76–136; Padraic Kenney, *Rebuilding Poland: Workers and Communists, 1945–1950* (Ithaca, N.Y., 1997), 6.

19. APUFSBIaO, s.d. 8597, l. 33.

20. The October Revolution was theirs, too, because the textile workers had done so much to bring about and then defend it. During the autumn of 1917—a moment of acute class consciousness on Russian shop floors—general strikes erupted in major branches of industry as workers endeavored to convey their rejection of the Provisional Government and their support for a class dictatorship of the soviets. Significantly, the largest general strike at the time was by the textile workers of the Ivanovo-Kineshma Region. Diane P. Koenker and William G. Rosenberg, *Strikes and Revolution in Russia, 1917* (Princeton, N.J., 1989), 292–298.

21. These articles defined and criminalized anti-Soviet and counterrevolutionary speech and behavior. *Ugolovnyi kodeks RSFSR: Redaktsii 1926 goda s izmeneniiami do 1 iulia 1931 goda* (Moscow, 1931).

22. GARF, f. 5457, op. 16, d. 163, l. 226ob. ("defenders"); APUFSBIO, s.d. 289-p, l. 87 ("the slogans").

23. Steve Smith, "Class and Gender: Women's Strikes in St. Petersburg, 1895–1917, and in Shanghai, 1895–1927," *Social History* 19, no. 2 (1994): 141–168 (quote, 142). I say "reemergence of class" because class was a potent category of social identity on shop floors in 1917. Koenker and Rosenberg, *Strikes and Revolution;* David Mandel, "October in the Ivanovo-Kineshma Industrial Region," in *Revolution in Russia: Reassessments of 1917*, ed. Edith Regain Frankel, Jonathan Frankel, and Baruch Knei-Paz (Cambridge, England, 1992), 157–187.

24. This, too, was subversive because the party long endeavored to monopolize class "as a means of political legitimation." David L. Hoffmann, *Peasant Metropolis: Social Identities in Moscow, 1929–1941* (Ithaca, N.Y., 1994), 211.

25. Orlando Figes and Boris Kolonitskii, *Interpreting the Russian Revolution: The Language and Symbols of 1917* (New Haven, Conn., 1999), 108 (quote); Sarah Davies, "'Us against Them': Social Identity in Soviet Russia, 1934–41," *Russian Review* 56, no. 1 (1997): 70–89.

26. On the washroom as a "club" where workers traditionally gathered to discuss their concerns and plan protests, and on shop-floor gender conflict, see Diane P. Koenker, "Men against Women on the Shop Floor in Early Soviet Russia: Gender and Class in the Socialist Workplace," *American Historical Review* 100, no. 5 (1995): 1438–1464; and Jeffrey J. Rossman, "Worker Resistance under Stalin: Class and Gender in the Textile Mills of the Ivanovo Industrial Region, 1928–1932" (Ph.D. diss., University of California, Berkeley, 1997), 18–30.

27. Judging by the frequency of complaints against them, peasant migrants from distant regions seem to have been a visible minority—perhaps 10 percent of the labor force—in at least some textile mills. N. Semenov, *Litso fabrichnykh rabochikh prozhivaiushchikh v derevniakh i politprosvetrabota sredi nikh* (Moscow-Leningrad, 1929), 35. The other groups were much smaller. On the eve of the FFYP, only 1.3 percent of IIR factory workers were classified as seasonal workers. GARF/RR2, f. 374, op. 20, d. 25, l. 70. *Lishentsy,* who were purged from the ranks of the trade union in 1929 and among the first to be sent to the Labor Exchange during the mass layoffs that occurred the same year, had a negligible presence on the shop floor. *Golos tekstilei* (hereafter, *GT*), 1/15/29, 4; TsDNIIO, f. 327, op. 5, d. 162, l. 9.

28. Although the shop-floor view of who could legitimately claim to be a worker was infused with official values, the party maintained that anyone who opposed one or another aspect of the revolution "from above" was an enemy of the working class. As a rule, textile workers disagreed with this assessment and condemned efforts to portray their leaders in such terms.

29. Familial references served a similar function in nineteenth-century European labor struggles and in protests by Russian workers and peasants through 1917. Sonya O. Rose, "Gender and Labor History: The Nineteenth-Century Legacy," *International Review of Social History* 38, supplement 1 (1993): 159; Barbara Alpern Engel, "Women, Men, and the Languages of Peasant Resistance, 1870–1907," in *Culture in Flux: Lower-Class Values, Practices, and Resistance in Late Imperial Russia,* ed. Stephen P. Frank and Mark D. Steinberg (Princeton, N.J., 1994), 34–53; Anne Bobroff-Hajal, *Working Women in Russia Under the Hunger Tsars: Political Activism and Daily Life* (Brooklyn, N.Y., 1994).

30. See, for example, Merle Fainsod, *Smolensk under Soviet Rule* (London, 1958); Alex Inkeles and Raymond Bauer, *The Soviet Citizen: Daily Life in a Totalitarian Society* (Cambridge, Mass., 1959); and Solomon M. Schwarz, *Labor in the Soviet Union* (London, 1953).

31. Moshe Lewin, *The Making of the Soviet System: Essays in the Social History of Interwar Russia* (New York, 1985), 221–223, 257; Lewin, "On Soviet Industrialization," in *Social Dimensions of Soviet Industrialization,* ed. William G. Rosenberg and Lewis H. Siegelbaum (Bloomington, Ind., 1993), 282.

32. Classic revisionist titles include Sheila Fitzpatrick, *Education and Social Mobility in the Soviet Union, 1921–1934* (Cambridge, England, 1979); Hiroaki Kuromiya, *Stalin's Industrial Revolution: Politics and Workers, 1928–1932*

(Cambridge, England, 1988); Lynne Viola, *The Best Sons of the Fatherland: Workers in the Vanguard of Soviet Collectivization* (Oxford, 1987); and William J. Chase, *Workers, Society and the Soviet State: Labor and Life in Moscow, 1918–1929* (Chicago, 1987), especially chap. 8. For a late-model version of revisionism, see Kenneth M. Straus, *Factory and Community in Stalin's Russia: The Making of an Industrial Working Class* (Pittsburgh, Pa., 1997).

33. Donald Filtzer, *Soviet Workers and Stalinist Industrialization: The Formation of Modern Soviet Production Relations, 1929–1941* (London, 1986). Vladimir Andrle advanced arguments similar to Filtzer's, but without discerning the collective shop-floor resistance that took place during the FFYP. Andrle, *Workers in Stalin's Russia: Industrialization and Social Change in a Planned Economy* (New York, 1988). The NEP, or New Economic Policy, era was the period from 1921 to 1927 when the USSR endeavored to advance toward socialism in an evolutionary instead of a revolutionary manner. Under the NEP, all but the "commanding heights" of the economy were in private hands, and exchange between town and village was governed, in principle, by the market rather than the state.

34. Stephen Kotkin, *Magnetic Mountain: Stalinism as a Civilization* (Berkeley, 1995), chap. 5.

35. Jochen Hellbeck, "Fashioning the Stalinist Soul: The Diary of Stepan Podlubnyi, 1931–9," in *Stalinism: New Directions,* ed. Sheila Fitzpatrick (New York, 2000), 77–116 (quotes, 82, 111, 104).

36. Jochen Hellbeck, "Speaking Out: Languages of Affirmation and Dissent in Stalinist Russia," in *The Resistance Debate in Russian and Soviet History,* eds. Michael David-Fox, Peter Holquist, and Marshall Poe (Bloomington, Ind., 2003), 108.

37. On the "neo-totalitarian" school, see Thomas Dodman, "The Fate of Red October," *History Workshop Journal* 56, no. 1 (2003): 258–267.

38. Sheila Fitzpatrick, "Ascribing Class: The Construction of Social Identity in Soviet Russia," in *Stalinism: New Directions,* 20–46 (quotes, 20, 39). Reading Fitzpatrick's otherwise masterful study of everyday life under Stalin, one is hard-pressed to find any indication that most able-bodied Soviet adults spent nearly half their waking hours engaged in one or another form of wage labor during the 1930s. Although Fitzpatrick justifies the omission by claiming that the experience of work was too diverse to warrant inclusion in a study focused on commonalities, her decision to reduce the experience of workers to their role as consumers and to ignore the sphere of production seems rather to spring from her assumption that social identity was, at least in the Stalinist context, ascribed by the state. Sheila Fitzpatrick, *Everyday Stalinism: Ordinary Life in Extraordinary Times* (Oxford, 1999), 11.

39. See, for example, the editors' introduction and the essays by Diane P. Koenker, Stephen Kotkin, Chris Ward, and Gábor T. Rittersporn in *Making Workers Soviet: Power, Class, and Identity,* ed. Lewis H. Siegelbaum and Ronald Grigor Suny (Ithaca, N.Y., 1994).

40. Koenker, "Men against Women," 1461–1462 ("a proletarian . . . exploitation"); Koenker, "Class and Consciousness in a Socialist Society: Workers in the Printing Trades during NEP," in *Russia in the Era of NEP: Explorations in Soviet Society and Culture*, ed. Sheila Fitzpatrick, Alexander Rabinowitch, and Richard Stites (Bloomington, Ind., 1991), 53 ("class"); Kotkin, *Magnetic Mountain*, 226 ("irrational . . . psychopathic"), 236 ("opposition").

41. Hellbeck, "Speaking Out," 106–107; Michael David-Fox, "Whither Resistance?" in *Resistance Debate*, 235 ("transform"); David-Fox, "Masquerade: Sources, Resistance and Early Soviet Political Culture," *Trondheim Studies on East European Cultures and Societies*, no. 1 (May 1999): 32 ("fictional"). Although she has written persuasively about peasant resistance, Fitzpatrick deserves at least candidate membership in the resistance to resistance club. Having argued in a seminal early monograph (*Education and Social Mobility*) that Soviet workers viewed the revolution "from above" as a fulfillment of the October Revolution because it made available to them an otherwise unattainable degree of upward mobility, in recent work she predictably dismisses the significance of resistance by these same workers. Fitzpatrick, *Everyday Stalinism*, 224.

42. Hellbeck, "Speaking Out," 134 ("the chorus"), 136 ("self-marginalization"); Peter Fritzsche, "On the Subjects of Resistance," in *Resistance Debate*, 216 ("dissenting").

43. David-Fox, "Masquerade," 12–14 ("the emerging," 14); David-Fox, "Whither Resistance," 236 ("the culture"); Fritzsche, "On the Subjects," 215 ("the false").

44. Fritzsche, "On the Subjects," 214 ("all," "distorted"). Moshe Lewin pointed out long ago that the Stalin regime relied increasingly on the security police after 1928 "to master the chaos" caused by revolution "from above." *Making of the Soviet System*, 265. For a brilliant account of what the party and its enforcers had to contend with in the countryside, see Lynne Viola, *Peasant Rebels under Stalin: Collectivization and the Culture of Peasant Resistance* (Oxford, 1996).

45. Typically filled out by a member of the factory committee, which was the organ that represented the trade union at enterprise level, strike reports were written by hand on a preprinted "Form for the Recording of a Strike." The existence of such forms suggests that strikes were more common in Soviet industry than previously assumed. For examples, see GAIO, f. 1276, op. 1, d. 28. For examples of OGPU reports on labor unrest, see GAIO, f. 1276, op. 23, dd. 2–4, 6–7, 9–10.

46. *Raiony Ivanovskoi promyshlennoi oblasti* (hereafter, *Raiony IPO*) (Moscow-Ivanovo, 1933), 1:9, 26–27; *Istoriia goroda Ivanova* (Ivanovo, 1962), 2:142; *Narodnoe khoziaistvo SSSR: statisticheskii spravochnik* (Moscow, 1932), 72–75; *Trud i profdvizhenie v Ivanovskoi promyshlennoi oblasti: statisticheskii spravochnik* (Ivanovo, 1929), 4–7; Davies, *Soviet Economy*, 526; *GT*, 4/14/29, 2 ("calico"). All statistics are as of 1929; regional rankings are as of 1930. The capital of the Ivanovo-Voznesensk Region—and, subsequently, of the IIR—

was known formally as Ivanovo-Voznesensk and colloquially as Ivanovo until 1932, when the colloquial name became the formal name as well. In this book, it will only be referred to as Ivanovo.

47. Chris Ward, *Russia's Cotton Workers and the New Economic Policy: Shop-floor Culture and State Policy, 1921–1929* (Cambridge, England, 1990), 85; *Deviatyi vsesoiuznyi s"ezd professional'nykh soiuzov SSSR: stenograficheskii otchet* (Moscow, 1933), 632; *Narodnoe khoziaistvo SSSR*, 19; *Sotsialisticheskoe stroitel'stvo SSSR: statisticheskii ezhegodnik* (Moscow, 1934), 34; RGASPI, f. 81, op. 3, d. 49, l. 125.

48. *Narodnoe khoziaistvo Ivanovskoi promyshlennoi oblasti [IPO]: statistiko-ekonomicheskii spravochnik* (Ivanovo, 1932), 6; David Mandel, "The Ivanovo-Kineshma Workers in War and Revolution," in *Strikes, Social Conflict and the First World War: An International Perspective*, ed. Leopold Haimson and Giulio Sapelli (Milan, 1992), 501–502.

49. Korneev, *Tekstil'naia promyshlennost*, 187; *Trud i profdvizhenie*, 4; *Raiony IPO*, 1:29; *Vsesoiuznaia perepis naseleniia 1926 goda* (hereafter, *1926 Census*; Moscow, 1929–1931), 34:124–125; 19:434, 451, 474, 561. On craft identity, see Chris Ward, "Languages of Trade or a Language of Class? Work Culture in Russian Cotton Mills in the 1920s," in *Making Workers Soviet*, 194–219.

50. A. G. Rashin, *Zhenskii trud v SSSR* (Moscow, 1928), 8; Rashin, "Dinamika promyshlennykh kadrov SSSR za 1917–1958 gg.," in *Izmeneniia v chislennosti i sostave sovetskogo rabochego klassa: sbornik statei*, ed. D. A. Baevskii (Moscow, 1961), 61; *Trud i profdvizhenie*, 86; GARF, f. 5457, op. 12, d. 200, l. 14.

51. Engel, "Women, Men, and the Languages of Peasant Resistance"; Lynne Viola, "*Bab'i Bunty* and Peasant Women's Protest during Collectivization," *Russian Review* 45, no. 1 (1986): 23–42; Bobroff-Hajal, *Working Women*.

52. *1926 Census*, 19:434, 451, 474, 561. According to this source, the crafts of card tender, picker tender, and mule spinner employed roughly equal numbers of men and women.

53. A. Rashin, *Sostav fabrichno-zavodskogo proletariata SSSR* (Moscow, 1930), 166; V. V. Il'inskii, *Ivanovskii tekstil'shchik: sostav i sotsial'naia kharakteristika rabochikh-tekstil'shchikov v Ivanovskoi promyshlennoi oblasti* (Ivanovo, 1930), 18–20 (quote, 19). According to Il'inskii (21–22), the typical IIR operative had *stazh* in 1929 of 13.7 years (for male operatives, the figure was 14.7 years; for women, 13.2 years). According to Rashin (168), *stazh* for the average Soviet worker at this time was just twelve years.

54. Il'inskii, *Ivanovskii tekstil'shchik*, 22–24; Rashin, *Sostav*, 13–14, 168. Cotton and linen mills boasted relatively low rates of labor turnover even during the FFYP. *Narodnoe khoziaistvo SSSR*, 449–451. On the party's ambivalence about labor-force stability, see the speech delivered by Kaganovich at a May 1932 conference on the crisis in the textile industry. RGASPI, f. 81, op. 3, d. 49, 133–134.

55. Il'inskii, *Ivanovskii tekstil'shchik*, 40–41; Ward, *Russia's Cotton Workers*, 199–204.

56. Il'inskii, *Ivanovskii tekstil'shchik*, 43, 45–48, 53; Rashin, *Sostav*, xv–xvi. According to Il'inskii (p. 45) and contrary to Bolshevik assumptions, there was little difference in the literacy rate between urban and rural mills as a whole.

57. Statistics are from Il'inskii, *Ivanovskii tekstil'shchik*, 53. The pathologies of the working-class family posed a threat to labor-force productivity and thus were condemned by the trade union as the program of forced capital accumulation got under way. For example, see *GT*, 2/17/28, 5; 2/19/28, 5; 3/3/28, 5; 4/21/28, 5; 4/27/28, 6; 5/6/28, 5; 9/14/28, 5; and 9/20/28, 5.

58. *1926 Census*, 56:x–xi, 21, 23, 25. The same study found that 82.9 percent of the families of Moscow metalworkers were headed by a husband-wife dyad, and that only 4 percent were headed by a single parent. For Moscow factory workers as a whole, the figures were 74.1 percent and 11.5 percent, respectively. *1926 Census*, 56:9, 11, 13, 21, 23, 25.

59. Il'inskii, *Ivanovskii tekstil'shchik*, 55–61; *1926 Census*, 53:210; M. O. Braginskii, *Zhilishchnyi vopros v tekstil'noi promyshlennosti* (Moscow, 1927); *Narodnoe khoziaistvo IPO*, 34–35; GARF, f. 5457, op. 12, d. 23, ll. 164–165 ("politically"). Municipal housing consisted mostly of the former homes of merchants and industrialists. Cooperative housing was new construction in which workers themselves invested. Il'inskii, *Ivanovskii tekstil'shchik*, 56–57.

60. The census definition is imperfect because property tended to be registered in the name of male rather than female family members, and because there were various subjective as well as objective ways in which a worker could be "tied" to the land.

61. Il'inskii, *Ivanovskii tekstil'shchik*, 25–26, 28; Rashin, *Sostav*, 167.

62. Il'inskii, *Ivanovskii tekstil'shchik*, 28–30, 32, 38–39; Semenov, *Litso*, 30. *Stazh* figures (from Rashin, *Sostav*, 38) are for the IIR cotton industry. Data from a 1932 analysis of Vichuga's mills confirmed that workers with ties to the land were among the industry's most experienced. TsDNIIO, f. 327, op. 5, d. 162, l. 9.

63. Semenov, *Litso*, 10–12, 14–15. According to Semenov (p. 12), the typical rural operative was a veteran female worker—most likely, a weaver—with a family of her own.

64. Il'inskii, *Ivanovskii tekstil'shchik*, 62–64; Rashin, *Sostav*, 169; RGASPI, f. 89, op. 3, d. 8, ll. 38–39.

65. Mandel, "The Ivanovo-Kineshma Workers," 498–499.

66. Koenker and Rosenberg, *Strikes and Revolution*, 292–298; William B. Husband, "Local Industry in Upheaval: The Ivanovo-Kineshma Textile Strike of 1917," *Slavic Review* 47, no. 2 (1988): 448–463.

67. William B. Husband, *Revolution in the Factory: The Birth of the Soviet Textile Industry, 1917–1920* (Oxford, 1990), 47–121, 166 ("economic"); *Trud v SSSR*, 94; Korneev, *Tekstil'naia promyshlennost*, 111. Employment in, and an-

nual output of, the textile industry declined by more than two-thirds from 1913 to 1921, with most of the decline taking place during the Civil War. *SSSR za 15 let: statisticheskie materialy po narodnomu khoziaisvu* (Moscow, 1932), 94; Clarke, *Soviet Economic Facts,* 80.

68. This policy, a cornerstone of the NEP known as the *smychka,* posited an ideological and economic alliance between town and village. Its abandonment, in 1928, signaled the onset of revolution "from above."

69. Ward, *Russia's Cotton Workers,* 197.

70. On the emasculation of state policy under the NEP, see Ward, *Russia's Cotton Workers,* 197, 261, 264. On the rhetoric of class war, see Kuromiya, *Stalin's Industrial Revolution,* 316–318.

1. The Workers Mobilize

1. The NEP in agriculture—a policy that relied on market mechanisms to coax grain out of the peasantry—was all but formally abolished in January 1928 when Stalin responded to a shortfall in state grain procurements by abruptly shifting to a policy of forced requisitioning.

2. *Sobranie zakonov i rasporiazhenii Raboche-Krest'ianskogo Pravitel'stva SSSR, izdavaemoe Upravleniem Delami Sovnarkomov SSSR i STO,* no. 61 (Moscow, 1927), 613, 662; GARF, f. 5451, op. 12, d. 459, ll. 166, 181, 203; f. 5457, op. 16, d. 63, l. 228ob.; TsDNIIO, f. 2, op. 11, d. 39, l. 21. By October 1, 1928, twenty-six mills employing 118,200 workers had implemented round-the-clock production. By the same date in 1930, more than one hundred mills employing 347,600 workers had made the switch. GARF, f. 5451, op. 12, d. 459, l. 163; f. 5457, op. 23, d. 97, l. 13.

3. GARF, f. 5451, op. 12, d. 459, ll. 163, 203; f. 5457, op. 12, d. 23, ll. 96, 100; op. 16, d. 61, l. 129; d. 63, l. 225; RGASPI, f. 17, op. 32, d. 131, ll. 4–5; op. 85, d. 305, l. 5. The night shift increased employment in the mills where it was introduced by one-fourth, and output by one-sixth. GARF, f. 5451, op. 12, d. 459, l. 163; f. 5457, op. 13, d. 13, l. 42.

4. GARF, f. 5451, op. 12, d. 459, l. 184; f. 5457, op. 16, d. 63, l. 250 ("to get"); d. 85, l. 17; *GT,* 2/15/28, 5 ("This"); 6/7/28, 5; 6/8/28, 5; *VIII s"ezd professional'nykh soiuzov SSSR (10–24 dekabria 1928 g.). Plenumy i sektsii. Polnyi stenograficheskii otchet* (Moscow, 1929), 78.

5. GARF, f. 5457, op. 16, d. 61, l. 129 ("the severe"); op. 12, d. 48, l. 24 ("under").

6. GARF, f. 5457, op. 12, d. 23, l. 165 ("counterrevolutionary," "transgressions"); op. 16, d. 173, ll. 14–15; RGASPI, f. 17, op. 85, d. 305, l. 75 (Kaganovich, Mel'nichanskii).

7. GARF, f. 5451, op. 12, d. 459, l. 181; RGASPI, f. 17, op. 32, d. 131, l. 14; TsDNIIO, f. 2, op. 11, d. 220, l. 26.

8. GARF, f. 5451, op. 12, d. 459, ll. 201–203; f. 5457, op. 16, d. 61, l. 41; op. 13, d. 13, l. 19; RGASPI, f. 17, op. 32, d. 131, ll. 5–6; *GT,* 5/15/28, 4;

5/25/28, 4; 12/14/28, 3; 1/16/29, 3. On the risks of night work, see S. N. Cherkinskii, V. S. Shopen, R. I. Ryzhikov, et al., *Rabota tkachikh v nochnoi smene (Opyt issledovaniia utomliaemosti, proizvoditel'nosti i sanitarnykh uslovii truda v sviazi s perekhodom na semichasovoi rabochii den* (Moscow, 1929). As of 1928, mills were able to fulfill only 30 percent of the demand for on-the-job child care—a situation that provoked myriad complaints from female workers. GARF, f. 5457, op. 12, d. 200, l. 24; d. 48, l. 21.

9. RGASPI, f. 17, op. 32, d. 131, ll. 5–6, 15; GARF, f. 5451, op. 12, d. 459, ll. 182–183, 202; f. 5457, op. 16, d. 61, ll. 41ob., 129; d. 71, ll. 3 (quote; report by Main Directorate of the Textile Industry), 6; d. 72, l. 8; *GT,* 5/15/28, 4. According to an industry official, the ban affected 12 percent of operatives, one-quarter to one-third of whom categorically refused to work a day shift. GARF, f. 5457, op. 12, d. 23, l. 279.

10. *GT,* 1/3/29; TsDNIIO, f. 2, op. 11, d. 39, ll. 308–309 (Krasilova); d. 184, l. 4; f. 327, op. 4, d. 196, l. 12 (Red Perekop); RGASPI, f. 17, op. 85, d. 305, l. 38. The domestic burdens of female workers were a constant source of concern in the trade union, which asserted that women "had been liberated only on paper" and worried that this situation undermined their workplace productivity. GARF, f. 5457, op. 12, d. 48, l. 21 (quote); d. 200, ll. 21–24.

11. RGASPI, f. 17, op. 85, d. 236, l. 10; GARF, f. 5457, op. 16, d. 63, ll. 224, 228–228ob., 236–236ob., 252; d. 72, ll. 7–8, 140; f. 5451, op. 12, d. 459, l. 185; TsDNIIO, f. 2, op. 11, d. 39, l. 309; d. 220, ll. 22, 25–27; Semenov, *Litso,* 36, 51–53 (quotes); A. V. Shipulina, "Sotsialisticheskoe sorevnovanie Ivanovskikh rabochikh v gody pervoi piatiletke," *Uchenye zapiski Gor'kovskogo pedagogicheskogo instituta* 50, sb. no. 8 (Seriia istoricheskaia, 1965): 24.

12. GARF, f. 5451, op. 12, d. 459, ll. 181–182, 186; f. 5457, op. 12, d. 197, ll. 77–78, 81; op. 13, d. 252, l. 2ob.; op. 16, d. 63, ll. 228ob., 254; d. 72, l. 138; Semenov, *Litso,* 36, 51, 53.

13. RGASPI, f. 17, op. 32, d. 131, l. 3; GARF, f. 5451, op. 12, d. 459, ll. 180–181, 202; f. 5457, op. 16, d. 61, l. 129.

14. *GT,* 9/8/28, 4; TsDNIIO, f. 2, op. 11, d. 184, l. 24; GARF, f. 5457, op. 16, d. 62, l. 4 ("the tense," "the unceasing"); f. 5451, op. 12, d. 459, ll. 186, 203 ("lessened"; trade-union report); RGASPI, f. 17, op. 85, d. 236, ll. 5–6 ("in the end"; OGPU report), 10.

15. GARF, f. 5451, op. 12, d. 459, ll. 164, 188.

16. RGASPI, f. 17, op. 85, d. 236, l. 7; GARF, f. 5457, op. 13, d. 252, ll. 1–1ob. Between 1914 and 1928, average workloads in the Russian cotton industry rose 18 percent in spinning, 46 percent in weaving, and 80 percent in finishing sheds. Most of these gains were achieved during the last three years of the NEP. The FFYP called for workloads to rise by at least another 40 percent. GARF, f. 5457, op. 13, d. 252, ll. 1–1ob.

17. GARF, f. 5451, op. 12, d. 459, ll. 163–165, 189–190, 192, 202–203; f. 5457, op. 12, d. 23, ll. 81, 100; op. 13, d. 252, ll. 1ob., 3, 4ob.–5, 6ob.–7; op. 16, d. 63, ll. 225, 253; d. 72, l. 8; RGASPI, f. 17, op. 85, d. 236, l. 10.

18. GARF, f. 5451, op. 12, d. 459, ll. 164, 192–194 (quote).

19. RGASPI, f. 17, op. 85, d. 217, l. 100; d. 236, l. 10; *GT,* 1/18/28, 4; GARF, f. 5457, op. 13, d. 252, l. 1ob.

20. GARF, f. 5451, op. 12, d. 459, ll. 165 (quote), 194–195, 204.

21. RGASPI, f. 17, op. 85, d. 311, l. 13 (Vichuga, Ivanovo); TsDNIIO, f. 2, op. 11, d. 163, l. 17; d. 222, ll. 4 (Sereda), 20–22 (Teikovo, Navoloki).

22. TsDNIIO, f. 2, op. 11, d. 222, ll. 4–5, 20–21, 25–27.

23. TsDNIIO, f. 2, op. 11, d. 222, ll. 1, 18–19.

24. RGASPI, f. 17, op. 85, d. 311, ll. 28–30; d. 325, l. 28; APUFSBIaO, s.d. 8597, ll. 93 ("wringing," "on the backs"), 69ob. ("toss"), 102; GARF, f. 5451, op. 12, d. 459, ll. 181, 185 ("impossible"); f. 5457, op. 16, d. 61, ll. 103–104; d. 72, l. 138.

25. TsDNIIO, f. 2, op. 11, d. 162, ll. 42–44; GARF, f. 5457, op. 12, d. 23, l. 259; RGASPI, f. 17, op. 85, d. 236, l. 10; d. 311, l. 29.

26. TsDNIIO, f. 2, op. 11, d. 162, ll. 42–44 (quote); RGASPI, f. 17, op. 85, d. 236, l. 10.

27. TsDNIIO, f. 2, op. 11, d. 162, ll. 43–44 (quotes); RGASPI, f. 17, op. 85, d. 236, ll. 24, 30.

28. TsDNIIO, f. 2, op. 11, d. 162, l. 45; d. 39, ll. 19, 22.

29. TsDNIIO, f. 2, op. 11, d. 39, l. 22.

30. TsDNIIO, f. 2, op. 11, d. 222, ll. 53, 55 (Suslov, Kisiakov); d. 163, l. 16 (Katin); RGASPI, f. 17, op. 85, d. 236, l. 9.

31. TsDNIIO, f. 2, op. 11, d. 39, ll. 19 (Teikovo), 32; d. 162, l. 497; d. 163, l. 16 (Gorki-Pavlovo); d. 222, ll. 12–13 (Lezhnevo); RGASPI, f. 17, op. 85, d. 236, ll. 9–10 (Kineshma), 65; d. 311, ll. 28–30, 42; GAIO, f. 1276, op. 1, d. 28, ll. 127–127ob.

32. TsDNIIO, f. 2, op. 11, d. 163, l. 2 (Salandin); d. 222, l. 54 (Kineshma); RGASPI, f. 17, op. 85, d. 307, ll. 13–14 (Vanchikov).

33. RGASPI, f. 17, op. 85, d. 236, l. 9 ("to fight"); TsDNIIO, f. 2, op. 11, d. 39, ll. 19–20 ("brute," "to enserf"). On gender conflict between weavers and overlookers on the eve of the FFYP, see Rossman, "Worker Resistance under Stalin," 18–30.

34. GARF, f. 5457, op. 12, d. 23, ll. 290–292; op. 16, d. 63, l. 254.

35. RGASPI, f. 17, op. 85, d. 325, l. 28; d. 297, ll. 72–73; d. 307, l. 20; GARF, f. 5457, op. 16, d. 61, l. 102 (quote).

36. GARF, f. 5457, op. 16, d. 61, ll. 103–104; TsDNIIO, f. 2, op. 11, d. 222, ll. 45, 50–51 (quote); GAIO, f. 119, op. 4, d. 2, l. 7; d. 3, l. 34ob.

37. GAIO, f. 1276, op. 1, d. 28, ll. 121–121ob.; TsDNIIO, f. 2, op. 11, d. 163, l. 16 (quote).

38. GAIO, f. 119, op. 4, d. 3, ll. 10–11; f. 1276, op. 1, d. 28, ll. 124–124ob.; TsDNIIO, f. 2, op. 11, d. 162, ll. 496–497 (quote); RGASPI, f. 17, op. 85, d. 236, l. 7.

39. TsDNIIO, f. 2, op. 11, d. 39, ll. 22, 260; GARF, f. 5457, op. 12, d. 23, l. 260; op. 16, d. 63, ll. 2, 17, 20, 225; RGASPI, f. 17, op. 85, d. 236, l. 10; GAIO, f. 119, op. 4, d. 2, ll. 16, 38; *GT,* 9/8/28, 4.

40. GARF, f. 5457, op. 16, d. 63, l. 17; d. 68, ll. 1, 4–6; TsDNIIO, f. 2, op. 11,

d. 39, ll. 260–261; d. 163, l. 112; RGASPI, f. 17, op. 85, d. 307, l. 65; *GT,* 9/8/28, 4.

41. GARF, f. 5457, op. 12, d. 23, l. 97; op. 16, d. 63, l. 18 (quote); RGASPI, f. 17, op. 85, d. 305, l. 39.

42. RGASPI, f. 17, op. 85, d. 305, l. 39; TsDNIIO, f. 2, op. 11, d. 39, l. 261.

43. GARF, f. 5457, op. 16, d. 63, ll. 18–19; RGASPI, f. 17, op. 85, d. 307, l. 65 (block quote); TsDNIIO, f. 2, op. 11, d. 39, ll. 261–263 (other quotes); GAIO, f. 1276, op. 1, d. 28, ll. 150–150ob.

44. RGASPI, f. 17, op. 85, d. 236, l. 21; d. 305, l. 39; d. 307, ll. 64–65; GARF, f. 5451, op. 12, d. 821, l. 19; f. 5457, op. 16, d. 63, ll. 18–19, 226ob.; GAIO, f. 119, op. 4, d. 3, l. 39; f. 1276, op. 1, d. 28, ll. 150–150ob.; TsDNIIO, f. 2, op. 11, d. 39, ll. 260–261, 263.

45. TsDNIIO, f. 2, op. 11, d. 39, l. 262; GAIO, f. 1276, op. 1, d. 28, ll. 150–150ob.; RGASPI, f. 17, op. 85, d. 236, l. 21; GARF, f. 5457, op. 16, d. 63, l. 19.

46. RGASPI, f. 17, op. 85, d. 236, l. 21.

47. RGASPI, f. 17, op. 85, d. 236, l. 22; TsDNIIO, f. 2, op. 11, d. 39, ll. 262–263.

48. RGASPI, f. 17, op. 85, d. 236, l. 22; TsDNIIO, f. 2, op. 11, d. 39, l. 263; GARF, f. 5457, op. 16, d. 63, l. 19. As of April 1929, the typical mule spinner was forty-one years old, had twenty-three years of experience on the shop floor, and earned three rubles, ten kopecks per day. Only overlookers had statistics more impressive. Rashin, *Sostav fabrichno-zavodskogo,* 75, 94.

49. RGASPI, f. 17, op. 85, d. 236, l. 22; GARF, f. 5457, op. 16, d. 63, l. 19. Apparently, the peasant speaker was unaware that Stalin had already abandoned the *smychka.*

50. GARF, f. 5457, op. 16, d. 63, l. 225; d. 68, l. 1; TsDNIIO, f. 2, op. 11, d. 39, l. 263.

51. RGASPI, f. 17, op. 85, d. 236, ll. 23–25 (quote), 30; GARF, f. 5457, op. 16, d. 68, l. 2.

52. GARF, f. 5457, op. 16, d. 63, l. 19; d. 68, ll. 3–4; RGASPI, f. 17, op. 85, d. 236, ll. 30–55ob.; d. 307, l. 65.

53. TsDNIIO, f. 2, op. 11, d. 39, l. 264; d. 163, ll. 112, 117–119; d. 184, ll. 3–5, 46–47, 174; *GT,* 9/8/28, 4 ("mistake," "the evil"); GARF, f. 5457, op. 12, d. 23, ll. 97 ("harm . . . state"), 110; op. 16, d. 63, l. 21; RGASPI, f. 17, op. 85, d. 305, ll. 39–40.

54. RGASPI, f. 17, op. 85, d. 307, ll. 67–68; d. 236, ll. 10–11; d. 305, ll. 39, 52–53; TsDNIIO, f. 2, op. 11, d. 39, ll. 264, 308–309; d. 184, l. 168.

55. RGASPI, f. 17, op. 85, d. 305, ll. 2, 6.

56. GARF, f. 5457, op. 16, d. 63, l. 254 ("with"); d. 72, ll. 10–11 (other quotes); op. 12, d. 23, ll. 290–292, 309.

57. RGASPI, f. 17, op. 85, d. 236, l. 11.

58. GARF, f. 5457, op. 16, d. 63, l. 229.

59. RGASPI, f. 17, op. 85, d. 311, l. 62; TsDNIIO, f. 2, op. 11, d. 39, ll. 19, 30–31, 82 (Teikovo, Iuzha); d. 222, ll. 64–65 (Shuia, Rodniki); GARF, f. 5457, op. 16, d. 62, ll. 1ob., 16–16ob., 22–22ob. (Kostroma).

60. GARF, f. 5457, op. 16, d. 62, ll. 1, 22ob.; d. 72, l. 8; RGASPI, f. 17, op. 85, d. 307, ll. 31–32 (May events), 40, 43–45 (summer events); d. 311, ll. 133–134.

61. TsDNIIO, f. 2, op. 11, d. 39, ll. 280–281 (quotes); GAIO, f. 119, op. 4, d. 2, l. 31; RGASPI, f. 17, op. 85, d. 311, l. 113. Cooperatives, a major source of staples for Soviet workers, typically were based inside, or near, enterprises. They raised funds by selling shares to eligible employees, then used these funds to purchase goods from state supply agencies and local producers. Each month the cooperative was obliged to distribute a portion of its purchases to shareholders. While cooperatives had the best prices, the range of goods offered was limited; as a result, workers also relied on state stores and private traders to fulfill their needs. Julie Hessler, *A Social History of Soviet Trade: Trade Policy, Retail Practices, and Consumption, 1917–1953* (Princeton, N.J., 2004).

62. GARF, f. 5457, op. 16, d. 72, l. 8 ("a wave"); d. 62, l. 76 ("the most").

63. GARF, f. 5457, op. 16, d. 62, ll. 74–75ob. (quotes); d. 61, ll. 149–152; RGASPI, f. 17, op. 85, d. 307, ll. 65–66; TsDNIIO, f. 2, op. 11, d. 39, l. 280.

64. TsDNIIO, f. 2, op. 11, d. 39, ll. 280–282, 306–307; d. 184, ll. 9–11, 15, 18ob., 20, 22–25, 33, 44–45, 52ob., 68, 130, 149, 162–164 (quotes), 166, 168, 170, 174, 179–180.

65. TsDNIIO, f. 2, op. 11, d. 184, l. 170.

66. TsDNIIO, f. 2, op. 11, d. 184, ll. 4 (Golubev), 9–10, 15–16, 22–23, 41–45, 54–54ob., 145–146, 149–150, 160–161, 168 (Kokhma weaver); d. 39, ll. 282 ("our"), 305–306.

67. TsDNIIO, f. 2, op. 11, d. 184, ll. 9–11.

68. TsDNIIO, f. 2, op. 11, d. 39, ll. 283–285 (peasants); GARF, f. 5457, op. 12, d. 23, l. 120 (troops).

69. GARF, f. 5457, op. 16, d. 63, l. 228ob. (rank-and-file Communist); RGASPI, f. 17, op. 85, d. 305, ll. 2–6, 8 (Mel'nichanskii).

70. RGASPI, f. 17, op. 85, d. 305, ll. 3, 14, 16–17, 25, 35–36, 40; GARF, f. 5457, op. 16, d. 61, l. 50 (quote; Riazan Region trade-union bureau); d. 75, l. 47.

71. TsDNIIO, f. 2, op. 11, d. 39, ll. 305 (italics in original), 307–308. The memorandum is dated October 13, 1928.

72. On Russia's first workers' soviet, see Abraham Ascher, *The Revolution of 1905: Russia in Disarray* (Stanford, Calif., 1988), 145–150. On the general strike of autumn 1917, see Koenker and Rosenberg, *Strikes and Revolution*, 292–298; Mandel, "October in the Ivanovo-Kineshma Industrial Region," 157–187; and Husband, "Local Industry in Upheaval," 448–463.

73. TsDNIIO, f. 2, op. 11, d. 39, l. 306 ("very tense"); TsDNIIO, f. 2, op. 11, d. 184, ll. 144–145 (other quotes), 147–151.

74. TsDNIIO, f. 2, op. 11, ll. 145–146.

75. TsDNIIO, f. 2, op. 11, d. 184, l. 28.

76. TsDNIIO, f. 2, op. 11, d. 39, ll. 305–306 ("deceiving," "having"); d. 184, ll. 18ob.–22 ("fourth"), 24, 26–28.

77. TsDNIIO, f. 2, op. 11, d. 184, ll. 20, 22–26 (quotes).

78. TsDNIIO, f. 2, op. 11, d. 162, ll. 20, 22–24, 130, 149; GARF, f. 5457, op. 16, d. 173, l. 14; op. 12, d. 197, ll. 5, 20 (quote), 76–79, 101.

79. TsDNIIO, f. 2, op. 11, d. 184, ll. 53–54 ("rumors"), 68 ("panic"), 33–34 ("a mass"), 179–180.

80. TsDNIIO, f. 2, op. 11, d. 184, ll. 52, 54.

81. TsDNIIO, f. 2, op. 11, d. 184, l. 54ob. The Soviet Union exported 289,000 tons of grain during fiscal year (FY) 1927–1928, which was 86 percent less than it exported in FY 1926–1927. Grain exports virtually ceased during the fourth calendar quarter of 1928 and resumed at a modest level in 1929, when 178,000 tons were exported. The next year, grain exports skyrocketed to 4.8 million tons—a figure that was surpassed in 1931. Clarke, *Soviet Economic Facts*, 46.

82. TsDNIIO, f. 2, op. 11, d. 184, ll. 54ob.–55.

83. TsDNIIO, f. 2, op. 11, d. 162, ll. 2–4ob. Scholars who claim that the party successfully deployed the rhetoric of the Civil War to mobilize the shop floor for revolution "from above" should take heed of Kolotilov's remarks, which demonstrate that on workers' minds at this juncture was the popular suffering rather than the class heroism of that conflict.

84. TsDNIIO, f. 2, op. 11, d. 162, ll. 9–10.

85. TsDNIIO, f. 2, op. 11, d. 162, l. 10ob.

86. GAIO, f. 1276, op. 23, d. 4, l. 230; TsDNIIO, f. 2, op. 11, d. 162, ll. 11–11ob. (quotes).

87. TsDNIIO, f. 2, op. 11, d. 162, l. 11.

88. TsDNIIO, f. 2, op. 11, d. 162, ll. 13–14.

89. TsDNIIO, f. 2, op. 11, d. 162, l. 14.

90. TsDNIIO, f. 2, op. 11, d. 162, ll. 14ob.–15.

91. TsDNIIO, f. 2, op. 11, d. 162, l. 14ob.

92. GARF, f. 5457, op. 16. d. 63, l. 227ob.; TsDNIIO, f. 2, op. 11, d. 162, l. 15 (quotes; italics added).

93. TsDNIIO, f. 2, op. 11, d. 162, ll. 15ob.–16ob.

94. TsDNIIO, f. 2, op. 11, d. 162, ll. 20ob.–21ob.

95. GARF, f. 5457, op. 12, d. 23, ll. 308ob., 322.

96. GARF, f. 5457, op. 12, d. 23, l. 57.

97. TsDNIIO, f. 2, op. 12, d. 65, l. 102. On implementation of the rationing system across the USSR, see Elena Osokina, *Our Daily Bread: Socialist Distribution and the Art of Survival in Stalin's Russia, 1927–1941* (Armonk, N.Y., 2001), 35–41.

98. GAIO, f. 119, op. 4, d. 2, l. 61ob. ("sharp"). On the emergence of the Stalinist supply hierarchy, see Elena Osokina, *Ierarkhiia potrebleniia: O zhizni liudei v usloviiakh Stalinskogo snabzheniia, 1928–1935gg.* (Moscow, 1993).

99. *VIII s"ezd professional'nykh soiuzov*, 417, 476, 481; GARF, f. 5457, op. 16, d. 63, l. 228ob. (quote).

100. During the first nine months of 1928, 17,000 operatives participated in ninety-six strikes. RGASPI, f. 17, op. 85, d. 169, ll. 170, 252; d. 305, l. 14.

101. Naum Jasny, *Soviet Industrialization, 1928–1952* (Chicago, 1961), 73.

2. The Klepikov Affair

1. GARF, f. 5457, op. 16, d. 63, ll. 226ob., 228–229, 248ob.
2. GARF, f. 5457, op. 16, d. 63, ll. 226ob., 228–228ob., 236–236ob., 247–251.
3. GARF, f. 5457, op. 16, d. 63, ll. 226ob.–227ob.
4. GARF, f. 5457, op. 16, d. 63, l. 227ob.
5. APUFSBIO, s.d. 289-p, ll. 10, 50–50ob., 98; s.d. 9391-p, l. 49; GARF, f. 5457, op. 16, d. 63, l. 227ob. As of 1928, the Rodniki Mill employed 12,167 workers. GARF, f. 5457, op. 16, d. 62, l. 41.
6. APUFSBIO, s.d. 289-p, ll. 2, 10; s.d. 9391-p, ll. 95 ("For . . . administration"), 49ob. ("an extreme").
7. Mikhail Klepikov, interview with author, Moscow, 8/29/94; APUFSBIO, s.d. 289-p, II. 50–50ob.
8. On worker-authors, their role as cultural mediators, and the themes in their writings, see Mark D. Steinberg, "Worker-Authors and the Cult of the Person," in *Cultures in Flux: Lower-Class Values, Practices, and Resistance in Late Imperial Russia*, ed. Stephen P. Frank and Mark D. Steinberg (Princeton, N.J., 1994), 168–184 (quote, 171). On the worker-activist as cultural mediator, see Reginald E. Zelnik, "Introduction: Kanatchikov's *Story of My Life* as Document and Literature," in *A Radical Worker in Tsarist Russia: The Autobiography of Semën Ivanovich Kanatchikov*, trans. and ed. Reginald E. Zelnik (Stanford, Calif., 1986), xx–xxi; and Jeffrey Brooks, "Competing Modes of Popular Discourse: Individualism and Class Consciousness in the Russian Print Media, 1880–1928," in *Culture et Révolution*, ed. Marc Ferro, Sheila Fitzpatrick, Sydney Monas, and Jutta Scherrer (Paris, 1989), 77–79.
9. GARF, f. 5457, op. 12, d. 23, l. 114; APUFSBIO, s.d. 289-p, ll. 2, 4.
10. APUFSBIO, s.d. 9391-p, l. 4ob. ("The current . . . people"), 50, 83, 95, 128. On shop-floor unrest during the closing months of the Civil War, see Jonathan Aves, *Workers against Lenin: Labour Protest and the Bolshevik Dictatorship* (London, 1996). Among the unpopular policies associated with war communism were forced grain requisitioning, the suppression of private trade, and the labor militarization.
11. TsDNIIO, f. 2, op. 11, d. 184, l. 156 (piece rates); APUFSBIO, s.d. 289-p, l. 95 (campaign speech). On the implementation of piece rates, see Ward, *Russia's Cotton Workers*, 171–175.
12. APUFSBIO, s.d. 289-p, ll. 2, 94–95. On workers' disaffection with the NEP, see Chase, *Workers, Society, and the Soviet State*.
13. APUFSBIO, s.d. 289-p, l. 58.
14. APUFSBIO, s.d. 289-p, ll. 2, 96 (quote). Klepikov's remarks echoed those made by striking workers after the Bolsheviks disbanded Menshevik- and Socialist-Revolutionary-dominated soviets in 1918. Vladimir Brovkin, "Workers' Unrest and the Bolsheviks' Response in 1919," *Slavic Review* 49, no. 3 (1990): 350–373. The Kornilov affair was a right-wing coup attempt that the Bolsheviks helped to defeat in August 1917. Aleksandr Kerenskii was the

prime minister of the provisional government that the Bolsheviks overthrew in October 1917.

15. RGASPI, f. 17, op. 87, d. 200, l. 107ob.; APUFSBIO, s.d. 289-p, ll. 5, 30 (quotes).

16. APUFSBIO, s.d. 289-p, ll. 58–59. Klepikov's son became a Komsomol anyway, but by 1930 had resigned or been expelled from the organization's ranks. Aleksei Arakcheev was a favorite of Aleksandr I, at whose request he established military colonies that were reviled for their intense regimentation and draconian discipline. Dmitrii Trepov was the governor-general of St. Petersburg whom the populist Vera Zasulich endeavored to assassinate in 1878 in retaliation for Trepov's having ordered the beating of a political prisoner. Petr Stolypin was the prime minister who oversaw the repression of rebels and terrorists after the 1905 Revolution.

17. APUFSBIO, s.d. 289-p, ll. 3–4 (quotes), 93; Steinberg, "Worker-Authors," 182–183.

18. APUFSBIO, s.d. 289-p, ll. 2, 4–5, 30, 58, 94–95.

19. APUFSBIO, s.d. 289-p, l. 59 ("The factory . . . gendarmerie," "cruel," "Stalin . . . Solovki"); GARF, f. 5457, op. 16, d. 67, ll. 37–37ob. (other quotes). Solovki was a notorious Soviet labor camp.

20. APUFSBIO, f. 289-p, l. 59 ("the despotic"); GARF, f. 5457, op. 16, d. 67, l. 36ob. (other quotes).

21. APUFSBIO, s.d. 289-p, ll. 81–83 (poem), 48ob. ("what"), 60 ("loud"). The grammar and spelling errors in Klepikov's poems have not been translated.

22. GARF, f. 5457, op. 16, d. 67, ll. 38–38ob.

23. GARF, f. 5457, op. 16, d. 67, l. 35.

24. APUFSBIO, s.d. 289-p, l. 5 (Klepikov); GARF, f. 5457, op. 12, d. 23, l. 121 ("comrades-in-arms").

25. *GT*, 9/12/28, 3; TsDNIIO, f. 2, op. 11, d. 184, l. 44 ("which"). *Voice* was the logical place for the anti-Klepikov campaign to be waged because it was by far the most widely read newspaper in the industry. RGASPI, f. 17, op. 85, d. 325, l. 35.

26. GARF, f. 5457, op. 12, d. 23, ll. 114–119. The vote in favor of the anti-Klepikov resolution was unanimous. It probably was rigged.

27. TsDNIIO, f. 2, op. 11, d. 184, ll. 154–154ob.; GARF, f. 5457, op. 16, d. 63, ll. 227ob. (quote), 248.

28. TsDNIIO, f. 2, op. 11, d. 184, ll. 154–155.

29. TsDNIIO, f. 2, op. 11, d. 184, ll. 155–157.

30. TsDNIIO, f. 2, op. 11, d. 184, l. 157ob. ("not guilty"); GARF, f. 5457, op. 16, d. 63, l. 227ob. (other quotes).

31. *GT*, 11/17/28, 4; 11/20/28, 3.

32. *GT*, 1/11/29, 4; 12/30/28, 3.

33. APUFSBIO, s.d. 289-p, ll. 87–88. Kvas is a carbonated beverage made from fermented bread.

34. *GT*, 1/15/29, 4.

35. GARF, f. 5457, op. 16, d. 97, l. 33.
36. *GT*, 2/5/29, 4; 1/15/29, 4.
37. APUFSBIO, s.d. 289-p, l. 59.
38. APUFSBIO, s.d. 289-p, ll. 6, 51ob., 60 (quote).
39. APUFSBIO, s.d. 289-p, ll. 6 (quotes), 9a, 50ob., 55.
40. APUFSBIO, s.d. 289-p, ll. 10ob.–11.
41. APUFSBIO, s.d. 289-p, l. 48ob.
42. APUFSBIO, s.d. 289-p, ll. 48ob.–49.
43. APUFSBIO, s.d. 289-p, ll. 51ob. (quote), 61–63. Nothing is known about Klepikov's years in confinement, although one of his sons suspects that he did time at Vorkuta. At any rate, the family received word in 1933 that Klepikov had committed suicide in a Vladimir psychiatric hospital. In 1992, he was rehabilitated. Mikhail Klepikov, interview with author; APUFSBIO, s.d. 289-p, ll. 104–106; s.d. 9391-p, ll. 128–128ob.

3. The Liulin Affair

1. TsDNIIO, f. 327, op. 4, d. 500, l. 85; Page and Grant, "The Textile Industry of the Soviet Union," 36, 78.
2. APUFSBIaO, s.d. 8597, ll. 6, 62, 106; RGASPI, f. 17, op. 85, d. 325, l. 56.
3. APUFSBIaO, s.d. 8597, ll. 6, 70ob., 73 (quotes).
4. RGASPI, f. 17, op. 85, d. 325, l. 95; APUFSBIaO, s.d. 8597, l. 72ob. (quote). On lifestyle experimentation, see Anne E. Gorsuch, *Youth in Revolutionary Russia: Enthusiasts, Bohemians, Delinquents* (Bloomington, Ind., 2000).
5. APUFSBIaO, s.d. 8597, ll. 62, 89 (quote), 102; RGASPI, f. 17, op. 85, d. 325, ll. 56, 95. A memorandum by Central Party Committee investigators asserted that Liulin was a Communist until being purged, in 1921, for "antiparty misdemeanors." RGASPI, f. 17, op. 85, d. 325, l. 95. Other sources, however, including Liulin's own testimony, indicate that he never joined the party. RGASPI, f. 17, op. 85, d. 325, l. 56; APUFSBIaO, s.d. 8597, ll. 6, 62, 89.
6. RGASPI, f. 17, op. 85, d. 325, l. 56; GARF, f. 5457, op. 16, d. 63, l. 227ob.; APUFSBIaO, s.d. 8597, ll. 62, 65ob. ("Soviet"), 70ob. ("authority").
7. RGASPI, f. 17, op. 85, d. 307, ll. 40 ("panic"), 44 ("strike"); APUFSBIaO, s.d. 8597, ll. 70ob., 74ob., 76ob., 94 ("They . . . [cooperative]"); GARF, f. 5457, op. 16, d. 63, ll. 227ob. ("stands").
8. RGASPI, f. 17, op. 85, d. 307, ll. 65–66; APUFSBIaO, s.d. 8597, ll. 70ob., 73 (quote).
9. APUFSBIaO, s.d. 8597, ll. 20, 36, 43–45, 55ob., 91. Besides Liulin, another member of the delegation was thirty-one-year-old Vladimir Mednikov, an overlooker who had worked at the mill since before the October Revolution, and known Liulin "since childhood." A husband and father of three children, Mednikov served in the Imperial Army during the Great War, and in the Red

Army during the Civil War. He "sympathize[d] with Soviet power," and was a party member from 1925 to 1926. APUFSBIaO, s.d. 8597, ll. 18, 70–70ob. The sources offer no details about the other delegates, other than that one was a woman and that another was a Communist who was soon expelled from the delegation's ranks.

10. APUFSBIaO, s.d. 8597, l. 55ob.; RGASPI, f. 17, op. 85, d. 325, l. 40 ("an overwhelming"); d. 307, ll. 65–66 (block quote, Central Party Committee report; italics in original).

11. RGASPI, f. 17, op. 85, d. 325, ll. 30 ("masters"), 40–42; d. 307, l. 66 ("categorically").

12. RGASPI, f. 17, op. 85, d. 297, l. 57.

13. APUFSBIaO, s.d. 8597, ll. 21–22.

14. APUFSBIaO, s.d. 8597, l. 21.

15. RGASPI, f. 17, op. 85, d. 297, l. 57; APUFSBIaO, s.d. 8597, ll. 21–22 (quotes).

16. APUFSBIaO, s.d. 8597, ll. 18–19.

17. APUFSBIaO, s.d. 8597, ll. 55ob., 94–95; RGASPI, f. 17, op. 85, d. 325, ll. 6–7, 29.

18. APUFSBIaO, s.d. 8597, l. 22.

19. APUFSBIaO, s.d. 8597, ll. 22 (quotes), 26.

20. APUFSBIaO, s.d. 8597, l. 20; RGASPI, f. 17, op. 85, d. 325, ll. 4–5, 11 (quotes); GARF, f. 5457, op. 16, d. 78, ll. 23–24.

21. APUFSBIaO, s.d. 8597, ll. 20–23 (italics added).

22. APUFSBIaO, s.d. 8597, ll. 24–26.

23. APUFSBIaO, s.d. 8597, ll. 31–34 (italics added).

24. APUFSBIaO, s.d. 8597, ll. 34–36.

25. APUFSBIaO, s.d. 8597, ll. 43–45; RGASPI, f. 17, op. 85, d. 325, l. 5 (quote).

26. RGASPI, f. 17, op. 85, d. 297, l. 57; d. 325, l. 6 (quote).

27. GARF, f. 5457, op. 16, d. 78, l. 23.

28. RGASPI, f. 17, op. 85, d. 305, ll. 1–75 ("very," 6; "The workers . . . all," 35).

29. RGASPI, f. 17, op. 85, d. 325, l. 56.

30. RGASPI, f. 17, op. 85, d. 325, ll. 9, 31; APUFSBIaO, s.d. 8597, l. 56.

31. RGASPI, f. 17, op. 85, d. 325, ll. 9, 16–17, 31, 33, 48, 56.

32. RGASPI, f. 17, op. 85, d. 325, ll. 21–22. "Bourgeois specialists" were managers and technicians who had received their training and first been employed in industry before the October Revolution.

33. RGASPI, f. 17, op. 85, d. 325, ll. 17, 39, 50, 57 ("not"); APUFSBIaO, s.d. 8597, l. 56; GT, 1/24/29, 3 ("a bandit"). Miller made himself even more unpopular when he got into a shouting match with Liulin's supporters. "You're all counterrevolutionaries!" he told them. "We'll make you work twelve hours! We'll squeeze you like a lemon!" RGASPI, f. 17, op. 85, d. 325, l. 57.

34. RGASPI, f. 17, op. 85, d. 325, l. 95. On the Comintern: "We have to force Stalin to stop taking the Soviet money-box abroad for agitation and propaganda. Workers there live 65 percent better than the Russians."

35. RGASPI, f. 17, op. 85, d. 325, l. 95. Rightists were well aware that the textile industry was in crisis, and it was no coincidence that their stronghold was the Moscow Party Committee, which oversaw numerous mills and opposed Stalin, in part, because of the anticipated impact of his program on light industry. Cohen, *Bukharin and the Bolshevik Revolution,* 234, 297.
36. APUFSBIaO, s.d. 8597, l. 72ob.
37. RGASPI, f. 17, op. 85, d. 325, ll. 31 (quote), 57–58; APUFSBIaO, s.d. 8597, l. 56.
38. RGASPI, f. 17, op. 85, d. 325, l. 58.
39. RGASPI, f. 17, op. 85, d. 325, l. 32; APUFSBIaO, s.d. 8597, ll. 56–56ob.; *GT,* 12/7/28, 3; 12/14/28, 3 (retraction).
40. RGASPI, f. 17, op. 85, d. 325, ll. 52, 32, 49.
41. RGASPI, f. 17, op. 85, d. 325, ll. 49–50, 52.
42. RGASPI, f. 17, op. 85, d. 325, ll. 49, 52.
43. RGASPI, f. 17, op. 85, d. 325, ll. 37, 52.
44. APUFSBIaO, s.d. 8597, l. 56ob. ("extraordinary"); RGASPI, f. 17, op. 85, d. 325, ll. 49, 52 (other quotes).
45. RGASPI, f. 17, op. 85, d. 325, ll. 54, 58 (quote).
46. RGASPI, f. 17, op. 85, d. 325, l. 54.
47. RGASPI, f. 17, op. 85, d. 325, ll. 37, 54, 58 (quotes).
48. RGASPI, f. 17, op. 85, d. 325, ll. 49, 53–54; *GT,* 1/24/29, 3 (quote).
49. RGASPI, f. 17, op. 85, d. 325, ll. 53, 66 (quote).
50. RGASPI, f. 17, op. 85, d. 325, ll. 36–38, 41.
51. RGASPI, f. 17, op. 85, d. 325, l. 38; APUFSBIaO, s.d. 8597, ll. 56ob.–58ob. (quotes).
52. RGASPI, f. 17, op. 85, d. 325, ll. 28–30; APUFSBIaO, s.d. 8597, ll. 53, 55ob.–59ob. (quotes). *Samokritika* was the principle that workers had the right to offer constructive criticism of their superiors. The term "Liulin type" is from an April 1930 OGPU report on labor unrest in Sereda. GAIO, f. 1276, op. 23, d. 4, l. 236.
53. RGASPI, f. 17, op. 85, d. 325, ll. 12–13, 15–16, 34–36, 38.
54. RGASPI, f. 17, op. 85, d. 325, ll. 49–50, 52–54.
55. RGASPI, f. 17, op. 85, d. 325, ll. 53 (quote), 66.
56. APUFSBIaO, s.d. 8597, l. 73 ("routine"); RGASPI, f. 17, op. 85, d. 325, l. 73 (other quotes). On the Central Institute of Labor, see Beissinger, *Scientific Management,* chaps. 1–4. Liulin refused an opportunity to visit the Lenin mausoleum: "I didn't go . . . because [Lenin's] not an icon and I don't intend to worship him. It isn't right to turn a corpse into an idol." RGASPI, f. 17, op. 85, d. 325, l. 95.
57. RGASPI, f. 17., op. 85, d. 325, ll. 73, 95ob. A witness claimed to have been told by Liulin that he was already a member of a party that had cells in Moscow and "in almost all the factories in Iaroslavl." APUFSBIaO, s.d. 8597, l. 66ob. More likely, Liulin had longstanding contact with leftists who, like himself, were disillusioned with the Bolsheviks.

58. RGASPI, f. 17, op. 85, d. 325, ll. 32, 73.
59. RGASPI, f. 17, op. 85, d. 325, ll. 32, 35, 39. Evidence from Red Perekop suggests that about 40 percent of operatives subscribed to *Voice*. RGASPI, f. 17, op. 85, d. 325, l. 35.
60. *GT,* 12/30/28, 3.
61. *GT,* 12/30/28, 3.
62. RGASPI, f. 17, op. 85, d. 325, l. 74; *GT,* 1/15/29, 4.
63. *GT,* 1/15/29, 4.
64. *GT,* 1/15/29, 4.
65. *GT,* 1/15/29, 4.
66. *GT,* 1/19/29, 3.
67. *GT,* 1/19/29, 1, 3.
68. RGASPI, f. 17, op. 85, d. 325, l. 68.
69. RGASPI, f. 17, op. 85, d. 325, l. 68. Liulin contradicted Voronova by denying that the trade union defended the workers' interests, and by asserting that food shortages were caused by grain exports rather than, as Voronova claimed, poor harvests. Ibid. Privately, Liulin also accused party leaders of hypocrisy. "In the press, they call the workers who are fighting for a wage increase 'self-seekers' . . . [but] the 'self-seekers' are the Rykovs, the Kalinins, and the others who get a big salary and ride around in automobiles, boozing it up with *artistes*." APUFSBIaO, s.d. 8597, l. 85ob. Aleksei Rykov was chairman of the Council of People's Commissars, and Mikhail Kalinin was president of the Soviet Union.
70. RGASPI, f. 17, op. 85, d. 325, ll. 68–69. The sources do not indicate how many voted for or against the resolutions.
71. *GT,* 1/24/29, 3 (quotes); RGASPI, f. 17, op. 85, d. 325, l. 69.
72. *GT,* 1/24/29, 3.
73. *GT,* 1/29/29, 4; 2/3/29, 4; 2/5/29, 4 (quotes).
74. *GT,* 1/30/29, 3 (Lytochkin); 2/5/29, 4; 2/6/29, 4 ("correct").
75. TsDNIIO, f. 327, op. 4, d. 48, l. 14 ("be . . . enemy"); RGASPI, f. 17, op. 85, d. 325, l. 75 ("they").
76. TsDNIIO, f. 327, op. 4, d. 48, l. 13; *GT,* 2/5/29, 4 (Nazarov); RGASPI, f. 17, op. 85, d. 325, ll. 71–72, 75–76 (Antropov, Gol'dberg).
77. RGASPI, f. 17, op. 85, d. 325, ll. 75–76, 71–72. The fact that the resolution passed unanimously suggests that the vote was rigged, or that voting against it was not an option.
78. *GT,* 2/5/29, 4.
79. RGASPI, f. 17, op. 85, d. 325, l. 78. On "specialist baiting," see Kuromiya, *Stalin's Industrial Revolution,* 106.
80. GARF, f. 374, op. 27, d. 1639, l. 3.
81. GARF, f. 374, op. 27, d. 1639, ll. 2 (quote), 4, 7. On the 1929–1930 party purge, see Kuromiya, *Stalin's Industrial Revolution,* 35–40.
82. *GT,* 3/3/29, 4; GARF, f. 5457, op. 16, d. 63, l. 226ob. (quotes).
83. TsDNIIO, f. 327, op. 4, d. 48, l. 14. On the Sixteenth Party Conference, see

Leonard Schapiro, *The Communist Party of the Soviet Union* (New York, 1971), 379–381.

84. TsDNIIO, f. 327, op. 4, d. 48, l. 14; *GT,* 6/14/29, 2 ("The state"); APUFSBIaO, s.d. 8597, ll. 60, 96 (other quotes).

85. APUFSBIaO, s.d. 8597, l. 66ob. (Bobrov); *GT,* 6/14/29, 2.

86. *GT,* 6/14/29, 2; TsDNIIO, f. 327, op. 4, d. 48, l. 14 (quote); APUFSBIaO, f. 8597, l. 97.

87. APUFSBIaO, s.d. 8597, ll. 67ob.–68ob.

88. APUFSBIaO, s.d. 8597, ll. 1–2 (quote), 62, 93, 109. Liulin was posthumously rehabilitated in 1993 (l. 118).

89. TsDNIIO, f. 327, op. 4, d. 48, l. 14 (district party committee); *GT,* 6/14/29, 2.

90. RGASPI, f. 17, op. 85, d. 297, ll. 25, 56. The block quote draws from each of three versions of the confiscated leaflet.

91. APUFSBIaO, s.d. 8597, ll. 105–106; RGASPI, f. 17, op. 85, d. 297, ll. 54–54ob. (quote). The sources do not reveal how the conference delegates were selected, or how many voted for or against the resolution.

92. See Kuromiya, *Stalin's Industrial Revolution.*

4. Battle at the Point of Production

1. During these years, the OGPU sent reports on shop-floor unrest to the IIR Party Committee, Soviet Executive Committee, and Council of Trade Unions. Often these reports noted that agents were "investigating" a disturbance, "neutralizing" a "ringleader," or taking other "Chekist measures" to restore order. For examples of such reports, see GAIO, f. 1276, op. 23, dd. 2–4, 6–7, 9–10.

2. Overall employment in the Soviet textile industry declined 5.3 percent in 1929 (from 718,800 to 680,900), and by another 5.3 percent in 1930 (to 645,100). *Trud v SSSR,* 94. In the IIR, the decline was steeper: 10.3 percent in 1929 (from 269,755 to 242,085), and 14.4 percent in 1930 (to 207,144). *Narodnoe khoziaistvo Ivanovskoi promyshlennoi oblasti: Statistiko-ekonomicheskii spravochnik* (Ivanovo-Voznesensk, 1932), 353–354. The data on strike activity underscores the effect of the layoffs. During fiscal year (FY) 1927–1928, Ivanovo-Voznesensk Region mills suffered twenty-five strikes, in which 3,084 workers participated and 3,183.5 work days were lost. FY 1928–1929, by contrast, witnessed only six strikes, 153 strikers, and thirty-two lost work days. By 1930, strike activity again was on the rise. GAIO, f. 1276, op. 1, d. 28, l. 160; TsDNIIO, f. 327, op. 4, d. 157, l. 1.

3. GARF, f. 393, op. 2, d. 1865, l. 17; TsDNIIO, f. 2, op. 12, d. 54, l. 107 (quote). For factory workers, the new ration was either twelve kilograms of flour per month or six hundred grams of bread per day; for dependents, either eight kilograms of flour per month or four hundred grams of bread per day. TsDNIIO, f. 2, op. 12, d. 65, l. 102. The leadership of the trade union criticized the step taken by Ivanovo's cooperatives, saying that purging supply rolls

of workers with ties to the land was unfair and inflammatory. GARF, f. 5457, op. 13, d. 9, ll. 109, 124; *GT,* 3/12/29, 5.

4. TsDNIIO, f. 2, op. 12, d. 54, l. 97 ("lead"); d. 65, ll. 104–105 (other quotes).

5. GARF, f. 393, op. 2, d. 1865, l. 19; f. 5457, op. 13, d. 86, l. 20 ("Why . . . state?"); TsDNIIO, f. 2, op. 12, d. 54, ll. 97 ("blabbering . . . collapse"), 101 ("semi-starvation"), 107; d. 65, ll. 104–105 ("the true"), 148; d. 74, l. 16.

6. TsDNIIO, f. 2, op. 12, d. 65, ll. 102–106 (quotes; italics in original), 144; GARF, f. 393, op. 2, d. 1865, l. 28ob.; f. 3316, op. 1, d. 425, l. 196.

7. TsDNIIO, f. 2, op. 12, d. 54, ll. 55, 108–109 ("correctness," "secure"), 124–125; d. 59, l. 19ob.; d. 65, l. 109 (Smirnov) d. 74, ll. 7–7ob. (Malin); f. 327, op. 4, d. 59, l. 1; GAIO, f. 1276, op. 23, d. 4, l. 230.

8. GARF, f. 5457, op. 13, d. 86, l. 20 ("What's"); d. 9, l. 109 ("The norm"). Regional workers spoke with awe about food supplies in Moscow and Leningrad. GARF, f. 3316, op. 1, d. 425, l. 55; f. 5457, op. 13, d. 9, l. 120. Still, a Norwegian diplomat noted in 1929 that "the shortage of food-stuffs in Leningrad and Moscow has reached an appalling stage." Queues for "bread, butter, sugar, and eggs" lasted "many hours," while staples such as flour, coffee, tea, and macaroni were "unobtainable." D. Cameron Watt, ed., *British Documents on Foreign Affairs: Reports and Papers from the Foreign Office Confidential Prints,* Part II, Series A (Frederick, Md., 1986), 9:207–208.

9. TsDNIIO, f. 2, op. 12, d. 65, l. 106 ("a rather," "anti-Soviet"); d. 54, l. 108 ("the mood"); GARF, f. 393, op. 2, d. 1865, ll. 17–17ob. ("bagmen"), 21, 26, 31; *GT,* 2/23/29, 3; 2/24/29, 1 ("there"). Mill towns such as Kineshma, Sereda, Teikovo, and Vichuga were "second-tier" insofar as they tended to be supplied more poorly than the regional capital, Ivanovo.

10. RGASPI, f. 558, op. 1, d. 5388, ll. 111–112 (cited in R. W. Davies, M. B. Tauger, and S. G. Wheatcroft, "Stalin, Grain Stocks and the Famine of 1932–1933," *Slavic Review* 54, no. 3 [1995]: 648). Grain procurements in 1929 exceeded the previous year's by almost 50 percent. Clarke, *Soviet Economic Facts,* 113.

11. *Itogi XVI s"ezda VKP(b)* (Moscow, 1930), 98–99, 106–107, 110; GARF, f. 3316, op. 1, d. 448, ll. 44–45; TsDNIIO, f. 327, op. 4, d. 157, l. 1ob.; GAIO, f. 1276, op. 23, d. 4, ll. 302 ("sharp"), 325, 342–343, 360 ("tense").

12. GAIO, f. 1276, op. 23, d. 4, ll. 209 (Shuia), 277 ("colossal"), 179 (Teikovo, Nerl), 360; GARF, f. 3316, op. 1, d. 446, l. 134 ("the party").

13. GAIO, f. 1276, op. 23, d. 4, ll. 260, 315 (italics in original).

14. GAIO, f. 1276, op. 23, d. 4, ll. 305 (quotes), 316.

15. GAIO, f. 1276, op. 23, d. 4, l. 317.

16. GAIO, f. 1276, op. 23, d. 4, l. 339.

17. GARF, f. 393, op. 2, d. 1876, ll. 131, 194; f. 5457, op. 14, d. 78, l. 45; op. 16, d. 97, l. 162; GAIO, f. 1276, op. 23, d. 4, l. 403; d. 3, l. 110 (Ivanovo); TsDNIIO, f. 327, op. 4, d. 166, l. 3 (Shuia). On closed workers' cooperatives, see Hessler, *A Social History of Soviet Trade.*

18. GARF, f. 393, op. 2, d. 1876, l. 131; GAIO, f. 1276, op. 23, d. 3, l. 127; d. 7, ll. 12–13 (Profintern); d. 4, l. 404 (Kovrov); TsDNIIO, f. 327, op. 4, d. 59, l. 17 (Perekop).

19. GARF, f. 5457, op. 16, d. 97, l. 33; GAIO, f. 1276, op. 23, d. 3, l. 116 (quote).

20. GARF, f. 5457, op. 13, d. 252, ll. 1ob.–3ob. (quote) Raw cotton was in short supply because the government was importing less of it to conserve hard currency. After peaking at 163,000 tons in FY 1926–1927, cotton imports fell to 145,000 tons in FY 1927–1928, 115,000 tons in 1929, and 58,000 tons in 1930. Domestic cotton, the output of which rose during this period, was lower in quality and often could not serve as a replacement. Clarke, *Soviet Economic Facts*, 48, 116.

21. GARF, f. 5457, op. 13, d. 86, l. 27 (Sereda); d. 220, l. 58; op. 16, d. 97, l. 33 ("counterplans," "unrealistic"); GAIO, f. 1276, op. 23, d. 3, l. 90 (Zakharov); d. 2, ll. 68, 90, 95–95ob.; TsDNIIO, f. 327, op. 4, d. 195, ll. 61, 64–65; d. 561, l. 69.

22. TsDNIIO, f. 2, op. 12, d. 54, l. 101 (Navoloki); d. 66, ll. 30, 32 (Malin); GAIO, f. 1276, op. 23, d. 2, l. 86 (Dzerzhinskii).

23. GARF, f. 393, op. 2, d. 1865, l. 17; f. 3316, op. 1, d. 425, ll. 196 (Gavrilov-Posad), 222; GAIO, f. 1276, op. 23, d. 4, l. 81; d. 2, ll. 194, 210 (Gavrilov-Iam).

24. GARF, f. 5457, op. 13, d. 57, l. 27ob.; TsDNIIO, f. 2, op. 12, d. 54, l. 101; GAIO, f. 1276, op. 23, d. 4, l. 26 (quote); d. 2, l. 136.

25. TsDNIIO, f. 2, op. 12, d. 54, ll. 101–102; d. 59, l. 6ob. (Zaitseva); GAIO, f. 1276, op. 23, d. 2, l. 214ob.; d. 4, ll. 29–31, 210 (Pershin).

26. GAIO, f. 1276, op. 23, d. 4, ll. 102 ("They . . . work!"), 64 ("You've . . . wages!"), 153; d. 3, l. 10.

27. GARF, f. 5457, op. 13, d. 86, l. 10 (quote); GAIO, f. 1276, op. 23, d. 2, l. 86.

28. GAIO, f. 1276, op. 23, d. 4, ll. 39, 103, 139; d. 2, ll. 68, 70–70ob. (quote), 145, 181–182; op. 1, d. 28, ll. 31–31ob.; GARF, f. 5457, op. 13, d. 57, ll. 69, 71–72; *GT*, 3/15/29, 1, 3.

29. TsDNIIO, f. 2, op. 12, d. 65, ll. 105–106.

30. GAIO, f. 1276, op. 1, d. 28, ll. 17–17ob., 31–31ob. (quote); op. 23, d. 2, ll. 44–45, 54–54ob., 122; d. 3, l. 99; GARF, f. 5457, op. 13, d. 317, l. 74. The outcome of a job action in March 1930 by forty veteran female weavers at the Navoloki Mill was not reported. GAIO, f. 1276, op. 23, d. 4, ll. 120, 124–125.

31. TsDNIIO, f. 2, op. 12, d. 74, ll. 6ob.–7 (Ivanovo); d. 66, l. 30 (Kineshma); f. 327, op. 4, d. 67, l. 96 (Gus-Khrustal'nyi); GAIO, f. 1276, op. 23, d. 2, ll. 18–18ob., 248 (Kamenka); d. 4, l. 226.

32. TsDNIIO, f. 2, op. 12, d. 54, ll. 101–102.

33. GAIO, f. 1276, op. 23, d. 2, ll. 139–140 (Pistsovo); d. 4, l. 107 (Lakinskii); TsDNIIO, f. 2, op. 12, d. 54, ll. 99–100 (lyrics).

34. TsDNIIO, f. 327, op. 4, d. 195, ll. 64–65; d. 555, l. 28 ("class"); f. 2, op. 12, d. 65, l. 105 (Balashov); GAIO, f. 1276, op. 23, d. 4, ll. 29, 246–248 (Kamenka).

35. TsDNIIO, f. 327, op. 4, d. 195, l. 64; GARF, f. 5457, op. 14, d. 103, l. 34; GAIO, f. 1276, op. 23, d. 7, l. 317 (quote).

36. GAIO, f. 1276, op. 23, d. 2, ll. 141–142.

37. TsDNIIO, f. 2, op. 12, d. 65, l. 124 (quotes; italics in original); GARF, f. 5457, op. 13, d. 57, l. 28.

38. GAIO, f. 1276, op. 23, d. 2, ll. 24–24ob.; TsDNIIO, f. 2, op. 12, d. 65, l. 106; GARF, f. 5457, op. 13, d. 57, ll. 60 ("the anti-proletarian"), 61–74, 85–88; *GT,* 10/9/29, 1.

39. E. L. Bondarenko, *Razvitie sotsialisticheskogo sorevnovaniia v khlopchatobu-mazhnoi promyshlennosti SSSR* (Moscow, 1953), 5; Shipulina, "Sotsialistich-eskoe sorevnovanie," 26–27; Svetlana Semenovna Sadina, *Partiino-sovetskaia periodicheskaia pechat v bor'be za razvitie massovogo sotsialisticheskogo sorev-novaniia tekstil'shchikov v gody pervoi piatiletki, 1928–1932gg.* (Leningrad, 1977), 15.

40. Bondarenko, *Razvitie,* 5; Shipulina, "Sotsialisticheskoe sorevnovanie," 30–31; Sadina, *Periodicheskaia pechat,* 15; TsDNIIO, f. 327, op. 4, d. 55, l. 63; GARF, f. 5457, op. 13, d. 18, l. 71; d. 202, ll. 4–5; *GT,* 9/4/29, 3; 9/26/29, 4; 10/9/29, 1; *Serp i molot* (Shuia; hereafter, *SiM*), 5/25/29, 2 (quote).

41. TsDNIIO, f. 327, op. 4, d. 67, ll. 199 ("the most"), 95 ("kulak-counterrevo-lutionary"); *SiM,* 5/21/29, 1–2; 5/24/29, 2; 5/30/29, 2; 6/13/29, 2.

42. GARF, f. 5457, op. 13, d. 18, l. 71; op. 14, d. 78, l. 62; *SiM,* 6/13/29 ("The Soviet"), 2; 6/4/29, 3 ("There's"); 5/30/29, 2; TsDNIIO, f. 327, op. 4, d. 67, l. 96; d. 195, ll. 61, 64; d. 561, l. 71; GAIO, f. 1276, op. 23, d. 2, l. 160; d. 3, ll. 122–124.

43. GARF, f. 5457, op. 16, d. 78, l. 73 (italics in original).

44. *GT,* 10/26/29, 1 ("manifestation"); GARF, f. 5457, op. 13, d. 57, l. 69 ("categorically"); TsDNIIO, f. 327, op. 4, d. 67, l. 96 (other quotes).

45. GARF, f. 5457, op. 13, d. 57, l. 48 ("the strong," "were"); op. 16, d. 63, ll. 100–101; TsDNIIO, f. 327, op. 4, d. 561, l. 71 ("For").

46. *GT,* 9/26/29, 4. Most operatives who became shock workers did so to secure privileges or to avoid incurring the wrath of superiors. Hence the trade union's concern that "pseudo–shock workers" had infiltrated the ranks. Sadina, *Peri-odicheskaia pechat,* 17; Shipulina, "Sotsialisticheskoe sorevnovanie," 32; GARF, f. 5457, op. 14, d. 78, ll. 1, 60; op. 16, d. 87, ll. 4–5 (quote); d. 97, l. 30; *SiM,* 5/21/29, 2.

47. *SiM,* 6/4/29, 3; GAIO, f. 1276, op. 23, d. 3, l. 26 (Ivanovo); d. 2, ll. 166, 180–180ob., 211 (Iakovlevskoe); GARF, f. 5457, op. 13, d. 18, l. 71; d. 202, ll. 4–5 (Tutaev); TsDNIIO, f. 327, op. 4, d, 55, l. 63; *GT,* 9/26/29, 4. While some young workers opposed socialist competition out of fear of retaliation, others did so out of respect for their shop-floor elders. The former often looked to the latter for guidance in such matters. GARF, f. 5457, op. 13, d. 202, ll. 4–5; GAIO, f. 1283, op. 1, d. 275, l. 6.

48. GAIO, f. 1276, op. 23, d. 7, l. 112 (Iuzha); d. 2, ll. 161–161ob. (Gorelev); GARF, f. 5457, op. 16, d. 97, l. 33.

49. TsDNIIO, f. 327, op. 4, d. 56, l. 33; *SiM,* 5/21/29, 2; 5/24/29, 2; 5/30/29, 2; 6/4/29, 3; 6/11/29, 2 (quotes).

50. RGASPI, f. 17, op. 85, d. 236, l. 4 (Central Party Committee); *Trud,* 7/3/29 (Gozhev, cited in Filtzer, *Soviet Workers and Stalinist Industrialization,* 77); TsDNIIO, f. 327, op. 4, d. 55, l. 63 (IIR Party Committee); GARF, f. 5457, op. 23, d. 199, l. 59. The official view was that peasant workers bore most of the responsibility for the deterioration of morale in—and the poor performance of—the mills. GARF, f. 5457, op. 13, d. 13, l. 7; d. 14, ll. 5–6; d. 18, l. 32ob.; *GT,* 2/9/29, 1. By contrast, a cautious defense of peasant workers and their contribution to the industry appeared in Semenov, *Litso,* 46–50, 52–53.

51. TsDNIIO, f. 327, op. 4, d. 55, l. 63 (Iakovlevskoe); d. 59, l. 17 ("the idea"); d. 67, l. 118 (Karabanovo); *SiM,* 5/25/29, 2 (Shuia); 5/24/29, 2; 6/4/29, 3; GAIO, f. 1276, op. 23, d. 7, l. 11 (Profintern); d. 2, ll. 24–24ob., 160; d. 3, ll. 26, 153–154; d. 4, l. 138 (Krasnye tkachi); APUFSBIaO, s.d. 8597, ll. 97, 73 ("the tenth"). The vote on socialist competition at the Novye Gorki Mill was not even close: 20 in favor, 980 opposed. GAIO, f. 1276, op. 23, d. 4, l. 145.

52. Shipulina, "Sotsialisticheskoe sorevnovanie," 28–29; GARF, f. 5457, op. 13, d. 18, ll. 68, 71; GAIO, f. 1276, op. 23, d. 2, ll. 166, 180–180ob.; d. 7, ll. 146–147 (suicides); *Trud,* 7/3/29 (Gozhev; cited in Filtzer, *Soviet Workers,* 77–78).

53. GARF, f. 5457, op. 13, d. 13, ll. 6–9; d. 57, l. 23ob.; *Voprosy truda v tsifrakh: statisticheskii spravochnik za 1927–1930gg.* (Moscow, 1930), 46. The number of unemployed Soviet textile workers rose almost 50 percent between April 1928 and May 1929—from 54,900 to 80,000. GARF, f. 5457, op. 13, d. 13, ll. 10–11. In the IIR, the unemployment rate among textile workers climbed from 4 percent in October 1928 to 8.1 percent a year later. In the industry as a whole, the figures were 7.3 and 10.5 percent, respectively. GARF, f. 5457, op. 13, d. 326, ll. 392, 398.

54. TsDNIIO, f. 2, op. 12, d. 54, l. 99 (Vichuga, Ivanovo, "exploiters"); d. 74, l. 17 (Iuzha, "bloodsuckers"); GARF, f. 5457, op. 13, d. 86, l. 5; Semenov, *Litso,* 51.

55. GARF, f. 5457, op. 13, d. 86, l. 29 (Sereda); TsDNIIO, f. 2, op. 12, d. 54, l. 101 (Kineshma); Semenov, *Litso,* 58–59.

56. TsDNIIO, f. 2, op. 12, d. 65, ll. 88–89, 100.

57. GARF, f. 5457, op. 13, d. 13, ll. 6–7; d. 18, l. 63; d. 252, ll. 1–3ob.; op. 16, d. 87, l. 2; d. 88. ll. 1–3; *GT,* 3/10/29, 6.

58. TsDNIIO, f. 2, op. 12, d. 54, ll. 107, 109; d. 65, ll. 102, 104–105 (quotes).

59. GARF, f. 5457, op. 13, d. 86, ll. 4, 31; TsDNIIO, f. 2, op. 12, d. 54, ll. 56 (Kharitonov), 107–108 (other quotes); d. 65, l. 109; f. 327, op. 4, d. 67, l. 96.

60. GAIO, f. 1276, op. 23, d. 2, l. 136 ("abominable"); d. 4, l. 81 (other quotes).

61. GAIO, f. 1276, op. 23, d. 4, l. 86; d. 2, ll. 210, 204 (quotes).

62. GARF, f. 5457, op. 16, d. 78, ll. 142–142ob. (Mel'nichanskii), 102ob. (Pereslavl); GAIO, f. 1276, op. 23, d. 4, ll. 140, 162.

63. GARF, f. 5457, op. 13, d. 57, l. 27ob.; d. 86, ll. 18, 28–31 (quote), 39, 45; TsDNIIO, f. 2, op. 12, d. 59, ll. 15ob.–16; d. 65, l. 104; *SiM*, 5/30/29, 2.

64. TsDNIIO, f. 2, op. 12, d. 59, l. 17; GAIO, f. 1276, op. 23, d. 3, l. 105; *GT*, 2/27/29, 3; 4/14/29, 3; GARF, f. 3316, op., d. 425, l. 222; d. 426, l. 31 (letter).

65. GAIO, f. 1276, op. 23, d. 4, ll. 45, 197 (Sereda), 236, 251, 144 (Perekop); TsDNIIO, f. 327, op. 4, d. 166, l. 3.

66. GARF, f. 5457, op. 23, d. 74, ll. 26–27.

67. GARF, f. 5457, op. 23, d. 74, ll. 27–29.

68. GARF, f. 5457, op. 23, d. 74, l. 23; RGASPI, f. 17, op. 85, d. 305, ll. 7–8 (quotes).

69. RGASPI, f. 17, op. 85, d. 305, ll. 8, 66; *GT*, 11/4/28, 1; *Itogi XVI s"ezda*, 253.

70. *GT*, 6/22/29, 3; GARF, f. 5457, op. 12, d. 23, l. 38; op. 13, d. 13, l. 45; op. 16, d. 72, l. 9. The real wages of Soviet workers are estimated to have declined by almost 50 percent from 1928 to 1932. John Barber, "The Standard of Living of Soviet Industrial Workers, 1928–1941," in Charles Bettelheim, ed., *L'Industrialisation de L'URSS dans les Années Trente* (Paris, 1982), 116.

71. TsDNIIO, f. 2, op. 11, d. 39, l. 306; d. 184, l. 15; GARF, f. 5457, op. 12, d. 48, l. 30; d. 23, ll. 108, 320ob.; op. 13, d. 18, l. 40ob.; *GT*, 12/8/28, 3; 12/7/28, 3 (quotes).

72. TsDNIIO, f. 2, op. 12, d. 66, l. 32; d. 54, ll. 55–56 (quote); f. 327, op. 4, d. 56, l. 72; *GT*, 11/30/29, 4.

73. TsDNIIO, f. 327, op. 4, d. 195, ll. 78–81; f. 2, op. 12, d. 54, l. 97 (quote).

74. GARF, f. 5457, op. 13, d. 86, ll. 13, 28; d. 317, l. 74; TsDNIIO, f. 2, op. 12, d. 54, ll. 101–102; d. 74, l. 167ob.; GAIO, f. 1276, op. 1, d. 28, ll. 31–31ob.; op. 23, d. 2, ll. 68–68ob., 86, 107–107ob., 123–123ob., 136, 138, 165, 214ob.; d. 3, ll. 10, 18.

75. GAIO, f. 1276, op. 23, d. 3, ll. 52, 56–58.

76. GAIO, f. 1276, op. 23, d. 4, l. 93.

77. GAIO, f. 1276, op. 23, d. 4, l. 139.

78. GARF, f. 5457, op. 13, d. 57, ll. 27ob.–28.

79. TsDNIIO, f. 327, op. 4, d. 56, ll. 71 (Great Ivanovo, Nogin); *GT*, 12/11/29, 3; GAIO, f. 1276, op. 23, d. 2, l. 184 (Zinov'ev).

80. GAIO, f. 1276, op. 23, d. 4, ll. 221, 238, 225–226 (quotes). When Prostiakova was reprimanded by the factory committee chairman, subsequently her coworkers vowed to defend her.

81. GAIO, f. 1276, op. 23, d. 4, l. 140. The outcome of the strike, which prompted the intervention of the district party committee, was not reported.

82. GARF, f. 3316, op. 1, d. 425, l. 161 (letter); GAIO, f. 1276, op. 23, d. 4, ll. 346 (Krasnoshchekov), 106 (Perekop). The Soviet government raised 9.4 percent of net revenue from the sale of domestic bonds in FY 1929/30. Davies, *Soviet Economy*, 534.

83. GAIO, f. 1276, op. 23, d. 4, ll. 173–176, 230, 339–340 (quote, 175); d. 3, l. 154; GARF, f. 393, op. 2, d. 1876, ll. 29, 488; f. 5457, op. 16, d. 97, l. 31; TsDNIIO, f. 327, op. 4, d. 195, l. 61; *GT*, 10/9/29, 1.

84. GAIO, f. 1276, op. 23, d. 4, ll. 174–175.

85. GAIO, f. 1276, op. 23, d. 3, l. 149 ("the money"); d. 4, ll. 174–175 (other quotes).

86. RGASPI, f. 17, op. 85, d. 305, l. 10 (quote); GARF, f. 5457, op. 13, d. 13, ll. 9–10, 42; op. 23, d. 228, l. 1; *VIII s"ezd professional'nykh soiuzov SSSR*, 416.

87. RGASPI, f. 17, op. 85, d. 236, l. 20; TsDNIIO, f. 2, op. 11, d. 39, l. 282; GARF, f. 5457, op. 13, d. 86, ll. 20, 22; op. 14, d. 78, ll. 50, 53; op. 16, d. 88, ll. 1–2ob.; op. 23, d. 228, l. 4; *Otchety TsK, TsKK i delegatsii VKP(b) v IKKI XVI s"ezdu VKP(b)* (Moscow, 1930), 240–241. The idling of most mills during the summer of 1930 caused Soviet output of cotton cloth to decline by more than half compared to the same period of the previous year. Davies, *Soviet Economy*, 515.

88. GAIO, f. 1276, op. 23, d. 4, l. 230. The compensation issue was so sensitive that it was decided by the Politburo, which decreed that all furloughed operatives be paid two-thirds of the current tariff rate and exempted from the social-insurance tax. RGASPI, f. 17, op. 3, d. 783, l. 10.

89. GAIO, f. 1276, op. 23, d. 4, ll. 148, 180–181 (Sosnevo), 238 (Zinov'ev).

90. GAIO, f. 1276, op. 23, d. 4, l. 236.

91. GAIO, f. 1276, op. 23, d. 4, ll. 236–236ob.

92. TsDNIIO, f. 327, op. 5, d. 162, l. 9; GAIO, f. 1276, op. 23, d. 4, ll. 306, 338 (quotes).

93. GAIO, f. 1276, op. 23, d. 4, ll. 339–340.

94. GAIO, f. 1276, op. 23, d. 4, ll. 171–172.

95. GAIO, f. 1276, op. 23, d. 4, ll. 171–172. Given that the Rostov Mill was still in operation as of 1933, it seems that the workers' rearguard action in defense of their livelihood was successful. *Raiony IPO*, 2:206.

96. GAIO, f. 1276, op. 23, d. 3, ll. 109, 117 (italics added). Given that the Sosnevo Mill was still in operation as of 1933, the protesters apparently prevailed. *Raiony IPO*, 2:76.

97. GAIO, f. 1276, op. 23, d. 3, l. 175. The party ignored the workers' protests, and, by 1933, the Korolev Mill was out of operation. *Raiony IPO*, 2:76.

98. GAIO, f. 1276, op. 23, d. 7, ll. 62–64.

99. GARF, f. 3316, op. 1, d. 446, l. 106 (unpublished letter, italics in original); GAIO, f. 1276, op. 23, d. 4, l. 138 (Larionova).

100. Western diplomatic and Soviet sources make clear that the crisis of shop-floor morale was confined neither to the textile industry nor to the IIR. See, for example, Watt, *British Documents on Foreign Affairs*, 9:275–277; 10:123, 157–158, 167; 16:333–334; GARF, f. 1235, op. 141, d. 583, l. 85; f. 3316, op. 1, d. 425, ll. 57–59, 159–161; d. 426, ll. 36–38, 92, 133; d. 446, ll. 102, 104–106, 127–129, 160–162, 166, 211–212, 231, 233–235; and d. 448, ll. 19–20, 40–41, 62, 102–106.

101. Watt, *British Documents on Foreign Affairs*, 10:167.

5. To the Brink of Rebellion

1. The FFYP was declared by the party to have been completed in four years and three months. It began on October 1, 1928, and ended on December 31, 1932.

2. TsDNIIO, f. 327, op. 4, d. 157, l. 1; d. 449, l. 151. The 1931 figure includes participants in "conflicts" as well as "strikes"; authorities recorded 91 of the former, and 116 of the latter. Figures for earlier years cover strikes only: there were twenty-three in 1929, and fifty-five in 1930. A Russian scholar who has worked in the central archive of the security police—to which the author of this book has been denied access—reports that there were sixty-six strikes in the Soviet textile industry during the first quarter of 1929, and ninety-two during the first quarter of 1930. The surge in labor unrest thus was not confined to IIR mills. Osokina, *Our Daily Bread,* 53.

3. *Itogi XVI s"ezda VKP(b),* 107.

4. GAIO, f. 1276, op. 23, d. 7, ll. 39, 82, 88, 103, 106, 110 (quotes).

5. GAIO, f. 1276, op. 23, d. 7, ll. 82–83 (Vichuga), 88, 93–94 (Kineshma).

6. GAIO, f. 1276, op. 23, d. 7, ll. 196–197, 214, 230 (quote).

7. GAIO, f. 1276, op. 23, d. 7, ll. 249, 271 (Ivanovo, Kokhma), 330; d. 6, l. 148 (Kostroma); APUFSBIO, s.d. 8535-p, l. 31 (Teikovo).

8. GAIO, f. 1276, op. 23, d. 7, ll. 83, 85–87, 103, 214, 222, 230; d. 6, l. 139ob. (quotes).

9. GARF/RR2, f. 406, op. 8, d. 852, ll. 1–5ob; TsDNIIO, f. 327, op. 4, d. 515, l. 8; GAIO, f. 1276, op. 23, d. 7, l. 235.

10. GAIO, f. 1276, op. 23, d. 7, ll. 322–323 (quotes), 330–331.

11. TsDNIIO, f. 327, op. 4, d. 449, l. 6; d. 515, ll. 7–10; GARF, f. 5451, op. 42, d. 250, l. 16 (quote); f. 5457, op. 23, d. 74, ll. 39–40. As of December 1930, the 264,200 employees of IIR textile mills were distributed among supply rolls as follows: special category, 0; first category, 58,600 (22.2 percent); second category, 149,300 (56.5 percent); third category, 56,330 (21.3 percent). Bread norms for workers in the special, first, and second categories were identical in 1931, but norms for other products, such as meat and groats, varied. By the middle of that year, cooperatives had little other than bread and sugar in stock, and virtually ceased giving out rations for dependents. Workers in the third category received small ration packets that were assembled and had to be supplied entirely from local sources. GARF, f. 5457, op. 15, d. 79, ll. 65, 75; op. 23, d. 74, l. 35.

12. GARF, f. 374, op. 27, d. 1988, l. 84; f. 5451, op. 16, d. 261, ll. 135–136; TsDNIIO, f. 327, op. 4, d. 515, ll. 17, 146, d. 516, l. 26; GAIO, f. 1276, op. 23, d. 10, ll. 23–24, 42.

13. TsDNIIO, f. 327, op. 4, d. 481, ll. 12–13 (quote), 22–26, 28.

14. RGAE, f. 1562, op. 15, d. 680, ll. 357ob., 383ob., 345ob. Food was by far the largest expense faced by Soviet workers at this time.

15. RGAE, f. 1562, op. 15, d. 735, ll. 269ob., 271ob., 272ob., 273ob.

16. GAIO, f. 1276, op. 23, d. 9, ll. 1–2.
17. GAIO, f. 1276, op. 23, d. 3, ll. 5–6 (OGPU), 13, 26 (Zinov'ev); TsDNIIO, f. 327, op. 4, d. 59, l. 17 (Perekop).
18. GAIO, f. 1276, op. 23, d. 3, l. 3; d. 4, l. 390 (quotes).
19. GAIO, f. 1276, op. 23, d. 4, l. 393 (Vinogradov); d. 3, l. 7 (other quotes).
20. GAIO, f. 1276, op. 23, d. 3, l. 4.
21. GAIO, f. 1276, op. 23, d. 3, ll. 24–25. One of the women who spearheaded this protest was a former member of the Socialist-Revolutionary Party.
22. GAIO, f. 1276, op. 23, d. 3, ll. 34–35. One of the strike's organizers was the former candidate party member Kokina; one of its opponents, current candidate party member Bakulinskaia.
23. GAIO, f. 1276, op. 23, d. 3, l. 32.
24. GAIO, f. 1276, op. 23, d. 3, l. 15 (Smirnov); GARF, f. 393, op. 2, d. 1876, l. 131. According to the latter source, the OGPU moved expeditiously in Kineshma "to expose the initiators who roused the workers to organized demonstration."
25. GAIO, f. 1276, op. 23, d. 3, ll. 102, 108, 116 (quotes). Protests also were reported at the Teikovo Combine, prompting the OGPU to take unspecified "Chekist measures" (ll. 103, 131).
26. GAIO, f. 1276, op. 23, d. 3, l. 128. A similar protest was reported at the Gavrilov-Iam Mill (ll. 136, 145, 151). In Kineshma and Iaroslavl, discontent over wage arrears was exacerbated when cooperatives refused to distribute goods to those who had fallen behind in their dues—a practice, warned the OGPU, that "put workers under the threat of hunger" (l. 127).
27. GAIO, f. 1276, op. 23, d. 3, ll. 126, 81.
28. GAIO, f. 1276, op. 23, d. 7, ll. 357 (Kovrov), 106, 91, 97, 132 (Gorki-Pavlovo). The all-factory strike was followed by the identification and, most likely, arrest of its leaders, and by the sacking of the mill's director and the chairmen of the factory committee and party cell.
29. GAIO, f. 1276, op. 23, d. 7, ll. 221–222. When the protest ended, the OGPU arrested the "instigators."
30. GAIO, f. 1276, op. 23, d. 7, ll. 241 ("mass"), 322 ("unhealthy"), 288 ("we're"), 293, 296–298, 326, 330–331 (Chigunkina), 306 ("Sharp"), 335–336; d. 10, ll. 1, 17–18.
31. GAIO, f. 1276, op. 23, d. 10, ll. 14, 23, 26, 28 (quote); TsDNIIO, f. 327, op. 4, d. 516, ll. 25, 27.
32. GAIO, f. 1276, op. 23, d. 7, ll. 327, 332; d. 10, l. 39.
33. GAIO, f. 1276, op. 23, d. 7, ll. 57–58.
34. GAIO, f. 1276, op. 23, d. 7, l. 59.
35. GAIO, f. 1276, op. 23, d. 9, ll. 60, 70 (Nogin); d. 7, ll. 99, 231–232 (Zinov'ev).
36. GAIO, f. 1276, op. 23, d. 7, ll. 329, 359; d. 10, ll. 17, 32; TsDNIIO, f. 327, op. 4, d. 515, l. 17.
37. GARF, f. 5457, op. 23, d. 74, ll. 31–32, 34; GAIO, f. 1276, op. 23, d. 7, l. 313.

38. I. V. Stalin, *Works* (Moscow, 1955), 13:57–62; GAIO, f. 2888, op. 1, d. 49, l. 58. Statistics are from the First State Cotton Trust, which supervised mills in Teikovo and Vichuga.

39. GARF, f. 5457, op. 23, d. 74, ll. 37–39; GAIO, f. 2888, op. 1, d. 49, l. 58.

40. GAIO, f. 1283, op. 1, d. 459, ll. 111–114.

41. GARF, f. 5457, op. 23, d. 228, ll. 1–9, 16, 19–20; TsDNIIO, f. 327, op. 4, d. 515, l. 66; GAIO, f. 1283, op. 1, d. 459, ll. 107, 111; d. 461, l. 3.

42. TsDNIIO, f. 327, op. 4, d. 515, ll. 67–68 (quotes), 145; d. 516, ll. 24–26; GAIO, f. 1276, op. 23, d. 10, l. 36; f. 1283, op. 1, d. 459, l. 110.

43. GAIO, f. 2888, op. 1, d. 49, l. 46; f. 1283, op. 1, d. 461, ll. 3–6; d. 459, ll. 108, 110–112; GARF/RR2, f. 390, op. 11, d. 115, "Kon"iunktura po trudu za 11 mes. 1931 g. po khlopchatobumazhnoi promyshlennosti."

44. GARF, f. 5451, op. 16, d. 261, l. 136 (quote); TsDNIIO, f. 327, op. 4, d. 516, l. 26; d. 503, ll. 3–5.

45. TsDNIIO, f. 327, op. 5, d. 162, l. 82.

46. TsDNIIO, f. 327, op. 4, d. 515, l. 143.

47. TsDNIIO, f. 327, op. 4, d. 515, l. 143 (quote); RGAE, f. 1562, op. 15, d. 735, ll. 269ob., 271ob. Goods sold in the socialized sector of the economy were, on average, 62 percent more expensive in the first half of 1932 than in 1928. In the unregulated sphere of private trade, agricultural goods were almost nine times more expensive on April 1, 1932, than they had been four years earlier. R. W. Davies, *Crisis and Progress in the Soviet Economy, 1931–1933* (Cambridge, Mass., 1996), 553, 556.

48. GARF, f. 5457, op. 23, d. 74, ll. 32–33.

49. I. P. Borisov and L. S. Kheifets, *Chto dala funktsionalka na fabrike imeni Lakina* (Ivanovo-Voznesensk, 1931), 2, 6–7, 16, 21, 23–24, 49, 51–57, 62.

50. Borisov and Kheifets, *Chto dala funktsionalka,* 2, 5, 8–14, 16–18, 35–39, 47, 50–57, 60–61; GARF/RR2, f. 390, op. 11, d. 115, "Kon"iunktura"; GAIO, f. 1276, op. 23, d. 7, l. 76.

51. GARF/RR2, f. 390, op. 11, d. 115, "Kon"iunktura"; TsDNIIO, f. 327, op. 4, d. 351, l. 1; Borisov and Kheifets, *Chto dala funktsionalka,* 10–11 ("a combat"), 6–7 ("the class"), 12–13; Ivan Chuev, *V boiakh za funktsionalku* (Ivanovo-Voznesensk, 1931), 8–9 ("the most"), 10–15; GAIO, f. 1276, op. 23, d. 7, ll. 76–78.

52. Kuromiya, *Stalin's Industrial Revolution,* 242; GAIO, f. 1276, op. 23, d. 7, ll. 76–78 (quotes).

53. GARF, f. 5457, op. 23, d. 74, l. 34; d. 47, ll. 5ob. ("a negative"), 29, 78ob.–79ob., 82, 95ob., 98 ("the most").

54. GAIO, f. 1276, op. 23, d. 7, ll. 150–151.

55. GAIO, f. 1276, op. 23, d. 7, ll. 174–175.

56. GAIO, f. 1276, op. 23, d. 7, ll. 113, 230.

57. GAIO, f. 1276, op. 23, d. 7, ll. 285–286 (quotes), 361; d. 10, l. 17.

58. *Lubianka: Stalin i Glavnoe upravlenie gosbezopasnosti NKVD, 1937–1938* (Moscow, 2004), 120–121. I am indebted to Leonid Vaintraub for bringing this source to my attention.

59. GARF/RR2, f. 390, op. 11, d. 115, "Kon"iunktura"; Kuromiya, *Stalin's Industrial Revolution*, 243; Chuev, *V boiakh za funktsionalku*, 29; TsDNIIO, f. 327, op. 4, d. 500, l. 41; d. 503, l. 1; d. 515, l. 25; d. 555, ll. 12–13.

60. GAIO. f. 1276, op. 23, d. 7, ll. 91, 146, 365.

61. GAIO. f. 1276, op. 23, d. 7, ll. 208–209.

62. *Trud v SSSR*, 94; GARF/RR2, f. 390, op. 11, d. 115, "Kon"iunktura"; GARF, f. 5457, op. 23, d. 74, ll. 23–25, 41; d. 228, l. 16; TsDNIIO, f. 327, op. 4, d. 500, ll. 103–105; d. 515, l. 11; GAIO, f. 1276, op. 23, d. 7, ll. 22, 223; *Narodnoe khoziaistvo Ivanovskoi promyshlennoi oblasti*, 368–369. The expansion of the textile industry at this time was not unique, for "[t]he year 1931 witnessed the most rapid influx of new workers into industrial labor in the history of Soviet industrialization." Kuromiya, *Stalin's Industrial Revolution*, 290.

63. GARF/RR2, f. 390, op. 11, d. 115, "Kon"iunktura"; *Sostav novykh millionov chlenov profsoiuzov* (Moscow, 1933), 62–63, 96–97; GARF, f. 5457, op. 23, d. 74, l. 24; GAIO, f. 1276, op. 23, d. 9, l. 1; f. 1283, op. 1, d. 459, ll. 52–54; f. 2888, op. 1, d. 49, ll. 70–72.

64. GARF/RR2, f. 390, op. 11, d. 115, "Kon"iunktura"; GARF, f. 5457, op. 23, d. 74, l. 25.

65. Because the *samkritika* campaign often was implemented in name only, workers continued the longstanding—and much safer—tradition of voicing complaints against local officials by writing individual and collective letters to government leaders. This tradition seems to have been nurtured by Moscow, which routinely launched investigations into accusations leveled by such means. GAIO, f. 1276, op. 23, d. 6, ll. 87–88ob., 102, 138–139ob., 148, 173–174ob.

66. GAIO, f. 1276, op. 23, d. 7, ll. 13 (Profintern), 367 (Gusev); GARF, f. 3316, op. 1, d. 446, ll. 38–39 (letter).

67. TsDNIIO, f. 327, op. 5, d. 92, l. 130 (Gus-Khrustal'nyi); d. 152, l. 39 (Novikov); op. 4, d. 507, l. 61 (propagandists). An official noted that comments such as Novikov's could be heard often at the combine's "party, Komsomol, and worker assemblies" (l. 48).

68. TsDNIIO, f. 327, op. 4, d. 507, ll. 3, 48 ("growth"), 78 ("the Social"); d. 515, l. 41 (Belov; italics added); GARF, f. 5457, op. 13, d. 220, l. 22 ("the crisis").

69. GAIO, f. 1276, op. 23, d. 3, ll. 132–134. Krasavina's letter was intercepted by Leningrad Communists, who organized a collective response and reported her to the authorities.

70. TsDNIIO, f. 327, op. 4, d. 516, l. 27; GAIO, f. 1276, op. 23, d. 7, l. 172 (quote; italics added).

71. GAIO, f. 1276, op. 23, d. 7, l. 256.

72. GAIO, f. 1276, op. 23, d. 7, ll. 88, 13 (Radnoshkina, Kozlov), 160 (Kineshma; italics added), 153–154 (peasants).

73. GARF, f. 5457, op. 12, d. 23, l. 165 (trade union); d. 201, ll. 1–3, 10–11, 14; op. 13, d. 220, ll. 9, 28ob., 37ob., 38ob., 40–41ob. (atheism lecturer),

49–50, 58; *GT*, 2/27/29, 4; 4/27/29, 5; 6/8/29, 1; TsDNIIO, f. 327, op. 4, d. 507, l. 76.

74. *GT*, 6/29/29, 5 ("divine"); GARF, f. 5457, op. 13, d. 204, l. 46 ("Before"); d. 220, l. 50 (other quotes).

75. GARF, f. 374, op. 27, d. 1988, l. 61.

6. The Teikovo Strike

1. RGASPI, f. 81, op. 3, d. 213, ll. 49–51; GARF, f. 5451, op. 42, d. 250, l. 148; f. 374, op. 27, d. 1988, l. 93. The only Soviet workers whose rations were left untouched were "underground workers, workers in high-temperature shops, and workers in newly constructed enterprises of the first supply roll." GARF, f. 5451, op. 42, d. 250, l. 148. The decree affected 400,000 workers in the IIR, almost all of whom were on the second or third supply rolls. GARF, f. 374, op. 27, d. 1988, l. 93.

2. GARF, f. 374, op. 27, d. 1988, ll. 63 ("hunger"), 69 ("We'll"; spoken by an Ivanovo metalworker). For a brief description of the labor unrest that took place outside the IIR at this time, see GARF, f. 5451, op. 42, d. 250, ll. 17–18.

3. TsDNIIO, f. 327, op. 4, d. 516, l. 22.

4. TsDNIIO, f. 327, op. 4, d. 516, l. 22.

5. TsDNIIO, f. 327, op. 4, d. 516, l. 23.

6. *Raiony IPO*, 2:247, 250; I. I. Zimin, "Teikovo: Khronika sobytii i dokumentov (Dokumenty i materialy s 1931g. po 1941 god: Kniga 5)," typescript, 1960, Muzei Teikovskogo khlopchatobumazhnogo kombinata, Teikovo, 42, 44–46; TsDNIIO, f. 327, op. 4, d. 452, l. 15. Nikolai Kochnev, "Diary," 3/1/32, 3/17/32, 3/31/32, and c. 4/1/32, cited in Vladimir Smirnov, "Iz zapisei Nikolaia Grigor'evicha Kochneva (1932 god): Dnevnik, zapiski, dokumenty" (n.d., photocopy). I am indebted to the Smirnov family for the latter source. The Teikovo Combine employed about five thousand operatives, 63 percent of whom were women. *Raiony IPO*, 2:250; TsDNIIO, f. 327, op. 5, d. 172, unnumbered page showing gender breakdown of the labor force.

7. APUFSBIO, s.d. 8535-p, ll. 2ob.–3ob. (Novikov; "A dependent"), 31–32 ("I knew"), 18ob. According to the testimony of an acquaintance, Chernov often was elected to serve as a delegate to local conferences because he was viewed as "a true defender of the toiling masses." Chernov's authority sprang in part from his passion for ridiculing party members and criticizing the government's effort to finance industrialization at the shop floor's expense. A second-generation worker, he lived with his wife and three children in a private home in town (ll. 2, 30ob.–31).

8. GARF, f. 374, op. 27, d. 1988, l. 88; APUFSBIO, s.d. 7951-p, ll. 2–2ob., 27ob.; s.d. 8535-p, ll. 18ob., 32; s.d. 8551-p, l. 22 (quote). The offspring of local workers, Shishkin joined the machine shop as a fitter in 1911, fought in the Imperial Army during World War I, and rose to the rank of Red Army commander during the Civil War. In 1919, he served briefly under the com-

mand of the anarchist Nestor Makhno, a sometime ally and sometime enemy of the Bolsheviks. After being discharged from the army in 1921, Shishkin returned to the Teikovo Combine, where he employed his personal authority to taunt party members and to condemn policies—for example, compulsory state bond campaigns and dekulakization—that undermined workers' standard of living. He lived with his wife and only child in a private home in town. APUFSBIO, s.d. 7951-p, 2, 8–10, 14–16, 27ob., 49; s.d. 8535-p, l. 10ob., 12–12ob., 22, 25; s.d. 8543-p, ll. 22–24, 31.

9. Kochnev, "Diary," 4/9/32.

10. APUFSBIO, s.d. 7951-p, l. 2ob. (quote); s.d. 8535-p, ll. 21, 23; TsDNIIO, f. 327, op. 5, d. 152, l. 35. Anan'ev moved to Teikovo at age twelve when his father took a job at the combine as a weaving overlooker. After working for several years on his father's work team, he volunteered, during the Civil War, for service in a requisitioning battalion. In 1921, he settled into a job as a carpenter at the combine. Ten years later, he became an assistant fitter and a shock worker. He lived with his wife and five children in a private home in town.

11. APUFSBIO, s.d. 8583-p, tom 1, ll. 15ob.–16ob. ("None"); s.d. 8551-p, ll. 28–28ob. ("Stop . . . what?"), 35ob., 56. Lavrent'eva was the offspring of local peasants; Asafov, of local workers. Neither had children, and both lived with their spouses in private homes in town.

12. APUFSBIO, s.d. 7951-p, ll. 14–14ob. A "twenty-five thousander" was a worker who had been mobilized by the party in 1930 to collectivize the peasantry.

13. APUFSBIO, s.d. 7951-p, ll. 2ob.–3, 28; s.d. 8535-p, ll. 21, 27; s.d. 8543-p, ll. 19, 22; s.d. 8551-p, ll. 5ob., 35ob., 56; s.d. 8583-p, tom 1, ll. 2, 15ob., 27.

14. GARF, f. 374, op. 27, d. 1988, l. 88; APUFSBIO, s.d. 7951-p, l. 3; s.d. 8535-p, ll. 3ob. ("You"), 18ob., 21; s.d. 8551-p, ll. 18, 20, 30ob. ("Stop"), 26ob. ("stop"); RGASPI, f. 81, op. 3, d. 213, ll. 64–67.

15. APUFSBIO, s.d. 7951-p, ll. 14–16.

16. APUFSBIO, s.d. 7951-p, l. 5 (Shishkin); 8535-p, l. 3ob. ("It's"); s.d. 8551-p, l. 25ob.; Kochnev, "Diary," 4/17/32 (other quotes).

17. APUFSBIO, s.d. 7951-p, ll. 3–4; s.d. 8535-p, ll. 18ob., 21; s.d. 8551-p, ll. 20, 64; GARF, f. 1235, op. 141, d. 1352, l. 12; RGASPI, f. 81, op. 3, d. 213, ll. 64–67.

18. APUFSBIO, s.d. 7951-p, ll. 4 (quote), 11.

19. RGASPI, f. 81, op. 3, d. 213, ll. 69–71; APUFSBIO, s.d. 8535-p, l. 27 ("it's"); s.d. 8543-p, ll. 39ob. ("the workers"), 19 ("workers," "Soon"), 17 ("we"), 38. Lipin worked as a cobbler until 1914, when he was drafted into the Imperial Army. After spending most of World War I in a German prison camp, he returned, in 1918, to Teikovo. APUFSBIO, s.d. 8543-p, ll. 15, 59.

20. APUFSBIO, s.d. 8551-p, 18ob. ("It's"), 3, 4ob.–5ob. (other quotes).

21. APUFSBIO, s.d. 8551-p, 5ob. ("We've gone"), 8ob. ("I explained"); 20–21 ("The Communists and the OGPU," "The policy," "We must overthrow"),

18 ("The new"), 63 ("During"), 56 ("This regime"); 40ob. ("They live"); s.d. 8535-p, ll. 4ob. ("We must reduce"), 23 ("We must declare"); s.d. 7951-p, l. 6 ("Year"); s.d. 8583-p, tom 1, l. 3ob. ("If bread"). Khudiakov's father was a spinner who was dismissed from the Teikovo Combine and blacklisted for participating in a violent strike there in 1896. In his youth, Khudiakov apprenticed with a tradesman, worked as a shop assistant, landed a job as a packer at the combine, and eventually joined a calico-printing artel. After service in the Imperial Army, he returned, in 1918, to Teikovo, where he worked as a guard at the combine until retiring in 1929. A lifelong bachelor, he lived in a private home in town. APUFSBIO, s.d. 8551-p, ll. 3–5ob., 9ob.–10ob., 12ob., 29ob.; s.d. 8583-p, tom 1, l. 2ob.; s.d. 8543-p, l. 12.

22. APUFSBIO, s.d. 7951-p, ll. 5–6 ("Soviet power," "patently"), 8; s.d. 8551-p, l. 5ob. ("the workers"); s.d. 8535-p, ll. 4ob. ("purely"), 23; s.d. 8583-p, tom 1, l. 3ob.

23. APUFSBIO, s.d. 8551-p, ll. 3ob., 5ob.–6ob. ("tradesman"), 18 ("mere"); s.d. 8535-p, l. 29 ("commanded").

24. APUFSBIO, s.d. 8551-p, ll. 5ob.–6ob., 18 (quote). The offspring of local peasants, Matiushkin served in the Red Army during the Civil War. He lived with his wife and seven children in a private home in town (l. 17).

25. APUFSBIO, s.d. 8551-p, ll. 19, 56 (quotes). Balashev hailed from the local peasantry, served in the Red Army, and quit the party in 1929 after being reprimanded for sending a complaint "to *Pravda* about the suppression of *samokritika* in Teikovo." He lived with his wife and four children in rented quarters. Letkov, the offspring of Suzdal peasants, lived with his wife and seven children in a private home in town (ll. 19–20 [quote], 56).

26. APUFSBIO, s.d. 8583-p, tom 1, ll. 3ob., 9ob. The offspring of peasants, Gradusov moved to Teikovo as a child when his father got a job at the combine. He became a baker's assistant at age twelve, and a spinner at age twenty. After spending most of World War I in an Austrian prison camp, he returned to Teikovo in 1918 and volunteered to serve in the Cheka (security police). After enrollment in the party and studies in Moscow, he served as a commissar in regional Cheka bureaus. Demobilized in 1922, he found adjustment to civilian life difficult. Although he landed a job as a spinner, he was convicted of petty theft and expelled from the party as a "demoralized element." At this juncture, he suffered a nervous breakdown that landed him in a psychiatric hospital. After recovery, he took a job in the combine's finishing shed. When cost reductions eliminated his job in 1931, he was forced to work as a guard in the warehouse; the next year, he lost that job as well. At the time of the strike, he was working as a cesspit cleaner to help his wife, a mill hand since 1912, support their family of four. They lived in a communal apartment in town. APUFSBIO, s.d. 8583-p, tom 1, ll. 2–3ob., 33 (quote), 36, 42–42ob.; tom 2, ll. 1, 5, 18–19, 21, 23, 40.

27. APUFSBIO, s.d. 8583-p, tom 1, ll. 3ob.; s.d. 8535-p, ll. 2, 4ob.–5ob. ("long," "Our," "We"), 23–24, 27, 29; s.d. 8551-p, l. 43ob. ("Khudiakov's"), 56

("ours"); Kochnev, "Diary," n.d. ("Gradusov"). Among the protestors who gave testimony about Gradusov was the fifty-three-year-old pensioner Ivan Bagashkov, a former spinner and World War I veteran who lived in a private home in town with his wife and three children. APUFSBIO, s.d. 8551-p, l. 43.

28. APUFSBIO, s.d. 8535-p, ll. 25–26 (block quote; italics added). Brief and largely inaccurate accounts of the IIR strike wave surfaced in the émigré press and in diplomatic cables. See, for example, *Sotsialisticheskii vestnik*, 7/23/32; 11/26/32; *Biulleten oppozitsii*, 1932, no. 29/30; and Watt, ed., *British Documents on Foreign Affairs*, 16:93, 146.

29. GARF, f. 374, op. 27, d. 1988, ll. 93–92. Italics indicate words that were edited by hand into this typewritten report. The term "strike" was excised from the final draft of the reprimand that the Central Party Committee sent to the IIR Party Committee in the aftermath of the unrest. Politburo member Lazar Kaganovich seems to have been responsible for the excision. RGASPI, f. 81, op. 3, d. 213, ll. 80–81, 84–85.

30. APUFSBIO, s.d. 8535-p, l. 24 (Anan'ev); TsDNIIO, f. 327, op. 4, d. 449, l. 92 ("could"); Kochnev, "Diary," 4/17/32 (other quotes). Trained as a spinner, Maleeva became a Bolshevik in 1917. After working full-time as a party functionary during the Civil War, she returned to the shop floor. She was respected by workers and officials alike, and in 1925 was elected to lead a strike committee with Khudiakov. Shortly thereafter, she took a full-time job with the regional bureau trade-union. APUFSBIO, s.d. 8551, ll. 29–29ob.

31. APUFSBIO, s.d. 8535-p, l. 5ob.

32. GARF, f. 374, op. 27, d. 1988, l. 87; APUFSBIO, s.d. 7951-p, l. 6; s.d. 8535-p, ll. 5ob., 21, 24–25 ("former"); s.d. 8583-p, tom 1, ll. 3ob.–4ob. ("anti-Soviet," "nonworker"), 9ob.–10; s.d. 8543-p, l. 23; s.d. 8551-p, ll. 6ob., 36ob.–37ob., 56.

33. APUFSBIO, s.d. 7951-p, l. 14; s.d. 8551-p, ll. 21, 27ob., 30.

34. APUFSBIO, s.d. 8535-p, l. 6ob.

35. Semenov, who had worked at the combine since 1915, served as a Red Guard in 1917 and volunteered for the Red Army during the Civil War. His parents were local peasants, and he lived with his wife and two children in a private home in town. APUFSBIO, s.d. 8551-p, l. 15.

36. APUFSBIO, s.d. 8535-p, l. 21; s.d. 8543-p, ll. 8ob., 24, 31ob. ("very"); s.d. 8551-p, ll. 6ob., 16, 37ob. ("It's"), 21 ("We've . . . power"), 27ob.; s.d. 7951-p, ll. 20ob., 28 ("Comrades").

37. APUFSBIO, s.d. 8543-p, l. 24 ("We've"); s.d. 8535-p, l. 22 ("The regime," "Soviet"); s.d. 8551-p, ll. 6ob., 19, 21–22 ("many," "In . . . situation"), 27ob.; s.d. 7951-p, l. 28 ("We'll").

38. APUFSBIO, s.d. 8551-p, ll. 8ob.–9ob. (Khudiakov), 15ob.–16.

39. APUFSBIO, s.d. 7951-p, l. 28; s.d. 8535-p, ll. 21, 27; s.d. 8543-p, l. 18 (Andrianov); s.d. 8551-p, l. 15ob. (Vakhrovskii); s.d. 8950-p, ll. 3, 18.

40. GARF, f. 374, op. 27, d. 1988, l. 86; APUFSBIO, s.d. 7951-p, l. 20ob.; s.d. 8535-p, ll. 5ob., 12–12ob. (Shishkin), 21, 24, 27; s.d. 8543-p, l. 22; s.d. 8551-p, ll. 6ob., 32ob.–33, 37ob.–38ob.; s.d. 8583-p, tom 1, l. 4ob.

41. APUFSBIO, s.d. 7951-p, ll. 14ob.–15; s.d. 8535-p, ll. 7ob. (Shishkin, "We won't," Chernov), 24 (Gradusov), 27–28; s.d. 8543-p, ll. 9, 23; s.d. 8551-p, ll. 26ob., 33–33ob., 56; s.d. 8583-p, tom 1, l. 9ob.

42. APUFSBIO, s.d. 8535-p, ll. 27–28 (Matrosov); s.d. 7951-p, l. 15 (Shishkin's wife); s.d. 8551-p, l. 38ob.; RGASPI, f. 81, op. 3, d. 213, ll. 64–67 ("liberated"). Matrosov, whose parents were local peasants, worked as a weaver from 1894 to 1910, and as a lugger until his retirement in the 1920s. He and his wife lived in a private home in town. APUFSBIO, s.d. 8535-p, l. 27.

43. APUFSBIO, s.d. 7951-p, l. 18ob., 20ob. (Shishkin); s.d. 8535-p, ll. 7ob.–8ob., 12, 21, 24–26, 28 ("an absolute"); s.d. 8551-p, ll. 26ob., 38ob.–39ob., 56; s.d. 8583-p, tom 1, ll. 4ob., 15ob.

44. APUFSBIO, s.d. 8535-p, l. 12.

45. APUFSBIO, s.d. 8583-p, tom 1, ll. 9ob. ("out"), 4ob. ("bread," "to bring"); s.d. 8535-p, ll. 12, 24, 28; s.d. 8543-p, ll. 30ob., 58–60, 64–67ob.; s.d. 8551-p, l. 7ob.; s.d. 8950-p, l. 3. On the strategic deployment of children in lower-class protests, see Engel, "Women, Men, and the Languages of Peasant Resistance," 43. Gornostaev, the offspring of tradesmen and a former *lishenets*, served in the Imperial Army during World War I. He lived with his wife and four children in a private home in town. APUFSBIO, s.d. 8543-p, ll. 8, 59. Kozyrin's father was a cobbler who owned a workshop and store in Teikovo before the Revolution. After serving in the Imperial Army during World War I, Kozyrin founded a workshop of his own. Because he was a petty trader, he was temporarily deprived of his civil rights by Soviet authorities. He lived with his wife and six children in a private home in town. APUFSBIO, s.d. 8543-p, ll. 32–32ob., 58.

46. GARF, f. 374, op. 27, d. 1988, l. 87.

47. APUFSBIO, s.d. 7951-p, ll. 7–8. The archival sources do not confirm that peat-bog workers were on strike at this time, but these workers protested frequently in 1930–1931 against dismal work and living conditions and likely would have been receptive to appeals from the Teikovo strikers. GAIO, f. 1276, op. 23, d. 2, ll. 40, 105; d. 3, l. 39; d. 7, ll. 170, 332.

48. APUFSBIO, s.d. 7951-p, l. 5; s.d. 8535-p, l. 17ob.; s.d. 8551-p, l. 22.

49. APUFSBIO, s.d. 8551-p, ll. 39ob. (shouts), 27ob.–28ob. ("Whoever"), 22 ("The arrest"), 56, 62; s.d. 8535-p, ll. 8ob. ("There's no"), 19ob., 24–26 (Vakhrovskii); s.d. 7951-p, ll. 7, 18ob. ("We haven't"), 21ob.; s.d. 8543-p, ll. 16, 24 ("Since"); s.d. 8583-p, tom 1, ll. 5ob., 10–11ob., 15ob., 21.

50. APUFSBIO, s.d. 8535-p, l. 25; s.d. 8551-p, l. 28ob.; s.d. 8583-p, tom 1, ll. 5ob. (quotes), 21.

51. APUFSBIO, s.d. 8535-p, ll. 19ob.–20ob. ("It's . . . us"); s.d. 8583-p, tom 1, l. 16ob. ("Come . . . else"); s.d. 8551-p, ll. 26–28ob. ("accused"). Syrov-Shishkinov was the son of local workers; Romanov, of poor peasants. Both were married, had several children, and lived in private homes in town. APUFSBIO, s.d. 8535-p, 1–19; s.d. 8551-p, l. 26.

52. APUFSBIO, s.d. 7951-p, ll. 18ob., 28; s.d. 8535-p, l. 25; s.d. 8583-p, tom 1, ll. 4ob.–5ob., 21; s.d. 8551-p, ll. 17ob.–18.

53. APUFSBIO, s.d. 8551-p, l. 39ob. On carnival, see Pam Morris, ed., *The Bakhtin Reader: Selected Writings of Bakhtin, Medvedev and Voloshinov* (London, 1994), 199–200, 209, 220–221, 225–226, 229, 244 (quote).

54. GARF, f. 374, op. 27, d. 1988, ll. 87–86; APUFSBIO, s.d. 7951-p, l. 15.

55. APUFSBIO, s.d. 8583-p, tom 1, ll. 4ob.–5ob. ("I"), 9–9ob. ("rank-and-file"), 10, 11ob., 21; s.d. 8535-p, ll. 15ob. ("Come"), 19ob.–20ob., 25–26; s.d. 8551-p, ll. 15ob., 25ob.; s.d. 7951-p, l. 7 ("When . . . part").

56. APUFSBIO, s.d. 8551-p, ll. 22, 29, 62; s.d. 8535-p, ll. 20ob. (quote), 25.

57. APUFSBIO, s.d. 8535-p, ll. 8ob., 15ob., 25–26; s.d. 8583-p, tom 1, ll. 5ob., 21; RGASPI, f. 81, op. 3, d. 213, ll. 3–15; Mikhail Vladimirovich Smirnov, interview with author, Ivanovo, 4/20/94; Natalia Ivanovna Golubeva, interview with author, Ankudinovo, Ivanovo Region, 5/2/94 (quote; eyewitness account).

58. APUFSBIO, s.d. 7951-p, l. 11; s.d. 8551-p, ll. 16 ("Why," "that *lishentsy,*"), 22, 31; s.d. 8583-p, tom 1, l. 10ob. ("against").

59. APUFSBIO, s.d. 7951-p, l. 7; s.d. 8535-p, l. 15ob.; s.d. 8551-p, ll. 15ob., 22, 27ob., 39ob.; GARF, f. 374, op. 27, d. 1988, l. 87; RGASPI, f. 81, op. 3, d. 213, ll. 3–15.

60. APUFSBIO, s.d. 8535-p, l. 15ob.; s.d. 8551-p, ll. 15ob., 39ob.; s.d. 8583-p, tom 1, l. 10.

61. APUFSBIO, s.d. 8535-p, ll. 15ob.–17ob. ("If," "Since . . . ourselves"), 19ob.; s.d. 8551-p, l. 18; s.d. 8583-p, tom 1, l. 21; GARF, f. 374, op. 27, d. 1988, l. 87 ("the overwhelming," "completely"); RGASPI, f. 81, op. 3, d. 213, ll. 3–15.

62. Arrests were carried out during the third week of April. Afraid of provoking another disturbance, the OGPU seized Shishkin and Chernov last. Most of those taken into custody were released after questioning, but the defendants were imprisoned and interrogated several times. Indictments were filed within two months, and sentences were handed down by an OGPU court on July 2, 1932. APUFSBIO, s.d. 7951-p, l. 80; s.d. 8535-p, ll. 17ob.–18, 21; s.d. 8551-p, ll. 25–26, 30, 47; s.d. 8583-p, tom 2, l. 15. Although a former party member by the name of Piskunov was arrested for being a "ringleader" of the strike, the archival sources shed no light on what role, if any, he played in it. TsDNIIO, f. 327, op. 5, d. 152, l. 43.

63. APUFSBIO, s.d. 7951-p, ll. 49, 54–55; s.d. 8535-p, ll. 11ob., 34, 37; s.d. 8543-p, ll. 55, 61–62; s.d. 8551-p, ll. 61, 67, 69; s.d. 8583-p, tom 1, ll. 10–11, 33, 37; s.d. 8950-p, ll. 18, 20, 22. The defendants, all of whom were rehabilitated in 1989–1990, were convicted under Articles 58 and 59 of the Criminal Code, which criminalized "anti-Soviet" and "counterrevolutionary" speech and behavior. Their sentences carried a term of three years.

64. Most strike leaders and most rank-and-file strikers for whom biographical information is available were married and had children.

65. APUFSBIO, s.d. 7951-p, ll. 13 ("I believe that"), 8 ("I believe there"); s.d. 8551-p, ll. 9ob., 13 (Khudiakov).

66. APUFSBIO, s.d. 8535-p, l. 29; s.d. 8543-p, l. 12 ("a Social"); s.d. 8551-p, ll. 3–5ob. ("I . . . socialist"), 9ob.–10ob. Khudiakov elaborated his views under OGPU interrogation.

67. APUFSBIO, s.d. 7951-p, ll. 11–12.

68. On worker resistance in Teikovo under the old regime, see V. A. Babichev, I. I. Zimin, and V. M. Smirnov, *Teikovskii khlopchatobumazhnyi: istoricheskii ocherk* (Iaroslavl, 1966), 12–14, 16–27, 31–32, 40; and David Pretty, "Neither Peasant nor Proletarian: The Workers of the Ivanovo-Voznesensk Region, 1885–1910" (Ph.D. diss., Brown University, 1997).

69. APUFSBIO, s.d. 8535-p, ll. 9ob., 25; s.d. 8551-p, l. 8ob.; s.d. 8583-p, tom 1, ll. 5ob., 10. Although the strike leaders emerged spontaneously, it should be noted that three of them—Chernov, Gradusov, and Mokeeva—had spearheaded protests against the severe bread shortages of autumn 1928, and that two others—Khudiakov and Maleeva—had served on a strike committee in 1925. TsDNIIO, f. 2, op. 11, d. 184, ll. 9, 144–145; APUFSBID, s.d. 8551-p, ll. 3ob., 29ob.

70. GARF, f. 374, op. 27, d. 1988, ll. 88–86; TsDNIIO, f. 327, op. 4, d. 366, l. 31; APUFSBIO, s.d. 8535-p, l. 30ob.; s.d. 8583-p, tom 1, l. 10ob.; Kochnev, "Diary," 4/17/32.

71. GARF, f. 374, op. 27, d. 1988, l. 86; TsDNIIO, f. 327, op. 4, d. 449, l. 161.

72. RGASPI, f. 81, op. 3, d. 213, ll. 64–67, 77–78; GARF, f. 374, op. 27, d. 1988, l. 93.

73. The OGPU was deeply involved in the official response to the IIR strike wave. Having defined the organization's tasks as reconnaissance, recruitment, and "demoralization," the regional bureau rushed ten special agents and twenty-two political officers into the field when the strikes began. Of these, seventeen went to Vichuga, five to Teikovo, four to Rodniki, and three each to Sereda and Lezhnevo. Assisted by their colleagues at the local level, they secured state property, dispersed crowds, arrested fourteen "anti-Soviet workers," recruited twenty informants, and added 149 names to the OGPU catalog of "anti-Soviet elements." These actions prevented the "mass discontent" reported on the shop floors of Iaroslavl, Ivanovo, Kokhma, Navoloki, Nerekhta, Rodniki, and Sereda from crystallizing into strikes. TsDNIIO, f. 327, op. 4, d. 449, l. 130; RGASPI, f. 81, op. 3, d. 213, ll. 3–15, 69–71, 77–78.

74. Kochnev, "Diary," 4/21/32.

75. That the most prominent Teikovo striker, Shishkin, was a veteran male worker from the machine shop was not unusual. Shishkin felt compelled to lead the strike because it was "we, the fitters, who started it." APUFSBIO, s.d. 7951-p, l. 8. Notwithstanding, such claims we have seen that departments that employed mostly women—such as the weaving shed—idled production at roughly the same time as the machine shop, and played a crucial role in enforcing the strike.

7. The Vichuga Uprising

1. Enterprises in Vichuga included the Nogin Mill (7,439 workers), the Red Profintern Mill (7,494 workers), the Shagov Amalgamated Mill (2,529 workers), and Machine-Building Plant No. 6 (425 workers). In terms of equipment and staff, the Nogin and Red Profintern mills were among the largest in the IIR. Statistically, Vichuga's mills were typical: a majority (68 percent) of the workers employed in them were women; a small minority (7.6 percent) of these workers were Communists; and most (62 percent) of these Communists were men. Also typical was that the majority of Vichuga's operatives were veterans of the labor force. The fact that ties to the land were weakest at the two mills that spearheaded the Vichuga strike illustrates the hollowness of the Bolshevik claim that labor unrest was a function of such ties. At the Shagov, one in nine operatives reported ties to the land; at the Nogin, one in five. *Raiony IPO*, 2:26; TsDNIIO, f. 327, op. 4, d. 603, pages showing mill employment levels in 1932; op. 5, d. 162, l. 9; GARF, f. 5457, op. 23, d. 199, l. 59.

2. *Raiony IPO*, 1:52; GAIO, f. 1276, op. 23, d. 7, ll. 253–255; GARF, f. 374, op. 27, d. 1988, ll. 114, 84–83; TsDNIIO, f. 327, op. 4, d. 449, ll. 2–7, 45, 130, 138–139 (quote, 6).

3. RGASPI, f. 81, op. 3, d. 213, ll. 72–76.

4. RGASPI, f. 81, op. 3, d. 213, ll. 72–76.

5. RGASPI, f. 81, op. 3, d. 213, ll. 72–76.

6. RGASPI, f. 81, op. 3, d. 213, ll. 3–15, 72–76 (quotes); TsDNIIO, f. 327, op. 4, d. 449, l. 145. One reason for the district party committee's inaction was that the local food-supply organization had significantly underreported the number of families that had been denied flour.

7. RGASPI, f. 81, op. 3, d. 213, ll. 3–15, 72–76.

8. RGASPI, f. 81, op. 3, d. 213, ll. 3–15, 50–51, 62, 72–76; GARF, f. 374, op. 27, d. 1988, l. 92.

9. RGASPI, f. 81, op. 3, d. 213, ll. 3–15, 72–76.

10. GARF, f. 374, op. 27, d. 1988, l. 92; RGASPI, f. 81, op. 3, d. 213, ll. 3–15, 64–67, 72–76.

11. RGASPI, f. 81, op. 3, d. 213, ll. 3–15, 64–67, 72–76; GARF, f. 374, op. 27, d. 1988, l. 92; TsDNIIO, f. 327, op. 4, d. 516, l. 24.

12. GARF, f. 374, op. 27, d. 1988, ll. 89–88; RGASPI, f. 81, op. 3, d. 213, ll. 3–15, 64–67; TsDNIIO, f. 327, op. 4, d. 449, l. 5.

13. GARF, f. 374, op. 27, d. 1988, l. 92; RGASPI, f. 81, op. 3, d. 213, ll. 3–15, 64–67, 72–77.

14. RGASPI, f. 81, op. 3, d. 213, ll. 3–15, 64–67, 72–77; GARF, f. 374, op. 27, d. 1988, ll. 92–91.

15. GARF, f. 374, op. 27, d. 1988, ll. 92–91; RGASPI, f. 81, op. 3, d. 213, ll. 3–15, 72–76. One source states that workers at the Kamenka Mill, eighteen kilometers north of Vichuga, also struck on this day. RGASPI, f. 81, op. 3, d. 213, ll. 64–67.

16. GARF, f. 374, op. 27, d. 1988, ll. 91, 89; TsDNIIO, f. 327, op. 4, d. 509, l. 68; op. 5, d. 162, l. 146; RGASPI, f. 81, op. 3, d. 213, ll. 3–15, 64–67, 90–92.
17. GARF, f. 374, op. 27, d. 1988, l. 89; TsDNIIO, f. 327, op. 4, d. 449, l. 145; RGASPI, f. 81, op. 3, d. 213, ll. 3–15, 64–67, 90–92.
18. TsDNIIO, f. 327, op. 4, d. 449, l. 5 ("counterrevolutionary"; block quote); RGASPI, f. 81, op. 3, d. 213, ll. 3–15 (other quotes).
19. GARF, f. 374, op. 27, d. 1988, l. 91; RGASPI, f. 81, op. 3, d. 213, ll. 3–15, 64–67, 93–95. Damage to equipment and attacks against party and nonparty opponents of the job action took place on this day when strikers from Shagov Mill No. 1 and No. 3 broke into Mill No. 2.
20. GARF, f. 374, op. 27, d. 1988, l. 91; APUFSBIO, s.d. 8537-p, ll. 13–13ob. (quotes); RGASPI, f. 81, op. 3, d. 213, ll. 64–67, 72–76.
21. RGASPI, f. 81, op. 3, d. 213, ll. 64–67, 72–76, 93–95; APUFSBIO, s.d. 8537-p, ll. 5, 7ob.–8ob., 13ob.–14, 17. Korotkov grew up in a poor peasant family in a village near Vichuga and entered the labor force at age twelve when he landed a job as a warp drawer at one of the Morokin (later, Shagov) mills. His tenure on the shop floor was interrupted by two stints in the Imperial Army and by the collapse of the economy in 1918. After several years of employment in Khar'kov Region, he returned, in 1921, to Vichuga, where he organized a workers' cooperative and earned a living as a stove setter. While dabbling in petty trade in 1929, he was convicted of purchasing stolen goods and exiled to Enisei Region. After returning to Vichuga eighteen months later, he took a job as a warp drawer at the Nogin Mill. He lived with his wife and five children in a private home in town. APUFSBIO, s.d. 8537-p, ll. 5–5ob., 8ob., 13ob., 17, 19, 33ob–35, 37.
22. GARF, f. 374, op. 27, d. 1988, l. 91; RGASPI, f. 81, op. 3, d. 213, ll. 3–15, 72–76; APUFSBIO, s.d. 8537-p, ll. 8ob. ("Comrade . . . you"), 12.
23. GARF, f. 374, op. 27, d. 1988, l. 91; APUFSBIO, s.d. 8537-p, l. 8ob. ("Comrades . . . Mill!"); RGASPI, f. 81, op. 3, d. 213, ll. 3–15, 64–67, 72–76.
24. GARF, f. 374, op. 27, d. 1988, l. 91; TsDNIIO, f. 327, op. 4, d. 449, l. 5 ("all . . . class"); RGASPI, f. 81, op. 3, d. 213, ll. 3–15, 64–67, 72–76, 85, 90–92.
25. RGASPI, f. 81, op. 3, d. 213, ll. 3–15, 64–67, 72–76.
26. RGASPI, f. 81, op. 3, d. 213, ll. 3–15; GARF, f. 374, op. 27, d. 1988, l. 91; TsDNIIO, f. 327, op. 5, d. 162, ll. 137–138 (quote). Unfortunately, the metalworkers' perspective is barely illuminated by the archival sources. Although their rations also were cut at this time, they seem to have enjoyed privileges—or a *sense* of privilege—that prevented them from identifying with the crowd of mostly female textile workers who endeavored to win their support. TsDNIIO, f. 327, op. 5, d. 162, ll. 137–138. Perhaps not too much should be read into the metalworkers' aloofness from the strike, however, since they constituted only about 2 percent of Vichuga's industrial labor force, and since there is evidence that their counterparts in Ivanovo sympathized with the strikers' demand. *Raiony IPO*, 2:26; GARF, f. 274, op. 27, d. 1988, l. 69.

27. APUFSBIO, s.d. 8537-p, ll. 7ob.–9; GARF, f. 374, op. 27, d. 1988, l. 91; RGASPI, f. 81, op. 3, d. 213, ll. 3–15, 64–67, 72–76.

28. GARF, f. 374, op. 27, d. 1988, ll. 60, 31–30; RGASPI, f. 81, op. 3, d. 213, ll. 3–15, 34–37, 90–92.

29. RGASPI, f. 81, op. 3, d. 213, ll. 3–15, 64–67, 72–76; TsDNIIO, f. 327, op. 5, d. 162, ll. 137–138.

30. RGASPI, f. 81, op. 3, d. 213, ll. 3–15, 72–76.

31. RGASPI, f. 81, op. 3, d. 213, ll. 72–76. After interrogating scores of witnesses, the OGPU concluded in a July 1932 report to Kaganovich that "the Vichuga events" did not, in fact, appear to have been organized by "a counterrevolutionary organization." RGASPI, f. 81, op. 3, d. 213, ll. 93–95.

32. GARF, f. 374, op. 27, d. 1988, ll. 91–90; RGASPI, f. 81, op. 3, d. 213, ll. 3–15, 34–37, 64–67, 72–76.

33. GARF, f. 374, op. 27, d. 1988, ll. 90, 31; APUFSBIO, s.d. 8537-p, l. 9; d. 8545-p, l. 2ob.; RGASPI, f. 81, op. 3, d. 213, ll. 3–15, 34–37, 64–67, 72–76.

34. RGASPI, f. 81, op. 3, d. 213, ll. 3–15, 34–37, 64–67, 72–76; GARF, f. 374, op. 27, d. 1988, ll. 90, 31; APUFSBIO, s.d. 8537-p, l. 9; s.d. 8545-p, ll. 2ob., 7ob.–8ob. (quotes). According to Pavel Finoedov, a Komsomol, the two men who led the search for Iurkin were eighteen-year-old Nikolai Nikitin, a migrant from the Kazan Region who had briefly apprenticed as a chef at the Nogin's factory kitchen, and Sozin, a worker who lived in the same (nearby) village as Iurkin. Nikitin admitted that he observed the assault, but claimed that he did not participate. Two other witnesses placed Nikitin outside the police station. Although the investigation did not clarify Nikitin's precise role, he was an attractive target for prosecution: young, orphaned, unemployed, and vaguely critical of the regime, he could easily be depicted as one of the "class-alien and hooligan elements" whom the party blamed for the uprising. APUFSBIO, s.d. 8545-p, ll. 2–2ob., 4ob.–8ob., 10ob.; GARF, f. 374, op. 27, d. 1988, l. 90; RGASPI, f. 81, op. 3, d. 213, ll. 3–15, 72–76.

35. RGASPI, f. 81, op. 3, d. 213, ll. 34–37 (quote); APUFSBIO, s.d. 8545-p, ll. 7ob.–8ob.; s.d. 8537-p, l. 9. The junior officer's rifle was not loaded.

36. GARF, f. 374, op. 27, d. 1988, ll. 90, 31; RGASPI, f. 81, op. 3, d. 213, ll. 3–15, 34–37, 64–67, 72–76, 90–92; TsDNIIO, f. 327, op. 5, d. 162, l. 146. Questioned later about his failure to intervene, Vorkuev lamely asserted that "a policeman kept me out" of the building. TsDNIIO, f. 327, op. 4, d. 509, l. 68.

37. RGASPI, f. 81, op. 3, d. 213, ll. 3–15, 34–37, 64–67, 72–76; GARF, f. 374, op. 27, d. 1988, ll. 90, 57, 31. Besides Itkin, nine male officers and one female typist were at work in the OGPU building when the strikers set upon it.

38. RGASPI, f. 81, op. 3, d. 213, ll. 3–15, 34–37, 64–67, 72–76.

39. RGASPI, f. 81, op. 3, d. 213, ll. 3–15, 34–37, 64–67, 72–76; GARF, f. 374, op. 27, d. 1988, ll. 90, 57; APUFSBIO, s.d. 8537-p, l. 9. Kaganovich immediately ordered an investigation into the use of force. Later, Central Party Committee investigators branded the firing of weapons "a great political mistake." RGASPI, f. 81, op. 3, d. 213, ll. 3–15, 90–92.

40. GARF, f. 374, op. 27, d. 1988, ll. 90, 31; RGASPI, f. 81, op. 3, d. 213, ll. 3–15, 34–37, 64–67, 72–76; APUFSBIO, s.d. 8545-p, l. 3; TsDNIIO, f. 327, op. 4, d. 449, ll. 5, 89. On April 11, strikers in Lezhnevo awaited delivery of a letter or telegram from their counterparts in Vichuga. RGASPI, f. 81, op. 3, d. 213, ll. 64–67.

41. TsDNIIO, f. 327, op. 4, d. 449, l. 5; RGASPI, f. 81, op. 3, d. 213, ll. 3–15, 64–67, 69–71, 72–76. The sabotaging of the factory boilers was particularly dangerous because party cells had ordered their members to defend them "by all means" necessary—a task in which they were assisted by armed OGPU officers. RGASPI, f. 81, op. 3, d. 213, ll. 3–15, 69–71.

42. GARF, f. 374, op. 27, d. 1988, ll. 90 ("political," "a tactical," "class-alien"), 31; Nina Dmitrievna Guseva, interview with author, Kineshma, 5/23/94 ("a full-fledged"); TsDNIIO, f. 327, op. 4, d. 449, l. 141; RGASPI, f. 81, op. 3, d. 213, ll. 3–15; APUFSBIO, s.d. 8545-p, l. 2ob.

43. RGASPI, f. 81, op. 3, d. 213, ll. 3–15. These same distinctions do not seem to have been drawn by the district's embittered peasants, two of whom—the twenty-five-year-old Reutskii and the forty-two-year-old Poliakov—posed as Vichuga "rebels," laid siege to their village soviet, and visited "reprisals" on its detested chairman. RGASPI, f. 81, op. 3, d. 213, ll. 93–95.

44. RGASPI, f. 81, op. 3, d. 213, ll. 3–15, 34–37, 64–67, 90–92; GARF, f. 374, op. 27, d. 1988, ll. 90, 37. The OGPU investigation of the shooting came to the following conclusions. First, confronted by an "extraordinarily tense" "situation," the officers had used their weapons only after "other measures to prevent the complete devastation of the building and the plundering of documents" had failed. Second, the three casualties probably were struck by bullets that ricocheted off a building on the opposite side of the street. Finally, as the senior official on the scene and the author of the order to fire warning shots, Golubev of the regional OGPU bureau bore responsibility for the tragedy. RGASPI, f. 81, op. 3, d. 213, ll. 3–15, 34–37.

45. RGASPI, f. 81, op. 3, d. 213, ll. 3–15, 34–37, 89–92. Forty to fifty individuals were admitted to the hospital for strike-related injuries.

46. GARF, f. 374, op. 27, d. 1988, l. 31; TsDNIIO, f. 327, op. 4, d. 449, l. 141.

47. GARF, f. 374, op. 27, d. 1988, l. 31. After being assaulted by the demonstrators, El'zov made it to safety on his own.

48. GARF, f. 374, op. 27, d. 1988, ll. 31–30 (quotes); TsDNIIO, f. 327, op. 4, d. 509, l. 68.

49. GARF, f. 374, op. 27, d. 1988, ll. 31–30; RGASPI, f. 81, op. 3, d. 213, l. 79.

50. GARF, f. 374, op. 27, d. 1988, ll. 31–30; RGASPI, f. 81, op. 3, d. 213, l. 79.

51. GARF, f. 374, op. 27, d. 1988, ll. 31–30 (quote); RGASPI, f. 81, op. 3, d. 213, l. 79.

52. GARF, f. 374, op. 27, d. 1988, ll. 31–30 (quotes); RGASPI, f. 81, op. 3, d. 213, ll. 69–71, 79.

53. APUFSBIO, s.d. 8537-p, l. 11ob.; RGASPI, f. 81, op. 3, d. 213, ll. 3–15, 64–67, 72–76. The OGPU persuaded three hundred employees of the Red Profintern Mill—about 4 percent of the enterprise's labor force—to return to

work on this day, which may explain why the most serious of the morning's clashes between strikers and their opponents took place there. RGASPI, f. 81, op. 3, d. 213, ll. 69–71, 72–76.

54. APUFSBIO, s.d. 8537-p, ll. 9, 11ob.

55. APUFSBIO, s.d. 8537-p, ll. 11ob., 14, 17ob.

56. RGASPI, f. 81, op. 3, d. 213, ll. 3–15, 64–67, 72–76; APUFSBIO, s.d. 8537-p, l. 11ob.

57. APUFSBIO, s.d. 8537-p, l. 11ob.; RGASPI, f. 81, op. 3, d. 213, ll. 3–15, 64–67, 72–76.

58. APUFSBIO, s.d. 8537-p, ll. 9–10, 11ob.–12, 17ob.; RGASPI, f. 81, op. 3, d. 213, ll. 3–15, 64–67, 72–76.

59. RGASPI, f. 81, op. 3, d. 213, ll. 3–15, 72–76. It is not clear why the women on the commission that drafted the telegram did not sign it. As for those who did, Golubev was a warp drawer, Obukhov was a Nogin operative and "a Trotskyite who had been excluded from the party," and Kostkin was a fitter in the machine shop of the Red Profintern Mill. APUFSBIO, s.d. 8537-p, ll. 8ob., 12; RGASPI, f. 81, op. 3, d. 213, ll. 3–15.

60. RGASPI, f. 81, op. 3, d. 213, ll. 3–15, 72–76.

61. GARF, f. 374, op. 27, d. 1988, l. 90; RGASPI, f. 81, op. 3, d. 213, ll. 3–15.

62. GARF, f. 374, op. 27, d. 1988, l. 90; RGASPI, f. 81, op. 3, d. 213, ll. 3–15 ("all"), 69–71 ("strike"); Gennadii Shutov, "Delo 'Filosofii': Dokumental'nyi ocherk," *Ivanovo-Voznesensk: Regional'naia gazeta Rossiiskogo soiuza promyshlennikov i predprinimatelei*, nos. 2–3 (35–36) (February 1994), 15; Marco Carynnyk, Lubomyr Y. Luciuk, and Bohdan S. Kordan, eds., *The Foreign Office and the Famine: British Documents on Ukraine and the Great Famine of 1932–1933* (Kingston, Ontario, 1988), 6; Guseva, interview.

63. RGASPI, f. 81, op. 3, d. 213, ll. 3–15. Perhaps in response to the appearance of railroad workers in the crowd, the OGPU placed "traveling agents" on all trains passing through the IIR (ll. 69–71).

64. GARF, f. 374, op. 27, d. 1988, l. 90; RGASPI, f. 81, op. 3, d. 213, ll. 72–76.

65. RGASPI, f. 81, op. 3, d. 213, ll. 3–15. In a revealing display of the hierarchy of institutional power under Stalin, Kaganovich's delegation included not a single member of the trade union.

66. RGASPI, f. 81, op. 3, d. 213, ll. 3–15.

67. RGASPI, f. 81, op. 3, d. 213, ll. 3–15; APUFSBIO, s.d. 8537-p, ll. 10, 12 (quote), 17ob.

68. RGASPI, f. 81, op. 3, d. 213, ll. 3–15 (quotes); APUFSBIO, s.d. 8537-p, ll. 10, 12–12ob.

69. APUFSBIO, s.d. 8537-p, ll. 10, 12ob. ("listened"); RGASPI, f. 81, op. 3, d. 213, ll. 3–15, 89; GARF, f. 374, op. 27, d. 1988, l. 90.

70. RGASPI, f. 81, op. 3, d. 213, ll. 3–15 (quote); TsDNIIO, f. 327, op. 4, d. 506, ll. 1–4, 10–11, 20; op. 5, d. 162, l. 139; Shutov, "Delo 'Filosofii,'" 15; Gennadii Kapitonovich Shutov, interview with author, Ivanovo, 3/28/94.

71. RGASPI, f. 81, op. 3, d. 213, ll. 1–15, 89.

72. RGASPI, f. 81, op. 3, d. 213, ll. 3–15, 31–32. It is not clear how the worker-delegates were chosen, what portion of them were Communists, or how much involvement, if any, they had in the strike.

73. RGASPI, f. 81, op. 3, d. 213, ll. 3–16, 33.

74. RGASPI, f. 81, op. 3, d. 213, ll. 31–32. A crucial lesson of the IIR strike wave that the resolution ignored was that the textile workers' "glorious revolutionary traditions" dictated resistance to—rather than support for—Stalin's program of forced capital accumulation.

75. RGASPI, f. 81, op. 3, d. 213, ll. 2–15.

76. RGASPI, f. 81, op. 3, d. 213, ll. 3–15, 69–71, 77–78, 80, 89–95; APUFSBIO, s.d. 8537-p, l. 42; s.d. 8545-p, l. 17. Also targeted for arrest were those identified as having perpetrated acts of violence.

77. RGASPI, f. 81, op. 3, d. 213, ll. 3–15, 93–95; APUFSBIO, s.d. 8537-p, ll. 5, 7ob–8, 11, 13, 16 ("fit"), 17, 19–21, 42; s.d. 8545-p, ll. 2, 4–10, 12–14, 17ob. Korotkov, who ended up at the Murmansk labor camp, gained his freedom in January 1934. Nikitin served his term of exile in Arkhangel'sk. Both men were rehabilitated in 1989. APUFSBIO, s.d. 8537-p, ll. 22, 32–35, 39–40, 42–42ob.; s.d. 8545-p, l. 15, 17–17ob. Iurkin was also convicted, but his fate is unknown.

78. Guseva, interview ("tense"); TsDNIIO, f. 327, op. 5, d. 162, l. 139 ("depression"); op. 4, d. 449, l. 141. As in Teikovo, the "overwhelming majority" of Komsomols and Communists did not participate in the strike. Instead, they reported for work or served in brigades assigned to defend the mills. Fearful, lacking effective leadership, and having in some instances been ordered not to clash with the strikers, most party members stood aside when workers sabotaged equipment or assaulted strikebreakers. A small minority, however, overtly sided with the protesters. Among party-affiliated individuals, those most likely to oppose the strike were the Komsomols, and those most likely to support it were Communists who had three or more children to feed. Many of the non-party working wives of rank-and-file Communists—especially those employed in the weaving sheds—also sided with the strikers. RGASPI, f. 81, op. 3, d. 213, ll. 3–15, 85, 90–92; GARF, f. 374, op. 27, d. 1988, ll. 89–88; TsDNIIO, d. 327, op. 4, d. 449, ll. 5, 93; d. 507, ll. 29–30.

79. Regional officials concluded that reduced bread rations never would have triggered "a movement of this scale" had it not been for the relentless deterioration of living standards. TsDNIIO, f. 327, op. 4, d. 449, ll. 93, 101.

80. GARF, f. 374, op. 27, d. 1988, l. 89; TsDNIIO, f. 327, op. 4, d. 449, ll. 93 ("there"), 141 ("We . . . well"); op. 5, d. 162, ll. 139–140 ("During . . . corners").

81. RGASPI, f. 81, op. 3, d. 213, ll. 31–32.

82. Guseva, interview ("My God"); Shutov, interview; Shutov, "Delo 'Filosofii,'" 15. The violence may explain why Guseva recalled seeing adults of both sexes—but no children—on the streets during the strike.

Conclusion

1. RGASPI, f. 81, op. 3, d. 213, l. 90 (block quote); f. 89, op. 3, d. 8, l. 6 ("attached"; speech to Lezhnevo party conference); d. 7, ll. 7 ("to justify"), 2 ("The policy").

2. RGASPI, f. 81, op. 3, d. 8, ll. 6 ("an extraordinarily"), 2; TsDNIIO, f. 327, op. 5, d. 972, l. 24 ("the debris"; Central Party Committee letter to IIR Party Committee). The vehicle for the public humiliation of these officials was a front-page *Pravda* editorial that Stalin ridiculed as "politically harmful" insofar as it "gave foreign correspondents the opportunity to write about 'a new Kronstadt' that supposedly forced" the party to reverse course economically. Although its subject was the incompetence of officials in the towns where the strikes occurred rather than the strikes themselves, the editorial painted a vivid portrait of shop-floor discontent. For having inadvertently supplied ammunition to the enemies of Soviet power, its author—Iaroslavskii—was stripped of his position on the newspaper's editorial board. "Perestroit'sia nado nemedlenno," *Pravda*, 5/31/32, 1; *Stalin i Kaganovich. Perepiska. 1931–1936gg.* (Moscow, 2001), 139 (quotes), 145, 147. I am indebted to David Brandenberger for bringing the latter source to my attention.

3. The mantra of party leaders in the aftermath of the strike wave was that plan fulfillment depended on resolution of the food-supply crisis. See, for example, Iaroslavskii's July 1932 speech to rank-and-file Communists in Moscow. RGASPI, f. 89, op. 3, d. 98, l. 2.

4. Davies, Tauger, and Wheatcroft, "Stalin, Grain Stocks," 651 ("industrial"), 652, 656; Davies, *Crisis*, 209–228, 292–300, 301 ("fantastic"). The reforms implemented in the aftermath of the April 1932 strike wave were a response not merely to that event, but to "the growing economic crisis" of which the strike wave was the most dramatic illustration. Davies, *Crisis*, 189–191, 301 (quote); Oleg Khlevniuk, "30-e gody. Krizisy, reformy, nasilie," *Svobodnaia mysl*, no. 17 (1991): 75–87.

5. Davies, *Crisis*, 292 (quote), 293–301; Eugène Zaleski, *Stalinist Planning for Economic Growth, 1933–1952* (Chapel Hill, N.C., 1980), 105; Jasny, *Soviet Industrialization*, 149–176. The coercive measures included the law of August 7, 1932, which threatened peasants with execution for stealing so much as a stalk of grain from the fields, and the creation four months later of an internal passport system, which—like serfdom before it—virtually bound peasants to the land. Davies, *Crisis*, 242, 290–291. The textile industry was a beneficiary of the new approach to planning, which resulted in higher long-term rates of investment in the means of consumption. Korneev, *Tekstil'naia*, 159–160.

6. Unsheathed in October 1932, the carrots came in the form of higher wages for Soviet textile workers and higher ration levels for IIR textile workers. GARF, f. 5457, op. 23, d. 264, l. 2; RGASPI, f. 17, op. 3, d. 902, ll. 33–35; d. 928, ll. 68–69; TsDNIIO, f. 327, op. 5, d. 1090, l. 62. Given Kaganovich's out-of-character insistence at a May 1932 conference that textile workers' living standard be improved, the carrots apparently were sown by the workers

whose strikes Kaganovich had just suppressed. RGASPI, f. 81, op. 3, d. 149, ll. 135–137, 141–143. As for the sticks, these took the form of decrees issued in late 1932 that granted managers the authority to fire workers for absenteeism and absolute control over the distribution of rations. Davies, *Crisis,* 287–289. While the carrot-and-stick approach was effective, strikes nearly erupted again in the IIR—including in Ivanovo itself—during the terrible winter of 1932–1933. RGAE, f. 8043, op. 11, d. 73, l. 163 (Central Party Committee report to Stalin). I am indebted to Julie Hessler for this citation.

7. For examples of labor unrest elsewhere, see GARF, f. 5451, op. 42, d. 250, ll. 17–18; RGAE, f. 8043, op. 11, d. 56, ll. 151–152; d. 57, ll. 285–290; and Osokina, *Our Daily Bread,* 52–58.

8. *Trud v SSSR,* 94. Employment in IIR mills fell by roughly the same amount. *Raiony IPO,* 1:28–29.

9. When Iaroslavskii visited the IIR in the aftermath of the April 1932 strike wave, he endeavored to rally rank-and-file Communists by reminding them of the crucial role played by the region's workers in the October Revolution. If only he had appreciated the irony of the dilemma facing the party: it was precisely these workers' authorship of the Revolution that informed—indeed, legitimated—their condemnation of its betrayal. RGASPI, f. 89, op. 3, d. 7, l. 7; d. 8, l. 35.

10. GARF, f. 374, op. 27, d. 1988, l. 69. A showpiece of the FFYP and reportedly the largest enterprise of its kind in the world, the Mixed Yarn Combine was, ironically, one of the "giants" whose usefulness the speaker questioned.

11. GARF, f. 374, op. 27, d. 1988, l. 67. Investigations carried out in the aftermath of the IIR strike wave estimated that single-parent-families were living on "less than half a pound of bread per day" per person. RGASPI, f. 81, op. 3, d. 213, ll. 3–15, 90–92. The plight of these families was conveyed to Lenin's widow, Nadezhda Krupskaia, in a November 1932 letter from a weaver whose husband's death left her family on the brink of starvation. "Do something, madam!" she demanded. "Alleviate our inhuman suffering and thus enable us to appreciate what we achieved in the Revolution." TsDNIIO, f. 327, op. 5, d. 92, l. 130.

12. Regional rankings are as of 1930. *Narodnoe khoziaistvo SSSR,* 72–75. The Kremlin was rumored to have stationed "fleets of lorries . . . at various points in Moscow" in the aftermath of the April 1932 strike wave in case disturbances broke out in or near the capital. Marco Carynnyk, Luciuk, and Kordan, eds., *The Foreign Office and the Famine,* 6.

13. GARF, f. 1235, op. 141, d. 1352, l. 13 ("command[ed]"); f. 374, op. 27, d. 1988, ll. 70–61; TsDNIIO, f. 327, op. 4, d. 507, ll. 7, 11, 29, 34, 43, 48–49 ("five . . . corpses"), 61, 63, 65, 70, 78, 84; d. 508, l. 14; d. 509, l. 25; d. 515, ll. 25 ("hunger"), 4–5 ("up . . . party," "the workers . . . regime"), 38, 42; op. 5, d. 152, ll. 39, 43; GAIO, f. 1276, op. 23, d. 10, l. 131.

14. There was an exodus from the mills of veteran workers—especially those with ties to the land—in the months following the strike wave, and an influx of new workers in 1934, when more balanced planning resulted in a 12.6 percent

surge in employment in the Soviet cotton and linen industries. GARF, f. 374, op. 27, d. 1988, ll. 67–66, 63, 61; TsDNIIO, f. 327, op. 4, d. 507, ll. 4, 18, 72, 75–76; *Trud v SSSR*, 94.

15. Davies, *Crisis*, 292 (quote), 293–301; Jasny, *Soviet Industrialization*, 149–176. Although living standards improved from 1934 to 1938, at no point during these years did they "regain, let alone surpass the level of the 1920s." Barber, "The Standard of Living of Soviet Industrial Workers," 109.

16. Robert Conquest, *The Great Terror: A Reassessment* (Oxford, 1990), 218–219.

17. RGASPI, f. 81, op. 3, d. 229, ll. 13–17. Kolotilov's "confession" is a classic example of the genre of security police sources that—in contrast to those cited elsewhere in this book—were manufactured out of whole cloth and reflected, in Michael David-Fox's felicitous phrase, "the culture of masking and unmasking that emerged out of Soviet communism's didactic thrust." David-Fox, "Whither Resistance?," 236.

18. RGASPI, f. 81, op. 3, d. 229, l. 17.

19. APUFSBIO, s.d. 7951-p, ll. 74–75. The annihilation of officials such as Kolotilov and of workers such as Shishkin was a crucial step in the legitimation of Stalin's tyranny—and in the emergence on Soviet soil of full-blown totalitarianism. The memory of the workers' rejection of the revolution "from above" had to be repressed, and the meanings attached to the ineradicable traces of this memory had to be monopolized. The means by which these were accomplished—mass murder—differed in degree, though not kind, from the means by which the October Revolution was "fulfilled."

20. For a brilliant account of how the "divergence of ideology and reality" under Communism gave rise to "a distinctive working-class consciousness" that was ever "potentially threatening to the existing order," see Michael Burawoy, "Reflections on the Class Consciousness of Hungarian Steelworkers," *Politics and Society* 17, no. 1 (1989): 1–34 (quotes, 24, 21). Like the Russian strike wave of January 1921, the East German workers' uprising of June 1953, the Hungarian Revolution of 1956, the Novocherkassk strike of June 1962, the Prague Spring of 1968, and the Polish Solidarity movement of 1980–1981, the events recounted on the pages of this book illustrate the validity of Burawoy's observation that "[t]he Russian Revolution of 1917 remain[ed] undigested" under Communism, "always ready to take revenge on the body that swallowed it" (26).

Appendix

1. Sources for the Appendix include Ward, *Russia's Cotton Workers*, 51–88; Tamara K. Hareven and Randolph Langenbach, *Amoskeag: Life and Work in an American Factory-City* (Hanover, N.H., 1978), 34–38; V. R. Barve, *Complete Textile Encyclopedia* (Bombay, 1967); and *Illustrated Catalogue of Cotton Machinery Built by Howard & Bullough American Machine Company, Ltd.* (Boston, 1909).

Acknowledgments

I am grateful for the love and support of my wife, Cori Field, and of our children, Thea, Phoebe, and Elliot.

I thank those who read one version or another of the manuscript and gave me ideas on how to make it better: David Brandenberger, Cori Field, Bob Geraci, Kyrill Kunakovich Chuck McCurdy, Kathleen McDermott, Nicholas Riasanovsky, Yuri Slezkine, Kathleen Valenzi, Reginald Zelnik, the anonymous members of my department's third-year review committee, and Harvard University Press's anonymous outside reviewers. I also offer these individuals my apologies for refusing to heed much of their superb advice.

Thanks and apologies also to those who commented on portions of the manuscript: Andrea Graziosi, Page Herrlinger, Manfred Hildermeier, David Hoffmann, William Husband, Hiroaki Kuromiya, David Mandel, Ben Nathans, Max Okenfuss, Henry Reichman, Gábor Rittersporn, William Rosenberg, Rochelle Ruthchild, Kurt Schultz, David Shearer, and Lewis Siegelbaum.

For their moral and intellectual support at critical junctures, I am indebted to Golfo Alexopoulos, Donald Filtzer, Wendy Goldman, Brian Taylor, and Lynne Viola.

For their advice and encouragement along the way, I am grateful to Samuel Baron, Jeffrey Burds, Alon Confino, Sarah Davies, Brigid Doherty, Sheila Fitzpatrick, Oleg Khlevniuk, Diane Koenker, Stephen Kotkin, Yanni Kotsonis, and Donald Raleigh.

For making my every trip to Ivanovo a success, many thanks to Sergei Tachenov. And for taking good care of me and my wife while there, the same to Tonia and Olia Dmitrieva, and to Natasha Tachenova.

For sharing their knowledge of the Ivanovo Region with me, I am grateful to Nikolai Patrikeev, Al'bina and Mikhail Smirnov, Aleksandr Smirnov, and Genadii Shutov.

Many individuals shared their expertise with me as I wrote this book. Those to whom I am especially indebted for having done so include John Barber, Eduard Beliaev, R. W. Davies, Julie Hessler, Terry Martin, David Pretty, Lewis Siegelbaum, and Chris Ward.

Leonid Vaintraub has been there for me time and again with advice and assistance. Ogromnoe spasibo, Lenia.

For his superb work on the maps, my thanks to Bill Nelson.

Just as the workers who are the subject of this book fought to maintain their living standard, so also a number of organizations fought hard to maintain mine. Research support came in the form of a Fulbright-Hays Dissertation Research Fellowship and a fellowship from the International Research and Exchanges Board, with funds provided by the National Endowment for the Humanities, the U.S. Information Agency, and the U.S. Department of State, which administers the Russian, Eurasian, and East European Research Program (Title VIII). The dissertation was written with support from the Mellon Foundation, and the manuscript revised with a postdoctoral fellowship from Harvard's Davis Center for Russian and Eurasian Studies and a Sesquicentennial Fellowship from the University of Virginia. I am grateful to each of these organizations for their support.

I owe a special debt to the employees of the archives and libraries in which I worked, including the Center for Documentation of the Contemporary History of Ivanovo Region (especially Viacheslav Terent'ev and Nadezhda Makarova); the State Archive of Ivanovo Region (especially Liudmilla Briuletova and Nadezhda Kochanova); both branches of the State Archive of the Russian Federation (especially Boris Sadovnikov); the Russian State Archive of Socio-Political History; the Russian State Archive of the Economy; the archives of the Federal Security Service in Ivanovo and Iaroslavl; the Russian State Library; the State Public Historical Library; and the Ivanovo Region Scientific Library.

Earlier drafts of chapters 2, 6, and 7 appeared in, respectively, *Jahrbücher für Geschichte Osteuropas* 44, no. 3 (1996), *The Russian Review* 56, no. 1 (1997), and *Contending with Stalinism: Soviet Power and Popular Resistance in the 1930s*, ed. Lynne Viola (Ithaca, N.Y., 2002). I am grateful for having been granted permission to publish this material again.

I am indebted to the distinguished scholars with whom I had the benefit of training, including Susanna Barrows, Victoria Bonnell, Gene Brucker, Gregory Freeze, Boris Gasparov, Daniel Orlovsky, Randolph Starn, and Mark David Steinberg.

My greatest professional debt is to my former graduate adviser, Reginald E. Zelnik. One of the great historians and mentors of his generation, Reggie was taken from this world—tragically and unexpectedly—as I put the finishing touches on the manuscript. This book is dedicated to his memory.

Index